T0328127

FOREIGN BANKS AND GLOBAL FINANCE IN MODERN CHINA

In this wide-ranging study, Ghassan Moazzin sheds critical new light on the history of foreign banks in late nineteenth- and early twentieth-century China, a time that saw a substantial influx of foreign financial institutions into China and a rapid increase of both China's foreign trade and its interactions with international capital markets. Drawing on a broad range of German, English, Japanese and Chinese primary sources, including business records, government documents and personal papers, Moazzin reconstructs how during this period foreign banks facilitated China's financial integration into the first global economy and provided the financial infrastructure required for modern economic globalization in China. *Foreign Banks and Global Finance in Modern China* shows the key role international finance and foreign banks and capital markets played at important turning points in modern Chinese history.

GHASSAN MOAZZIN is Assistant Professor at the University of Hong Kong. His research focuses on the economic and business history of modern China. He received his BA and PhD from the University of Cambridge.

CAMBRIDGE STUDIES IN THE EMERGENCE OF GLOBAL
ENTERPRISE

Editors
Louis Galambos, The Johns Hopkins University
Geoffrey Jones, Harvard Business School
Susie J. Pak, St. John's University

The world economy has experienced a series of globalizations in the past two centuries, and each has been accompanied and shaped by business enterprises, their national political contexts, and new sets of international institutions. Cambridge Studies in the Emergence of Global Enterprise focuses on those business firms that have given the global economy many of its most salient characteristics, particularly regarding how they have fostered new technology, new corporate cultures, new networks of communication, and new strategies and structures designed to meet global competition. All the while, they have accommodated changes in national and international regulations, environmental standards, and cultural norms. This is a history that needs to be understood because we all have a stake in the performance and problems of global enterprise.

A complete list of titles in the series can be found at:
www.cambridge.org/globalenterprise

FOREIGN BANKS AND GLOBAL FINANCE IN MODERN CHINA

Banking on the Chinese Frontier, 1870–1919

GHASSAN MOAZZIN
The University of Hong Kong

CAMBRIDGE
UNIVERSITY PRESS

Shaftesbury Road, Cambridge CB2 8EA, United Kingdom

One Liberty Plaza, 20th Floor, New York, NY 10006, USA

477 Williamstown Road, Port Melbourne, VIC 3207, Australia

314–321, 3rd Floor, Plot 3, Splendor Forum, Jasola District Centre, New Delhi – 110025, India

103 Penang Road, #05–06/07, Visioncrest Commercial, Singapore 238467

Cambridge University Press is part of Cambridge University Press & Assessment, a department of the University of Cambridge.

We share the University's mission to contribute to society through the pursuit of education, learning and research at the highest international levels of excellence.

www.cambridge.org
Information on this title: www.cambridge.org/9781009016940

DOI: 10.1017/9781009037891

© Ghassan Moazzin 2022

This publication is in copyright. Subject to statutory exception and to the provisions of relevant collective licensing agreements, no reproduction of any part may take place without the written permission of Cambridge University Press & Assessment.

First published 2022
First paperback edition 2023

A catalogue record for this publication is available from the British Library

ISBN   978-1-316-51703-1   Hardback
ISBN   978-1-009-01694-0   Paperback

Cambridge University Press & Assessment has no responsibility for the persistence or accuracy of URLs for external or third-party internet websites referred to in this publication and does not guarantee that any content on such websites is, or will remain, accurate or appropriate.

Für meine Eltern
Ahmed Taufik Moazzin und Sophia Moazzin
und für meine Geschwister
Rim und Hischam

CONTENTS

FIGURES

TABLES

ACKNOWLEDGEMENTS

I started work on this book as a doctoral student at the University of Cambridge under the supervision of Hans van de Ven. My deep debts of gratitude to Hans go back further to my undergraduate days though, when, as my director of studies, he helped me develop my interest in Chinese history and encouraged me to pursue doctoral research. Later, as my doctoral supervisor, he listened to and answered my many questions, guided me through the challenges of doctoral research, read and commented on multiple drafts and was always generous with his time and advice. My second expression of gratitude is due to Mao Haijian, now at the University of Macau. During my doctoral research, he kindly accepted me as his student, introduced me to a wonderful group of scholars and students at East China Normal University, enabled me to spend an extended period of time in China and continuously offered comments and advice on my research.

In Cambridge, I am also indebted to Joseph McDermott, who read early versions of the manuscript and often took time out of his busy schedule for long discussions. I have learned so much from these discussions. Adam Chau posed important questions and always reminded me to step away from the sources and think about the larger implications of my research. I also benefited from the help of Imre Galambos, Paul Hartle, the late Philip Oliver, Leon Rocha, Natasha Sabbah, Roel Sterckx, Emma Wu and Boping Yuan. I am similarly grateful to Julia Lovell, who provided encouragement but also important comments on my work during its early stages. Many fellow graduate students and friends at Cambridge also offered encouragement and help, most importantly Chen Kuan-Jen, Vivian Chih, Hajni Elias, John Feng, Fu Yang, He Jiani, Naomi Kojen, Li Chen, Lin Zhenru, Bill Moriarty, Rudolph Ng, Avital Rom, Shu Sheng-chih, Wang Shuxi and Wu Rong. In Shanghai, my thanks go to my *tongmen* Li Wenjie, Zhou Jian, Chen Xiaohan, Fu Liang, Ji Chen, Liu Bensen, Liang Chunge, Luo Zhenyu, Wang Yan and Zhao Songjie, who many times went out of their way to facilitate my research. In Taibei, I am thankful to Chen Yung-fa, who hosted me during my visit to the Academia Sinica, and to Lin Man-houng and Chang Ning for many helpful discussions. After my doctoral studies, I moved to the University of Tokyo as a Japan Society for the Promotion of Science (JSPS) postdoctoral fellow. There, Tetsuji Okazaki kindly hosted me at the Graduate School of Economics and provided much guidance. I am also thankful to Michael Schiltz, who read different parts of the manuscript and provided critical comments. In Japan, I am also indebted to Simon Bytheway, Andrew Kissane, Makiko Sawaguchi, Tomoko Shiroyama, Alessandro Trani and Koji Yamamoto for help and encouragement.

At the University of Hong Kong, Angela Leung and Helen Siu welcomed me to the Hong Kong Institute for the Humanities and Social Sciences and were always generous with their time and advice. At the Institute, I also benefited much from my discussions with Ching May Bo, Daniel Chua, James Kung, Li Ji, Izumi Nakayama, David Palmer, John D. Wong and Zhang Chaoxiong. I am also grateful to Yvonne Chan, Joan Cheng, May Chiu, Terrie Ip, Louis Kwong, Louise Mak, Hilson Ng, Roy Yiu and Zhang Xueqian for all the help they have rendered me since I joined the University of Hong Kong. At the Department of History, I thank Bert Becker, Julia Bowes, John Carroll, Peter Cunich, Frank Dikötter, Elizabeth LaCouture, Alastair McClure, Robert Peckham, David Pomfret, Oscar Sanchez-Sibony, Charles Schencking, Devika Shankar, Priscilla Song and Xu Guoqi for welcoming me to the department and for their support and collegiality. At HKU Business School, I profited much from discussions with Chen Zhiwu and Ma Chicheng. When the pandemic hit Hong Kong and the world, John Wong had the brilliant idea of organizing a regular reading group together with our colleague Michael Ng at the Faculty of Law. Soon, we were also joined remotely by Koji Hirata. John, Koji and Michael all read large parts of the book manuscript and provided detailed feedback, for which I am very grateful.

Like many other junior historians, I have benefited greatly from the encouragement and counsel of Elisabeth Köll, who has supported this project for a long time and read and commented on the entire manuscript. Brett Sheehan also commented on parts of the manuscript and has provided much advice over the years. I am also thankful to many others who at different stages read and commented on earlier drafts of all or parts of this book: Youssef Cassis, Christopher Clark, Parks Coble, Sherman Cochran, Sheldon Garon, Geoffrey Jones, Elisabeth Kaske, the late Christopher Kobrak, Debin Ma, Andrea McElderry, Micah Muscolino, Duncan Needham and Shirley Ye. For help and support in various forms, I am also grateful to Felix Boecking, Hubert Bonin, Cheng Linsun, Peter A. Crush, Du Xuncheng, Renate Jährling, Kwan Man Bun, Bernd Martin, Meng Zhongjie, Klaus Mühlhahn, Roger Nougaret, Neil Rollings, Glenda Sluga, Wen-hsin Yeh and Xie Junmei. While writing this book, I also had the good fortune of enjoying the camaraderie of Benedikt Bäther, Chen Tao, Austin Dean, Hsia Ke-chin, Mujeeb Khan, Toby Lincoln, Matthew Lowenstein, George Mak, Kwong Chi Man, Philip Thai, Fei-Hsien Wang, Wang Lianming and Dong Yan.

A full studentship from the Arts and Humanities Research Council in the United Kingdom (award reference: 1229431) enabled me to carry out my doctoral research. Grants from the German Academic Exchange Service (DAAD), the British Council, the China Scholarship Council, the Chiang Ching-kuo Foundation (grant no. DD017-U-15), the Faculty of Asian and Middle Eastern Studies, University of Cambridge and St Catharine's College, University of Cambridge provided further financial support during my doctoral studies. Thereafter, a JSPS postdoctoral fellowship, JSPS KAKENHI grant number JP17F17310, and a Hang Seng Bank Golden Jubilee Education Fund for Research grant provided additional assistance. A second grant from the Hang Seng Bank Golden Jubilee Education Fund for Research supported the publication of this book. I am most grateful to all these organizations and bodies for their assistance.

I would also like to thank the staff at the First Historical Archives of China, Beijing; Shanghai Municipal Archives; Tianjin Municipal Archives; Archiv des Studienwerk Deutsches Leben in Ostasian, Munich; Bundesarchiv, Lichterfelde, Berlin; Bundesarchiv/Militärarchiv, Freiburg; Geheimes Staatsarchiv Preußischer Kulturbesitz, Berlin; Hausarchiv Sal. Oppenheim Bank, Cologne; Faculty of Asian and Middle Eastern Studies Library, University of Cambridge; St Catharine's College Library, University of Cambridge; Cambridge University Library; Shanghai Municipal Library; East China Normal University Library, Shanghai; Library of the Si-Mian Institute for Advanced Studies in Humanities, East China Normal University, Shanghai; The University of Hong Kong Libraries; Library of Economics, University of Tokyo; National Diet Library, Tokyo; National Library of China, Beijing; Kuo Ting-yee Library, Academia Sinica, Taibei; Archives, Institute of Modern History, Academia Sinica, Taibei; Politisches Archiv des Auswärtigen Amts, Berlin; Staatsbibliothek zu Berlin; HSBC Group Archives, London; and The National Archives, Kew. I would like to reserve a special word of thanks for Martin Müller and Reinhard Frost at the Historical Archive of Deutsche Bank, Frankfurt am Main, who opened the archives for me during my numerous visits and were always ready to answer my questions and fetch even the most obscure source I wished to consult.

An earlier version of some of the material in Chapter 2 previously appeared in 'Sino-Foreign Business Networks: Foreign and Chinese Banks in the Chinese Banking Sector, 1890–1911', *Modern Asian Studies* 54, no. 3 (2020), pp. 970–1004. A previous version of some of the material in Chapter 5 was previously published in 'Investing in the New Republic: Multinational Banks, Political Risk, and the Chinese Revolution of 1911', *Business History Review* 94, no. 3 (2020), pp. 507–34. A prior version of a small portion of material that appears in Chapter 6 was first published in 'From Globalization to Liquidation: The Deutsch-Asiatische Bank and the First World War in China', *Cross-Currents: East Asian History and Culture Review E-Journal* no. 16 (2015), pp. 52–76.

At Cambridge University Press, I would like to express my thanks to Michael Watson, Emily Plater, Stephanie Taylor and Malini Soupramanian for their guidance and assistance during the publication process. The reviewers' reports for the Press helped me improve the manuscript in many ways. I am grateful to Lou Galambos, Geoffrey Jones and especially Susie Pak for their support and for including my book in the Cambridge Studies in the Emergence of Global Enterprise series. I would also like to thank Colleen Berry and Sally Evans-Darby for their expert editorial support and Cynthia Col for creating the book's index.

It would have been impossible to complete this book without the unconditional love and support of my parents, Ahmed Taufik Moazzin and Sophia Moazzin, and my siblings, Rim and Hischam. While I am glad that my mother and siblings can finally view what I have been working on for so long, my father unfortunately did not live to see me begin or finish work on this book. However, his seemingly unshakeable trust and confidence in his children stayed with me throughout. I dedicate this book to my parents and siblings with love and gratitude. Finally, ever since I met Luk Sing Yi shortly after arriving in Hong Kong, her humour, love, companionship and support have not only helped me complete this book, but have also made my life immeasurably more joyful.

NOTES AND CONVENTIONS

This book uses Chinese standard *pinyin* for the romanization of Chinese names of places and people (i.e. Guangzhou instead of Canton and Li Hongzhang instead of Li Hungchang). The only exception I have made is Sun Yat-sen, as many readers will be more familiar with this version of the Chinese revolutionary leader's name. I have used traditional Chinese characters throughout the book. For Chinese and Japanese names of people, the Chinese characters or Kanji are provided when the names are first used.

In late nineteenth- and early twentieth-century China, many currency units were used. The transactions in Chinese currency readers will encounter in this book were made in silver, which at the time was measured in various tael units depending on purpose and locality. These tael units differed somewhat in terms of their fineness and weight. The most important tael units were the Kuping tael (used by the Chinese imperial treasury), the Haiguan tael (used by the Chinese Maritime Customs Service) and the Shanghai tael (which dominated international commerce). Taels of silver could be paid in uncoined silver, minor silver coins or silver dollars. For more on Chinese currency during this period, see Morse, *Trade and Administration of China*, ch. 5; Vissering, *On Chinese Currency*, 5–6, appendix A; and Wei, *The Currency Problem in China*, ch. 3. Unless stated otherwise, all translations from the German and Chinese are my own.

ABBREVIATIONS

AIMC	Chen Xiafei 陳霞飛 and Han Rongfang 韓榮芳, eds. *Archives of China's Imperial Maritime Customs Confidential Correspondence between Robert Hart and James Duncan Campbell 1874–1907*, 3 vols. Beijing: Foreign Language Press, 1990–3
AIMH	Archives of the Institute of Modern History, Taibei
AMCS	Chen Xiafei 陳霞飛, comp. *Zhongguo haiguan mi dang* 中國海關密檔 (The Secret Archives of the Chinese Imperial Maritime Customs Service), 9 vols. Beijing: Zhonghua shuju, 1990–5
BA/MA	Bundesarchiv/Militärarchiv (Federal Military Archives of Germany), Freiburg
BArch	Bundesarchiv Lichterfelde (Federal Archives of Germany, Lichterfelde), Berlin
BBC	*Berliner Börsen-Courier*
BBZ	*Berliner Börsen-Zeitung*
BCC	British and Chinese Corporation
CCR	Chinese Central Railways
DAB	Deutsch-Asiatische Bank
GStA	Geheimes Staatsarchiv, Preussischer Kulturbesitz (Secret State Archives, Prussian Cultural Heritage), Berlin
HADB	Historical Archive of Deutsche Bank, Frankfurt am Main
HSBC	Hongkong and Shanghai Banking Corporation
HSO	Hausarchiv Sal. Oppenheim Bank (Archives of the Bank Sal. Oppenheim), Cologne
IGPK	John King Fairbank, Katherine Frost Bruner and Elizabeth Macleod Matheson, comp. *The I.G. in Peking: Letters of Robert Hart, Chinese Maritime Customs, 1868–1907*, 2 vols. Cambridge, MA: Harvard University Press, 1975
KfAG	Konsortium für Asiatische Geschäfte (Consortium for Asiatic Business)
LHZQJ	Gu Tinglong 顧廷龍 and Daiyi 戴逸, comp. *Li Hongzhang quanji* 李鴻章全集 (The Complete Works of Li Hongzhang), 39 vols. Hefei: Anhui jiaoyu chubanshe, 2008
MJZQJ	Ma Jianzhong 馬建忠. *Ma Jianzhong quanji* 馬建忠全集 (The Collected Works of Ma Jianzhong). Beijing: Zhonghua shuju, 2013
MYCQJ	Ma Yinchu 馬寅初. *Ma Yinchu quanji* 馬寅初全集 (The Complete Works of Ma Yinchu), 15 vols. Hangzhou: Zhejiang renmin chubanshe, 1999

PAAA   Politisches Archiv des Auswärtigen Amtes (Political Archives of
        the German Foreign Office), Berlin
PHSL   Huang Jianhui, ed. *Shanxi piaohao shiliao* 山西票號史料
        (Historical Materials on Shanxi Piaohao). Taiyuan: Shanxi jingji
        chubanshe, 2002
PVH   Johannes Hürter, comp. *Paul von Hintze: Marineoffizier,
        Diplomat, Staatssekretär. Dokumente einer Karriere zwischen
        Militär und Politik, 1903–1918*. Munich: Harald Boldt Verlag im
        R. Oldenbourg Verlag, 1998
QWSL   Zhongguo renmin gonghe guo caizheng bu 中國人民共和國財政
        部 and Zhongguo renmin yinhang zonghang 中國人民銀行總行,
        comp. *Qingdai waizhaishi ziliao (1853–1911)* 清代外債史資料
        (1853–1911) (Materials on the History of Foreign Debt in the
        Qing Dynasty (1853–1911)), 3 vols. Beijing: Zhongguo renmin
        gonghe guo caizheng bu, Zhongguo renmin yinhang zonghang,
        1988
SHQZSL Zhongguo Renmin Yinhang Shanghai shi fenhang 中國人民銀
        行上海市分行, comp. *Shanghai qianzhuang shiliao* 上海錢莊
        史料 (Historical Materials on Qianzhuang Banks in Shanghai).
        Shanghai: Shanghai renmin chubanshe, 1960, reprint 1978
StuDeO-Archiv   Archiv – Studienwerk Deutsches Leben in Ostasien, Munich
StuDeO-Bibl.   Bibliothek – Studienwerk Deutsches Leben in Ostasien, Munich
SZSQJ   Guangdong sheng shehui kexue yuan lishi yanjiushi 廣東省社會
        科學院歷史研究室, comp. *Sun Zhongshan quanji* 孫中山全集
        (The Complete Works of Sun Yat-sen), 11 vols. Beijing:
        Zhonghua shuju, 1981–6
TDS   Tianjin shi danggangguan 天津市檔案館, comp. *Yuan Shikai
        Tianjin dangan shiliao xuanbian* 袁世凱天津檔案史料選編
        (Selected Sources from the Tianjin Municipal Archives about
        Yuan Shikai). Tianjin: Tianjin dangan chubanshe, 1990
TMA   Tianjin Municipal Archives, Tianjin
TNA   The National Archives, Kew
WTHJ   Xie Junmei 謝俊美, comp. *Weng Tonghe ji* 翁同龢集 (The
        Collected Works of Weng Tonghe), 2 vols. Beijing: Zhonghua
        shuju, 2005
WTHRJ   Chen Yijie 陳義杰, comp. *Weng Tonghe riji* 翁同龢日記 (The
        Diary of Weng Tonghe), 6 vols. Beijing: Zhonghua shuju, 1989–98
YSKQJ   Luo Baoshan 骆宝善 and Liu Lusheng 刘路生, comp. *Yuan Shikai
        quanji* 袁世凱全集 (The Collected Works of Yuan Shikai), 36
        vols. Zhengzhou: Henan daxue chubanshe, 2013
ZJTS   Mi Rucheng 宓如成, comp. *Zhongguo jindai tielu shi ziliao
        (1863–1911)* 中國近代鐵路史資料 (1863–1911) (Materials on

the History of Modern Chinese Railways (1863–1911)), 3 vols. Beijing: Zhonghua shuju, 1963

ZZDQJ   Yuan Shuyi 苑書義, Sun Huafeng 孙华峰 and Li Bingxin 李秉新, comp. *Zhang Zhidong quanji* 張之洞全集 (The Complete Works of Zhang Zhidong), 12 vols. Shijiazhuang: Hebei renmin chubanshe, 1998

Opened Chinese Ports in 1914

○ Opened Chinese Ports

⊕ Opened Chinese Ports with Deutsch-Asiatische Bank Branch or Agency in 1914

Rehe
Chengde   Huludao   Shenyang (Mukden)
                       Yingkou (Newchwang)
Zhangjiakou   Dadonggou
⊕ Beijing Qinhuangdao Fengtian (Tatungkow)
Zhili   ⊕ Tianjin   Dalian
           Longkou   Lüshun
                        (Port Arthur)   KOREA
                        Weihaiwei

Shanxi   ⊕ Jinan   Yantai
           Shandong   (Chefoo)
                        ⊕ Qingdao (Tsingtao)

                                Yellow
                                  Sea
C   H   I   N   A
Shaanxi   Henan   Jiangsu

                Nanjing Zhenjiang (Chinkiang)
                Anhui
Yichang   Hubei   Wuhu   Suzhou   ⊕ Shanghai
          Hankou
○ Shashi ⊕   Hangzhou   Ningbo
                        Zhejiang
          Jiujiang
Yueyang

Changsha   Wenzhou   East
          Jiangxi   China
Hunan   Sandu   Sea
          Fujian   Fuzhou

          Xiamen (Amoy)

Guangxi   Guangdong   Taiwan
Wuzhou   Sanshui   1895 to Japan
                  Shantou (Swatow)
Nanning   Jiangmen Guangzhou (Canton)
Lappa (Hengqin Dao) Hong Kong
Beihai   Kowloon

          Zhanjiang (Kwangchowwan)

                        South
                        China
          Qiongzhou   Sea

                                N

0   200 km
0   200 miles

Figure 0.1 Opened Chinese Ports in 1914

Introduction

This book is about the activities of foreign banks in China between the late nineteenth century and the end of the First World War. During this period, foreign banks were major players in Chinese finance. They financed the rapidly growing international trade of China, cooperated closely with Chinese banks and provided the Chinese state with capital that allowed China to pay for wars, fund industrialization projects and maintain political stability. In *Foreign Banks and Global Finance in Modern China*, I try to answer the question of how foreign banks rose to such prominence in China and what role they played in facilitating China's financial integration into the global economy. Most importantly, I show that the interaction between foreign banks and Chinese officials and entrepreneurs led to the rapid internationalization of Chinese finance, both in terms of the banking sector of the China coast and in Chinese public finance, during the last two decades of the Qing dynasty and the first years of the Chinese republic. Although I contend that foreign banks as intermediary institutions played an important part in this process of internationalization, the evidence presented in the following chapters will also make clear the important role of Chinese actors and agency for the operations of foreign banks in China.

In studying the history of foreign banking in modern China, this book particularly follows the history of the Deutsch-Asiatische Bank (Dehua Yinhang 德華銀行, DAB), a leading German bank operating in China during the last two decades of the Qing dynasty and the early years of the republican period. The DAB's history in many ways exemplifies the activities and development of foreign banks operating in modern China throughout this period. After its establishment as a private joint-stock bank in 1889 in Shanghai, the DAB became both the most important German bank in China and one of the most important international financial institutions operating in East Asia. When the DAB started to operate in China during the 1890s, Chinese foreign trade was growing rapidly and the bank became involved in the financing of foreign trade. It also maintained important business relations with Chinese banks and attracted deposits from foreign and Chinese customers. After China's crushing defeat in the First Sino-Japanese War, Chinese officials became more open to the use of foreign capital and the DAB started to play

1

an important role in floating loans for the Chinese government on the German capital market. By 1914, the DAB connected most of China's major economic hubs with Germany and had also extended its branch network to East and Southeast Asia to facilitate its business in China. Eventually, however, the bank fell victim to the turmoil of the First World War, when it was liquidated by the Chinese government.

The history of the DAB, from its opening in Shanghai in 1890 to its eventual demise during the First World War, takes us through the period in modern China's history when foreign banks rose to a position of unprecedented significance both for the Chinese state and the local Chinese banking sector on the China coast. Between the 1890s, when China's foreign trade started to grow at a previously unmatched rate, and the First World War that saw the end of this rapid growth in trade and the rise of modern Chinese banks, foreign banks played a unique role in the banking sector of the China coast by financing foreign trade and supplying both Chinese banks and the Chinese state with capital. The DAB's history therefore constitutes a useful case-study for understanding the rise of international banking in China at the turn of the twentieth century.

In many ways, *Foreign Banks and Global Finance in Modern China* builds on recent scholarship by scholars outside the field of Chinese history. Scholars of global history have highlighted the important role the integration of inter-national financial markets and global flows of capital played during the first era of modern globalization in the nineteenth and early twentieth centuries.[1] At the same time, business historians like Geoffrey Jones have emphasized the decisive impact modern multinational banks had on the creation of the first global economy between the early nineteenth century and the First World War by supplying the financial infrastructure that facilitated the unprecedented global economic integration during this period.[2] Financial historians have also stressed that international banks provided the infrastructure for international payments, capital flows and trade for the first era of globalization during the nineteenth and early twentieth centuries, and have emphasized the importance

---

[1] Osterhammel, *Transformation of the World*, pp. 730–44; O'Rourke and Williamson, *History and Globalization*, pp. 207–46. For a discussion of the differences between modern globalization and earlier phases of globalization, see Bayly, *Birth of the Modern World*, pp. 23–85.

[2] See Jones, *Multinationals and Global Capitalism*, pp. 19–20, 109, 113–14, 144 and 285; and Jones, ed., *Banks as Multinationals*. The first global economy mainly differed from earlier global economic interaction because of the unprecedented global economic integration it saw and the new technologies of transportation and communication that made large-scale global trade and capital flows possible. These processes accelerated during the second half of the nineteenth century and declined after 1914. See Jones, *Multinationals and Global Capitalism*, pp. 18–19; Jones, *Entrepreneurship and Multinationals*, pp. 2–5; Jones, 'Globalization', pp. 143–7; Obstfeld and Taylor, *Global Capital Markets*, pp. 23–5; Findlay and O'Rourke, 'Commodity Market Integration', pp. 13–64.

of this infrastructure and the services of these banks for the rapid growth and integration of the global economy, including in Asia.[3]

However, if we look at China and the activities of foreign banks in the modern Chinese economy, we find that the specific role these foreign banks in China and their interaction with Chinese actors played in the internationalization of Chinese finance and China's financial connections to the global economy until today remain understudied. This lack of historical research into the activities of foreign banks in modern China can be explained by three factors. First, and most importantly, views that see foreign banks as part of foreign imperialism in China still loom large in the historiography of late Qing and republican China, generating an often simplistic picture of the activities of foreign banks. Second, many of the records relevant to the activities of foreign bankers in China are written in different languages and scattered across different archives, and have often only recently become available to historians. This has made it difficult for historians to engage with the history of foreign banks in modern China beyond a superficial level. Third, the China-centred approach that long dominated Western scholarship of China has tended to lead Western historians of China to shift their focus away from foreign influences on China's modern history.[4]

Only in recent years have historians of China started to use a more global perspective to engage with China's modern history. William Kirby has argued that during the republican period 'nothing mattered more' than China's foreign relations, which became 'all penetrating, all permeating, all prevailing ... forcing their way into every part of Chinese society'. Kirby sees the first Chinese republic as the start of a process of internationalization that is still ongoing in China today.[5] Hans van de Ven has argued that China witnessed its own 'onrush of modern globalization' during the late nineteenth and early twentieth centuries.[6] He has challenged historians to recognize the perspective of 'globalization ... as an opportunity to bring back the foreign as a significant factor in modern Chinese history' that allows us to focus on 'networks, interactions, mutual exploitations, and rupture' instead of simplistic 'binary dichotomies between China and the West'.[7] R. Bin Wong, Kenneth Pomeranz and others have also urged historians to break away from Eurocentric interpretations of China's economic development and to take the 'Chinese experience' into serious account when analysing the evolution of economic globalization.[8] Yet, despite these

---

[3] See Nishimura, Suzuki and Akagawa, 'Jobun', pp. i–xiii; and Nishimura, Michie and Suzuki, 'Introduction', pp. 1–12.

[4] See Cohen, *Discovering History in China.*

[5] Kirby, 'Internationalization of China', pp. 433–58.

[6] Van de Ven, 'Modern Globalization', pp. 167–94.

[7] Van de Ven, 'Globalizing Chinese History', p. 1.

[8] Quote from Wong, *China Transformed*, p. 10; Pomeranz, *The Great Divergence*; Blue and Brook, 'Introduction', pp. 1–9.

efforts of historians to understand the economic aspects of the first era of modern globalization and place the history of modern China in a global context, we still know very little about how China was financially integrated into the first global economy during this era.

This book aims to shed light on this question through an exploration of the role foreign, and particularly German, bankers played in the process of modern economic globalization in China during the late nineteenth and early twentieth centuries. While this book primarily follows the activities of foreign bankers in late Qing and early republican China, it situates the role the DAB and other foreign banks played during this period within the context of the longer development of China's public finance and Chinese credit markets. It specifically focusses on the interaction between foreign bankers and Chinese actors within the Chinese political and economic sphere. This book thereby aims to paint a more nuanced picture of the history of foreign banks in modern China than before that both highlights the role played by Chinese agency and stresses the importance of cooperation, conflict and shifting relations of power between foreign and Chinese actors. Ultimately, I argue that the DAB and other foreign banks acted as intermediary institutions that financially connected the Chinese economy to Western economies and facilitated its financial integration into the first global economy.

Foreign Banks and the Paradigm of Imperialism

As I have pointed out already, arguably the most important reason why our understanding of the history of foreign banking in China is relatively limited is that much of the previous scholarship on foreign banks in modern China has looked at them mainly as part of foreign imperialism. The origin of historical discourses that interpret foreign banks in modern China mainly in these terms can be traced back to the republican period and the rise of Chinese nationalism.[9] Chinese bankers like Chen Guangfu 陳光甫 criticized foreign banks as being part of the 'foreign economic invasion' of China and for absorbing Chinese capital and not caring about the development of Chinese industries.[10] Ma Yinchu 馬寅初, one of the most important Chinese economists of the republican period, accused foreign banks of having seized China's economic rights by 'absorbing the private savings of the people... safeguarding the government's tax revenue ...[and] managing foreign remittances' in China.[11] Popular opinion also turned against foreign banks, with newspapers

[9] On the rise of Chinese nationalism during the Republican period, see Zarrow, *China in War*, pp. 145–247.
[10] Chen Guangfu, 'Chen xiansheng zai Zhongguo Yinhang zhi yanjiuhui yanjiang: Zhanshi yingzhihou yinhangjie zhi xinshiming', February 1932, in Shanghai Commercial and Savings Bank, *Chen Guangfu Xiansheng*, p. 87.
[11] Ma Yinchu, 'Zhongguo jingji gaizao', 1935, *MYCQJ*, vol. 8, pp. 130–1.

criticizing Chinese customers' belief in the trustworthiness and stability of foreign banks and accusing foreign banks of being harmful to Chinese sovereignty and China's economy.[12]

After 1949, criticism of foreign banks in terms of the imperialist domination of China reached new heights. Starting from the 1960s, financial historians in China like Hong Jiaguan 洪葭管 categorized foreign banks as 'an important means for carrying out imperialism's brutal domination over China'.[13] During the 1990s and 2000s Wang Jingyu 汪敬虞 published several articles that investigated the role of foreign banks in modern China, largely based on research into articles from newspapers, a limited number of Chinese published primary sources and Western secondary literature. While these were more detailed, nuanced studies that pointed out that foreign banks did introduce some financial innovations into China and spurred on the development of Chinese capitalism, Wang maintained that foreign banks were mainly 'important tools for the economic invasion of China' by the West.[14] Even the most recent Chinese studies on foreign banking in China follow these views. While they are at times more balanced, start to see foreign banks as part of Chinese finance and admit that foreign banks at times cooperated with Chinese actors and provided an institutional model for modern Chinese banks, they generally continue to see foreign banks as 'the tools and main medium used by imperialism for seeking profits in China'. Moreover, these recent studies largely continue to rely on a limited array of sources and thus also fail to break much new ground in terms of the activities of foreign banks.[15] Besides the insistence on seeing foreign banks as manifestations of foreign imperialism, a further common problem of Chinese-language scholarship on foreign banking in modern China is that it does not use foreign archival sources, which makes it difficult to develop a nuanced picture of the activities of foreign officials, diplomats, bankers or any other foreign actors.

---

[12] Xiao, 'Guoren ji yinggai bian xinli', *Shenbao* (11 June 1935); Wang, 'Zai Hua waiguo yinhang gaishu', *Dagongbao (Jingji Zhoubao)* (7 August 1935).

[13] Hong, 'Cong Huifeng yinhang', p. 35. Also see his other articles collected in Hong, *Zai jinrong shiyuan dili manbu.*

[14] For the quote see Wang, '19 shiji moye waiguo zai Hua', p. 63. For a collection of these articles see Wang, *Waiguo ziben zai jindai Zhongguo.* Also see Wang, *Jindai Zhongguo ziben zhuyi.* For another study on foreign banking in modern China from this period that is based on a very limited number of primary sources and follows the paradigm of imperialism, see Heilongjiang jinrong lishi bianxie zu, *Hua E daosheng yinhang.*

[15] Quote from Jiang and Jiang, *Jindai Zhongguo waishang yinhang,* p. 344. Also see Guo, *Jindai Riben yinhang zai hua*; Wu, *Huifeng yinhang*; Song, *Jindai Shanghai waishang yinhang.* In Taiwan, scholars like Wang Yejian 王業鍵 have largely followed historians in mainland China in their view of foreign banks as 'tools of the imperialist countries for extending their political and economic power'. See Wang, 'Zhongguo jindai huobi', pp. 234–5.

Generally, Chinese-language literature on foreign banks frequently implicitly or explicitly blurs the line between such banks as independent financial institutions and Western governments, thereby suggesting that foreign banks essentially acted in accordance with and as a component of these governments' imperialist policies. If one tries to sum up the criticism that the work of historians like Hong Jiaguan, Wang Jingyu and much of the other Chinese-language scholarship commonly puts forward against foreign banks, one can identify three main areas of criticism: first, foreign banks are criticized for their involvement in raising loans for the Chinese government. These loans are said to have been detrimental to China because of their supposedly unfair and harmful loan conditions, such as high interest rates and a low issue price for the issued bonds. At the same time, the involvement of foreign banks in these loans is seen as part of their home governments' policy of furthering their control over China. Moreover, railway loans provided to the Chinese government by the banks are criticized as paving the way for foreign governments to establish spheres of influence in China.[16] Chinese historians working on the history of China's foreign debt have generally agreed with this view.[17] Second, foreign banks are viewed as dominating China's international remittances and the management of foreign exchange rates and controlling China's trade finance and the banking sector of the treaty ports. In their interaction with Chinese financial institutions, they are largely seen as having occupied the dominant and superior position. Third, foreign banks and their activities are seen as part of the incursion of foreign capital into China that inhibited the normal development of the Chinese economy. While foreign capital spurred on the development of Chinese capitalism, it also suppressed the normal development of capitalism in China and is seen as inevitably being in competition and confrontation with Chinese capital.[18]

There is relatively little Western-language scholarship that specifically deals with foreign financial institutions in modern China. Frank King's history of the Hongkong and Shanghai Banking Corporation (HSBC) arguably still remains the most influential study on the history of a foreign financial institution in China.[19] As a commissioned institutional history, it mainly focusses on and meticulously and comprehensively depicts the activities of the HSBC in China, but – partly because of its almost exclusive reliance on Western sources – neglects both the Chinese side of the history of the bank and the impact that interaction between the foreign bankers and Chinese elites had on China's financial internationalization. More specialist studies deal with the

---

[16] For this argument also see Mi, *Diguo zhuyi*.
[17] Xu et al., *Qingdai waizhai shilun*; Xu et al., *Cong bainian quru*, 4 vols; Ma, *Waizhai yu wan Qing zhengju*; Ma, *Wan Qing waizhai shi*.
[18] On this aspect also see Xu and Wu, *Zhongguo ziben zhuyi*, pp. 16–21.
[19] King, *History of the Hongkong and Shanghai Banking Corporation*, 4 vols.

relationship between foreign bankers in China and their home governments.[20] Several smaller studies that touch upon the activities of foreign banks in China exist, but they remain too narrow either by just focussing on a very specific aspect of foreign banking or by only employing a very limited number of primary sources. Generally, these studies also still see foreign banks in modern China as 'colonial and imperial banks'.[21] German banking in modern China remains understudied and mainly limited to a commissioned institutional history,[22] the study of financial imperialism[23] and narrow technical scholarship that fails to advance any broader arguments about foreign banking in modern China.[24] Moreover, non-Chinese-language studies of foreign banks in modern China also mostly do not make use of Chinese primary sources, so that such studies are not able to adequately reconstruct the motivations, decisions and actions of Chinese actors.

Thus, most of the existing literature on foreign banks in modern China either follows the imperialism paradigm that sees banks as part of the imperialist domination of China or tacitly accepts or does not properly challenge this view when writing about the institutional history or specific aspects of foreign

---

[20] McLean, 'British Banking'; Dayer, *Bankers and Diplomats*. Neither of these studies draws on Chinese sources and both are limited to a Western perspective, providing very little insight into the interaction between Western bankers and Chinese elites.

[21] Quote from Bonin, 'Introduction – Issues Regarding Asian Imperial Banking', p. 2. Also see, for example, Crisp, 'The Russo-Chinese Bank', pp. 197–212; and Quested, *The Russo-Chinese Bank*.

[22] See Müller-Jabusch, *Deutsch-Asiatische Bank*. This commissioned history of the DAB published in 1940 is the only major monograph that exclusively deals with the history of the DAB. The author's analysis is limited to an overview of the bank's history and mainly praises the activities of the German bankers without critically engaging with them.

[23] See Barth, *Imperialismen*. Writing mainly from a political history perspective, Barth also covers the DAB to some extent in his monograph on the connection between German overseas banks and German imperialism during the period from 1870 to 1914. Barth shows that there existed differences in the motivation and goals for overseas expansion between the German government and German bankers and demonstrates that the latter were willing to cooperate with non-German banks irrespective of European political developments. Yet, because of his insistence on seeing the activities of the bankers as financial imperialism and as his study is only based on Western sources, he fails to adequately account for Chinese agency and generally sees the activities of German bankers in a negative light.

[24] Akagawa, 'German Banks in East Asia', pp. 1–20. This article is based on a very limited number of sources from the Historical Archive of Deutsche Bank. It mainly focusses on the capital flows between different branches of the DAB in 1906. Largely based on the same limited group of primary sources and existing secondary literature but also lacking the use of Chinese primary sources, Akagawa also published a longer book chapter in Japanese that provides a mostly descriptive overview of some of the history, business areas and development and financial technicalities of German banking in Asia. See Akagawa, 'Doitsu ginkō', pp. 999–1209. Similar to the journal article, this book chapter does not advance a broader argument about the activities of foreign bankers in modern China.

banks. In the absence of broader works on the history of foreign banks in modern China that go beyond this paradigm and employ a wide range of both Chinese and Western primary sources, most of the existing scholarship neglects Sino-foreign interaction and Chinese agency when explaining the activities of foreign bankers. As a consequence, our understanding of foreign banking in modern China largely remains stuck in a victimization narrative that mainly emphasizes exploitation and confrontation and fails to properly account for other kinds of interaction between foreign bankers and Chinese actors, such as cooperation based on common benefits, competition and changing power relations. This narrative also fails to explain the wider implications of China's financial internationalization.

In recent years, some historians have started to correct this one-sided view of the imperialism paradigm on foreign banks in China. Leading a group of historians studying international banking in Asia, Nishimura Shizuya 西村閑也, Suzuki Toshio 鈴木俊夫 and Akagawa Motoaki 赤川元章 have argued against the use of ideologically and negatively charged terms like 'colonial banks' for describing the operations of international banks. Instead, terminology like 'international banks' that more accurately reflects the operations of these banks should be used.[25] While the main focus of the research of this group of historians is on international banking in Asia in general – in particular the specific technicalities of trade finance, international remittances and the internal operations of international banks – and not the role these banks played in their host economies, they acknowledge that historians of international banking have to 'recognise the existence of long-established banking traditions and payments networks outside Europe and areas of European settlement' and investigate the interaction of foreign bankers with these local structures if they wish to properly study the activities of international banks, including in Asia.[26]

Studies more specifically focussed on foreign banking in China have also begun to challenge the imperialism paradigm. In his study of the loan business between foreign and Chinese banks in Shanghai and Hankou before 1914,

[25] Nishimura, Suzuki and Akagawa, 'Jobun', pp. x–xii. Most likely because of their focus on the international monetary mechanism, the authors prefer the term 'international bank'. However, in the case of China, I find that the term 'foreign bank' is most straightforward and useful.

[26] Nishimura, Michie and Suzuki, 'Introduction', pp. 1–2. The group of historians discussed in this paragraph originated in a Japanese research seminar on international banking founded by Nishimura Shizyua and Suzuki Toshio, which led to the two edited volumes whose introductions are referenced in this paragraph. See Nishimura, Ranald and Suzuki, *The Origins of International Banking in Asia*; and Nishimura, Suzuki and Akagawa, *Kokusai ginkō to Ajia*. For a very recent excellent English-language work that builds on the work of this group of historians and focuses on the technicalities of trade finance between Asia and Europe and the related hedging of exchange risks, see Schiltz, *Accounting for the Fall of Silver*.

Nishimura Shizuya suggested that power relationships between these banks were much less one-sided than previously thought and proposed that foreign and Chinese banks depended on each other to effectively finance China's foreign trade.[27] Niv Horesh's recent revisionist work on the currency issuance of British banks in China shows that the bank notes issued by these banks were not detrimental to China's economic development but rather limited in their impact on the Chinese economy and only responded to Chinese demands for stable paper currency in the absence of a central government that could meet this need.[28]

Foreign Banks on the Chinese Frontier

This book builds on these revisionist studies and hopes to contribute to the more balanced understanding of foreign banks in modern China they have started to put forward by following the history of the DAB during the late Qing and early republican period, and by combining both Western and Chinese sources. However, *Foreign Banks and Global Finance in Modern China* goes a step further and proposes a new conceptual framework for transcending simplistic or stereotypical interpretations of the history of foreign banking in modern China. It introduces the concept of the 'frontier bank' to depict the varied activities and interactions of foreign banks on the China coast, explain the position they occupied in late Qing and early republican China and highlight the important role the DAB and other foreign banks played in financially integrating China into the first global economy through processes of conflict, cooperation and competition with both Chinese and foreign actors.[29]

Scholars have for some time drawn attention to the frontier as a space of global interaction and exchange. Some have described the frontier as a 'contact zone', which they see as 'a space in which peoples geographically and historically separated come into contact with each other and establish ongoing relations'.[30] Others have conceptualized the frontier as a 'middle ground',

---

[27] Nishimura, 'Chop Loans', pp. 109–32.

[28] Horesh, *Shanghai's Bund*. Horesh also points out the impact of Chinese agency on British bank note issuance, but does so only with a focus on Chinese nationalism and anti-foreign bank sentiments and policies in the 1920s and 1930s. See pp. 13, 130, 151–2.

[29] My understanding and conceptualization of the 'frontier bank' is informed by studies of investment and businesses operating in frontier regions of nineteenth-century North America. See, for example, Erickson, *Banking in Frontier Iowa*, Kerr, *Scottish Capital* and Gallaher, 'First Bank in Iowa' (in the latter article the term 'frontier bank' appears in the American context). For an example of a frontier institution in nineteenth- and twentieth-century China that 'operated with considerable independence in the frontier zone between weak Chinese regimes and overstretched European empires', see van de Ven, *Breaking with the Past*, especially pp. 4–5 (quotation on p. 4).

[30] Pratt, *Imperial Eyes*, quote on p. 6.

a space that lies at the intersection of different empires, cultures and populations, where foreigners and indigenous people meet, power relations are complex and interdependence leads to cooperation, exchanges and accommodation.[31] In the Chinese context, Christian Henriot and Robert Bickers have argued that following the creation of the treaty system in the 1840s, East Asia became a 'wild frontier zone'. In China, '[f]ar from sharply demarcating a new frontier between Qing and foreign, the treaty system in fact led to the creation of new grey areas of contested sovereignty and control'. Within this system, 'entrepreneurial Chinese . . . saw how advantageous the new system could be to those who were well placed to make use of it'. It was a 'system [that] was founded on collaboration, and on agency'. Indeed, rather than only serving foreign interests, in this frontier region 'a clear distinction between aggressor and exploited can hardly be effectively identified, because of the wholesale interpenetration of interests, because of the multiplicity of actors operating under the shadow of any one state, and because of the way in which the treaty system actually worked in practice'. On the Chinese frontier, foreign power overlapped and interacted with and could be limited by local Chinese power. Importantly, Henriot and Bickers call for an 'internationalis-[ation] and denationalis[ation]' of the history of the treaty ports and point out that 'the treaty system, broadly defined, effectively replaced the state as the defining organisational framework for East Asia's international relations, and the treaty system and its citizens were international'.[32]

The DAB, other foreign banks and their Chinese interlocutors operated on this frontier in the economic hubs of China's treaty port economy along the China coast.[33] I use the term frontier bank to describe foreign banks to highlight both the complex nature of the environment they operated in and the fact that these banks exemplified much of the ambiguity of the frontier on China's coast. They were foreign institutions connected to their home economies, but also formed an important part of the Chinese economy. They were chiefly managed by foreigners, but very much depended on their Chinese staff, partners and

---

[31] White, *The Middle Ground.*

[32] Henriot and Bickers, 'Introduction', pp. 1–11. On the necessity for economic cooperation in the treaty port of Shanghai and the significant economic advantages Chinese actors could derive from Sino-foreign interaction, also see Bergère, *Shanghai: China's Gateway*, pp. 4–5.

[33] On the treaty port economy, see So, 'Modern China's Treaty Port Economy', pp. 1–27. I follow So's understanding that modern China's treaty port economy extended not only to China's treaty ports and their hinterland, but also included other economic centres along the China coast such as Beijing, Hong Kong and Jinan that were not treaty ports but provided a similar 'politically and legally stable environment'. Unless otherwise stated, in this book the 'banking sector' refers to the banking sector of the Chinese treaty port economy. In China, the activities of foreign banks were limited to this treaty port economy centered on the China coast. For an overview of the locations of foreign banks in China that illustrates this, see, for example, Bell and Woodhead, *The China Year Book, 1912*, p. 302. On foreign residence in China more generally, see Allen and Donnithorne, *Western Enterprise*, pp. 14, 265. On the special case of Beijing, see Nield, *Places*, pp. 186-7.

Chinese institution in order to interact with the Chinese economy. Their branch networks spanned both their home economies and the treaty port economy of the Chinese frontier and thus connected the two. They were truly international institutions that operated at the intersection of different empires, financial and commercial networks and capital and commodity flows on the Chinese frontier. The concept of the frontier bank allows for an understanding of foreign banks in modern China that accounts for these institutional ambiguities.

The frontier region offered the DAB and other foreign banks many business opportunities, but also imposed its own specific set of limitations on these banks' operations. It was on the China coast that the motivations, interests and visions of German bankers, investors and diplomats met with the realities of the China market. The distance between Germany and China, the vast and mostly unknown expanse that lay beyond the frontier and the limited knowledge that existed about China in Germany opened up a grand space for imagination of huge markets and possibilities for profits in China. As a frontier bank, the DAB often had to act as a mediator between these visions – including their own directors in Germany – and the realities and limitations of operating a foreign bank and investing in China.

At the same time, operating on the edges of the Chinese economy meant that the DAB as a frontier bank was always subject to both the spatial limitations of the economic hubs it operated in and to the institutional barriers erected by Chinese merchants and bankers and the Chinese state. As a consequence, it often depended on entering into strategic cooperation with Western and Chinese governments, officials, diplomats, bankers and businesspeople to operate its business in the banking sector of China's coast and to gain the opportunity of providing loans to the Chinese central or provincial governments. Finally, conceptualizing the DAB as a frontier bank can help explain the role the bank fulfilled while operating in a frontier region where flows of capital and commodities, different forms of currencies, law and institutions, and the interests of different empires converged. Together with other foreign banks, the DAB played a crucial role in using its global network of branches and correspondent banks to facilitate the flow of capital and commodities that passed through the frontier region.

Being situated at such a converging point of capital and commodities provided foreign banks with manifold opportunities for business and profit. At the same time, operating at the frontier, the DAB often had to mediate among different interest groups and could easily become subject to conflicts, whether tensions between Western powers in China or the struggles of different factions of the Chinese court or public. From the frontier region of the China coast the bank's business extended into many different areas of Chinese politics and finance and connected China to the wider world. At the same time, the frontier's specific limitations also always compelled the bank to build up networks of cooperation with foreign and Chinese actors to operate its business. Nevertheless, I argue that, despite the limitations, it was their position as frontier banks operating on China's frontier that allowed the DAB and other foreign banks to act as intermediary institutions that financially connected China, both in terms of the banking sector and public finance, to the global economy.

With regards to interactions and power relations between foreign and Chinese actors in the financial sphere of the Chinese frontier, a further important characteristic of the frontier that this book will shed light on was that shifts in the political or economic constellations on the frontier could open up or close spaces of Chinese agency and change the power dynamics on the Chinese coast. While I highlight the importance of Chinese agency and the complexities and changing nature of power relations between Chinese and foreign actors, I also show that timing and contingency could be key in determining these power relations and the space for Chinese agency. For example, while growing financial internationalization and relative political stability during the last years of the Qing dynasty allowed Chinese officials to win increasingly favourable terms for foreign loans from foreign banks, this ability was diminished after 1911 because of the fall of the Qing dynasty and the ensuing political instability in China.

When following the activities of foreign banks on the Chinese frontier in the late nineteenth and early twentieth centuries, *Foreign Banks and Global Finance in Modern China* focusses on the themes of financial internationalization, transnational networks, the conflict between nationalism and economic globalization, and risk. The first and most important theme of this book is what I call the financial internationalization of China. Drawing on William Kirby's theme of internationalization in the republican period, I argue that during the time between the 1890s and the First World War, Chinese finance went through an unprecedented phase of rapid internationalization.[34] Within this timespan, the frontier of the China coast was the main stage for China's accelerated engagement with foreign banks, capital and capital markets. Before the 1890s, a limited number of mainly British foreign banks had entered China and China's foreign trade had only grown at a steady pace. In contrast, the two and a half decades before the First World War saw an unprecedented influx of foreign banks and foreign capital from different countries into the banking sector of China's treaty port economy, accompanied by a rapid growth in China's foreign trade with different countries facilitated by these foreign banks. As a result, foreign banks and capital came to play an important role in the Chinese banking sector, for example in inter-bank lending or the financing of China's foreign trade. Moreover, these developments resulted in hitherto unseen growth in the amount and diversity of transnational capital flows between China and other economies and the cheapening of credit in the banking sector. During the same period, both the Chinese central government

---

[34] Kirby, 'The Internationalization of China'.

and provincial governments increasingly relied on using foreign capital. Since the 1850s, China had occasionally resorted to foreign borrowing from mainly British sources. However, after the Sino-Japanese War of 1894/5, indemnity payments and the high cost of the Qing's reform efforts led to a dramatic increase in the amount of Chinese foreign borrowing and engagement with foreign capital markets. This was accompanied by increasing competition of foreign financiers in the Chinese loan business and a greater diversity of the sources of Chinese foreign borrowing, which allowed China to borrow large sums of money on favourable terms, so that foreign borrowing became an important part of Chinese public finance.

The result was that by 1914 the Chinese frontier had become a space for the confluence of international capital flows and global financial connections. Both the banking sector of China's coastal areas and Chinese public finance were so closely connected to international flows of capital and capital markets that it had become part of the international financial system, and occurrences like financial crises or wars in other parts of the world profoundly influenced Chinese finance. I argue that it was the rapid inflow of foreign banks into the Chinese treaty port economy during the last two decades of the Qing dynasty and the first years of the new Chinese republic, together with the unprecedented growth of China's foreign trade and engagement with foreign capital markets during this period, that caused the full-fledged internationalization of Chinese finance. While we will see that foreign banks and their activities on the Chinese frontier were central to this process of financial internationalization, *Foreign Banks and Global Finance in Modern China* also shows how Chinese bankers and officials grew increasingly familiar with and managed to exploit these international financial connections, whether by integrating foreign banks into existing banking networks and tapping sources of foreign capital or by efficiently using and at times even manipulating foreign investors. More broadly, by shedding light on China's growing global financial entanglements during the late nineteenth and early twentieth centuries, this book also reveals the crucial role international finance played at important junctures of modern Chinese history, such as the 1911 revolution or the First World War. As will become clear in the following chapters, 'following the money' can provide us with a fresh perspective on key events in modern Chinese history.[35]

A second theme that I pursue in this book is that of transnational networks. The history of the DAB and other foreign banks involves both physical and social transnational networks. Physical networks like the global branch

---

[35] Here I follow Austin Dean's recent work on modern Chinese currency reform, which makes a similar point about the importance of 'following the money' and looking at modern Chinese history from a financial perspective: Dean, *China and the End*, pp. 1–8, 185.

network of the DAB and the bank's connection to the branch networks of the major German banks provided the financial infrastructure that made capital flows between Germany and China possible. Social networks that involved foreign and Chinese officials, diplomats, bankers and merchants were equally important for German bankers operating in China. German bankers involved in China relied on social networks to attain information, establish business contacts and facilitate their banking operation, whether in the local banking sector or in the realm of international finance. This book sees transnational networks mainly as 'instrumental', meaning networks that are created and maintained by different parties not because of some intrinsic value of building a network but because all sides derive certain clear-cut benefits and advantages from it. This does not mean that transnational networks did not create or build upon amicable feelings, but this book mainly sees common benefits, objectives and interests among the participants as the basis for transnational networks.[36]

Economic profits often stood at the centre of these networks, and the objectifying effect of money made it easier for foreign and Chinese actors to identify common benefits and achieve common objectives through cooperation and compromise.[37] Therefore, Sino-foreign cooperation was often easier to achieve in the economic than in the political realm, where it was more difficult to overcome differences in political interests, culture and ritual. Such Sino-foreign networks held together by the cooperative creation of profits can be traced back to the Canton System of the early nineteenth century.[38] As I argue, by connecting and integrating different Chinese and foreign institutions, practices and elites, transnational networks were a crucial element of modern Sino-foreign economic interactions on the Chinese frontier and played an important role both in the operation of foreign banks and in China's financial internationalization at the turn of the twentieth century, and in modern globalization in late Qing and early republican China more generally.[39]

The third theme that appears in the following chapters is the relationship between nationalism and economic globalization in the late nineteenth and early twentieth centuries. Attentive to recent criticisms of writing history

[36] My conceptualization of transnational networks, including the distinction between physical and social networks, the understanding of 'instrumental' networks and the role of networks in 'controlling conflict and fostering cooperation', builds on Casson, *Entrepreneurship*, pp. 115–49.
[37] On the objectifying effect of money, see Simmel, *Die Philosophie des Geldes*; on cooperation based on common benefits, see Axelrod, *Evolution of Cooperation*.
[38] See Wong, *Global Trade in the Nineteenth Century*.
[39] On the importance of transnational networks for modern globalization, also see van de Ven, 'Robert Hart and Gustav Detring', pp. 631–62. For an account that stresses the importance of transnational networks – made up of both foreign and Chinese actors, who bridged what he calls the 'Chinese/foreign divide' – for the functioning of the key treaty port of Shanghai, see Wasserstrom, 'Cosmopolitan Connections'.

from a global perspective,[40] this book not only pays attention to the growing financial connections between the Chinese and other economies, but also notes the conflicts that these growing connections could engender between the proponents and beneficiaries of globalization and their nationalist detractors. In the case of the German bankers, this was most prominently reflected in their relationship to the German government. The German government supported the establishment of a German bank in China that unified German banking interests primarily to strengthen the independence of German commerce from British banks. German bankers, by contrast, were more interested in the general profitability of the bank's business in China and not willing to support German commerce for purely national reasons. Thus, the bankers' prioritization of economic profit before national interests meant that the relationship between the German government and the DAB was marked as much by conflict as it was by cooperation. On the Chinese side, the conflict between national interests and economic globalization manifested itself in the relationship between Chinese officials and foreign banks and capital. While cooperation with foreign banks and the use of cheap foreign capital that came with it was often welcomed by and of great benefit to Chinese reformers who wanted to finance China's modernization, it also meant that these officials became targets of criticism from conservative officials and increasingly vocal Chinese nationalists. Thus, this book shows that economic globalization did not only foster transnational cooperation and interdependence but could also fuel tension and conflict between, on the one hand, transnational elites open to using the new opportunities globalization provided and, on the other, more sceptical national institutions and interest groups. As we will see, the Chinese frontier often became the space where these tensions manifested themselves.

The last theme that appears in the following chapters is that of risk.[41] This is not surprising given that banks continuously have to take on and deal with risks, such as risk of illiquidity or loan loss, and 'their business is unimaginable without risks'.[42] This was even more so the case given that the DAB and other foreign banks in China operated in a foreign country.[43] While the activities of foreign banks in late nineteenth- and early twentieth-century China have often been explained as being largely driven by the imperialist policies of their home

---

[40] Jeremy Adelman has argued that global historians need to pay more attention to disintegration, conflict and other negative consequences of globalization. See Adelman, 'What Is Global History Now?'. For a critique of Adelman, and Adelman's reply to the critique, see Drayton and Motadel, 'Discussion: The Futures of Global History', pp. 1–21.

[41] For a good introduction to the significance of risk as a theme in business history, see Scranton and Fridenson, *Reimagining Business History*, pp. 222–6.

[42] Schönhärl, 'Introduction', p. 3.

[43] On the general riskiness of modern multinational banking, see Jones, *British Multinational Banking*, pp. 61–2, 388.

governments, this book contends that the management of risk can be a more useful perspective for analysing and comprehending the actions of foreign banks and foreign financiers operating on the Chinese frontier. While not the sole driving force behind their actions, this book reveals that the management and minimization of risk was often an important element in the decision-making of foreign bankers.

As the book shows, there were primarily three forms of risk that played a role in the decisions of the bankers and the operations of the DAB as a foreign bank on the Chinese frontier. First, the risk of operating a foreign bank as a multinational company in a foreign and new market with different business practices, institutions and currencies was often at the centre of the German bankers' decision-making. As we will see, because of this risk, the DAB opted for a risk-averse approach in the running of its business, which, while curtailing its profits to a certain extent, eventually proved successful. Second, when negotiating and floating loans for the Chinese government, the assessment of China's sovereign risk and its integration into the international system of sovereign borrowing became crucial in determining on what terms the bankers were willing to float Chinese loans. Finally, with the collapse of the Qing dynasty and the outbreak of the First World War, managing the increasing political risk of operating a foreign bank and investing in China became a significant challenge for the bankers. Foreign financiers managed the instability and increased political risk that followed the fall of the Qing by making demands for more foreign supervision of Chinese public finance. However, in the case of the First World War, the German bankers proved unable to contain the political risk connected to the outbreak of the war, and China's entry into the war eventually led to the end of the DAB's operations in China.

China and Economic Globalization

Foreign Banks and Global Finance in Modern China also addresses wider issues within modern Chinese economic and business history and the history of modern economic globalization.

Previous debates among historians regarding the role of foreign businesses and investment in the modern Chinese economy mainly revolved around the question of whether the foreign presence helped the development of the Chinese economy or was part of foreign imperialism and hindered Chinese economic development.[44] These debates remained largely inconclusive and the scholars involved were later criticized for trying to generalize and reach too

---

[44] For positive assessments of foreign businesses and investment, see Hou, *Foreign Investment*, and Dernberger, 'The Role of the Foreigner', pp. 19–47. For an example of a more negative assessment see Esherick, 'Harvard on China', pp. 9–16.

broad and absolute conclusions.[45] More recent studies on Sino-foreign economic relations have more specifically dealt with the impact of foreign trade on the Chinese economy. Hao Yanping and Robert Gardella have shown that Chinese merchants and manufacturers were very adept at cooperating with foreign merchants and adjusting to China's increased integration with the world economy.[46] Lin Man-houng followed their lead and discussed the interplay of China's domestic economy with the modern world economy, showing that the rapid economic development in China's treaty ports also created increased demand for products from the wider Chinese economy.[47] However, despite the fact that we have recently witnessed a 'mini-explosion' in English-language scholarship on the history of modern Chinese banking, we still know very little about the role foreign banks played in the Chinese economy and the impact they had on both Chinese public finance and banking.[48]

This book aims to address this historiographical omission and explore the connections between foreign banks and China's public finance and the domestic banking sector in China's treaty ports by examining the mutual interactions between foreign bankers and different Chinese actors and institutions. Contributing to the work of scholars like Gardella and Lin, I show that Chinese financial and business networks and Chinese officials were able to integrate foreign banks and the access to foreign capital these banks provided into existing Chinese structures of commerce and public finance. Following the work of Brett Sheehan,[49] the book argues that absolute judgement about the beneficial or detrimental effects of the foreign influence on China's modern economy are unlikely to do justice to the multi-faceted nature of the operations of German bankers, their interaction with Chinese actors and more generally the impact of the foreign presence on China's economic development. Therefore, rather than providing an absolute verdict on the influence of the foreign presence on China's economy, this book aims to provide a study of foreign banking in modern China that broadens our view of the activities of foreign banks by showing that cooperation was as much part of the interaction of foreign banks with Chinese actors as was conflict, and that even exploitation was more often mutual than one-sided. Thereby, it hopes to contribute to a more nuanced understanding of the role foreign banks and foreign influence more generally played in the history of China's modern economy.

[45] Cochran, *Big Business*, pp. 4–6; Wright, 'Imperialism and the Chinese Economy', pp. 36–45.
[46] Hao, *Commercial Revolution*; Gardella, *Harvesting Mountains*.
[47] Lin, 'China's "Dual Economy"', pp. 179–97.
[48] Sheehan, 'The History of Chinese Money', pp. 1–2. Sheehan mainly refers to Sheehan, *Trust in Troubled Times*; Cheng, *Banking in Modern China*; and Ji, *A History of Modern Shanghai Banking*.
[49] Sheehan, *Industrial Eden*, pp. 5–6.

Contextualizing the role of the DAB and other foreign financial institutions within the long-term development of Chinese public finance and China's credit markets can also contribute to our understanding of the reasons for the Great Divergence in economic development between Western Europe and East Asia.[50] Building on the recent work of Loren Brandt, Ma Debin, Thomas Rawski and He Wenkai, I suggest that institutional differences between China and Western Europe were most likely an important factor in the origins and persistence of the Great Divergence.[51] This book shows that through the role they played in Chinese public finance and the Chinese banking sector, foreign banks were an important factor in the Chinese economy from the second half of the nineteenth century, when, in the aftermath of the two opium wars and China's forced opening to the West, China's foreign commercial relations increased and Chinese reformers began their efforts to industrialize China, to the 1920s, when modern Chinese banks started to emerge in great numbers. I argue that the main reason why foreign banks could rise to such prominence during this period was that they filled an 'institutional void' – a common feature of emerging markets – in this case left vacant by the absence of effective globally operating modern Chinese banking institutions.[52] Moreover, foreign banks operated in the special institutional environment of the treaty ports and

[50] The now classic study on the topic, which, however, dismisses institutional factors, is Pomeranz, *Great Divergence*. For an overview of the debate, see Parthasarathi and Pomeranz, 'The Great Divergence Debate', pp. 19–37.

[51] Brandt, Ma and Rawski, 'From Divergence to Convergence', pp. 45–123. On the connection between the Great Divergence and the development of Chinese financial institutions, see Ma, 'The Rise of a Financial Revolution'. In his comparative study of the success and failure of the institutional development of modern public finance in England, Japan and China, Wenkai He also, if only briefly, connects institutional differences in the development of fiscal institutions to the Great Divergence. However, he does so from the perspective of state capacity and not economic growth and development. See He, *Paths toward the Modern Fiscal State*, p. 22. More specifically in relation to bank note issuance by British banks, Horesh also draws attention to the importance of institutions for economic growth. See Horesh, *Shanghai's Bund*, chapters 1 and 2. Cheng's study of modern Chinese banking briefly and somewhat superficially points out that existing financial institutions in China before the rise of modern Chinese banks were insufficient for modern economic development, for example because of the small capitalization of some of these institutions. See Cheng, *Banking in Modern China*, pp. 22–3.

[52] On such 'institutional voids' as a common feature of the business history of emerging markets, see Austin, Dávila and Jones, 'The Alternative Business History', pp. 537–69. The term goes back to Khanna and Palepu, 'Why Focused Strategies May Be Wrong', pp. 41–51. Some of the literature on institutional voids has been criticized for neglecting local institutional arrangements and implying an inherent superiority of Western institutions. See Mair, Marti and Ventresca, 'Building Inclusive Markets in Rural Bangladesh: How Intermediaries Work Institutional Voids', *Academy of Management Journal* 55, No. 4 (2012): 819–50 (who see institutional voids as 'analytical spaces at the interface of several [existing local] institutional spheres' and stress the importance of local contexts) and Bothello, Nason and Schnyder, 'Institutional Voids and Organization Studies',

not within the institutional framework of the Chinese economy. Therefore, their activities and the Chinese demand for their services can also help us identify larger institutional imperfections in the Chinese economy, such as insufficient property rights and the lack of a functioning market for public debt, which hindered China's industrialization and contributed to the persistence of the Great Divergence during the nineteenth and twentieth centuries. Thus, studying the history of foreign banking in late nineteenth- and early twentieth-century China might help us answer larger questions about the role institutional insufficiencies in the development of Chinese financial institutions and the Chinese economy more broadly played in the origin and persistence of the Great Divergence.

Finally, this study also engages with larger questions about economic globalization and the first global economy of the nineteenth and early twentieth century. First, the case of the DAB contributes to our understanding of the role multinational enterprises played as 'facilitators of globalization' in the nineteenth and early twentieth centuries, especially in the financial realm, but also reveals how multinational enterprises had to adapt their business practices and institutional structures after entering a foreign emerging market like China.[53] Moreover, narratives still continue to dominate that describe the first global economy as a Western-dominated 'gentleman's club' of global capitalism, which some countries like Germany were allowed to join and to which others like China failed to gain entry because of their supposed rejection of global economic integration and lack of economic development along Western lines.[54] These views have increasingly been discredited as Eurocentric by global historians.[55] Still, the question remains – especially for the financial sphere – how two economies as different as those of China and Germany became part of the same global economy and were integrated into the web of global capital flows of the late nineteenth and early twentieth centuries.

This book argues that Western financial institutions and tools of public finance and credit played an important role in this process. However, it also shows that China's integration into the global web of capital flows and the making of the first global economy was always a process of negotiation

pp. 1499–512 (who focus on possible biases inherent in the use of the concept of institutional void). However, as Austin, Davila and Jones state, '[t]he term "void" should not ... be taken to mean total absence' or to 'imply that countries simply needed to import Western institutions to achieve successful economic modernization'. As I point out in this Introduction and as will become clear in the following chapters, I highlight the importance of interaction with Chinese institutions for foreign banks and stress that foreign banks need to be contextualized within the long-term development of Chinese fiscal and financial institutions.

[53] Geoffrey Jones uses this term for the role of multinational businesses in the first global economy; see Jones, *Entrepreneurship and Multinationals*, p. 4.

[54] Frieden, *Global Capitalism*, pp. 54–5.

[55] Wong, *China Transformed*; Frank, *ReOrient*.

between indigenous and foreign actors, markets and institutions, and not a one-way imposition of Western capitalism. While the history of German banking in China is only a small episode in the history of the first era of modern globalization, the question of how different financial institutions, networks, business practices and currencies could be negotiated across two very different economies was not unique to Sino-foreign financial relations. It also existed in many other places across the world where the financial infrastructure that made the integration of the first global economy possible emerged. Therefore, this study also stands as an example that contributes to our wider understanding of the history of economic globalization in the nineteenth and early twentieth centuries.

Chapter Summary

In the first chapter of this book I provide the background for the establishment of the DAB. By tracing the growing willingness of Chinese reformers and entrepreneurs to use foreign capital from the 1850s to the 1880s, I show that by 1885 there existed sufficient support in China for cooperation with foreign financial institutions. This new openness did not go unnoticed in Germany, where bankers since the 1870s had been interested in expanding their business into China. I follow the attempts of German bankers during the 1880s to get involved in the Chinese loan business and discuss differing opinions among German bankers and diplomats about the feasibility and profitability of establishing a German bank in China. While some reservations about the profitability of such a bank existed among German bankers, the strong support of the German government for such an institution and the realization that business with China was only possible through a branch network there eventually led to the founding of the DAB in 1889.

In Chapter 2, I first map out the business structure of the DAB. I then turn to the first decade of the DAB's activities in China's banking sector and explain the regular day-to-day business of the bank, with a focus on its business in financing China's foreign trade. I describe the difficulties the DAB encountered when trying to compete with and win over both German and other foreign customers from more established foreign banks like the HSBC. The chapter then discusses the connections the DAB established with Chinese bankers on the Chinese frontier. Using the case-study of China's financial centre Shanghai, I show that, despite what has often been claimed by scholars, foreign banks did not control and dominate the banking sector of China's treaty ports. In contrast, Chinese bankers and businesspeople integrated foreign banks into their own networks and thereby managed to generate large profits. The chapter then turns to a discussion of the development of the DAB's business during the early years of its operations, before concluding by discussing the acceleration of China's financial internationalization during the 1890s.

In Chapter 3, I turn my attention to the Anglo-German loans of 1896 and 1898, which were part of the indemnity loans China raised in Europe to pay for the Japanese indemnity after the Sino-Japanese War of 1894/5. I show that these loans were an important juncture in the internationalization of China's public finance and its integration into the international system of sovereign borrowing. Increasing competition among foreign financiers meant that, contrary to the assessment and expectations of the foreign bankers, China could now borrow foreign capital more cheaply than ever before. At the same time, once the previously used foreign-supervised Customs revenues were no longer available as a loan security, foreign bankers had to find new ways of evaluating China as a sovereign borrower, and eventually China was compelled to yield to the expectations of the bankers and bond markets when contracting the final indemnity loan. More broadly, the indemnity loans were not only the largest loans China had contracted so far and increased the importance of foreign capital for Chinese public finance. They also showed Chinese officials how easy it was to borrow large sums of money on foreign capital markets, thereby creating the basis for the accelerated foreign borrowing seen during the last decade of the Qing dynasty.

Chapter 4 traces the involvement of German bankers in modern Chinese railway finance. The chapter mainly focusses on the Tianjin-Pukou railway loans of 1908 and 1910, which were the most important railway loans the DAB was involved in. I use the case-study of the Tianjin-Pukou railway loan negotiations between 1898 and 1910, in particular the negotiations between foreign and Chinese negotiators in the contact zone of Tianjin, to discuss the significance of local intermediaries and transnational networks on the Chinese frontier for Chinese railway loan negotiations. Because of cooperation in transnational networks, a fading readiness of Western governments to get involved in loan negotiations after the turn of the century, the continued interest of foreign bankers in investing in China and a lack of understanding of Chinese finance by foreign financiers, Chinese negotiators were able to win increasingly favourable loan conditions during the last years of the Qing dynasty. As a result, the international bond market became a cheap and effective way of raising money for efforts in economic development in areas such as railway construction. The skill of Chinese negotiators in using the information asymmetry between foreign bankers, who knew very little about Chinese public finance, and Chinese negotiators, who by now had developed a good understanding of foreign capital markets, and the continued determination of foreign bankers to invest in China did not only mean that China could continue to increase its foreign borrowing at favourable terms and without foreign control, but it also led to many loans having insufficient guarantees.

In Chapter 5, I explore the 1911 revolution from the perspective of international finance. The chapter follows the German bankers' involvement in Chinese national politics during the 1911 revolution and its aftermath. By 1911 indemnity payments and excessive Chinese borrowing had rapidly increased the Qing government's financial burden. Therefore, the stance that foreign bankers took during and after the revolution from the beginning proved decisive for the ability of different factions to win power and stabilize the finances of the state. I argue that the decision of German and other foreign bankers to first remain neutral during the revolution and then support Yuan Shikai was an important factor shaping the course and outcome of the revolution with Yuan emerging victorious after the fall of the Qing dynasty. While the chapter shows that the Reorganisation Loan of 1913, which was floated by a consortium of foreign bankers for Yuan's new republican government, kept the new government afloat, it also demonstrates that the fall of the Qing and the ensuing political instability and increased political risk meant that China was no longer able to borrow at favourable conditions and had to agree to an extension of foreign control over Chinese public finance. Eventually, China had to pay the price for its increasing reliance on foreign debt during the preceding decades and the new republican government continued China's dependence on foreign debt.

Chapter 6 explores the fate of the DAB during the First World War, the breakdown of economic globalization in China and the involvement of China in Allied economic warfare. I first review the DAB's business and the internationalization of the banking sector of the treaty ports during the decade preceding the outbreak of war. I then follow the attempts of German bankers to maintain their business and keep China out of the war before China's declaration of war against Germany in 1917. The chapter shows that China's financial internationalization had developed to such a degree by 1914 that the outbreak of the war in Europe had a profoundly negative effect on the banking sector in China's treaty port economy and on Chinese public finance. The war in Europe also caused an unprecedented Chinese loss of confidence in foreign banks and financial centres like Shanghai for the first time witnessed runs on foreign banks that were alleviated only through support from Chinese banks. The end of cooperation among foreign banks meant that the Chinese state had to look to Japan for financial support, which came to dominate Chinese foreign borrowing during the war. While the German bankers at first tried to use the provision of loans to China to keep the Chinese government out of the war, they were eventually outbid by the Allies. China's entry into the war then sealed the fate of the DAB. The Chinese government initially only intended to stop the business of the bank for the duration of the war, but it eventually had to yield to Allied pressure to fully liquidate the bank, which not only dealt a decisive blow to the DAB but also damaged German commerce in China more generally.

Like elsewhere in the world, in China the First World War marked the end of a period of rapid global financial integration that had taken off in China in the 1890s. By 1914, Chinese finance had become internationalized and well connected to the global capital flows that were the basis of the first global economy. In the following chapters, I aim to demonstrate that German and other foreign bankers played a key role in making China's financial internationalization possible. I argue that foreign banks in China were not simply another form of imperialism but acted as intermediary institutions on the China coast and nodes within the emerging global network of capital flows and connected China with Western financial markets. They thereby supplied the financial infrastructure that made it possible for modern economic globalization to occur in China during the late nineteenth and early twentieth centuries. At the same time, I stress that interaction with Chinese actors and Chinese agency were always crucial to the operations of the DAB and other foreign banks. It is only through an understanding of this interaction that we can comprehend the growing interdependence between financial markets in China and Europe and China's engagement with international financial markets and capital flows during the first global economy of the nineteenth and early twentieth centuries.

A German Bank in China

Early Contact of German Bankers with China from the 1870s to the 1880s

On 16 July 1888, Simon Alfred von Oppenheim, offspring of the renowned German Oppenheim banking house, wrote to his father Eduard von Oppenheim about his travels in China:

> You were very right when already at the time of my departure you specifically called my attention to China and to what a German banker can learn there. As I already wrote to you previously, in the other parts of Asia, where the Englishman has the control, trade and all relating advantages in his hands and, supported by his government, will continue to hold them, there is no prospect of secure success for a German Bank. However, East Asia or more specifically China, needs to be named as the field for a German bank.[1]

Simon Alfred von Oppenheim had been sent on a world tour by his parents in 1887 and spent July 1888 travelling in China. There he met with German merchants and German ambassador to China Max von Brandt, and had an audience with Zhili governor-general Li Hongzhang 李鴻章.[2] He reported that not only German merchants but also Li Hongzhang would welcome a German bank sufficiently capitalized and accommodating in business. Convinced of China's increasing need for European capital, especially because of the growing Chinese interest in railway construction, and the preference of both German trading houses and German industry to have their business financed by a German bank, Oppenheim wrote to his father that 'the establishment of a German bank in China, soon, on a big scale and carried out on an accommodating basis, without any doubt seems to me to be a great thing'.[3]

---

[1] Simon Alfred von Oppenheim to Eduard von Oppenheim (16 July 1888) (underlined in the original), HSO, A VIII 114 Ostasiatische Geschäfte 1888–1914.

[2] Simon Alfred von Oppenheim to Eduard von Oppenheim (20 July 1888), HSO, A VIII 114 Ostasiatische Geschäfte 1888–1914; Simon Alfred von Oppenheim to Amalie Heuser and Eduard von Oppenheim (27 July 1888), HSO, A VIII 114 Ostasiatische Geschäfte 1888–1914. On the world tour, see Teichmann, *Mehr als eine Bank*, p. 107.

[3] Quote from Simon Alfred von Oppenheim to Eduard von Oppenheim (16 July 1888), HSO, A VIII 114 Ostasiatische Geschäfte 1888–1914; Simon Alfred von Oppenheim to Eduard von Oppenheim (20 July 1888), HSO, A VIII 114 Ostasiatische Geschäfte 1888–1914.

Simon Alfred advised his father to participate in the creation of a German bank in China, or, if a speedy establishment was not realized, to get involved in the China business on his own.[4]

While Simon Alfred von Oppenheim showed a particularly great enthusiasm for China, his letters reflect an interest among German bankers in China and the Chinese market that can be traced back as far as the 1870s. Before the Deutsch-Asiatische Bank (DAB) was established in 1889, there had been several attempts by German bankers to expand their business to China. While most of these attempts failed, they are important for understanding why and how German bankers established a bank in China. This chapter traces these attempts from the 1870s to the establishment of the DAB in 1889. The previous literature has mainly either over-emphasized the role of the German state in the establishment of the DAB or – while acknowledging the agency of German bankers to a certain extent – only discussed the bank's founding in the larger context of the expansion of German overseas banking in the late nineteenth century. Both strands of literature also solely view the bank's establishment from a German perspective and neglect the interdependence between the growing Chinese interest in foreign capital and the establishment of the bank.[5]

In contrast, this chapter focusses on the growing engagement of German bankers with China after 1870 and explains how the establishment of the DAB was a consequence of the growing interest of German bankers in China and their imaging of China as the market of the future, especially for German investment and industry. I also show how closely connected the wish of the German bankers to enter the China market was to the larger rise of German finance and the eagerness of German financiers to gain equal standing with their British peers. While this chapter acknowledges the role the German government played in the establishment of the DAB, particularly as an accelerating and unifying force, it demonstrates that the long-lasting interest of different German banking groups in China was the most important factor for the expansion of German banking to China.

Examination of the growing contact of German bankers with China during the period and the eventual establishment of the DAB also demonstrates that, while enjoying the support of the German state, the bank was a private bank controlled by its founding banks. It was not merely a 'quasi-independent semi-state bank', as is still claimed in some scholarly literature.[6] Finally, the chapter also situates the establishment of the bank within the larger development of

---

[4] Simon Alfred von Oppenheim to Eduard von Oppenheim (16 July 1888), HSO, A VIII 114 Ostasiatische Geschäfte 1888–1914.

[5] Stoecker, *Deutschland und China*, pp. 190–210; Barth, *Imperialismen*, pp. 24–42.

[6] This view is still common in the English scholarly literature. For the quote, see Otte, *The China Question*, p. 75. Also see Edwards, *British Diplomacy*, p. 4. This problem is also pointed out in Barth, *Imperialismen*, p. 41.

Chinese public finance and particularly the growing Chinese demand for foreign capital. As we will see, the increasing engagement of German bankers with China was not a one-sided effort, but developed parallel and in reaction to the increasing Chinese openness towards foreign capital and financial markets. German bankers were not only aware of the potential of the Chinese market, but also realized that doing business in China was only possible if China became open to using foreign capital, and if the German bankers could establish contacts with those Chinese officials willing to work with foreign banks to finance Chinese modernization projects.

This chapter first depicts the early interest of German bankers in the China market during the 1870s and early 1880s and the change of their primary interest from trade finance to investment in China, railway construction and direct business with the Chinese government. The chapter then turns to China and shows the growing interest of Chinese officials in using foreign capital, first mainly for military purposes but then increasingly for the funding of railways. We then follow the steps of a German study mission to China, which was dispatched to the China coast by German bankers and industrialists in 1886 to explore the possibilities for German investment there. While the mission returned to Germany without immediate results, afterwards it became clear that German bankers would only be able to enter the Chinese market if they established a German bank on the China coast. The last part of the chapter then explains how different German bank groups planned the founding of a German bank in China and how the German government unified and accelerated these efforts, which eventually led to the establishment of the DAB in 1889.

1.1   German Bankers and the Myth of the China Market

During the nineteenth century, the myth of China as a potentially large market for foreign products was widespread in Germany and the West.[7] So when a group of German bankers established the Deutsche Bank in 1870 to finance Germany's overseas trade and free it from its dependence on British finance, the 'special magic' that 'of old floated around the trade with the East' meant that Asia became a main priority for the newly established bank.[8] This was also the reason why the Deutsche Bank hired Hermann Wallich (Figure 1.1) as one of their first directors, who possessed direct experience in East Asian banking, having worked for the French bank Comptoir d'Escompte de Paris as the head of its Shanghai office between 1867 and 1870.[9]

---

[7] Leutner, 'Deutsche Vorstellungen über China', p. 422. For Britain, see Forman, *China and the Victorian Imagination*, pp. 5–6; for the United States, see Varg, 'Myth of the China Market', pp. 742–58.

[8] Helferrich, *Siemens*, 1:235.

[9] Helferrich, *Siemens*, 1:235; Wallich, 'Aus meinem Leben', pp. 85–104.

Figure 1.1 Hermann Wallich (1833–1928), 1875. Image courtesy of the Deutsche Bank AG, Historical Institute.

In preparation for the opening of branches in East Asia, Wallich asked one of his former German colleagues at the Comptoir d'Escompte de Paris, Julius Mammelsdorf, who had previously worked as the manager of the French bank's Yokohama branch, to draft a plan for the Deutsche Bank's expansion to East Asia.[10] In his report, Mammelsdorf praised the importance of East Asia as one of the 'richest and naturally most endowed areas in the world'. He continued that East Asia's products were 'very manifold and of great trade value' and described the continuous growth of East Asia's foreign trade. Mammelsdorf praised the potential for further growth of international trade with East Asia, which, he explained, possessed '450 Million inhabitants' and a 'richness of mines of all kinds'. Thus, Mammelsdorf felt that the bank could open up new fields of business for trade and industry in China. He then explained that Britain and British banks still dominated East Asian trade.

---

[10] Mammelsdorf, Untitled Report (1871), HADB, S3918.

Mammelsdorf emphasized the dependence of German traders on British finance, but expressed hope that a German bank could introduce German currency and trade finance to East Asia.

The report proposed that the Deutsche Bank should open three branches in East Asia in Yokohama, Shanghai and Hongkong. Mammelsdorf recognized Shanghai as the port with the greatest significance for China's export and import and saw it as the most important branch to be opened in East Asia, assigning to it 3 million of the total capital of 5.25 million German thalers he proposed for the East Asian branches. Mammelsdorf was optimistic that the three branches would return a very good profit and would play an important role in introducing the German currency in East Asia. His report shows the importance and enthusiasm that German bankers at the time attached to East Asia and China. Deutsche Bank director Georg von Siemens, who, with Wallich, was the driving force behind the Deutsche Bank's expansion to East Asia, mostly followed Mammelsdorf's report in his proposal to the supervising board of the Deutsche Bank in November 1871. Siemens proposed establishing overseas branches in London, Yokohama and Shanghai, assigning the highest capital of 2 million German thalers to the Shanghai branch.[11]

Following Siemens' proposal, the Deutsche Bank opened branches in Yokohama and Shanghai as their first branches outside of Germany in May 1872. However, the great expectations for the two branches in East Asia were not fulfilled. The global economic depression that started in 1873 had a detrimental effect on trade and led to speculation in tea and silk in China and an oversupply in European commodities in East Asia. At the same time, the falling silver prices caused by Germany's adoption of the gold standard in the same year negatively affected the business of the East Asian branches.[12] By 1875 the Shanghai branch had suffered losses of 245,611 reichsmark and the Yokohama branch losses of 190,821 reichsmark. To avoid further losses, the bank had closed its branches in East Asia by October 1875.[13] Thus the first attempt to establish German bank branches in China ended after only three years. While the Deutsche Bank pledged that it would continue its 'program for the support of German overseas trade',[14] this negative experience was undoubtedly part of the reason why it took another fifteen years for the next German bank to open for business in China.

---

[11] Helferrich, *Siemens*, 1:241–3.
[12] 'Vierter Geschäfts-Bericht der Direction der Deutschen Bank für die Zeit vom 1. Januar bis 31. December 1873' (April 1874), HADB, Geschäftsberichte, Deutsche Bank; Pohl, 'Ostasiengeschäft', pp. 475–6.
[13] 'Sechster Geschäfts-Bericht der Direction der Deutschen Bank für die Zeit vom 1. Januar bis 31. December 1875' (April 1876), HADB, Geschäftsberichte, Deutsche Bank.
[14] 'Sechster Geschäfts-Bericht der Direction der Deutschen Bank für die Zeit vom 1. Januar bis 31. December 1875' (April 1876), HADB, Geschäftsberichte, Deutsche Bank.

An important distinction between this first failure to establish a German bank in China in the 1870s and the interest of German bankers in China during the 1880s is that during the former period, the emphasis lay on financing overseas trade with China and not on providing loans directly to the Chinese government. The orders of the Deutsche Bank for its branches in East Asia especially stressed that the branches were to help finance trade between East Asia and other markets, and to introduce German currency there, but did not specifically mention any loan business with governments.[15]

This situation changed in the 1880s when German banking interests shifted from trade finance to providing direct loans to the Chinese government, and to what came to be known as the *Regierungsgeschäft* (government business), meaning the financing of purchases of industrial products by the Chinese government. In Germany, the large-scale nationalization of previously privately owned railways that began in the 1870s meant that large sums of capital were injected into the German economy, and government bonds with comparatively low interest rates of about 4 per cent replaced railway shares with high yields from 5 to 25 per cent. Moreover, the interest rates of Prussian and German state bonds were lowered through conversion and German corporation and stock exchange legislation made it difficult to float new industrial shares. These measures deprived German capital markets of objects for investment and speculation and led German investors to look abroad for investment opportunities that promised higher yields.[16] The German economic depression between 1873 and 1879 had also led German industrial firms to increasingly seek new opportunities to export their products to foreign markets, and German industrial exports continually grew until the First World War.[17] Many German industrialists saw China as a future market for their products, and manufacturers like Krupp, Mauser and Vulcan Stettin began selling arms and ships to China in the early 1870s.[18] More broadly, the decades after Germany's political unification in 1871 also saw its emergence as a major global economic power and capital exporter and the rise of Berlin as a leading international financial centre.[19]

---

[15] 'Geschäfts-Instruktion für die Agenturen der Deutschen Bank in Ost-Asien' (1872), reproduced in Pohl, 'Das Ostasiengeschäft der Deutschen Bank', p. 479.

[16] On German railway nationalization see Ziegler, *Eisenbahnen und Staat*, pp. 172–229. For the significant difference in yields between government bonds and railway shares, see Wehler, *Deutsche Gesellschaftsgeschichte*, p. 72. For the general surplus of capital in Germany, see Helfferich, *Siemens*, pp. 181–6; Tilly, 'Zur Entwicklung des Kapitalmarktes und Industrialisierung', pp. 155–6; Barth, *Imperialismen*, pp. 25–6.

[17] Wehler, *Gesellschaftsgeschichte*, pp. 561–7; Torp, *Globalisierung*, pp. 93–4.

[18] Ratenhof, *Chinapolitik*, pp. 71–88; Jing, *Mit Barbaren*, pp. 70–102.

[19] Torp, *Globalisierung*; Cassis, *Capitals of Capital*, ch. 3; Bersch, *Financial Globalization*, pp. 74–81.

These developments sparked the interests of both traditional German private banks and newly rising universal banks in the Chinese market, as they both were well connected to German industry through industrial financing and – often in consortia made up of several banks – undertook the floating of foreign bonds in Germany.[20] Most importantly, one of Germany's biggest banks, the Disconto-Gesellschaft, and its director Adolph von Hansemann (Figure 1.2), who had taken an interest in China since the 1870s, now made increasing efforts to expand their business to China.[21] According to his biographer Hermann Münch, the numerous works on China in both German and foreign languages in Hansemann's private library were testimony to his great interest in the Chinese market. In particular, the works of Ferdinand von Richthofen, a German geologist who had travelled in China between 1868 and 1872 and in his later publications discussed China's rich coal deposits and the importance of making them accessible through the construction of mines and railways, had a great influence on Hansemann's perception of China.[22] For Hansemann, who had close connections to Germany's steel and coal industries, this was an additional incentive for expanding his business to China.[23]

Hansemann's interest in both Chinese railway construction and government loans for China was the subject of a conversation he had with the German consul in Shanghai, Johann Heinrich Focke, in January 1882. During their meeting, they also discussed the possibility of establishing a German bank in China. Focke supported the establishment of such a bank and predicted a 'brilliant development' for it. After Focke mentioned that he would also discuss this issue with the Deutsche Bank, Hansemann expressed his willingness to cooperate with the Deutsche Bank in establishing a German bank in China. However, according to Hansemann, the Deutsche Bank reacted rather coldly to Focke's suggestion, most likely because of their previous failed attempt to establish branches in East Asia.[24]

Still, this did not mean that the Deutsche Bank was not interested in investments in China. In November 1882 Paul Jonas, board member of the Deutsche Bank, approached Emil Russell, a director at the Disconto-Gesellschaft, with a proposal to cooperate in the financing of Chinese railways. This resulted in a letter both banks sent to the Chinese minister to Berlin, Li

[20] On the connection of German banks to industry, see Wehler, Gesellschaftsgeschichte, pp. 622–32; Fohlin, Finance Capitalism and Germany's Rise. On the floating of foreign bonds, see Schaefer, Deutsche Portfolioinvestitionen im Ausland, pp. 28–40. On the involvement of German big banks in both industrial finance and international finance, see also Cassis, Capitals of Capital, p. 111.

[21] Disconto-Gesellschaft, Die Disconto-Gesellschaft, p. 82.

[22] Münch, Hansemann, pp. 217–18. On Richthofen see Wu, Empires of Coal, pp. 33–65.

[23] Münch, Hansemann, p. 273.

[24] Müller-Jabusch, Deutsch-Asiatische Bank, p. 8.

Figure 1.2 Adolph von Hansemann (1826–1903), ca.1900. Image courtesy of Deutsche Bank AG, Historical Institute.

Fengbao 李鳳苞, on 31 January 1883. They explained that they would 'respectfully offer their services' should the Chinese government decide to construct railways or grant concessions to construct railways. They stressed that any such railway would be constructed under the supervision and control of the Chinese government as a Chinese state railway. The banks with their 'manifold connections to the German railways and skilful railway technicians on the one hand, and to German industry engaged in railway construction on the other hand', could provide German capital, materials and engineers for such construction projects. They mentioned their long-standing business relations with the best German ironworks and proposed forming a consortium with these ironworks, conditioned on the approval of the Chinese government. This consortium could then supply the necessary materials, such as 'rails, points, bridges and other railway construction equipment and moreover locomotives and waggons' at set prices at the market rate. Finally, they offered to float a loan for the Chinese government in Germany to cover the construction costs.[25]

---

[25] Deutsche Bank und Disconto-Gesellschaft to Li Fengbao (31 January 1883), quoted in Stoecker, *Deutschland und China*, pp. 191–2.

The letter shows the willingness of the two most important German banks to enter the Chinese loan business. It also reveals the important role Chinese railway construction and possible orders of railway materials for German industrial firms played in the considerations of German bankers. What made railway construction so attractive for German bankers was that potential profits were not only limited to the financing of construction and the purchase of materials, but if a railway project generated large-scale orders for German industry, the banks could also profit from financing the manufacturing of railway equipment in Germany and from the commission for arranging the purchase for China. While Li Fengbao did not immediately reply to the offer of the German banks, they both were to continue their efforts to become involved in China's growing loan business. Eventually, it was only during the Sino-French War of 1884/5 that the Chinese government turned to German financiers for help. However, we can already see the great interest of German bankers in the China market before the war. Although the first attempt to establish a German bank had failed, the interest of German bankers in China continued and, beginning in the 1880s, shifted its focus from trade finance to investment in railway construction and the issuing of Chinese government loans.

1.2   Foreign Capital and the Chinese Search for Wealth and Power

Before we continue to follow the early contacts of German bankers with China, it is important to note that by the 1880s foreign capital had already started to play an important role both in the banking sector and foreign trade of Chinese treaty ports and in Chinese public finance. Foreign cash loans provided to Chinese merchants by Western merchant firms can be traced back as early as the Cohong (Gonghang 公行) system of the eighteenth and early nineteenth centuries.[26] Starting from the 1820s, other instruments of credit, such as bills of exchange, promissory notes, letters of credit, bank notes and drafts, also came into use and caused an 'expansion of credit' on the China coast.[27] Following the First Opium War and with the growth of China's foreign trade, the first foreign banks entered China. They were predominantly British foreign banks founded on the initiative of individual groups of merchants and investors. These foreign banks focussed on trade finance, which had so far been dominated by the big foreign merchant houses. By the 1860s, these new foreign banks had largely taken over the exchange business in China.[28] Yet, as the number of

---

[26] Chen, *Insolvency*.
[27] Hao, *Commercial Revolution*, pp. 72–111.
[28] Vinnai, *Die Entstehung der Überseebanken*, pp. 16–82; Kanada, 'Chūgoku kaikō-go no gaikoku ginkō', pp. 1559–61, 1574–5; Tamagna, *Banking and Finance in China*, pp. 24–5. As Vinnai points out, before 1839 the East India Company also played a significant role in Chinese trade finance. Kanada mentions that the Bank of Australasia might have already

foreign banks that focussed on providing specialized banking services remained small during this period, it was only after 1890 that the significance of foreign capital for Chinese finance reached its acme.[29] However, not only Chinese merchants, but increasingly also Chinese officials discovered the benefits of cheap foreign capital. From the early nineteenth century, rapidly increasing expenses from military costs, river conservancy works and disaster relief drained Chinese government reserves from 81,824,000 Kuping taels in 1777 to only 8,000,000 Kuping taels in 1850.[30] The outbreak of the Taiping Rebellion in 1851 further exacerbated these fiscal problems by cutting the government off from important sources of tax income and causing growing military expenses. By 1861, the government reserves had shrunk to only 1,521,784 Kuping taels.[31] To deal with this fiscal crisis, the Qing increased existing taxes, introduced the commercial *lijin* 釐金 tax and expanded the selling of official ranks. However, it also increasingly relied on foreign loans to raise funds and cover its growing expenses.[32]

The establishment of the foreign-led Imperial Maritime Customs Service in 1854 provided China with a new source of income that was transparent enough to be trusted by foreign merchants, bankers and investors.[33] This made it considerably easier for China to contract foreign loans and enabled it to borrow increasing amounts of foreign capital during the following decades. Qing China lacked a functioning domestic market for public debt.[34] Moreover, Chinese merchants mainly issued short-term loans and charged interest rates of 7–14 per cent or more per year.[35] Furthermore, they were reluctant to provide loans

had an agency agreement with a foreign merchant in Guangzhou before 1836, but does not provide further proof of this. The only long-lasting non-British bank that operated in China before the 1890s was the Comptoir d'Escompte de Paris (see Chapter 2, Table 2.2), in whose establishment the French government had played a role. However, the Comptoir d'Escompte de Paris did not unite all French financial interests in China like the DAB would do in Germany. On the Comptoir d'Escompte de Paris, see Stoskopf, 'La Fondation', pp. 395–411; Stoskopf, 'From the Private Bank to the Joint-Stock Bank'; and Brötel, *Frankreich im Fernen Osten*, pp. 266–72, 320–40. On the issue that French and British financial institutions in China did not unite the financial interests of their countries in the Chinese market, see also Barth, *Imperialismen*, p. 41.

[29] On the small number of foreign banks before 1890, see Tamagna, *Banking and Finance in China*, pp. 24–5 and Chapter 2 of the present volume.

[30] Ni, *Qingchao jiadao caizheng*, pp. 179, 380–1; Peng, *Shijiu shiji houbanqi de zhongguo*, pp. 107–8.

[31] Peng, *Shijiu shiji houbanqi de zhongguo*, pp. 104–8.

[32] Peng, *Shijiu shiji houbanqi de zhongguo*, pp. 109–26.

[33] Van de Ven, *Breaking with the Past*, pp. 133–8.

[34] Ma, 'Financial Revolution', p. 11; Van de Ven, *Breaking with the Past*, ch. 4.

[35] Tōa Dōbunkai Chōsa Hensanbu, *Shina kinyū kikan*, p. 449; Yang, *Money and Credit in China*, pp. 99–100; Xu, 'Jiawu zhongri zhanzheng qian', p. 108; Dzen, *Bankwesen in China*, p. 21; Du Ruilian 杜瑞聯 memorial (23 February 1877), *PHSL*, p. 110; Cen Yuying 岑毓英 memorial (1886/7), *PHSL*, p. 110.

to the government, being afraid that it would either not repay the loan on time or simply convert it into a donation.[36] Zeng Jize 曾紀澤, China's ambassador to Great Britain, explained that 'when China borrows money from its people, it usually lies and cheats. This causes the ignorant common people to be fearful when they hear news', so that in an emergency, China could not rely on its own people for the borrowing of money.[37] In contrast, Chinese officials were normally able to borrow large sums of money at the relatively low interest rate of around 8–10 per cent per year from foreign sources.[38] Therefore, foreign loans presented them with a welcome new measure for raising revenue. Zuo Zongtang 左宗棠, who contracted several foreign loans to fund his Western military expedition between 1867 and 1881, praised the willingness of foreign merchants to lend money: '[T]hey do not have the tendency of hoarding and profiteering that Chinese merchants have. Moreover, the more you borrow from them the lower is the interest you pay, which is also completely different from the attitudes of Chinese merchants.'[39] Between 1853 and 1884, China borrowed around 33 million Kuping taels from foreign sources.[40] Importantly, from 1874 the Chinese government also started to issue public loans on the London capital market, mainly with the help of the Hongkong and Shanghai Banking Corporation (HSBC), which made it possible for China to borrow even larger sums of money.[41] By 1884, borrowing foreign capital had become such a common practice for the government that the Board of Revenue included the income from foreign debt and the expenditure for its repayment as new categories in the accounts of China's state finance.[42]

During this period, foreign loans were mainly used for military purposes and the court maintained that 'the borrowing of foreign money is always only an emergency measure', urging officials to raise money otherwise if possible.[43] Yet, some Chinese reformers of the Self-Strengthening Movement (Ziqiang yundong 自强運動) in the 1870s also started to consider using foreign capital productively to finance China's modernization. This was especially the case in the field of railway construction, which was central to the efforts of Chinese reformers to pursue 'wealth and power', but required large sums of money not readily available in China. Starting from the 1870s, a group of officials led by

---

[36] Xu, 'Jiawu zhongri zhanzheng qian', p. 108.
[37] Zeng, diary entry (15 April 1879), in Wang, Zeng Jize, p. 192.
[38] Xu, Zhongguo jindai waizhai tongji, pp. 4–8.
[39] Zuo Zongtang memorial (10 January 1876), in Zuo, Zuo Zongtang quanji, 6:343. On Zuo's foreign loans, see Xu, Zhongguo jindai waizhai tongji, pp. 6–7.
[40] Xu et al., Cong bainian quru, 1:517–19.
[41] Van de Ven, Breaking with the Past, pp. 136–7; King, HSBC History, pp. 547–53.
[42] Ma, Wan Qing waizhaishi, pp. 76–7.
[43] Imperial Edict (31 January 1878), QWSL, 1:115. Also see Imperial Edict (June 1884), QWSL, 1:138. On the primacy of loans for military purposes before the mid-1880s, see Xu, Zhongguo jindai waizhai tongji, pp. 5–9.

Figure 1.3 Li Hongzhang 李鴻章 (1823–1901), 1870s. Image courtesy of the Metropolitan Museum of Art, New York (www.metmuseum.org/art/collection/search/261590).

Li Hongzhang (Figure 1.3) started to actively support the construction of railways.[44] However, the problem of how to raise the high construction costs for railways presented an important obstacle right from Li's earliest considerations of railway construction.[45]

In the late 1870s, Ma Jianzhong 馬建忠 and Xue Fucheng 薛福成, two members of Li's *mufu* staff, began to advocate using foreign capital to raise the necessary capital to construct railways.[46] Ma, who had lived and studied in Paris from 1876 to 1879, enthusiastically supported using foreign capital.

---

[44] Quote from Li Hongzhang to Prince Chun (Yi Xuan) (2 February 1881), *ZJTS*, 1:94; also see Li, *Zhongguo zaoqi de tielu*, pp. 4–32.

[45] Li, *Zhongguo zaoqi de tielu*, p. 27.

[46] Ma, *Qingmo minchu tielu*, pp. 18–24.

He argued that those criticizing the use of foreign debt 'do not know that among the Western countries there is not one that does not owe debts of several billion taels'. For him, borrowing foreign capital was fine if the interest rate was not excessively high and China repaid the loan on time. Unlike 'borrowing money for the payment of indemnities or interest of previous loans', using foreign loans to construct railways produced new revenue and would therefore be easily repaid.[47] While Xue was more cautious than Ma, he also argued that 'there is no alternative to borrowing foreign money' if China wanted to construct railways.[48] Li later stated that he had gained most of his knowledge about foreign borrowing from those who had spent periods of time abroad like Ma. At the same time, it was Xue who drafted many of the memorials that Li submitted to the throne about the use of foreign capital.[49]

In 1880 Liu Mingchuan 劉銘傳, a former general in Li's Huai army, made the first direct proposal to the throne to use foreign capital for railway construction.[50] Li then submitted a memorial drafted by Xue Fucheng to the emperor supporting Liu's views in December 1880.[51] After explaining that railways were essential for pursuing 'wealth and power', Li agreed with Liu that there was no alternative to borrowing foreign money if China wanted to build railways. Both Liu and Li argued that foreign capital was useful if it was employed for productive purposes that opened new streams of revenue such as the construction of railways. However, the court eventually forbade using foreign loans to construct railways, arguing that 'the required funds [for railway construction] can be up to several million, how we can obtain such large sums? If we borrow foreign money, then this will generate many corrupt practices'.[52] Evidently, the court was still anxious that using foreign debt might become widespread and escape its central control. Despite this early failure, the openness to using foreign capital for railway construction shown by Li, Liu and other officials became the basis for Chinese cooperation with foreign bankers beyond simple loans for military purposes.

Reformers like Ma also developed a critique of China's early foreign loans, which had mainly been handled by the HSBC. Ma criticized the fact there were 'not more than three or four foreign banks' in China that monopolized the Chinese loan business and offered China unfair loan conditions. 'Even if big foreign banks would send their representatives to China, it would be difficult for them to go beyond their [the foreign banks in the treaty ports] control.' Therefore, China needed to go to Europe directly and approach officials and

---

[47] Ma Jianzhong, 'Tiedao lun' (1879/1880), *MJZQJ*, pp. 16–23. On Ma Jianzhong, see Zhongyang yanjiuyuan jindaishi yanjiusuo, *Jindai zhongguo dui xifang*, p. 653.
[48] Xue Fucheng memorial (1880), in Ding and Wang, *Xue Fucheng xuanji*, p. 139.
[49] Ma, *Qingmo minchu tielu*, p. 23.
[50] Liu Mingchuan memorial (December 1880), *ZJTS*, pp. 86–7.
[51] Li Hongzhang memorial (31 December 1880), *ZJTS*, pp. 89–93.
[52] Imperial Edict (14 February 1881), *ZJTS*, pp. 102–3.

banks there about loans, so that it gained proper access to European capital markets and could fix the price and interest rates of the loans itself.[53] While the HSBC played an important role in mediating the issuance of China's first public loans, Ma recognized that China could raise money on better conditions if it could access foreign money markets more directly and if there existed more competition among foreign banks.

Ma's critique explains why Chinese reformers later welcomed the plans of German bankers to establish a bank in China, which would increase the competition among foreign banks there. More broadly, the increasing interest Chinese officials exhibited in using foreign capital shows that the entry of German and other foreign bankers into the China market was not a one-sided effort, but there also existed a growing interest among Chinese elites to engage with foreign financial institutes and markets. In the absence of Chinese institutions that could provide large sums of cheap capital, foreign banks and the capital markets they could access were able to fill an institutional void in the Chinese economy. As we will see, bankers in Germany followed this growing willingness of Chinese officials to use foreign capital for the purpose of modernizing China with great interest, and it played an important role in their assessment of the viability of investing and doing business in China.

1.3   The German Government and the Study Mission of 1886

It was during the Sino-French War of 1884/5 that China started to look beyond London to raise money for its war efforts. For this purpose, the new governor-general of Liangguang province, Zhang Zhidong 張之洞, started loan negotiations with the Deutsche Bank and the Disconto-Gesellschaft through the Chinese legation in Berlin.[54] The confidence of the German bankers in their ability to float a Chinese loan in Germany now also grew. While the HSBC was only willing to provide the German bankers with a small passive participation for any Chinese loans floated by the British bank in London during the war, the German bankers had no interest in merely participating in the subscription of the loan. They felt that 'the moment has come to start negotiations with the Hongkong Shanghai Bank in the direction that they and we make the deal [for a Chinese loan] together and on the basis of equality'. The German bankers were confident that the German market now was 'able to receive a Chinese loan'.[55]

---

[53] Ma Jianzhong, 'Jiezhai yi kai daolu shuo' (1879/1880), *MJZQJ*, pp. 24–30. As King explains when discussing early Chinese loans, China did not 'send its officials to London' to negotiate loans at the time. See King, *HSBC History*, 1:542.

[54] Xu to Disconto-Gesellschaft (18 December 1884), HADB, S2585; Xu to Deutsche Bank and Disconto-Gesellschaft (10 January 1885), HADB, S2585.

[55] Quote from Deutsche Bank (Berlin) to Deutsche Bank (London) (24 December 1884), HADB, S2585; Deutsche Bank (London) to Deutsche Bank (Berlin) (22 December 1884), HADB, S2585.

However, despite the Chinese interest in a loan provided by the German banks and the German bankers' grown confidence, the German bankers eventually failed to float a Chinese loan during the war and China once more raised necessary loans in London with the help of the HSBC and the British China firm Jardine, Matheson and Co.[56] There were two reasons for the German failure. First, as the London manager of the Deutsche Bank, Gustav Pietsch, pointed out, a key weakness of the German banks' position was that most loans were floated for the Chinese government after advances had been issued to the Chinese government by foreign banks and firms in China. Therefore, he felt that, in the absence of a branch or agent in China, the German banks would have difficulties contracting a loan with China.[57] This assessment was vindicated by the fact that eventually China cooperated with the HSBC and Jardine, two firms with a long-standing presence in China, in floating loans during the war. Second, while the German bankers considered cooperation with the HSBC in floating Chinese loans, they insisted on absolute parity with the British bankers 'in terms of the relationship to the Chinese government'.[58] However, the HSBC wished to maintain their monopoly position as 'banker to China' and handle all direct contact and contract the loan with the Chinese government alone. The bank generally showed little interest in the German offer for cooperation.[59] Thus cooperation with the HSBC, which could have provided the branch infrastructure and contacts in China the German bankers lacked, also seemed impossible for the moment.

After this failure, the German banks turned to the German Foreign Office for support. As early as March 1885, the Deutsche Bank had already written to the German minister in Beijing, Max von Brandt (Figure 1.4), and asked whether he could provide them with information about possible loans the Chinese government wished to contract. Brandt agreed, but he believed that it would 'most likely be those banking institutes that are established in China or at least have agencies there that will be approached by the Chinese government

---

[56] Wallich to Bulkeley-Johnson (13 June 1885), HADB, S2585; Matheson to Wallich (16 June 1885), HADB, S2585; 'Chinese Imperial Government Loan of 1885' (27 February 1885), HADB, S2585.

[57] Deutsche Bank (London) to Deutsche Bank (Berlin) (20 June 1885), HADB, S2585.

[58] Quote from Deutsche Bank (Berlin) to Koch (telegraph notes after Koch to Deutsche Bank (Berlin)) (1 July 1885), HADB, S2585; Deutsche Bank (Berlin) to Disconto-Gesellschaft (4 July 1885), HADB, S2585.

[59] Quote from Koch to Deutsche Bank (Berlin), Telegram No. 2 (2 July 1885), HADB, S2585; Koch to Deutsche Bank (Berlin), Telegram No. 1 (2 July 1885), HADB, S2585. In his correspondence with HSBC Hong Kong manager Thomas Jackson, David McLean, London manager of the HSBC, only mentions the offer of the German group to cooperate, but does not indicate any initiative from the side of the HSBC. See McLean to Jackson (1 July 1885), HSBC Group Archives, London, HQ HSBCK 0008-0001, 285. In their negotiations with the German bankers, the HSBC eventually rejected their request for parity. See Deutsche Bank (Berlin) to HSBC (London) (4 July 1885), HADB, S2585; HSBC to Deutsche Bank (Berlin) (6 July 1885), HADB, S2585.

Figure 1.4 Max von Brandt (1835–1920). From Exner, *China*.

or the provincial offices for the mediation of loans'.[60] This response reflected the great importance Brandt attached to the establishment of a German bank in China. While he was satisfied with the achievements of German merchants in China, he repeatedly complained to the Foreign Office and German Chancellor Otto von Bismarck about the lack of a German bank in China. On the one hand, Brandt believed that a sufficiently accommodating German bank institute was necessary to free German merchants from their dependency on British banks and merchant houses such as the HSBC or Jardine for trade financing. This was especially the case for German merchant houses that represented German industrial firms in China, since they needed to rely on British credit in the absence of a German bank. Consequently, Germany did not only 'suffer financial losses', but the reliance on British credit also 'weaken[ed] the national sentiment' of Germans involved in the China trade.[61] On the other hand, Brandt stressed that the lack of a German bank in China meant that German bankers were disadvantaged in the competition for loans, which were often tied to

---

[60] Brandt to Deutsche Bank (29 March 1885), HADB, S2585.
[61] Brandt to Bismarck (15 October 1886), BArch, R901/12986, pp. 4–5.

industrial purchases. This led to a loss of business for German industry, which could not rely on a strong German bank that brought them orders through the loans it contracted with China.[62] Consequently, Brandt became one of the driving forces behind the establishment of a German bank in China.

Brandt's support for the establishment of a German bank in China suited Bismarck's overall policy of strengthening and supporting German commerce abroad. While Bismarck had originally believed in free trade, from the 1870s he shifted to a more protectionist economic policy, both to appeal to conservative groups in Germany and to strengthen the German economy and find new markets for German exports after the start of the Great Depression in 1873.[63] The German government pursued three measures to strengthen German commerce abroad. First, it reformed and expanded the German diplomatic service, tasking it with the support of Germany's foreign trade. Second, it established state-subsidized shipping lines between Germany and China and Australia. Third, it supported the expansion of German overseas banking and particularly the establishment of a global German overseas bank. All these efforts were not only meant to simply support German overseas commerce. They were also specifically aimed at bolstering its independence from and helping it catch up with other countries, in particular Britain.[64] For Bismarck, China, with its 'vast and highly populated territory', was the overseas market that 'deserved the greatest interest'. As it would 'sooner or later' offer an important market for German industry, especially for railway construction, it would be essential for Germany to have a banking institution there.[65]

Now, following the failed attempt to float a Chinese loan during the Sino-French War or cooperate with British financiers for the floating of such loans, the German banks on 8 July 1885 approached the Foreign Office in Berlin for help. They explained that they had been interested in 'railway construction in China, and, in connection with this, the introduction of a Chinese loan on the German market' for several years. They mentioned that they had made relevant offers to the Chinese, especially with a view to opening a new market for German industry. They then turned to recent negotiations about a Chinese loan with the HSBC and explained that they had insisted on 'coming into direct contact with the Chinese government, not only because of our standing, but especially because in this way we can have real influence on the use of the money, especially with regards to the use of German industry and arrangement

---

[62] Brandt to Bismarck (15 October 1884), PAAA, R17.771, 11; Brandt to Bismarck (3 December 1884), PAAA, R17.771, pp. 17–19; Brandt to Bismarck (5 February 1885), PAAA, R17.771, pp. 44–6.

[63] Rose, 'Otto von Bismarck', pp. 84–5; Epkenhans, 'Bismarck und die Wirtschaft', p. 239; Canis, Bismarcks Aussenpolitik, pp. 209–10.

[64] Wehler, Bismarck und der Imperialismus, pp. 230–57.

[65] Bismarck to Boetticher (20 May 1888), BArch, R1501/102074, pp. 143–6.

of payments (the remittance of silver, etc.)'. However, the HSBC had insisted to alone be in direct contact with the Chinese government and handle the loan contract and transaction itself. Therefore, the German bankers felt they now needed to 'enter into direct negotiations [with the Chinese government] to open a suitable field of work for German capital and German industry in China'. They therefore asked Brandt to directly inform the Chinese government that German banks were ready to begin loan negotiations and believed that they could offer the same or better conditions than their British competitors.[66]

Brandt relayed the message to the Chinese government. However, this attempt to communicate with the Chinese government from Berlin through the German minister in Beijing also proved futile, as the Chinese government only thanked the banks for their offer and promised to come back to it if necessary. Brandt was certain that the two banks would fail in contracting a Chinese loan in this way. As foreign banks and agents in China made so many loan offers to the Chinese central and provincial governments, these did not need to enter into negotiations with banks in Europe. He therefore strongly recommended that the banks send an agent to China.[67] As we have seen from the offer Zhang Zhidong sought from the German banks and the writings of Ma Jianzhong, Brandt was wrong in thinking that Chinese officials were not interested in directly approaching European banks that were not present in China. However, Brandt was right that the lack of a branch or agent in China meant that the two German banks were at a disadvantage when it came to entering into direct negotiations with the Chinese government and to quickly reacting to Chinese loan requirements. Yet, at this point there do not seem to have existed concrete plans among German bankers for the establishment of a German bank in China yet.

Nevertheless, the two banks decided to send a study mission to China in 1885 to enter into more direct contact with China and the Chinese government. On 16 June 1885, the Deutsche Bank and the Disconto-Gesellschaft invited several German industrial firms, such as Krupp and Vulcan Stettin, to discuss 'railway construction overseas'. After a meeting on 24 June, the participants decided to send a study mission of three men to China to 'secure for the consortium the conclusion of loans, the provision of railway materials and the construction of railways' in China. To make such business deals possible, the study mission first was to 'acquire the necessary information and ... connections'. A second objective of the study mission was to find a suitable temporary or permanent agent for the interests of the consortium in China.[68] This study mission reflected

---

[66] Deutsche Bank and Disconto-Gesellschaft to Auswärtiges Amt (8 July 1885), PAAA, R17.771, pp. 74–80.
[67] Brandt to Bismarck (16 July 1885), PAAA, R17.771, pp. 99–102.
[68] Müller-Jabusch, *Deutsch-Asiatische Bank*, pp. 12–14.

the long-term interest of the banks and the involved industrial firms in Chinese railway construction. However, it was also the result of more recent developments in China.

After the end of the Sino-French War, news had reached Germany that China had now decided to construct railways. In June 1885, German industrialist Friedrich Hammacher forwarded a report by the German merchant Sammer from Tianjin to the Deutsche Bank. In the report, Sammer explained that with the beginning of the Sino-French War the party of Li Hongzhang, who was 'interested in the introduction of railways' but whose repeated railway proposals had been rejected, had now become the leading political party in China. Moreover, the father of the young emperor and head of the Chinese government, who was falsely called Prince Gong (Gong qinwang 恭親王) instead of Prince Chun (Chun qinwang 醇親王) by Sammer, was also interested in the construction of railways. This had already led to competition among several foreign firms, such as Jardine, Matheson & Co., for railway concessions. The Chinese were now becoming more and more convinced that 'railways are necessities of life for China'. Although there still existed opposition to railways among the common people in China, Sammer was certain that the Chinese 'government has to and will solve the railway questions sooner or later' and start the construction of railways. He was optimistic that the Germans could win the competition for railway concessions. However, he felt that uniting the big German banks in a syndicate to provide funds for Chinese railway construction was of key importance to achieve success.[69]

Sammer was correct insofar as in April 1884, after first conflicts with France, Prince Chun had replaced Prince Gong as the head of the Grand Council. He was a close ally of Li Hongzhang and had been persuaded by Li of the importance of building railways. This had already led to reports by Western newspapers in China that China would start the construction of railways.[70] In October 1885, Prince Chun and Li Hongzhang were put in charge of the new Board for Naval Affairs (Haijun yamen 海軍衙門), which also was to manage the construction of railways.[71] After the end of the Sino-French War, newspapers in Germany also reported that China had finally decided to 'swiftly start the construction of railways' with the help of foreign capital.[72] These factors all contributed to the dispatching of the study mission to China. The letter forwarded to the Deutsche Bank by Hammacher also shows how closely German commercial and industrial circles followed developments in China and how important the increasing openness of China towards railways was for

---

[69] Sammer to Hammacher (20 March 1885), HADB, S2585. The fact that the letter is located among other documents from June 1885 in the archives of the Deutsche Bank suggests that it was during June 1885 that the Deutsche Bank received the report.

[70] Li, *Zhongguo zaoqi de tielu*, pp. 57–9.

[71] Li, *Zhongguo zaoqi de tielu*, p. 61.

[72] *BBZ* (22 June 1885, evening edition).

these businesspeople. The dispatching of the study mission, ordered not only to conclude business deals but also to collect information, establish contacts to Chinese officials and hire an agent, was proof that the German bankers were drawn to China by these new developments and wished to understand them more clearly. It also showed that they realized the importance of establishing direct contacts with Chinese officials.

The study mission included August Heinrich Exner, Curt Erich and Karl Bethge. Exner and Erich were employees of Germany's two biggest banks, the Deutsche Bank and the Deutsche Disconto-Gesellschaft, respectively. Bethge was an engineer connected to Krupp.[73] The three representatives left Germany in January and first arrived in Hong Kong on 12 February. The German Foreign Office had promised the syndicate the support of the German minister and consuls in China for the study mission.[74] In China, the first important stop for the representatives was Tianjin, where they were introduced to Li Hongzhang by the German vice consul. On 14 March, they had a long audience with Li. The governor-general discussed the issuing of loans with the representatives and asked whether they would be willing to provide loans for mining projects and regulating the Yellow River. He also expressed his interest in the establishment of a German bank in China, just as he did two years later to Simon Alfred von Oppenheim.[75] When the discussion turned to the subject of railways, Li explained that China wanted to construct railways, but wanted to do so slowly and without borrowing money.[76]

As we have seen, despite this apparent hesitancy, Li was not opposed to using foreign loans to construct railways. After the establishment of the Board of Naval Affairs, Li quickly contracted a foreign loan for the extension of the Kaiping railways in 1887.[77] Moreover, both before and after 1886, Li often purchased foreign rails and other railway materials for his Kaiping railway project.[78] Therefore, Li's hesitant reply was not due to a general opposition to the use of foreign capital, but might have had other causes. One possibility is that he reacted hesitantly because of false reports that were circulating stating that the representatives wished to contract loans with China for the large sum of £35 million for war purposes and railway construction, but only under the condition that funds would be controlled by the German syndicate and used for material purchases in Germany.[79] Another possible reason for Li's hesitant

[73] Müller-Jabusch, *Deutsch-Asiatische Bank*, pp. 12–14.
[74] *North-China Herald* (24 February 1886); Müller-Jabusch, *Deutsch-Asiatische Bank*, pp. 14–15.
[75] Exner, *China*, pp. 119–23; Müller-Jabusch, *Deutsch-Asiatische Bank*, p. 17.
[76] Exner, *Einnahmequellen*, p. 35.
[77] Ma, *Wan Qing waizhaishi*, pp. 27–8.
[78] Perry Horace Kent, *Railway Enterprise in China*, pp. 23–35.
[79] *The Times* (London) (2 January 1886); *BBC* (4 January 1886, evening edition); *Journal des Débats* (3 January 1886); *North-China Herald* (6 January 1886).

response was that he might have simply wanted to avoid making early commitments to the representatives. In any case, even though Li had shown a general interest in cooperating with the German bankers, his reply with regards to the topic of railways naturally was a great disappointment to the study mission, whose main objective was focussed on the financing of railway construction and the provision of railway materials to China.

In Tianjin, the three representatives also met with the Chinese Customs Circuit Intendant (Daotai 道臺) Zhou Fu 周馥, who later went on to become governor of Shandong. Zhou complained to the bankers that he could not buy remittances to Germany in China and expressed his hope that a German bank in China would soon be established, which he would be happy to support.[80] As both Brandt and Simon Alfred von Oppenheim later stated, such Chinese support for the establishment of a German bank in China was most likely aimed at increasing the competition among foreign capitalists in China to obtain better terms for Chinese loans.[81]

On 16 March the three representatives left Tianjin for Beijing. Despite the help of Brandt, Prince Qing (Qing qinwang 慶親王) did not agree to meet them at the Chinese Foreign Office, the Zongli Yamen 總理衙門, and only informed Brandt again that he would contact him if China wished to raise a loan.[82] As the Inspector General of the Customs Service, Robert Hart, with whom the representatives also met, put it, 'the German Syndicate came, saw, and did not conquer'.[83] Most likely because there was nothing more the mission could do for the moment, Erich and Exner were eventually recalled to Germany in the summer and autumn of 1886.[84] Bethge stayed in China and would later act as agent for the German banks.[85] After Exner and Erich had returned to Germany, the consortium that had sent them to China met on 7 February 1887. Having read the reports of the study mission, it concluded that 'the preconditions, which had led to the forming of the consortium, at least for the moment do not exist'.[86] The members of the consortium felt that China would not build railways 'on a large scale' soon. Smaller railway lines that might be built in China were 'suitable for ... individual' members of the

---

[80] Exner, *China*, pp. 126–31; Müller-Jabusch, *Deutsch-Asiatische Bank*, pp. 18–19. For more on Zhou Fu, see Wang, *Shandong zhongyao lishi renwu*, pp. 193–5.

[81] Simon Alfred von Oppenheim to Eduard von Oppenheim (20 July 1888), HSO, A VIII 114 Ostasiatische Geschäfte 1888–1914; Brandt to Bismarck (24 July 1888), BArch, R901/12988, p. 3.

[82] Stoecker, *Deutschland und China*, p. 196.

[83] Quote from Hart to Campbell (3 April 1886), *IGPK*, 1:632. Hart mentions that he met with the representatives in his diary: Sir Robert Hart Diary (24 March 1886), *Special Collections and Archives, Queen's University Belfast*, MS.15.1.31.245.

[84] Berchem to Brandt (16 July 1886), in Stoecker, *Deutschland und China*, p. 278; Exner, *China*, pp. 208, 216; Stoecker, *Deutschland und China*, p. 197.

[85] Stoecker, *Deutschland und China*, p. 196.

[86] Müller-Jabusch, *Deutsch-Asiatische Bank*, p. 20.

consortium but did not require a 'consortium of such a size'.[87] However, the consortium was not disbanded and decided to stay in contact, while every member was given the right to act independently.[88]

Despite this rather negative assessment, it would be wrong to see the mission as a failure. The delegates succeeded in establishing important contacts in China, and with Bethge remaining in China, the consortium now had a representative there. Moreover, Exner 'collected a great amount of valuable materials' on the prospects of both the German financing of railways and the possible establishment of a German bank in China.[89] Exner later published two books based on his time in China – a study of the income of the Chinese state and a travel report.[90] His study of the income of the Chinese state was one of the first Western studies of China's public finance and became so influential that it was even translated into English.[91] It gave a very favourable picture of China's revenues and the ability of the Chinese state to contract and repay foreign loans. His travel report concluded that 'the construction of railways in China is a done deal' and just a matter of time.[92] He also reported that many Chinese reformers were in favour of railway construction and even provided some of their writings, such as the memorial of Liu Mingchuan, in German translation.[93] As such reports were scarce in Europe, they supported the already existing enthusiasm for railway construction in China. Moreover, the particular attention Exner pays to the new Chinese openness towards railways again reaffirms the importance of development in China for the thinking of German bankers. Finally, the delegates had also learned that there was Chinese support for the establishment of a German bank in China. They reported to the consortium in Germany that 'the precondition for everything planned, be it railways, business for German industry or loans, is the establishment of a German bank institute in China'.[94] This made the importance of establishing a German bank in China clear to the consortium that had sent the mission to China.[95] Exner later explained that the DAB's establishment was 'the first positive consequence' of the study mission to China.[96] The study mission represented a meeting of German financial and Chinese interests and actors

---

[87] Exner to Brandt (2 January 1887), PAAA, R9208/563, pp. 14–19.
[88] Müller-Jabusch, *Deutsch-Asiatische Bank*, p. 20.
[89] Brandt to Bismarck (15 October 1886), BArch, R901/12986, p. 2.
[90] Exner, *Einnahmequellen*; Exner, *China*.
[91] For the English translation, see Exner, 'The Sources of Revenue', pp. 276–91. Importantly, Exner's account preceded later prominent accounts, such as Jamieson, *Revenue and Expenditure of the Chinese Empire*.
[92] Exner, *China*, p. 241.
[93] Exner, *China*, pp. 242–62.
[94] Quote from Müller-Jabusch, *Deutsch-Asiatische Bank*, p. 17. Also see Exner, *Einnahmequellen*, p. 49.
[95] Münch, *Hansemann*, p. 218.
[96] Exner, *China*, p. viii.

on the Chinese frontier and laid the basis for the later establishment of a permanent presence of German bankers there.

1.4   The Establishment of the Deutsch-Asiatische Bank

After the return of the study mission, Brandt reiterated his conviction regarding the necessity of a German bank with sufficient capital in China to Bismarck, which for him was the 'necessary complementation' to the German state-subsidized shipping line. While several banks had expressed their interest in China to him, he believed that the 'diverging opinions and wishes' of different interested parties might hinder the emergence of any 'practical result'.[97] In Germany, the attempts of the German government to further the expansion of German overseas banking and the establishment of a global German overseas bank that could support German commerce abroad had not yielded any results by the middle of 1886. Yet, on 2 October the Deutsche Bank established the Deutsche Überseebank as a subsidiary firm without the participation of the German government.[98] As the Deutsche Bank explained to Brandt, they hoped to continue to use the connections the study mission had established in China. However, they did not think that the establishment of a bank in China was immediately possible, as such a bank would need to have its capital in silver currency, while German law only allowed stock companies with stock capital in German reichsmark. The Deutsche Bank believed that the Deutsche Überseebank, which was to focus its activities on South America for now, could later possibly extend its activities to East Asia.[99] The Deutsche Bank and the Disconto-Gesellschaft nevertheless maintained their interest in China. Bethge now acted as agent for the two banks and informed them about possible opportunities for loans.[100]

This stance of the Deutsche Bank and the Disconto-Gesellschaft changed in spring 1887, when a German consortium comprising the Berlin banks Warschauer & Co. and Berliner Handels-Gesellschaft and the Frankfurt bank Jacob S. H. Stern floated the first Chinese loan on the German capital market. While the sum of 5 million reichsmark was relatively small, the loan was enthusiastically received in Germany as the first introduction of a Chinese loan on the German capital market and 'the financial basis' for the engagement of German industry in China.[101] The loan was issued with an annual interest rate of 5.5 per cent and a repayment period of fifteen years. Li Hongzhang had

[97] Brandt to Bismarck (15 October 1886), BArch, R901/12986, pp. 3–5.
[98] Barth, *Imperialismen*, pp. 32–3.
[99] Deutsche Bank to Brandt (20 December 1886), PAAA, R9208/563, pp. 12–13.
[100] Disconto-Gesellschaft to Bethge (28 January 1887), HADB, S2586.
[101] *BBC* (9 April 1887, evening edition); *BBZ* (9 April 1887), in HADB, S2585; *BBC* (12 April 1887), in HADB, S2585. The quote is from the *Norddeutsche Allgemeine Zeitung* quoted in *BBC* (12 April 1887) and *BBZ* (9 April 1887).

contracted the loan with the German China firm Carlowitz & Co, who acted as agent for the Warschauer group. In his report to the throne, Li especially stressed that China had never been able to borrow foreign capital at such a low interest rate. Moreover, the German bankers had not even made it a requirement that Customs revenue must act as collateral.[102] Clearly, German bankers had already increased the competition among foreign financiers in China, which improved the loan terms China could obtain.[103] The floating of the loan was also proof that the German market was able to absorb Chinese loans and was the first public Chinese loan not floated in London.[104]

Reacting to their new German competition, the Deutsche Bank and the Disconto-Gesellschaft informed Bethge that they were happy to begin loan negotiations with the Chinese government.[105] They also tried to come to an understanding with the Warschauer group to cooperate for future Chinese loans. However, for now the competition between the Frankfurt house of Rothschild, who was a close ally of the Disconto-Gesellschaft and wished to join the loan business, and their Frankfurt competitors Jacob S. H. Stern, who belonged to the Warschauer group, prevented any cooperation.[106] This rivalry between the two Frankfurt banks became the main obstacle to bringing together two German bank groups during 1887. After the Chinese loan had been floated in Germany, the Foreign Office tried to unite the two German banking groups for future loans in China. Both Brandt and Bismarck believed that the two groups should cooperate and avoid any competition between German banks in China.[107] Ludwig Raschdau, a member of the Foreign Office, thereupon met with Disconto-Gesellschaft director Russell and asked him to unite all German banks in a loan consortium for China. Thereafter, Russell and Hugo Oppenheim, director of Warschauer & Co., met several times. In May 1887 Oppenheim agreed to talk to Jacob Stern and persuade him to forgo any further participation in the consortium.[108]

[102] Li Hongzhang memorial (31 January 1887), AIMH, 01-32-012-01-002; Warschauer to Deutsche Bank (12 November 1888), HADB, S2586.
[103] On this point, also see Brötel, *Frankreich im Fernen Osten*, pp. 292–3, 302–3. In his brief discussion of the issue, Brötel seems to overestimate the increased competition before 1895 based on a few loan offers that, except for the German 1887 loan, were eventually not realized.
[104] For an overview of Chinese public loans floated between 1874 and 1895, see King, *HSBC History*, 1:548–9, 557.
[105] Disconto-Gesellschaft to Bethge (22 April 1887), HADB, S2586.
[106] Deutsche Bank (Berlin) to Deutsche Bank (Hamburg) (30 April 1887), HADB, S2586; Wallich to Siemens (7 May 1887), HADB, S2586; Müller-Jabusch, *Deutsch-Asiatische Bank*, p. 25; Disconto-Gesellschaft, *Denkschrift*, p. 220.
[107] Warschauer & Co. to Brandt (28 July 1887), PAAA, R9208/563, p. 28; Rottenburg to Berchem (22 August 1887), BArch, R901/12986, p. 32.
[108] Wallich to Siemens (7 May 1887), HADB, S2586.

Members of the Foreign Office now also brought up the establishment of a global German overseas bank again. While Hansemann explained that the banks were still not in favour of establishing a global overseas bank, the Disconto-Gesellschaft and Deutsche Bank now planned to establish 'a bank with less capital [only] for China'. Besides the Frankfurt house of Rothschild, the Berlin private bank Bleichröder and the Norddeutsche Bank in Hamburg were also to join these plans.[109] Bismarck had promised early on to support such a German bank in China if it was established, but was not ready to take the initiative for its establishment himself.[110] However, despite the efforts of the Foreign Office, by July 1887 the two banking groups interested in China had still not been brought together.[111]

Bismarck and the Foreign Office grew impatient. As Hansemann later related, Bismarck now 'pushed for the realisation' of the bank project in China.[112] In November, Bismarck asked Franz von Burchard, the president of the Seehandlungsgesellschaft, a Prussian state bank, to mediate between the banks and fix the specifics of the future bank institute.[113] Burchard invited the bank group led by the Disconto-Gesellschaft, which also included the Deutsche Bank, Bleichröder and the Norddeutsche Bank, to negotiations on 9 and 10 November. The Disconto-Gesellschaft and the Deutsche Bank agreed to draw up a plan for the bank, which could then act as a basis for further negotiations. The Disconto-Gesellschaft also promised to begin discussions with the Rothschilds in Frankfurt, so that the three banks of the Warschauer group could soon join the consortium.[114]

When by the end of November still no agreement between the two groups had been reached, the Warschauer group, who had been complaining about the slow progress of the negotiations before, now took the initiative.[115] On 27 November 1887 they submitted a concrete proposal for the establishment of a German bank in China to the Foreign Office. The bank was to have a capital of 10 million reichsmark and was to be established in Shanghai. They explained that they were ready to follow the wishes of the Seehandlungsgesellschaft and unite with the other group. They, however, felt that the establishment of a German bank in China could 'bear ... no further delay' and were also willing to carry out the establishment of the bank on their own if necessary. A condition for a possible independent endeavour was that the German

[109] Foreign Office Note (30 April 1887), BArch, R901/12986, p. 15.
[110] Foreign Office Note (25 December 1886), BArch, R901/12986, p. 11.
[111] Berchem Note (15 May 1887), BArch, R901/12986, p. 16; Warschauer & Co. to Brandt (28 July 1887), PAAA, R9208/563, p. 28.
[112] Müller-Jabusch, *Deutsch-Asiatische Bank*, pp. 24–5.
[113] Scholz to Burchard (4 November 1887), GStA, I HA Rep. 109, No. 5363, pp. 1–2.
[114] Burchard to Scholz (10 November 1887), GStA, I HA Rep. 109, No. 5363, pp. 4–5.
[115] Warschauer & Co. to Brandt (5 May 1887), PAAA, R9208/563, p. 25; Warschauer & Co. to Brandt (28 July 1887), PAAA, R9208/563, pp. 28–9.

government would not support another bank group in the establishment of another competing German bank in China. They hoped that the German government would only support their bank in China and would also carry out its financial transactions between China and Germany through the bank.[116] The proposal not only showed that the Warschauer group was very determined to establish a bank in China, which must have increased the pressure on the other German bank group, but also indicated the importance they attached to the support of the German government.

On 2 December 1887, the group led by the Disconto-Gesellschaft submitted their own plan for a bank in China based on the negotiations in November with the Seehandlungsgesellschaft. Their plan was drafted by Deutsche Bank director Wallich and was more cautious than the proposal of the Warschauer group. Wallich possessed first-hand experience of working as a banker in China. Moreover, he was known as the 'conscience of the [Deutsche] Bank' and rather cautious in business.[117] This explains why the plan focussed on some of the risks involved in establishing a bank. While Wallich believed that there was 'no great danger' in establishing a bank in China, the opportunities for profits were limited because of the high expenses of such a bank and the existing competition in China. Nevertheless, the bank group was still willing to establish a bank in China to respond to the wishes of the Foreign Office for a bank institute that could assist German industry in opening a new market in China. Wallich insisted that it was a prerequisite for the establishment of such a bank that 'all interested German parties' needed to be united to avoid competition. Wallich saw the fluctuation of the market price of silver as one of the main problems a bank in China would face. Therefore, he hoped that the German government could issue a decree that allowed the bank to denominate its share capital in silver currency. As the bank was to be established in Shanghai, he proposed a capital of 5 million Shanghai taels.[118] Wallich's cautiousness, especially regarding the silver question, is understandable if we recall that the Deutsche Bank's first attempt to establish branches in China had partly failed because of the fall of the value of silver.[119] It was also strategically shrewder to show reluctance and caution when trying to persuade the government that a decree allowing the bank to denominate its share capital in silver currency was necessary. At the same time, Wallich's proposal taken together with the previous experience of the German bankers during the Sino-French

---

[116] Berliner Handelsgesellschaft to Auswärtiges Amt (28 November 1887), BArch, R901/12986, pp. 38–42.

[117] Hermann Wallich, 'Aus der Frühgeschichte der Deutschen Bank', p. 410.

[118] 'Promemoria in Sachen Gründung einer Deutsch-Chinesischen Bank', attachment to Wallich to Auswärtiges Amt (2 December 1887), BArch, R901/12986, pp. 48–58.

[119] On Wallich's cautiousness in the matter of establishing a German bank in China, also see Müller-Jabusch, Deutsch-Asiatische Bank, p. 27.

War shows that the German bankers understood that they were not entering a blank space without competition on the Chinese frontier.

At the end of November, Bismarck again asked Burchard to mediate between the groups. Referring to the quarrel between the two Frankfurt houses, Bismarck complained that 'personal resentments between two individual firms' could not inhibit an endeavour of such 'national importance'. In view of the proposal of the Warschauer group to establish a bank independently, he reiterated the importance of uniting German banking endeavours in China because of the 'national character' of competition there.[120] Burchard invited the representatives of the group led by the Disconto-Gesellschaft to a meeting on 5 December. During this meeting the banks finally agreed to cooperate with the Warschauer group, including the banking house of Jacob S. H. Stern, offering them one-third of the shares of the bank in China. Once the other group had agreed to enter the consortium for the bank, statutes were to be drawn up for the institute by Wallich, Russell, the delegates of the Warschauer group and the president of the Seehandlungsgesellschaft.[121] The Warschauer group promptly agreed to join the consortium.[122]

At the end of 1887, there finally existed a united consortium for the establishment of a German bank in China. The German government had certainly played an important role in bringing the banking groups together, but the willingness of the Warschauer group to act independently also added pressure to the Disconto group to comply, as it did not wish to have a German competitor in China. While the DAB was only officially established in February 1889, the agreement of the two bank groups was the key event for its establishment. From the end of 1887, the now-united banks already started to make preparations for the bank in China together, such as discussing the appointment of agents and interpreters.[123] The banks also acted together as a consortium and started to negotiate loans with Chinese government entities together.[124] In December 1887, the German Ministry of Justice also informed Burchard that the bank could be established as a bank with stock capital in silver, as the local currency in the consular district in China where the bank was to be established was also a silver currency.[125]

The year 1888 was used to work out the technicalities of establishing the bank.[126] While the plan of the Warschauer group had proposed a stock capital for the bank in reichsmark, the two groups eventually agreed on a capital of 5

---

[120] Bismarck to Burchard (30 November 1887), GStA, I HA Rep. 109, No. 5363, pp. 15–18.
[121] 'Protokoll' (5 December 1887), GStA, I HA Rep. 109, No. 5363, p. 62.
[122] Burchard Note (8 December 1887), GStA, I HA Rep. 109, No. 5363, p. 63.
[123] Warschauer & Co. to Deutsche Bank (25 July 1888), HADB, S2586; Warschauer & Co. to Deutsche Bank (12 November 1888), HADB, S2586.
[124] Warschauer & Co. to Deutsche Bank (9 March 1888), HADB, S2586.
[125] Wilke to Burchard (10 December 1887), GStA, I HA Rep. 109, pp. 75–6.
[126] Müller-Jabusch, Deutsch-Asiatische Bank, pp. 26–31.

million Shanghai taels, equal to around 20 million reichsmark, of which at first only 25 per cent was to be paid in.[127] This showed that the banks did not want to commit too much money and take too much of a risk when first establishing the bank. Before the bankers established the new bank, they asked the German government to support the bank in two ways. First, each time the bank elected a new chairman for their supervisory board, this chairman was to be confirmed by the German emperor. Second, the Seehandlungsgesellschaft was to take a small share of the stock capital and was to act as one of the subscription agents for the shares of the bank.[128] The purpose of both these requests was the elevation of the status of the bank. Bismarck agreed to the first request, stating that confirmation by the emperor would mean that the bank would 'receive the governmental recognition suitable to raise its reputation'.[129] Bismarck and Burchard also agreed to the participation of the Seehandlungsgesellschaft as shareholder and subscription agent.[130]

The solving of this last problem cleared the way for the new German bank in China. The DAB was established on 12 February 1889 by thirteen German banks with a share capital of 5 million Shanghai taels. The shareholder banks united most of German high finance. Besides those banks belonging to the original two bank groups and the Seehandlungsgesellschaft, the Bank für Handel & Industrie and Mendelssohn & Co. in Berlin also joined the bank. Eduard von Oppenheim, whose son had spoken so enthusiastically of the prospects of a German bank in China, also joined with his bank. Finally, the Bavarian Bayerische Hypotheken- und Wechselbank also joined the consortium with a small participation, as the German government had expressed their wish that a bank from Southern Germany should also be represented in the bank.[131] The Disconto-Gesellschaft received 16.1 per cent of the shares and became the biggest shareholder in the bank. The second biggest shareholders were the Deutsche Bank and Bleichröder with 11.1 per cent. Following the demand of the bankers, the Seehandlungsgesellschaft received the small amount of 3.5 per cent of the shares. However, the DAB was established as and remained an independent private joint-stock bank controlled by the

---

[127] 'Protokoll' (10 December 1887), GStA, I HA Rep. 109, No. 5363, p. 67; 'Protokoll' (19 December 1887), GStA, I HA Rep. 109, No. 5363, p. 79; 'Protokoll' (30 December 1887), GStA, I HA Rep. 109, No. 5363, pp. 82–83; Hansemann to Bismarck (5 December 1888) HSO, A VIII 114 Ostasiatische Geschäfte 1888–1914.

[128] 'Protokoll' (9 November 1888), HSO, A VIII 114 Ostasiatische Geschäfte 1888–1914.

[129] Bismarck to Consortium (5 January 1889), quoted in Müller-Jabusch, *Deutsch-Asiatische Bank*, p. 30.

[130] Rottenburg to Auswärtiges Amt (25 November 1888), BArch, R901/12988, p. 49; 'Protokoll' (23 January 1889), GStA, I HA Rep. 109, No. 5363, p. 158; Burchard to Scholz (1 February 1889), GStA, I HA Rep. 109, No. 5363, pp. 162–4.

[131] Russel to Berchem (12 February 1889), BArch, R901/12989, p. 29; 'Deutsch-Asiatische Bank betr.' (30 January 1889), BArch, R901/12989, p. 80; Oppenheim to Berchem (6 December 1888), BArch, R901/12988, pp. 71–2; *Deutscher Reichs-Anzeiger* (17 May 1889).

founding banks, and the Seehandlungsgesellschaft later sold its shares in the bank. Moreover, despite the relatively broad participation of German banks, Berlin's high finance and especially the Disconto-Gesellschaft were the most important forces in the DAB.[132]

In April 1890, the shareholder banks established the Konsortium für Asiatische Geschäfte (KfAG). This consortium included the same banks that had established the DAB, with the exception that the DAB itself took the place of the Seehandlungsgesellschaft and was given a share of 10 per cent in the consortium. The consortium was established to float Asian loans in Germany and, besides the famous Preußenkonsortium that floated loans for the German government, became one of the most important and prestigious German consortia.[133] In the following years the consortium and the DAB functioned as a dual structure, with the consortium taking over many of the big loans that the DAB negotiated and contracted in China. After two decades of failed attempts to gain a successful foothold in China for Germany's banks, the establishment of the DAB and the KfAG finally gave German bankers a broad and solid basis for their business in China. This made possible their increasing engagement with China and their rising importance for Chinese finance over the next twenty-five years.

1.5   Conclusion

As we have seen, German bankers had been interested in China and the supposedly large Chinese market since the 1870s. This enthusiasm was further spurred on by the growing Chinese interest to use foreign capital, construct railways and tap new sources of foreign finance beyond London and the HSBC in order to obtain better loan conditions through more competition among foreign banks and more direct access to foreign capital markets. At the same time, the growth of German banking and the German capital market meant that German banks were not willing to be only junior partners to British banks and firms engaged in China. The Sino-French War, the study mission to China and the first Chinese loan floated in Germany showed there were increasing possibilities for German financiers to issue loans to China and float Chinese bonds in Germany. However, each of these occasions had also demonstrated that at least an agent – or better, a bank – in China was necessary to compete with the established foreign banks and firms in China. While some banks like the Disconto-Gesellschaft in the early 1880s or later the Warschauer group expressed their interest in establishing a bank in China, others like the Deutsche Bank were more hesitant because of the existing competition in

---

[132] Müller-Jabusch, *Deutsch-Asiatische Bank*, pp. 31–2; 'Aufstellung der zur Generalversammlung vom 18.Juni 1909 hinterlegten Aktien der Deutsch-Asiatischen Bank' (18 June 1909), BArch, R901/4989, p. 136.
[133] Müller-Jabusch, *Deutsch-Asiatische Bank*, pp. 52–3.

China, the falling silver price and their previous negative experience with establishing a German bank in China.

Here, the German government to a certain extent played the role of a latecomer 'developmental state' wishing to support its own national economic development – in this case, German commerce in the Chinese market – to catch up and be able to compete with economically more developed countries like Britain.[134] The government acted as a unifying and accelerating element in bringing the banks together for the establishment of a German bank in China. However, the expectations that German bankers had for a bank in China were different from the German government's expectations. Since the 1880s, German banks had been mostly interested in issuing government loans and financing industrial projects for China and not in trade finance for German firms. Therefore, a German bank in China would ideally function as a vehicle and permanent agent for direct communication with the Chinese government. In contrast, the German government saw the bank as a key element in the building of a wider national commercial bloc in China that facilitated independent access for both German trade and industry to the Chinese market.[135] This contrast was reflected in the form the bank took after its establishment. While the bank unified German banking interests in China, the bankers initially only paid in a relatively small amount of the share capital. At the same time, the KfAG ensured that bigger loans could be taken over by the German banks if they wished. Thus, the bankers avoided taking on too much risk by committing a lot of capital in the bank. Yet, their limited commitment was sufficient to start establishing the infrastructure in China that allowed them to enter into direct contact with the Chinese government and effectively compete for loan contracts. This contrast between the relative risk-averseness of the bankers and the hope of the German government that the bank would financially accommodate the wishes of German trade and industry and cause the increased cooperation and cohesion of German commerce would lead to conflicts between the bank and the government over the following years.[136]

Despite the important role the German government played in shaping the form of the bank, its role should not be overestimated. German banks had a long-standing interest in China and the lack of a bank in China was an obvious and problematic disadvantage. Even if the German government had

---

[134] On the concept of the latecomer 'developmental state', see Gerschenkron, 'Economic Backwardness', pp. 5–30; and Woo-Cumings, *Developmental State*.

[135] Speaking about the establishment of German overseas banks in the 1880s more generally, Barth also notes the accelerating pressure of the German government, but also that eventually the private interests of German economic elites prevailed over the larger macroeconomic motives of the German state of supporting German exports. See Barth, *Imperialismen*, pp. 25, 41–2.

[136] For more on this, see Chapters 4 and 6.

taken no interest in China and overseas banking, it is difficult to imagine that the coming years would not have seen the establishment of a German bank in China. Especially the Warschauer group was keen to establish a bank in China, and other German banks would have needed to follow if they did not want to leave the Chinese market to their competitors. Therefore, there would have most likely been one or several, albeit smaller, German banks in China and they would have possibly been established later after the business for Chinese loans took off following the Sino-Japanese War of 1894/5. The influence of the German government should therefore only be seen as a shaping, but not necessarily decisive, factor in bringing about the establishment of a German bank in China. Moreover, the DAB was established as a private joint-stock bank and the involvement of the Seehandlungsgesellschaft was insignificant and had been invited by the bankers themselves. Nevertheless, the fact that, because of the unifying influence of the German government, the DAB united all of German high finance meant that the DAB brought a new type of foreign bank to the China coast. It differed from the HSBC and other foreign banks in China, which had mostly been established by smaller groups of merchants without the influence of their home governments, as it could speak for the entirety of German high finance and the entire German capital market. This advantage later helped the bank to establish itself as one of the leading foreign banks in China within a relatively short time after its founding.[137]

Finally, the early engagement of German bankers with China also reveals that the establishment of the DAB should not only be viewed in the context of the global expansion of German finance during the late nineteenth century, but also as part of the internationalization of Chinese finance and the growing interest of Chinese officials in foreign banks, capital and capital markets. As this chapter has shown, German bankers paid close attention to developments in China, and in their thinking and planning often reacted to the changes that took place there. Moreover, early on they realized the importance of establishing relations with important Chinese officials. The founding of the DAB itself was partly based on the experience of German bankers that it was necessary to have a permanent in-country presence and representatives in China, who could be in direct contact with the Chinese government and thus react promptly to new developments in China. Even before the DAB entered the China coast, the Chinese frontier attracted German financial interests and, in the form of the study mission, was a meeting ground for German and Chinese actors. The interdependent relationship between German bankers, who wished to use Germany's growing financial power for investments in China, and Chinese officials, who developed an ever-growing demand for foreign capital

---

[137] On this advantage of unity over the existing British and French banks 'thanks to the help of the [German] state's bureaucracy' (particularly for overcoming the British monopoly), also see Barth, *Imperialismen*, p. 41.

and tried to obtain better loan conditions by breaking the monopoly of the HSBC, was to continue after the establishment of the DAB. At the same time, despite the fact that before the 1890s relatively few foreign banks operated in China, the DAB's interactions with the HSBC and Wallich's concern about competition for a future German bank in China showed that the financial sphere of the Chinese frontier was a space not only of converging interests and interaction but also of competition and contention.

2

Entering the Chinese Banking Sector

Foreign Banks on the Chinese Frontier

This chapter examines the entry of the Deutsch-Asiatische Bank (DAB) into the banking sector of the China coast during the 1890s. While the loan business of the bank is covered in Chapter 3, this chapter will focus on the regular business of the bank, describing its function as an intermediary financial institution in the frontier region of China's treaty port economy. As such an intermediary institution, the bank not only financially connected China to the global economy by financing China's foreign trade and facilitating international capital flows, but also channelled its capital into the Chinese banking sector, connecting Chinese banks to global capital flows. This chapter will first describe the bank's establishment in Shanghai. It then turns to the bank's business in trade finance, explaining its competition with other foreign banks and its management of risk. The second part of the chapter uses the example of the Shanghai banking sector to examine the relationship of the DAB with Chinese banks and closes with a discussion of the risk-averse business strategy adopted by the DAB in the early years of its operations in China and the accelerated internationalization of the banking sector of China's treaty ports during the 1890s.[1]

This chapter focusses on both the 'outward internationalization' of German banking caused by its expansion to China and the 'inward internationalization' of the banking sector of the China coast due to the increasing influx of foreign banks, the growth of China's foreign trade and the increasing engagement of China with foreign capital markets.[2] Seeing the outward internationalization

---

[1] As explained in the Introduction, when I refer to the Chinese banking sector in this book, I mean the banking sector of China's treaty port economy. On the treaty port economy, see So, 'Modern China's Treaty Port Economy', pp. 1–27.

[2] On the concept of 'outward' and 'inward' internationalization, see Pintjens, 'The Internationalisation of the Belgian Banking', pp. 301–4. Pintjens sees 'outward internationalization' as the 'establishment of banking institutions of a given country in other countries'. For 'inward internationalization', besides the 'number of foreign banking institutions', he also takes into account a range of other factors feasible for his discussion of banking sector internationalization in the 1980s and 1990s but unfeasible for my discussion of late nineteenth- and early twentieth-century China here. Instead, as explained later, besides the influx of foreign banks, I also include the growth of transnational capital flows due to increasing foreign trade and greater interaction with foreign

of German banking as part of a larger process of economic globalization, I show that the extension of German banking to China did not simply involve the transplanting of German business structures and practices to the treaty ports, but always necessitated processes of localization like the adoption of new business practices or integration into existing Chinese business networks.[3] Regarding inward internationalization, I show the increasing importance of foreign banks and capital in the banking sector of the treaty port economy, which, together with China's rapidly growing foreign trade and increased sovereign borrowing, accelerated China's financial internationalization during the 1890s. This chapter shows that this inward internationalization of the banking sector of the treaty port economy was reflected in the number and in the invested capital of foreign banks in the Chinese banking sector, where these banks passed on part of their capital to Chinese banks.[4] I also stress the importance of the increased diversity of foreign banks in China, Sino-foreign networks and interactions between foreign and Chinese banks, and the increased diversity and accelerated growth of transnational capital flows between the treaty ports and other economies for China's financial internationalization.[5] Overall, this chapter highlights how foreign banks operated as frontier banks on the Chinese frontier. They played a key role in facilitating China's financial integration into the global economy. At the same time, their operations on the China coast necessitated adaptation to the Chinese business environment and interaction with their Chinese staff and partners.

2.1   Preparations in Berlin and Shanghai

When the DAB was established in 1889, the thirteen stockholder banks agreed on the statutes to govern the bank's business.[6] The statutes stated that the bank was established for 'conducting banking business and supporting trade between China and Germany'. The founding banks also made sure that the DAB did not become one of their competitors in Germany. Not only did they not establish a branch for the bank in Germany at this time, but the statutes

capital markets and the greater capital diversity of foreign banks and transnational capital flows.

[3] The simultaneity of the processes of globalization and localization is described in Robertson, 'Glocalization', pp. 25–44.

[4] These measures are selected from studies of banking sector internationalization. See, for example, Goldberg and Saunders, 'The Determinants of Foreign Banking Activity in the United States', pp. 17–32.

[5] On the importance of transnational capital flows, see Ramkishen S. Rajan, 'Booms and Busts in Private Capital Flows', pp. 3–8.

[6] 'Statut der Deutsch-Asiatischen Bank' (12 February 1889), HSO, A VIII 114 Ostasiatische Geschäfte 1888–1914.

also prohibited the DAB from taking on deposits or conducting current account business within Germany. Instead, the founding banks in Germany, the London agency of the Deutsche Bank and the London Rothschild house acted as correspondent banks for the DAB in Europe.[7] The founding banks guaranteed the acceptance credit of the DAB with the Seehandlungsgesellschaft in Berlin and the London house of Rothschild. In addition, the remaining founding banks provided the DAB with an acceptance credit of 10 million reichsmark (~£489,831) at their branches in Germany, which roughly equalled the capital of the shareholder banks not paid up yet.[8] This two-fold help by the founding banks enabled the DAB to start its business in trade finance. However, as we will see, having no branch network in Europe later became a problem for the bank and was criticized by some of their employees in China.

As the statutes also explained, the supervisory board (*Aufsichtsrat*) stood at the top of the bank and had far-reaching powers over the executive board (*Vorstand*) that comprised the directors of the bank in Berlin and China and carried out the direct management of the bank's affairs. The supervisory board appointed the directors and their deputies to the executive board. This also meant that the supervisory board appointed the directors of the branches of the DAB that carried out the main business of the bank on the ground in China. The supervisory board also remained in control of the people who could make executive decisions in China, as any binding decision made on behalf of the bank needed to be co-signed by at least one director or deputy-directors appointed by the supervisory board. The second signature also at least had to come from a member of the bank with a procuration given by the supervisory board. The supervisory board also fixed the instructions for the branches and agencies in China and decided on their establishment. With regards to the appointment of new employees, the last decision also remained with the supervisory board. The supervisory board was appointed yearly by the general assembly of the shareholders of the bank. However, the shares of the bank were only listed at the Berlin bourse in 1904, so for the next fifteen years the supervisory board was

---

[7] *North-China Herald* (3 January 1890). As discussed later, the first German branch of the DAB was established in Berlin in 1896.

[8] 'Aufsichtsratssitzung 6. November 1890' (6 November 1890), HADB, K07/010/I/01. When possible, currency conversions in this book were done using Rodney Edvinsson's Historical Currency Converter. See Edvinsson, *Historical Currency Converter*. When this was not possible, I used the exchange rate from Schneider et al., *Währungen der Welt IV*, and Schneider et al., *Währungen der Welt V*. Specifically to directly convert between Shanghai taels and pound sterling, I consulted Denzel, *Handbook of World Exchange Rates*, pp. 525–6.

made up and remained under the control of the founding banks.[9] This was reinforced by the stipulation that three quarters of the members of the supervisory board had to reside in Germany and all members had to reside in Europe. The structure of the bank reflected the strict control the founding banks wished to maintain to limit the risks of their investment.

Before the bank could start its business in Shanghai, it needed to find a first director that would set up and manage the affairs of the bank in China. According to one of the DAB's directors in Berlin, Curt Erich, the main difficulty in finding a suitable person was that the future first director needed to have a solid knowledge of banking, 'considerable experience with overseas business' and a formidable character that could be trusted.[10] Moreover, in Germany it was difficult to find bankers willing to leave behind their family and a secure career in Germany for a job in China with its different climate and business environment.[11]

While a German China merchant was also under consideration for the position for a while, the supervisory board appointed Ferdinand Rinkel, a banker of the Disconto-Gesellschaft, as first director of the bank in China. Rinkel had no experience in overseas banking. Therefore, the bank also appointed Moritz Kalb, who had worked for the British China firm Reiss & Co. in Shanghai, to act as Rinkel's advisor.[12] This choice not only reflected the difficulty of finding someone that had both expertise in banking and was familiar with business in East Asia, but also shows that the supervisory board preferred to pick one of their own bankers they knew and could trust instead of bringing in someone from outside.

Before Rinkel left for Shanghai, he was instructed how the bank was to operate.[13] According to these instructions, the first director, who was always also the manager of the bank's head branch in Shanghai, was responsible for the 'management of business' in China and for regularly checking the cash reserves and securities portfolio of the bank. He also had the power to dismiss

---

[9] Deutsch-Asiatische Bank to Zulassungsstelle an der Börse zu Berlin (4 July 1904), BArch, R3118/379, pp. 2–3. For a full list of the members of the supervisory and executive boards between 1889 and 1940, see Müller-Jabusch, *Deutsch-Asiatische Bank*, pp. 311–21. This list and surviving instructions for branches and agencies from 1904 ('Geschäfts-Anweisung für die Filialen Calcutta, Hongkong, Tientsin und Tsingtau und die Agenturen Hankow und Tsinanfu' (24 February 1904), BArch, R2/41689, pp. 34–5), combined with the establishment dates of the DAB's branches and agencies (Chapter 6, Table 6.2), clearly suggests that directors of full branches of the DAB in China were commonly also elected to the executive board either as full or deputy members.

[10] Erich to Brandt (3 March 1889), PAAA, R9208/563, pp. 111–12.

[11] Erich to Brandt (3 March 1889), PAAA, R9208/563, pp. 111–12.

[12] Focke to Bismarck (15 April 1889), BArch, R901/12989, pp. 121–2; Hugo Oppenheim to Auswärtiges Amt (27 June 1889), BArch, R901/12989, pp. 132–3.

[13] 'Geschäfts-Instruction für die Deutsch-Asiatische Bank' (18 September 1889), HSO, A VIII 114 Ostasiatische Geschäfte 1888–1914.

any employee, except for those with a procuration, who could only be dismissed with the consent of the supervisory board. The instructions also stressed the necessity of avoiding any unnecessary risk. The first clause explained that 'the basic condition of all conducted business is appropriate security for the bank'. This was reiterated in the second clause: 'In the administration and management of the bank greatest frugality is the guiding principle.' The bankers in China also were to report 'all important events concerning the bank as well as all conducted business' to the supervisory board each month. This general tone of caution continues throughout the instructions and again shows that the members of the supervisory board in Berlin wanted to remain in control of the business conducted in China.[14] The extant sources show that in China, the bank would come to have two types of offices: branches (*Filialen*) and agencies (*Agenturen*). While these sources do not provide a clear description of the differences between the two types of offices, they suggest that branches had a wider range of rights and competencies as opposed to agencies, which, for example, were not allowed to issue bills of exchange or cheques. This distinction was similar to other foreign banks in China. If necessary, agencies could be converted into branches.[15]

Rinkel and Kalb arrived in Shanghai on 5 November 1889 with five more German bank employees.[16] Rinkel continued what the German study mission had started and tried to establish contacts to important Chinese officials right away. He travelled to Tianjin and met with Li Hongzhang, who as before showed 'a lively interest in the establishment of the German [bank] institute'.[17] However, when Max von Brandt offered the possibility of a Chinese loan

---

[14] On this, also see Müller-Jabusch, *Deutsch-Asiatische Bank*, pp. 51–2. On the Shanghai manager also always being the first director of the bank, see 'Death of Mr. H. Figge', *North-China Herald* (21 November 1921) and Müller-Jabusch, *Deutsch-Asiatische Bank*, p. 66.

[15] The two different terms are frequently used in the yearly reports of the DAB before the First World War. See HADB, Geschäftsberichte, Deutsch-Asiatische Bank. On the different rights and competencies and the conversion of agencies into branches, see for instance 'Geschäfts-Anweisung für die Filialen Calcutta, Hongkong, Tientsin und Tsingtau und die Agenturen Hankow und Tsinanfu' (24 February 1904), BArch, R2/41689, pp. 34–5 and 'Protokoll des Geschäfts-Ausschusses' vom 13. September 1910', HADB, K07/010/I/ 01. For a similar distinction between branch and agency at the HSBC, see King, *HSBC History*, 1:123–5. As King points out, independent foreign firms that acted as agents for foreign banks could also be called 'agency'. However, my use of the word 'agency' in connection to the organization of a bank always refers to an office of a foreign bank staffed and controlled by that foreign bank. On agent agreements with foreign firms, see Chapter 6.

[16] Müller-Jabusch, *Deutsch-Asiatische Bank*, pp. 46–7.

[17] Quote from Brandt to Bismarck (20 November 1889), BArch, R901/12990, pp. 6–7; Moritz Kalb, 'Bericht ueber die Deutsch-Asiatische Bank in Shanghai nebst Erlaeuterungen' (1 July 1890), PAAA, R9208/563, 149:36 (hereafter cited as: Kalb, 'Bericht' (1 July 1890), PAAA, R9208/563).

floated by the DAB to the Chinese government, the Chinese authorities for the moment declined.[18] While Rinkel was away from Shanghai, preparations for the opening of the bank were made. A building for the bank was rented from Reuben Sassoon of the merchant firm David Sassoon, Sons & Co. for five years at 3,000 taels rent per year. The building was situated on the Shanghai Bund. In the spacious branch building, the offices of the bank and the private quarters of the manager were located, where parties could be held and guests hosted.[19] After the paid-up capital of the bank had been transferred to China, everything was ready for the opening of the bank.[20]

2.2   The Bankers of the Deutsch-Asiatische Bank

Before we turn to the opening of the DAB in Shanghai, it is useful to look at the bankers that ran the bank's business in China and explain their background, motivation for coming to China and the way they were recruited by the DAB (Figure 2.1). The five employees that came to China with Rinkel and Kalb were Arnold Ellert, Otto Messing, Erich Karbe, Otto Miretzky and Emil Gerecke. Ellert and Messing were given a procuration and therefore were the most senior employees after Rinkel.[21] While information on the activities of these bankers before entering the DAB is scarce, there is no evidence that any of them had experience of banking in China. For the bankers at home, the ideal banker for an overseas bank was 'trained in banking ... proficient in foreign languages and familiar with the conditions of foreign countries'. However, as such bankers were a rarity, one 'has to be satisfied if one can find part of these qualifications'.[22] As a consequence, the DAB 'occasionally hired people who were not bankers [Nichtbankiers]' but possessed overseas experience. According to Erich, the DAB was generally successful with this policy, although 'it cannot be overlooked, that ... in certain aspects the lack of schooling in the technicalities of banking of these men was noticeable'.[23]

At the same time, Erich's statement also implies that most of the employees of the DAB were bankers by training. As was the normal procedure for a German banker at the time, we can assume that these bankers had finished the *Einjähriges* after eleven years of school or even the *Abitur* and had then embarked on a three-year apprenticeship with a bank before becoming a full

---

[18] Zongli Yamen to Brandt (6 August 1890), AIMH, 01–32–014–02–004.
[19] Kalb, 'Bericht' (1 July 1890), PAAA, R9208/563, 149:10–11. On the location of the DAB's Shanghai branch, also see footnote 162.
[20] Müller-Jabusch, *Deutsch-Asiatische Bank*, pp. 53–4.
[21] Kalb, 'Bericht' (1 July 1890), PAAA, R9208/563, 149:19; Deutsch-Asiatische Bank to Auswärtiges Amt (January 1890), BArch, R901/12990, p. 11.
[22] Schoeller and Salomonsohn to Schinckel (17 June 1905), HADB, K01/781, pp. 129–30.
[23] Erich to Schinckel (3 June 1905), HADB, K01/781, p. 128.

Figure 2.1 Bankers of the DAB at a social gathering in Shanghai, ca.1900. Image courtesy of Deutsche Bank AG, Historical Institute (Sammlung Theodor Rehm).

bank employee.[24] The rise of joint-stock banks in Germany after 1870 opened up the banking profession to people from a wide range of middle-class backgrounds that could now enter a career in banking and even ascend to top positions within Germany's large banks.[25] For example, Franz Urbig, who we will meet later during the negotiations for the first Anglo-German indemnity loan, came from a modest non-banking background, but worked his way up the ranks of the Disconto-Gesellschaft and the DAB and later became a director of both banks.[26] Importantly, unlike their British colleagues, German bankers, even up to the high levels of high finance (*Hochfinanz*), as a social group remained largely separate from the ruling elite, including both the old aristocracy and university-trained upper civil servants. Unlike the 'gentlemanly capitalists' of the City of London, they mainly socialized among themselves and their contacts to the aristocracy, if they occasionally occurred, remained limited to a business relationship.[27]

Many of the employees of the DAB seem to have been directly recruited from the staff of the Deutsche Bank or the Disconto-Gesellschaft. As the

---

[24] Gall et al., *Die Deutsche Bank*, pp. 116–21.
[25] Reitmayer, *Bankiers im Kaiserreich*, pp. 120–47.
[26] On Urbig, see Müller-Jabusch, *Franz Urbig*; Urbig, *Aus dem Leben*.
[27] Reitmayer, *Bankiers*, pp. 83–4, 146–72, 247–72. For the 'gentlemanly capitalists' and the British case, see Cain and Hopkins, *British Imperialism: 1688–2000*, pp. 114–26.

Deutsche Bank had an agency in London and its employees there would have had expertise with overseas business, the London agency was an ideal place to recruit staff for the DAB and it seems that a significant number of DAB bankers had previously worked for the Deutsche Bank in London. For example, in early 1898 at least five of the nine German members of staff of the Shanghai branch had worked for the Deutsche Bank in London before coming to China.[28] Heinz Figge, who eventually became manager of the DAB's Shanghai branch, first joined the Deutsche Bank in Germany, then was transferred to its London office before joining the DAB.[29] There does not seem to have been one uniform procedure for the recruitment of staff. Hermann Wolff (Figure 2.4), a young banker that joined the DAB, related that after leaving the Deutsche Bank's London agency, he first joined the Deutsche Überseebank, the subsidiary bank of the Deutsche Bank in South America, hoping to be posted to Buenos Aires. However, he was then asked by a director of the Deutsche Überseebank to apply for a post at the DAB. This shows that German overseas banks exchanged their staff among each other. Wolff had to sit a five-hour exam that was reviewed by a commission of examiners made up of DAB supervisory board member Wallich and other bankers. After passing the test, Wolff negotiated his contract with Erich and left for China.[30] Urbig explained that he was recruited in a more informal way. When a temporary vacation replacement for the Shanghai directorship of the DAB was needed in 1895, Urbig, already working for the Disconto-Gesellschaft, was approached about this post by Erich and eventually persuaded to take the job during a holiday the two took together. He was then given a three-year period of leave from the Disconto-Gesellschaft and joined the DAB.[31]

The surviving evidence suggests that, when entering the DAB, bankers were given a contract for three years, which was automatically extended thereafter unless either the DAB or the banker wished to end the agreement. They were given up to a year of vacation after spending five years abroad. The starting salary of a banker was 2,000 Shanghai taels a year, which was equal to around 5,481 reichsmark, and gradually increased thereafter.[32] For a young German banker this was a high salary, given that the starting salary of a banker in

---

[28] Wolff, *40 Jahre Bankmann*, pp. 22–4, 33–6. Wolff states that after his arrival in Shanghai in January 1897 there first were seven and later nine German members of staff in the DAB branch there. As his statement about the five members of staff that had previously worked at the Deutsche Bank in London is made with reference to March 1898 – briefly before his departure for Hankou in May 1898 – it is most likely that there were nine German members of staff working at the DAB Shanghai branch at that time.

[29] 'Death of Mr. H. Figge', *North-China Herald* (21 November 1921).

[30] Wolff, *40 Jahre Bankmann*, pp. 18–20.

[31] Urbig, *Aus dem Leben*, p. 57.

[32] 'Vertrag Deutsch-Asiatische Bank in Berlin und Bernhard Kruse in London' (22 July 1905), HADB, Personalia, 365; 'Vertrag Deutsch-Asiatische Bank in Berlin and Albert Grothe in London' (17 February 1906), HADB, Personalia, N425. Conversion of Shanghai taels to reichmark according to exchange rate in 1905.

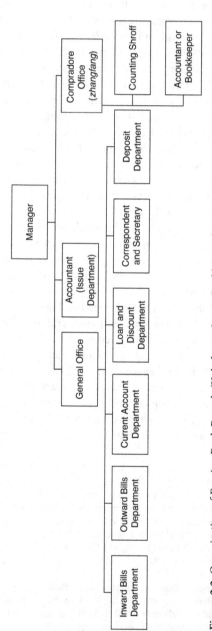

Figure 2.2 Organization of Foreign Bank Branch (Yokohama Specie Bank) in early twentieth-century Shanghai. Adapted from Tōa Dōbun Shoin Daigaku, *Shina Keizai zensho*, p. 947.

Germany was between 1,200 and 1,500 reichsmark, and even Franz Urbig, who then already occupied a relatively high position in the Disconto-Gesellschaft, stated that his salary in 1894 before joining the DAB had been only 5,000 reichsmark.[33] This high salary and the hope of amassing a large fortune was one of the attracting factors that drew young Germans to China.[34] More generally, a sense of adventure and the possibility of gaining a job that was both more interesting and more independent than an ordinary banking job at home was another motivation of many young German bankers that joined the DAB.[35] An example of such early independence is Hermann Wolff, who was made the first manager of the bank's agency in Hankou in 1898 and was 'proud and happy to have gained a fully independent position at the age of twenty-four'.[36]

2.3   The Deutsch-Asiatische Bank and Trade Finance

The DAB opened its doors in Shanghai on 2 January 1890.[37] It promised to conduct any 'banking and exchange business'. It also advertised itself as the representative and correspondent bank for its prominent German founding banks and listed the Deutsche Bank and N. M. Rothschild as its London bankers.[38] While the DAB's business comprised all kinds of normal bank business, such as business in deposits and cheques,[39] I will focus on the bank's business in trade finance and its business with Chinese banks. These areas of the bank's business were not only of importance for the bank, but also of greatest significance for its role as an intermediary institution and for the internationalization of the banking sector in the treaty ports. After a brief discussion of the inner organization of foreign banks in China, I will discuss trade finance in this section, before turning to a discussion of its relationship with Chinese banks in the next section.

While the remaining sources of the DAB do not give a clear description of the inner organization of the DAB branches, a Japanese economic survey from the early twentieth century provides an overview of the organizational structure of the Japanese Yokohama Specie Bank (Yokohama Shōkin Ginkō 横浜正金銀行, YSB) in Shanghai, a major foreign bank operating on the China coast. According to the survey, even though the structure of the inner organization of

---

[33] Gall, *Deutsche Bank*, p. 122; Urbig, *Aus dem Leben*, p. 70.
[34] Exner, *China*, pp. 68–9.
[35] Urbig, *Aus dem Leben*, p. 57; Wolff, *Bankmann*, p. 19.
[36] Wolff, *Bankmann*, p. 36.
[37] Kalb, 'Bericht' (1 July 1890), PAAA, R9208/563, 149:14.
[38] *The North-China Herald* (3 January 1890).
[39] Kalb, 'Bericht' (1 July 1890), PAAA, R9208/563, 149:14–32. Also see the advertisements of the DAB, for example 'Deutsch-Asiatische Bank', *North-China Herald* (9 January 1899), and an article by DAB banker August Reiß on the business of foreign banks in China: Reiß, 'Das Bankwesen in China', pp. 168–84.

foreign banks was naturally not exactly identical, one can use this example to infer the general structure of foreign bank branches in Shanghai (see Figure 2.2). The foreign manager of the branch sat at the head of the organization of the branch. The general office encompassed most of the departments of the branch. While the Inward Bills Department was responsible for the selling of bills of exchange, an important tool of international trade I will discuss later, the Outward Bills Department managed the buying of such bills. The current account department managed both current accounts and the buying and selling of foreign currency. The lending business of the bank was managed in the loan and discount department. As the survey points out, instead of a specific

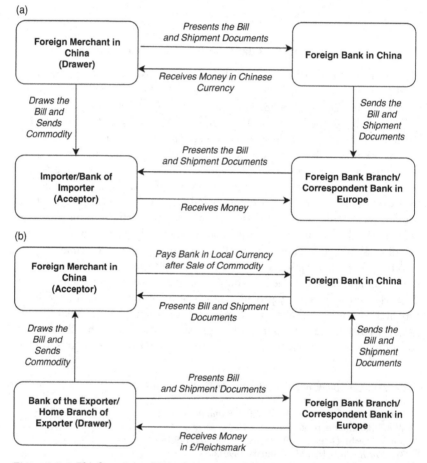

Figure 2.3 a. The financing of China's export trade; b. The financing of China's import trade (Source: See Footnote 45).

department for the management of loan securities, at the YSB this was jointly handled by the loan and discount and current account department. The correspondent and secretary handled the bank's correspondence and also carried out credit assessments. The deposit department managed deposits of those customers that did not have a current account with the bank. The accountant and comprador offices were separate from the general office. Besides the bank's accounting, the accountant also was in charge of the bank's note issuing. The comprador office, where the Chinese staff of the foreign banks worked, will be discussed later in this chapter using the example of the DAB.[40]

We will turn to the DAB's business in trade finance now. As we have seen, the statutes of the bank stated that it was to support trade between China and Germany. Trade finance and the involved foreign exchange transactions, although not exclusively between Germany and China, indeed became the most important business activity and source of profit for the bank.[41] While the founders of the DAB had mainly been interested in loans and railway investment, success in the day-to-day business of financing the 'export and import trade' became especially important as no large Chinese loans were contracted during the early years of the DAB's existence.[42] As explained in an article by DAB employee August Reiß, China's foreign trade was mainly financed using bills of exchange, which is 'an order [drawn by the drawer] on a given person or bank to pay a specified amount to the person and at the time named in the bill'.[43] As no Chinese banks with European branches existed that could finance trade and manage international remittances between China and Europe, this institutional void in the banking sector of the China coast was filled by foreign banks.[44] The DAB's role in the financing of import and export trade was that it bought bills drawn on Europe by exporters in China accompanied by the

---

[40] Tōa Dōbun Shoin Daigaku, *Shina keizai zensho*, pp. 946–9.

[41] How important trade finance was for the DAB from the start can already be seen in the overwhelming attention that Kalb pays to Chinese foreign trade and trade finance in his initial report to the supervisory board. See Kalb, 'Bericht' (1 July 1890), PAAA, R9208/563, 149:1–42.

[42] Rinkel, 'Bericht über die bisherige Geschäftstätigkeit' (February 1893), HSO, A VIII 114 Ostasiatische Geschäfte 1888–1914.

[43] Griffith, *Practical Bookkeeping*, p. 6.

[44] Jiang and Jiang also point out that foreign banks benefited from being able to make up for the deficiencies of the overseas operations of Chinese banks in fields like international remittances and foreign exchange. See Jiang and Jiang, *Jindai Zhongguo waishang yinhang*, pp. 343–4. This is also alluded to in Allen and Donnithorne, *Western Enterprise*, p. 102. Specifically in the context of foreign bank note issuance in Shanghai, Horesh speaks of an 'institutional vacuum' when discussing the city's imperfect financial system (which, however, he traces to failures on the part of both the Chinese government and the foreign Shanghai Municipal Council). He explains, though, that this 'vacuum was partly filled' not only by notes issued by foreign banks, but also by Chinese bank notes, thus he does not seem to see this supposed shortcoming as having been solely filled by foreign banks. See Horesh, *Bund and Beyond*, pp. 41, 48. In the context of exchange banking in East Asia, Schiltz also acknowledges the 'superior infrastructure and technologies' of foreign banks,

relevant shipping documents and issued bills and shipping documents to importers in China against payment (see Figure 2.3). In both cases, the shipping documents acted as security and only after the respective importer in China or Europe received them from the foreign bank or its correspondent bank against payment could he claim the shipped commodities. With export trade finance, the DAB would send the bill to one of its German branches or one of its European correspondent banks, which could discount it in the home market. With import trade finance, the DAB not only received the value of the bill but also interest at 5–8 per cent from the importer in China.[45]

Figure 2.4 Hermann Wolff (manager of the DAB in Hankou) with Chinese employees (1899). Image courtesy of Deutsche Bank AG, Historical Institute.

which he, however, sees as invertedly leading to the exploitation of indigenous institutions. See Schiltz, *Accounting*, p. 125. On this, also see footnote 90 in this chapter.

[45] For Reiß's article and its description of the foreign trade finance mechanism, see Reiß, 'Bankwesen', pp. 168–76. Figure 2.3 is based on Reiß's article and on the models in Denzel, *Handbook*, xviii–l. These two figures provide a general model of the mechanism for the financing of China's foreign trade. Naturally, such a figure cannot represent all the small varieties that existed within this mechanism. For these varieties, also see Reiß, 'Bankwesen', pp. 168–76. For a granular discussion of the technical details of trade finance between Europe and Asia in the nineteenth century, see Schiltz, *Accounting*, ch. 3.

Foreign banks also sold their own bills and telegraphic transfers drawn on their European branches or correspondent banks, which could be used by importers that directly paid exporters in Europe or for any other remittance to Europe.[46] All these international financial transactions involved a currency exchange transaction, meaning that the foreign bank earned money from the difference between the actual exchange rate and the exchange rate it offered to its customers.[47] Thus, foreign banks acted as intermediary institutions on the Chinese frontier that used their transnational networks of branches and correspondent banks to make transnational flows of capital between Europe and China and its different monetary systems possible and to finance China's foreign trade. Moreover, as we will see, foreign banks also provided Chinese banks with credit. Thereby, foreign banks also indirectly financed trade, as these Chinese banks funded the purchase of commodities by Chinese merchants outside the treaty ports.[48]

The assessment and limitation of risk was an important factor in managing the DAB's business in trade finance. As Kalb explained in a report to the supervisory board, in 1890 he and Rinkel started to create 'limit lists' (*Limitlisten*) for the buying of bills from foreign merchants. These lists would indicate up to what limit the bank would buy bills from foreign merchants. As Kalb explained, for a 'young banking institute' creating such lists was 'of great difficulty', as the bankers lacked the necessary experience in banking and trade in China. For the time being, Rinkel combined his knowledge of European firms with Kalb's knowledge of the reputation of foreign merchants in China to draw up these lists. Another important factor in the assessment of risk was the value of traded commodities acting as collateral for bills of exchange. Yet, the reputation of foreign merchants remained the most significant factor when deciding whether to buy a bill. While Kalb felt that bills hypothecated on commodities were safe, he also advocated that unlike other foreign banks, the DAB should not continue to do business with foreign merchants if problems with payments had occurred before.[49] This was again in line with the risk-averse business strategy of the DAB. Kalb's description is limited to the buying of bills in China, as the bank did not possess a branch in Europe at that time and the buying of bills there was done by the DAB's correspondent banks. However, the assessment of risk according to the reputation of the presenter of the bill and the value of the traded commodity was similar there.[50] A decisive factor in the degree of risk foreign banks took in the

[46] Müller-Jabusch, *Urbig*, pp. 44–6.
[47] Kalb, 'Bericht' (1 July 1890), PAAA, R9208/563, 149:15–16; Reiß, 'Bankwesen', pp. 178–80.
[48] Nishimura, 'Chop Loans', p. 128.
[49] Kalb, 'Bericht' (1 July 1890), PAAA, R9208/563, 149:17–18.
[50] Kalb, 'Bericht' (1 July 1890), PAAA, R9208/563, 149:19.

financing of China's trade was the fluctuating rate of silver. Changes and fluctuations in the silver exchange rate could cause exchange losses for these banks.[51] The fluctuation in the value of silver was so important to the DAB that nearly every yearly report would mention the development of the silver price.[52] Generally, the bank's early handling of risk was marked by both its lack of experience in the Chinese business and its cautious business approach.

Before the 1890s, foreign banking in China had been dominated by British banks.[53] When the DAB started its business in 1890, in Shanghai there existed five British banks and the French Comptoir National D'Escompte, which was the result of the reorganization of the French Comptoir D'Escompte de Paris after its failure in 1889. The French bank needed several years to recover from the failure and largely retreated from East Asia, where it was replaced by the Banque de L'Indochine from the mid-1890s.[54] Thus, on its entry into China, the DAB was not only the sole foreign bank that united the banking interests of an entire country, but because of the crisis of the French bank it was also the only formidable non-British bank in China. At first, the main aim of the bank was to win over German China merchants. However, 'in view of a German bank commencing business in China', in March 1890 the Hongkong and Shanghai Banking Corporation (HSBC) had opened a branch in Hamburg, Germany's main port for trade with China.[55] The Chartered Bank of India, Australia and China had also established an agency in Hamburg.[56] The HSBC now accepted and offered bills of exchange in reichsmark in China, which the German Foreign Office saw as a first 'success' caused by the establishment of the DAB.[57] After its arrival in China, the DAB also started to publish daily exchange rate notations for reichsmark in local newspapers, based on the exchange rate between pound sterling and reichsmark. Previously, such

---

[51] Reiß, 'Bankwesen', pp. 180–1.
[52] See HADB, Geschäftsberichte, Deutsch-Asiatische Bank.
[53] Tamagna, *Banking and Finance*, pp. 24–5.
[54] Kalb, 'Bericht' (1 July 1890), PAAA, R9208/563, 149:37; Brötel, *Frankreich im Fernen Osten*, pp. 320–32, 426–7; King, *HSBC History*, 1:261. As explained in Chapter 1, the French government had played a role in the founding of the Comptoir National D'Escompte, but the bank did not unite French financial interests in China like the DAB did for Germany. As mentioned in Chapter 1, footnote 28, on the Comptoir National D'Escompte, see Stoskopf, 'La Fondation', pp. 395–411; Stoskopf, 'From the Private Bank'; and Brötel, *Frankreich im Fernen Osten*, pp. 266–72, 320–40, and on French and British financial institutions in China not uniting their respective countries' financial interests in China, also see Barth, *Imperialismen*, p. 41.
[55] King, *HSBC History*, 2:538–9, quote from Minutes HSBC Board of Directors (14 February 1889) quoted on p. 538.
[56] Kalb, 'Bericht' (1 July 1890), PAAA, R9208/563, 149:3.
[57] Brandt to Bismarck (20 November 1889), BArch, R901/12990, pp. 7–8.

exchange rates had only been available for pounds sterling, francs and American gold dollars.[58]

As there were no Chinese financial institutions that published official foreign exchange rates for Chinese currencies, foreign banks – most importantly the HSBC – also set China's daily foreign exchange rates.[59] In Shanghai, foreign brokers acted as mediators between foreign banks and merchant houses in the exchange business. Driving horse-drawn carts, these brokers went back and forth between the foreign banks and merchants to see what exchange prices were offered and who wished to buy or sell bills and to negotiate between the banks and merchants. For this service they received a brokerage of usually 1/8 per cent. Brokers normally made around 1,000 taels a month but their monthly earnings could rise up to 30,000 taels and more at times. The brokers were organized in the 'Shanghai Exchange Brokers' Association', which worked together with the foreign banks in deciding who could be admitted as a broker. In 1908, there were around thirty foreign exchange brokers working in Shanghai. While our knowledge of the activities of such brokers is much more limited once we leave Shanghai, there were also foreign brokers working in other treaty ports like Hankou or Tianjin. In certain ways, their role as mediators can be compared to the role compradors played as mediators between foreign and Chinese banks, as discussed later.[60]

However, the bank could not just be content with introducing bills of exchange in reichsmark to China, but wished to take over as much of the direct financial transactions between China and Germany as possible itself. To compete with the HSBC and the Chartered Bank, the DAB offered favourable exchange rates for reichsmark bills to German merchants and tried to persuade them to entrust the DAB with their direct financial transactions with Germany. By July 1890, Kalb could already report that the DAB had managed to almost completely 'deprive these banks of the buying and selling of bills of exchange in reichsmark on the open market' in Shanghai. One reason for this success was that merchants preferred the bills the DAB sold, as the DAB's bills were drawn on the reputable Seehandlungsgesellschaft. Kalb also suspected that the two

---

[58] Focke, 'Promemoria betrifft die Errichtung der Deutsch-Asiatischen Bank in Shanghai' (February 1890), BArch, R901/12990, p. 33.

[59] On the setting of foreign exchange rates by foreign banks, see Jiang and Jiang, *Jindai Zhongguo waishang yinhang*, pp. 234–7; Schwarzer, Denzel and Zellfelder, 'Ostasiatische, indische und australische', p. 4; Mitsui Ginkō Shinkoku Shutchōin, *Mitsui Ginkō Shinkoku shutchoin*, p. 199; Gaimushō Tsūshōkyoku, *Honkon jijō*, p. 167; Arnold, *Commercial Handbook of China*, pp. 184–94; Uchida, *Shina kawase ron*, p. 113.

[60] Tōa Dōbun Shoin Daigaku, *Shina keizai zensho*, pp. 881–92. This book also comments on the fact that compradors were also a kind of broker. Besides Shanghai, it also briefly mentions the existence of brokers in Hankou and Tianjin. It says that there were over thirty brokers in Shanghai, although the members list of the Shanghai Exchange Brokers' Association it reproduces lists only twenty-eight.

banks had left this business to the DAB because it was not of great value to them. Besides buying and selling of reichsmark bills in Shanghai, the Hamburg correspondent bank of the DAB, the Norddeutsche Bank, also bought part of the bills drawn in Hamburg on Shanghai and sent them to the DAB for collection. It also used the DAB for the reimbursement of advances it issued to China merchants. Kalb was optimistic that the DAB would be able to gradually gain more of the business in bills of exchange drawn in Hamburg on Shanghai. He even reported that the DAB already carried out most financial transactions between North China and Germany and had taken over most of the financing for direct Chinese exports to Germany. However, Kalb also had to admit that the turnover of reichsmark bills between China and Germany was still so low that they could not create significant profits for the bank. While taking over the business in reichsmark bills was an important success for the bank, it should not be overestimated, as such bills had only recently been introduced in China and therefore the number of reichsmark bills in use was not high.[61]

In 1890, German direct trade with China only amounted to 3.5 per cent of China's total foreign trade.[62] According to Rinkel, the financing of this trade alone, which he saw as the main possible source of profits in the absence of larger loan business with the Chinese government, could not keep the bank alive. Yet, he also pointed out that in the early 1890s German merchants transported a portion of Shanghai's foreign trade much larger than that of the direct trade between Germany and China. The DAB also hoped to finance this larger portion of trade carried out by German merchants.[63] This, however, proved much more difficult than winning over the business in reichsmark bills, although 'every effort was made to pull over the German [merchant] houses' to the DAB. In July 1890, of the twenty-five German merchants in Shanghai, only nine had opened accounts with the DAB. Kalb also believed most of them still also had accounts with other banks, who often had long-standing relationships with German merchants and frequently bought their bills. For example, the German firm Arnold, Karberg & Co. opened an account with the DAB and also became the bank's agent in Hankou.[64] At the same time, it was also a member of the board of directors of the HSBC.[65] Smaller German firms, many of whom had worked with the HSBC, often told the bank they had no reason to change over to the DAB as the HSBC 'gives us all the facilities we could wish for'. Kalb suspected that these firms were given favourable facilities and credit by the HSBC 'to which they are hardly entitled' based on the standing of their

---

[61] Kalb, 'Bericht' (1 July 1890), PAAA, R9208/563, 149:3–4, 6, 16.
[62] Ratenhof, *Chinapolitik*, p. 565.
[63] Rinkel, 'Bericht über die bisherige Geschäftstätigkeit' (February 1893), HSO, A VIII 114 Ostasiatische Geschäfte 1888–1914.
[64] Kalb, 'Bericht' (1 July 1890), PAAA, R9208/563, 149:14, 20.
[65] King, *HSBC History*, 2:528.

business. He also believed that some were already indebted to the HSBC and therefore could not end their relationship with the HSBC. Maintaining the bank's cautious approach to business, the DAB refused to give such favourable credit to German firms if they felt these firms might not be able to repay their debt.[66] German merchants were not willing to change their allegiance to the DAB unless the bank offered better terms or facilities than their competitors. Besides the bank's cautiousness and consequential lack of generosity, another problem was that at least several of the large German firms active in East Asia possessed so much capital that they were usually able to finance their business themselves before the First World War.[67] All this, however, did not mean that the bank did not win important German customers. For example, the important German shipping firm Jebsen & Co. primarily cooperated with the DAB after the bank opened a branch in Hong Kong in 1900.[68] Moreover, despite its close connection to the HSBC and the fact that it also cooperated with other foreign banks, the prominent Bremen merchant firm Melchers & Co. also did business with the DAB.[69]

As the German bankers knew that the bank could not operate by just cooperating with German merchants, it was clear from the beginning that they also had to find customers among other foreign firms in China.[70] British firms proved reluctant to change to the DAB, as the German bankers could 'hardly offer more than the competition'. But British and also French firms accepted the DAB as an equal competitor to other foreign banks and started to purchase the bank's bills and sell their own bills to the bank if the DAB's rates were more favourable, so that the DAB also started to finance trade not carried out by German merchants.[71] The bank also tried to diverge non-British trade previously financed through London to Berlin, especially Russian tea exports from Hankou.[72] Before arriving in China, Rinkel had tried to win over Russian tea importers on a trip to Russia, and after its establishment the bank sent an agent to Hankou during the tea season in May and June to buy tea bills from Russian merchants.[73] For this purpose, an agency agreement with Arnold, Karberg & Co. was reached. The turnover in tea bills in Hankou amounted to £2.25 million (~46 million reichsmark) a year. While Kalb explained that it had been difficult to persuade Russian merchants that the financing of their tea imports would be cheaper if done through Berlin, the DAB quickly managed to

[66] Kalb, 'Bericht' (1 July 1890), PAAA, R9208/563, 149:14.
[67] Glade, *Bremen und der Ferne Osten*, pp. 114–15.
[68] Von Hänisch, *Jebsen & Co. Hongkong*, p. 440.
[69] Glade, *Bremen*, pp. 114–15. On Melchers & Co. and the HSBC, see King, *HSBC History*, vol. 1.
[70] Müller-Jabusch, *Deutsch-Asiatische Bank*, p. 50.
[71] Kalb, 'Bericht' (1 July 1890), PAAA, R9208/563, 149:15.
[72] Kalb, 'Bericht' (1 July 1890), PAAA, R9208/563, 149:6.
[73] Müller-Jabusch, *Deutsch-Asiatische Bank*, p. 50; Wolff, *Bankmann*, p. 38.

divert 4–5 million reichsmark (~£195,932 to £244,915) in tea bills from London to Berlin. Kalb hoped that eventually tea bills worth up to 30 million reichsmark (~£1.5 million) could be financed through Berlin, although, as elsewhere, the HSBC was the dominant foreign bank in Hankou with its own branch there.[74]

Generally, the DAB seems to have established itself relatively quickly in the business of trade finance. Despite the competition it was facing from other foreign banks, it gained equal standing with other foreign banks except the HSBC.[75] The DAB's lack of experience and connections to foreign merchants, its risk-averseness and its small paid-up capital to a certain extent inhibited its ability to compete with the HSBC. However, there existed a deeper structural problem that the bank's business in trade finance suffered from. In 1890, Kalb had already urged the directors and board members at home to open branches in Hong Kong, Bombay, Calcutta and Singapore, as these were the ports where trade – specifically German trade – was growing. He also recommended that the bank should open a branch in Berlin. This would allow the bank to discount bills drawn on Berlin without paying commission to its correspondent banks and gain direct market information from Europe.[76]

Rinkel also believed that the DAB needed to extend its branch network. In a more drastic manner than Kalb, he urged the supervisory board to see that the DAB had 'no ability to exist' without branches in London, Hamburg and Hong Kong. For him especially the establishment of a branch in London was necessary, as the DAB had to pay commission fees to its correspondent banks there. This decreased its competitiveness with those banks with branches in London, which remained the centre for financing trade between China and Europe. However, the supervisory board did not respond to his demands.[77] When Rinkel visited Germany in 1893 and reported to the supervisory board on the progress of the bank, he again reiterated the necessity of a branch in London, as it was the 'central point for traffic with Asia' where most of the financing of trade with China and India was carried out. Opening a branch in London would allow the bank to avoid paying commission, attract deposits and discount its own bills without depending on the acceptance credit of its shareholder banks. It would also enable the DAB to gain important information on the silver exchange rate and the commodities market in Europe.[78] The supervisory board members again maintained their reluctance to consider

---

[74] Kalb, 'Bericht' (1 July 1890), PAAA, R9208/563, 149:21.
[75] Kalb, 'Bericht' (1 July 1890), PAAA, R9208/563, 149:16.
[76] Kalb, 'Bericht' (1 July 1890), PAAA, R9208/563, 149:41–2.
[77] Brandt to Caprivi (20 April 1891), BArch, R901/12990, pp. 160–1.
[78] Rinkel, 'Bericht über die bisherige Geschäftstätigkeit' (February 1893), HSO, A VIII 114 Ostasiatische Geschäfte 1888–1914.

establishing a branch in London.[79] They most likely feared that such a branch would have competed with the branch of the Deutsche Bank in London and the London house of Rothschild.

Despite these problems, the DAB's business in trade finance took off quickly during the first decade of its existence. The bank profited both from Germany's growing trade with China and the general growth of China's foreign trade. In the 1890s Germany's yearly exports to China increased from 5.98 million Haiguan taels in 1890 to 10.12 million in 1899, and Chinese exports to Germany from 1.56 million Haiguan taels in 1890 to 11.5 million Haiguan taels in 1897. China's overall foreign trade grew from 214 million Haiguan taels in 1890 to 460 million Haiguan taels in 1899 (see Table 2.1). While the commission fees the bank had to pay to their correspondent banks in London and Germany might have made it less competitive, it nevertheless must have profited from its wide network of reputable correspondent banks in Germany that no other foreign bank in China could offer. The bank also profited from the reputation of its shareholder banks, the acceptance credit with which these banks had provided the DAB and the bank's status as the sole representative of German finance in China. Despite the critical tone of his report, in 1893 Rinkel explained to the supervisory board that because of the 'composition of our supervisory board' and the relative weakness of other foreign banks, the bank had already gained the full trust of foreign merchants and bills sold by the bank were 'currently the most popular ones in the market'.[80] This suggests that the bank's position as sole representative of German finance - as reflected in its supervisory board - helped it draw in

Table 2.1 *China's foreign trade and trade with Germany*

	German exports to China (in mill. Haiguan taels)	German imports from China (in mill. Haiguan taels)	China's foreign trade (in mill. Haiguan taels)
1890	5.98	1.56	214.2
1893	6.6	2.6	267.9
1895	7.08	5.4	290.2
1897	6.46	11.5	366.3
1899	10.12	5.8	460.5

Source: Ratenhof, *Chinapolitik*, p. 561; Hsiao, *China's Foreign Trade Statistics*, p. 23

[79] Brandt to Caprivi (20 April 1891), BArch, R901/12990, pp. 160–1.
[80] Rinkel, 'Bericht über die bisherige Geschäftstätigkeit' (February 1893), HSO, A VIII 114 Ostasiatische Geschäfte 1888–1914.

customers.[81] Finally, the bank also profited from the financial transactions of the German government between China and Germany after Bismarck had ordered the German legation and the German consulates in China to make use of the bank's services.[82]

The bank's business in trade finance and remittances grew swiftly during the 1890s, with the turnover in bills of exchange growing from 19,426,427 Shanghai taels in 1893 to 94,634,962 in 1897. The value of bills receivable bought from foreign merchants grew from 1,654,496 Shanghai taels in 1893 to 6,486,785 Shanghai taels in 1900.[83] While this number still paled in comparison with the HSBC, which in 1900 held bills receivable worth 49 million Shanghai taels, the growth of the DAB's dealings in bills of exchange was still significant given the comparatively small size of its branch network and paid-up capital.[84] Importantly, trade financing by the DAB and other foreign banks not only provided the financial basis for China's growing foreign trade, but also led to a continuous growth of transnational capital flows between China and European economies. As we will see, this became an important factor in the internationalization of the banking sector on the China coast.

In sum, by setting foreign exchange rates, managing international remittances and financing China's foreign trade, the DAB and other foreign banks filled an institutional void left vacant due to the absence of globally operating Chinese banking institutions.[85] Thereby, foreign banks acted as intermediary institutions that provided the financial infrastructure that made China's integration into the first global economy possible. The involvement of foreign banks in the treaty ports in the management of flows of capital between China and other economies also shows that not only in terms of trade, but also in terms of capital flows mediated by foreign banks, the frontier region of the China coast played an important role in China's integration into the global economy.

---

[81] Müller-Jabusch also describes how the composition of its supervisory board 'made it easier for the young bank to enter the business'. See Müller-Jabusch, *Deutsch-Asiatische Bank*, pp. 50–1.

[82] Bismarck to Brandt (5 March 1890), PAAA, R9208/563, p. 142.

[83] 'Bericht der Direction für das Geschäftsjahr 1893' (25 June 1894), PAAA, R9208/563, pp. 225–6; 'Bericht der Direction für das Geschäftsjahr 1897' (25 June 1898), HADB, Geschäftsberichte, Deutsch-Asiatische Bank.

[84] 'Abstract of Assets and Liabilities, Hongkong and Shanghai Banking Corporation, 31 December 1900', *The Economist*, 16 March 1901.

[85] It should be noted, though, that a network of Chinese financial institutions that could handle remittances did exist in East and Southeast Asia. See Harris, 'Overseas Chinese Remittance Firms', pp. 129–51. During the last years of the Qing dynasty, the He Sheng Yuan *piaohao* also made a short-lived and eventually unsuccessful attempt to establish a Chinese bank branch outside of China in Kobe. See Satō, 'He Sheng Yuan piaohao', pp. 114–27; Tatewaki, 'Senzen shio no zainichi gaikoku ginkō', pp. 43–74.

2.4   The Deutsch-Asiatische Bank and Chinese Banks

Besides their role as intermediary institutions that facilitated China's foreign trade, the DAB and other foreign banks also closely worked with Chinese banks. During the late Qing dynasty, there were primarily two forms of Chinese banks.[86] First, there were the *piaohao* 票號, which operated a country-wide network of branches and specialized in long-distance remittances. *Piaohao* also issued loans and received deposits. However, they seem to have had limited direct contact with foreign banks.[87] The second set of Chinese banking institutions were the *qianzhuang* 錢莊. These were local commercial banks that provided loans, accepted deposits and issued their own notes. *Qianzhuang* played a very important role as suppliers of credit for Chinese merchants involved in China's foreign trade and were also the main business partners of foreign banks in China's treaty port banking sector.[88] As we will see, *qianzhuang* received and supplied credit to foreign banks. Given that foreign banks mainly interacted with *qianzhuang*, I also use the term 'Chinese bank' to refer to *qianzhuang*.[89]

Foreign banks are commonly perceived as having dominated and controlled the banking sector of the treaty ports during the late Qing dynasty, most importantly by controlling the credit supply within the financial market. For example, writing about Shanghai, Wang Jingyu has argued that foreign banks 'controlled Shanghai's financial market and made Shanghai's *qianzhuang* [banks] their subordinates'. Thus, according to most previous scholarship, foreign banks were not integrated into the Chinese banking sector, but rather

---

[86] While the first modern Chinese banks modelled after Western banks started to appear during the last years of the Qing dynasty, they only became a significant factor in the Chinese banking sector after 1911. See Cheng, *Banking in Modern China*, chapters 1–3.

[87] On Shanxi *piaohao*, see Chen, *Shanxi piaozhuang kaolüe*. On the limited contact with foreign banks, see Zhang, *Wan Qing qianzhuang*, p. 119; Yasuda, *Shinkoku kinyū*, p. 28. Luman Wang gives some examples of contact between foreign banks and *piaohao* and emphasizes the importance of the *piaohao* remittance network for China's foreign trade. See Wang, *Money and Trade*, pp. 51–9.

[88] Pan, *Zhongguo qianzhuang gaiyao*. The standard work in English on *qianzhuang* is McElderry, *Old-Style Banks*. On *qianzhuang* being the main business partners of foreign banks, see Rawski, *Economic Growth in Prewar China*, pp. 130–1. While these local commercial banks were generally known as *qianzhuang* and also referred to by this name in Shanghai, they were called other names depending on the region or the size of the financial institution. The most important difference seems to have been that while the term *qianzhuang* was used in the Yangzi river region, the term *yinhao* was used in South (*Huanan* 華南) and North (*Huabei* 華北) China. On the different names used for *qianzhuang*, see Zhang, *Zhongguo jinrong tongshi*, p. 15; Tōa Dōbunkai Chōsa Hensanbu, *Shina kinyū kikan*, pp. 440–1; McElderry, *Old-Style Banks*, pp. 11–12.

[89] In the scholarly literature, the anachronistic and pejorative term 'native bank' is still often used to describe *qianzhuang*. However, I use the more accurate and appropriate terms of '*qianzhuang*' or 'Chinese bank'.

imposed their one-sided control on Chinese banks.[90] However, if we use Shanghai – the centre of China's foreign trade and an important centre of Chinese finance – as an example and have a closer look at the role foreign banks played in its banking sector, we not only see that foreign banks were integrated into existing networks and market structures, but also that the relationship between foreign and Chinese banks was one of interdependence rather than one-sided control.[91] Like other foreign firms, foreign banks had difficulties directly interacting with Chinese firms because of their lack of familiarity with the Chinese language and business environment. Therefore, the engagement of the DAB and other foreign banks with Chinese banks and merchants was managed by its Chinese staff, headed by a Chinese manager called comprador (Figure 2.5). While historical scholarship has moved away from views that see the compradors working for foreign firms mainly as supporters and beneficiaries of foreign imperialism, the notion that compradors constituted a specific class or group, whose 'primary capacity' was their work as a comprador for a foreign firm and whose primary characteristic was their 'compradorial background', still mostly prevails. Any other economic activities engaged in by a comprador have largely been understood as building on their work as a comprador for the foreign firm.[92] However, as the example of the DAB's Shanghai comprador will reveal, it is more useful to perceive the bank comprador simply as a position in a foreign bank filled by a Chinese entrepreneur. This position was neither their main occupation nor made up

[90] Quote from Wang, *Waiguo ziben zai jindai Zhongguo*, pp. 127–30. Also see, for example, McElderry, *Old-Style Banks*, pp. 3, 21–5; Zhang, *Wan Qing qianzhuang*, p. 64; Kong, *Jinrong piaohao shilun*, p. 99. A recent important exception that challenges such views by re-examining the importance of 'chop loans' for the Chinese money market is Nishimura, 'Chop Loans'. Susan Mann Jones, if only briefly, also casts doubt on the dominance of foreign banks. See Susan Mann Jones, 'Finance in Ningpo', p. 72. While referring to Nishimura's article, Schiltz's recent study on trade finance between Asia and Europe maintains that foreign banks were 'innately parasitic or even parasitoid' towards domestic financial institutions. See Schiltz, *Accounting*, p. 125.

[91] During the 1890s and early 1900s, Shanghai was the treaty port most important for China's foreign trade. During the same period, its only competitors in terms of its financial importance were Tianjin and Beijing. See Moazzin, 'Sino-Foreign Business Networks', p. 975.

[92] Hao Yanping, *Comprador*, quotes from pp. 89, 215. For a recent study of a comprador building businesses on the basis of his work for a foreign firm, see Kai Yiu Chan, *Business Expansion*, chapter 4. For an overview of the literature on compradors, see Nie, *Maiban*, pp. 3–15. In his brief overview of the comprador system, Frank King mainly discusses the HSBC's compradors' activities for the HSBC, but also mentions some of their outside business. See King, *HSBC History*, 1:509–18. A very recent addition to the literature is Kaori Abe's nuanced study of compradors in Hong Kong. While Abe acknowledges that some compradors worked as entrepreneurs before becoming compradors, she mainly discusses the enterprises of compradors as building on their role and work as compradors. Her discussion of the compradors' commercial networks also focuses on networks established between compradors. See Abe, *Chinese Middlemen*, chapters 3 and 4.

Figure 2.5 Chinese employees of the DAB in Shanghai, ca.1900. Image courtesy of
Deutsche Bank AG, Historical Institute.

the greater part of their business activities. Rather, taking on the position of
bank comprador in a foreign bank was a way for the Chinese entrepreneur to
complement their existing network of business enterprises with a connection
to a foreign bank. As we will see, Chinese entrepreneurs could use this
connection to a foreign bank to generate large profits and attain
a competitive advantage by exploiting information asymmetries between foreign and Chinese bankers and by integrating the foreign bank into their
business network.

   An important reason why the DAB and other foreign banks employed
a comprador seems to have been that this allowed them to use their working
capital and particularly their large deposits in the Chinese banking sector by
issuing loans to Chinese banks.[93] While the DAB received deposits from

[93] While acknowledging the role of chop loans as outlets for the working capital and in
particular deposits of foreign banks before 1911, McElderry suggests that investment in
government loans and industrial projects like railway construction gradually became an
alternative, and safer, outlet for foreign banks' capital. However, she overlooks that not
only were these irregular and not part of the day-to-day business of the foreign banks, but
also that such loans were mostly raised by issuing bonds on foreign capital markets and
did not come from the working capital of foreign banks. See McElderry, *Old-Style Banks*,
pp. 94–5. On the irregularity of the loan business, see, for example, Müller-Jabusch,
Deutsch-Asiatische Bank, p. 205. Nishimura is cautious with regards to the importance of

foreign sources, most of its deposits came from Chinese clients.[94] Foreign banks in China operated under extraterritoriality and, unlike Chinese banks, were therefore protected from intervention by the Chinese government.[95] This was especially significant because of the limited development of property rights in China and the tendency of the Chinese state for confiscation in times of crisis.[96] Therefore, foreign banks were the ideal place where rich officials and other individuals could deposit funds beyond the reach of the government. Reflecting on the activities of the DAB in China before the First World War, in 1933 Franz Urbig, at the time the president of the DAB's supervisory board, explained that extraterritoriality was the key factor that allowed the DAB to attract Chinese deposits and to accumulate working capital in excess of its stock capital.[97] Moreover, foreign banks were seen as more secure and trust-worthy than Chinese banks because of their large capitalization, which made it unlikely for them to fail and lose the deposits of their customers.[98] This led not only private customers but also Chinese government offices to deposit funds with the DAB.[99] In 1892, when discussing the deposit of certain government funds, a Tianjin official even remarked that the HSBC and DAB, the only two foreign banks in Tianjin at the time, were the only 'reliable banks' that could be trusted in Tianjin, so that he was only willing to deposit the government funds with these financial institutions.[100] In Beijing, foreign banks were also known to hold deposits from the Chinese government.[101] This popularity of foreign banks with Chinese depositors is all the more remarkable if we consider that these depositors would likely have been able to receive a higher return on their deposits with Chinese banks. For example, foreign banks seem to only have

chop loans for the business of foreign banks, but also acknowledges their importance as an outlet for surplus funds including deposits. See Nishimura, 'Chop Loans', p. 121. On this and for a more extended discussion of the sources of working capital of foreign banks, particularly their deposit business, and its role as a basis for chop loans, see Moazzin, 'Sino-Foreign Business Networks', pp. 970–1004, particularly pp. 978–82.

94 Kalb, 'Bericht' (1 July 1890), PAAA, R9208/563, 149:6, 31; 'The Shanghai Chromo- & Photo-Litographic Company, Limited' (2 August 1890), PAAA, R9208/563, p. 164; 'Bericht der Direction für das Geschäftsjahr 1893' (25 June 1894), PAAA, R9208/563, p. 225; Rinkel, 'Bericht über die bisherige Geschäftstätigkeit' (February 1893), HSO, A VIII 114 Ostasiatische Geschäfte 1888–1914.

95 King, 'Extra-Regional Banks', p. 378.

96 Brandt, Ma and Rawski, 'From Divergence to Convergence', pp. 78–9.

97 Franz Urbig, Untitled Report (23 October 1933), HADB, P08401.

98 Xiao, 'Guoren ji yinggai bian xinli', Shenbao (11 June 1935).

99 Rinkel, 'Bericht über die bisherige Geschäftstätigkeit' (February 1893), HSO, A VIII 114 Ostasiatische Geschäfte 1888–1914.

100 Quote from Li to Zongli Yamen (7 May 1892), AIMH, 01–32–016–03–004; Li to Zongli Yamen (9 January 1893), AIMH, 01–32–017–03–019. On the DAB and HSBC being the only foreign banks in Tianjin at the time, see Tōa Dōbun Shoin Daigaku, Shina keizai zensho, p. 984.

101 Shinkoku Chūtongun Shireibu, Pekin shi, p. 427.

been willing to pay between 2.5 per cent and 5.5 per cent in annual interest for fixed deposits. In contrast, *qianzhuang* offered between 4.8 per cent and 10.8 per cent in interest on their fixed deposits.[102] As no Chinese bank could offer the same security, secrecy and stability for deposits, this institutional void in the Chinese banking sector was filled by foreign banks. As a result, the DAB and other foreign banks received large deposits from Chinese sources.[103] This large deposit business might also have been the reason why foreign banks had a separate deposit department. By 1895, the DAB had accumulated 1,473,516 Shanghai taels in deposits, which at the time was more than the paid-up capital of the bank.[104]

Before the DAB could open its doors in Shanghai in 1890, a comprador had to be found for the bank to manage its business with Chinese banks. Because of his advisor Moritz Kalb's previous long experience as a merchant working as a co-owner of the British merchant firm Reiss and Co. in China, DAB Shanghai manager Ferdinand Rinkel asked Kalb to find a suitable person for the comprador post. Kalb recommended Xu Chunrong 許春榮, a merchant and banker he had 'known since 1872'. In choosing Xu, he was led by Xu's reputation and his personal knowledge and trust in Xu. In a report to the bank's directors in Berlin, Kalb emphasized that in his previous work as a China merchant, he had frequent large-scale business dealings with Xu and valued him as a 'diligent, assiduous and astute man . . . with whom I never had even the smallest argument. He always fulfilled his obligations [punctually] on the day, [accurately] to the last cent'. Kalb also explained that Xu was 'very influential', which would be very useful for the bank, especially for borrowing money from Chinese banks if necessary. After Rinkel had approved Kalb's choice, Kalb drew up a contract with Xu, as was common between foreign firms and their compradors. The contract fixed all of Xu's obligations towards the bank. He also had to provide a guarantee sum of 70,000 Shanghai taels, which was put up by his own firm Da Feng 大豐 and three Chinese banks. The DAB could terminate the contract at any time, while Xu had to give six months' notice if he wished to end the agreement.[105]

---

[102] Foreign banks and *qianzhuang* commonly offered fixed deposits for three months, six months or one year. For a sample of deposit interest rates and lengths for fixed deposits of foreign banks, see, for example, the foreign bank advertisements in *North-China Herald* (22 August 1890, 29 January 1892, 9 January 1899). On *qianzhuang* fixed deposit interest rates and lengths, see Pan, *Zhongguo qianzhuang*, pp. 69–71.

[103] Wagel, *Finance in China*, p. 260; Jiang and Jiang, *Jindai Zhongguo waishang yinhang*, pp. 246–9; Wang, *Waiguo ziben zai jindai Zhongguo*, pp. 177–81.

[104] 'Bericht der Direction für das Geschäftsjahr 1893' (27 June 1896), BArch, R8024/283, p. 1; Müller-Jabusch, *Deutsch-Asiatische Bank*, table opposite p. 326.

[105] Quotes from Kalb, 'Bericht' (1 July 1890), PAAA, R9208/563, 149:12–13; Müller-Jabusch, *Deutsch-Asiatische Bank*, pp. 46–7.

Xu was a very influential figure in Shanghai's foreign trade and finance. He was born in Huzhou in Zhejiang province in 1839, but his family came from the Zhenhai district in Ningbo.[106] After spending some time in Suzhou, he moved to Shanghai and, in the 1860s, became the manager of the Da Feng Company, which was owned by the Weng 翁 family of Ningbo. Da Feng became one of the first Chinese firms to sell imported foreign woven cloth in China. As Reiss & Co. imported British cloth products into China, Da Feng sold large parts of these imports on to Chinese customers. Kalb and Xu must have met through this business partnership. Most likely to further consolidate his relationship with Reiss & Co., he became the comprador of the company in 1870. As this position made him responsible for distributing the imported products of the foreign company, it guaranteed his access to these products in his capacity as the manager of Da Feng. The business of the company prospered, creating profits in the order of 30,000–40,000 Shanghai taels a year. As a result, Xu was able to purchase the rank of Daotai from the Chinese government, was the head of the Zhenhua Tang Trade Guild for Foreign Cloth (Zhenhua tang yangbu gongsuo 振華堂洋布公所) from 1877 to 1905 and became a secretary (yidong 議董) of the Shanghai Chamber of Commerce (Shanghai shangwu zonghui 上海商務總會). Around 1880, the Weng family withdrew its shares from the Da Feng Company and Xu became the company owner and worked as its manager until his retirement in 1905. Despite his later investment in banking, his main occupation remained his work with the Da Feng Company, which he turned from a small enterprise with an original stock capital of 3,000 Shanghai taels into a major trading company with an estimated capital of 200,000 Shanghai taels, according to Kalb in 1890.[107]

It is unclear when Xu became involved in banking, but he had already established seven qianzhuang in Shanghai by 1884. Xu's qianzhuang went bankrupt during a financial crisis caused by the Sino-French War. However, he subsequently opened several qianzhuang with other influential merchant families in Shanghai. Most importantly, he was connected through intermarriage to the Ye family, who also came from Zhenhai in Ningbo. Together the two families opened four qianzhuang, with a capital of 20,000 Shanghai taels each. Given their common ownership and the fact that each of these qianzhuang bore the character da (大, meaning 'big') in their names, they came to be known as the Sida qianzhuang 四大錢莊. They became so powerful that their bankruptcy was a major factor in the financial crisis that hit Shanghai after the revolution in 1911. Xu opened two more qianzhuang, each having a capital of

---

[106] This outline of Xu's life is based on Zhongguo shehui kexueyuan jingji yanjiu suo, *Shanghaishi mianbu shangye*, pp. 33–4; Wu, 'Shanghai waishang yinhang', pp. 273–6, 281–8; Hua, *Shanghai maiban*, pp. 64–5; Zhongguo Renmin Yinhang Shanghaishi fenhang, *SHQZSL*, pp. 33, 89–90, 743–5, 750–1.
[107] Kalb, 'Bericht' (1 July 1890), PAAA, R9208/563, 149:13.

20,000 Shanghai taels and also bearing the character *da* in their name together with two other influential families, most importantly the Xi family from Suzhou, who were also connected to the Xu family through intermarriage, and had a tradition of filling comprador positions in foreign banks. We know that in 1888, the *Yuda qianzhuang* 餘大錢莊, one of the four banks opened with the Ye family, had already been established and was a *huihua qianzhuang* 匯劃錢莊, the most powerful group of *qianzhuang* in Shanghai, and thus also a member of Shanghai's Money Trade Guild (Qianye zonggongsuo 錢業總公所). As Xu's other *qianzhuang* had the same capitalization, we must assume that they also became members of the Money Trade Guild.[108]

This sketch of Xu's life shows that he was not primarily a comprador, but had other more important business interests in trade and finance before he became the comprador of the DAB. Although he worked as a comprador for Reiss & Co., this only made up a small part of his business activities and he most likely only took up the position to re-enforce the already existing connection of the Da Feng Company with this foreign firm. As we will see, his decision to become the comprador of the DAB was most likely also not motivated by the official remuneration the post itself offered, but by Xu's wish to gain a connection to a foreign bank for his existing businesses and the possibility of exploiting the information asymmetry between him and the DAB to generate extra profits.

As comprador of the DAB, Xu was responsible for the entire Chinese staff he employed. He also guaranteed and was personally liable for all bills he accepted on behalf of the DAB from Chinese banks and for the cash reserves of the bank, which he managed under the supervision of the German cashier. His staff also evaluated the Chinese currencies and bullion the bank worked with, such as silver *sycee* and gold ingots. Apart from Xu, in 1890 the Chinese staff of the bank comprised the second comprador, three shroffs, who handled the money, book-keeping and other banking matters, one office clerk, four coolies and two guards that guarded the house day and night.[109] The office of Xu and his Chinese staff were in the same building as all the other offices of the German bankers.[110]

While Xu was the first comprador of the bank, Kalb pointed out that he only 'practices a kind of supervision' over the Chinese staff. The actual daily management of the Chinese business of the bank was carried out by Litchitching, who was employed by Xu as the second comprador of the bank

---

[108] On *huihua qianzhuang* and Shanghai's Money Trade Guild, see *SHQZSL*, pp. 9–11; Du, *Jindai Zhongguo qianye xiguanfa*, pp. 19–21; Yang, *Shanghai jinrong zuzhi gaiyao*, pp. 30–1, 52–3.

[109] Kalb, 'Bericht' (1 July 1890), PAAA, R9208/563, 149:12–13; August Reiß, 'Die Innere Organisation'.

[110] Kalb, 'Bericht' (1 July 1890), PAAA, R9208/563, 149:10.

and had already worked as comprador for the Deutsche Bank in the 1870s.[111] Wu Peichu 吳培初, who was a contemporary of Xu and later the comprador of the International Banking Corporation, also related that Xu only 'in the very beginning showed his face' at the DAB, but let Jiang Zhanggong 姜彰功, most likely one of his employees, carry out his daily work as comprador. Although Xu was officially comprador of the DAB until 1910, from 1898 his son Xu Xingquan 許杏泉 carried out his duties at the DAB, before officially becoming comprador of the DAB in 1911.[112] That Xu Chunrong was rarely, if ever, present at the DAB and only comprador in name shows that while he used his reputation and wealth to attain the comprador position at the DAB, working as a comprador for the DAB never became his main occupation. He rather delegated his work at the bank to others, while he must have been occupied with managing the Da Feng Company and overseeing his *qianzhuang* and other business interests. Thus, both Xu's network of other businesses and the fact that he seems never to have personally carried out his duties of being the DAB's comprador, having held the position in name only, suggest that rather than mainly seeing him as a comprador, it makes more sense to see Xu Chunrong as a banker and entrepreneur who also occupied the position of comprador in a foreign bank in order to acquire a connection to such a foreign bank.

Xu received a salary of 250 taels a month. While some foreign banks such as the HSBC paid their Chinese staff a separate salary, the sum Xu received from the DAB also had to cover the salaries of his staff.[113] As Kalb pointed out, this left Xu with 'little or nothing for himself'.[114] Hao Yanping has shown that besides their salary, the compradors of foreign trading firms in the nineteenth century received a commission of about 1–3 per cent for each transaction, which, however, decreased to between 0.5 and 1 per cent by the end of the nineteenth century. More importantly, they could earn large sums of money through 'squeeze', which meant the manipulation of transactions and duties carried out for the foreign firm, for example the artificial increase of the price of Chinese commodities purchased by the comprador for the firm.[115]

However, foreign bankers seem to have believed that the situation for bank compradors was rather different. According to Kalb, compradors working for foreign banks could 'gain almost no squeezes', which led him to the question: 'what purpose does it have for [Xu] to be comprador?' For Kalb, there were two

[111] Kalb, 'Bericht' (1 July 1890), PAAA, R9208/563, 149:13.
[112] Wu, 'Shanghai waishang yinhang', pp. 260, 263, 287. Because of the inaccuracies of German transcription of Chinese, it is unclear whether Jiang Zhanggong and Litchitching were identical persons, or whether Jiang was another employee of Xu.
[113] Kalb, 'Bericht' (1 July 1890), PAAA, R9208/563, 149:13; Wu, 'Shanghai waishang yinhang', p. 271.
[114] Kalb, 'Bericht' (1 July 1890), PAAA, R9208/563, 149:13.
[115] Hao, *Comprador*, pp. 90–4.

answers to this question. Most importantly, acting as comprador elevated Xu's reputation and allowed him to have one of his sons trained at the comprador office, who could then become the DAB's real comprador later. Second, Xu received a commission of 1/8 per cent for business in long-distance remittances between Chinese ports he did for the bank and could hope that his earnings from this commission would grow should the bank expand to other ports and thus enable him to engage in business with bills between Shanghai and other ports.[116] While Kalb's thinking was not wrong, a closer look at the work of the comprador and the DAB's interaction with Chinese banks reveals that Xu indeed profited in other, more significant ways from his connection to the DAB than those known and identified by Kalb.

The primary relationship of the DAB and other foreign banks to Chinese banks was via loans they provided to and received from *qianzhuang* banks. Since the 1860s, *qianzhuang* had used foreign capital primarily provided primarily by foreign banks. This was part of the 'expansion of credit' on the China coast.[117] In providing foreign capital for *qianzhuang*, foreign banks followed in the footsteps of and fulfilled a function and practice in the banking sector previously carried out by *piaohao* banks. *Piaohao* banks not only dominated China's domestic remittances, but were also the main providers of capital for the *qianzhuang* before foreign banks started to do so and continued to issue loans to the *qianzhuang* and cooperate with them thereafter.[118] Receiving loans from foreign banks was beneficial for *qianzhuang* not only because of the large quantities of foreign capital they could thus obtain, but also because of this capital's cheapness. While foreign banks were willing to lend their money for 7 per cent per annum or less, the average interest rate on the Chinese coast during the mid-nineteenth century, before the introduction of chop loans provided by foreign to Chinese banks, was still 12 per cent per annum.[119] At the same time, loans to Chinese banks were an important means for foreign banks to employ their working capital and large deposits in the market. To provide such loans, foreign banks in Shanghai participated in the inter-bank lending system of Chinese banks through the mediation of their comprador. In Shanghai, *qianzhuang* lent money to each other through one- or two-day short-term loans. For this purpose, representatives of the members of the Shanghai Money Trade Guild met twice a day to set

[116] Kalb, 'Bericht' (1 July 1890), PAAA, R9208/563, 149:11–13.
[117] Hao, *Commercial Revolution*, chapter 4. The only non-banks that Hao specifically mentions as suppliers of capital to *qianzhuang* were the foreign trading firms Jardine, Matheson & Co. and Renter, Brockelmann & Co. Also see *SHQZSL*, pp. 28–30.
[118] Chen, *Shanxi piaozhuang kaolüe*, pp. 69, 84; Kong, *Jinrong piaohao shilun*, p. 100; Wang, *Money and Trade*, pp. 48–51.
[119] Kalb, 'Bericht' (1 July 1890), PAAA, R9208/563, 149:25; W. Adams Oram to Hongkong and Shanghai Banking Corporation (Head Office) (30 May 1908), quoted in Nishimura, 'Chop Loans', p. 119; Hao, *Commercial Revolution*, p. 110.

the standard market interest rate for short-term inter-bank lending, which was also the standard interest rate for the money market in Shanghai. This market interest rate, called *yinchai* 銀拆, reflected the current money supply in Shanghai and could fluctuate between around 2 per cent and around 25 per cent, but the average *yinchai* interest rate between 1873 and 1911 was around 6.5 per cent (see Figure 2.6).[120] The DAB participated in this system through its comprador, who chose which *qianzhuang* had sufficient credit and then provided these *qianzhuang* with short-term loans. These loans were repayable after two days, but recallable by the foreign banks at any time. In exchange for the loan, the *qianzhuang* provided a promissory note, called a *zhuangpiao* 莊票, to the foreign bank that the comprador would accept and mark with his chop or seal as proof of his guarantee for the loan. These 'chop' loans (*chaikuan* 拆款) did not carry any real collateral. One of their primary purposes was that they were used and passed on to Chinese merchants by the *qianzhuang* and played an especially important role in the purchase of commodities by Chinese merchants in the hinterland.[121] Importantly, while

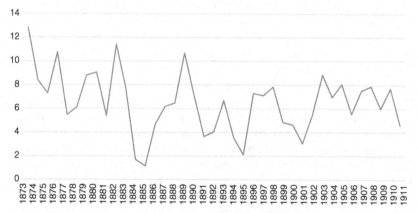

Figure 2.6 Shanghai *yinchai* interest rate yearly average, 1873–1911, in per cent. *Source*: Kong, *Nankai jingji*, pp. 479–80.

[120] Du, *Jindai Zhongguo qianye xiguanfa*, chapter 1; Yang, *Shanghai jinrong zuzhi*, pp. 54–9; McElderry, *Old-Style Banks*, pp. 42–5; Pan, *Zhongguo qianzhuang*, p. 62; Zhang, *Ge sheng jinrong*, p. 213. The average interest rate was calculated according to the annual averages for *yinchai* interest rates between 1873 and 1911 given in Kong, *Nankai jingji*, pp. 479–80.

[121] Kalb, 'Bericht' (1 July 1890), PAAA, R9208/563, 149:29; Nishimura, 'Chop Loans', pp. 115–16. On the chop loan mechanism, also see McElderry, *Old-Style Banks*, pp. 21–2; Hao, *Commercial Revolution*, pp. 77–80; and SHQZSL, pp. 29–30, 36.

the term 'chop loan' was normally exclusively used for loans issued by foreign banks, its Chinese equivalent *chaikuan* was also used for inter-bank lending between *qianzhuang*.[122]

These loans became very important for the business of the Shanghai *qianzhuang*. The total amount of chop loans provided by foreign banks in Shanghai could reach over 10 million Shanghai taels at any one time and individual *qianzhuang* sometimes took on chop loans of up to 800,000 Shanghai taels, despite the capital of *qianzhuang* only amounting to around 20–60,000 taels.[123] Yet, the importance of loans from foreign banks for *qianzhuang* should not be overestimated. Rather, borrowing from other *qianzhuang* seems to have been at least equally important for *qianzhuang*. For example, in 1896 the *Fukang qianzhuang* 福康錢莊 in Shanghai borrowed 92,660 Shanghai taels from *qianzhuang* in Shanghai and elsewhere and only 40,910 Shanghai taels from foreign banks. Similarly, in 1907 the *Shunkang qianzhuang* 順康錢莊 in Shanghai borrowed 122, 069 Shanghai taels from foreign banks, but also 101,865 Shanghai taels from other *qianzhuang* inside and outside of Shanghai.[124]

As the *qianzhuang* provided no real collateral for these loans, foreign banks had to trust the ability of their compradors to assess the credit of the Chinese banks. As mentioned before, the compradors provided a guarantee sum to the bank, but given the large amount of chop loans provided by foreign banks, this was not sufficient to cover any larger default of Chinese banks on their loans.[125] Therefore, the bank's granting of loans to Chinese banks mainly rested on its personal trust to the comprador. Another complicating factor were differences in business practices between Western and Chinese banks. Unlike foreign banks, *qianzhuang* had no large capitalization and mainly engaged in short-term lending 'that was often associated with extremely high risk'.[126] In contrast, we have seen that the DAB had instructed its bankers to avoid any unnecessary risk.[127] Still, for Kalb the chop loan business was 'very profitable and in my view not very dangerous', as he was certain that Xu would

---

[122] *SHQZL*, pp. 65, 474.

[123] Zhang, *Ge sheng jinrong*, pp. 213–14; von Glahn, *The Economic History of China*, p. 386.

[124] *SHQZSL*, pp. 788–9, 824–5. Nishimura Shizuya also uses these statistics and shows that the reliance of *qianzhuang* on foreign loans was not as strong as commonly assumed: Nishimura, 'Chop Loans', p. 123. However, he mistakenly reads *benbu tongye* 本埠同業 and *waibu tongye* 外埠同業 as meaning all non-foreign banks including *piaohao* banks, although these categories only mean *qianzhuang* and the statistics do not include loans from *piaohao*. See Nishimura, 'Chop Loans', pp. 122–3.

[125] On the possible insufficiency of the guarantee sum provided by compradors, also see King, *HSBC History*, 1:515.

[126] Quote from Wilson and Yang, 'Shanxi Piaohao', p. 442. For a comparison of the capitalization of foreign banks and *qianzhuang*, see Moazzin, 'Sino-Foreign Business Networks'.

[127] On this, also see Chapter 6.

only accept promissory notes from good banks since he had to guarantee for them.[128] Nevertheless, apart from their personal trust in their comprador, these loans were unsecured and thus the foreign bankers had to accept the higher risk they represented. Kalb reported that the general interest rate for loans in Shanghai in 1890 was 7 per cent per annum and that it was the comprador who reported the daily market interest rate to the bank and 'pledged to gain the best price [in terms of the interest rate] for loans' the bank provided to Chinese banks.[129]

However, Kalb was wrong to think that Xu had almost no opportunity to 'squeeze' and always reported the correct *yinchai* market interest rate and returned the best rate available to the bank. On the contrary, it was not the case that 'the interest on chop loans [issued by foreign banks] was the same as the interest charged on interbank loans';[130] instead, the compradors of foreign banks regularly manipulated the interest rate of the loans they were contracting for foreign banks. According to the famous Chinese banker Qin Runqing 秦潤卿, some compradors offered the loans from their foreign banks at interest rates below the market rate, thus allowing themselves and the *qianzhuang* to whom they lent the money to profit from the margin between the loan's interest rate and the market rate.[131] More commonly, compradors paid their foreign banks the interest rate for loans to Chinese banks according to the market rate, but charged a higher interest rate from the *qianzhuang* and kept the difference for themselves. Therefore, the interest rate that the compradors chose to offer on behalf of their foreign banks also invariably had an important impact on the cost of credit in the banking sector, although the *yinchai* interest rate set by the Chinese banks remained the most important guideline for interbank lending.[132]

We do not know exactly how large the margins were that the foreign bank compradors could earn by misinforming the bank about the real market interest rate or the real rate they offered when issuing chop loans to *qianzhuang*. However, by manipulating the interest rates of chop loans, compradors working for foreign banks could definitely generate extra profits, which, for example, were most likely much larger than the meagre salary or official commission for long-distance drafts Xu received from the DAB. That bank compradors could benefit in this way from their connection to foreign banks can mainly be explained in three ways. First, foreign banks had little knowledge of the actual inner workings of *qianzhuang*, so there existed an information asymmetry between the banks and their compradors, which the compradors

---

[128] Kalb, 'Bericht' (1 July 1890), PAAA, R9208/563, 149:29.
[129] Kalb, 'Bericht' (1 July 1890), PAAA, R9208/563, 149:12, 25.
[130] McElderry, *Old-Style Banks*, p. 21.
[131] *SHQZSL*, p. 38.
[132] Zhang, *Ge sheng jinrong*, p. 213; Dzen, *Das Bankwesen in China*, pp. 100, 107; Ma Yinchu, 'Zhonghua Yinhang lun' (1929), *MYCQJ*, 4:290–1.

and the Chinese banks they represented could exploit to deceive the foreign banks.[133] Second, the DAB and other foreign banks were excluded from Chinese guild organizations, which reinforced the information asymmetry. Although there exists evidence from Tianjin that foreign banks could be represented in Chinese merchant organizations by their compradors,[134] there is no evidence that foreign bankers were ever actively involved in such organizations, such as the Money Trade Guild in Shanghai. Therefore, they were also not involved in setting the interest rate for inter-bank lending, which would have allowed them to gain a full picture of the money supply in Shanghai. Finally, although Kalb had no knowledge of the interest manipulations of bank compradors, even if foreign bankers gained knowledge of such behaviour, they still had no alternative but to rely on compradors and *qianzhuang* to access the Chinese credit market.[135]

If we look at the wider business interests of Xu Chunrong, we can see that Xu could also benefit from his connection to the DAB in other ways. As he and his staff were in charge of choosing the banks the DAB granted loans, the Xu family could give preference to their own *qianzhuang* or those *qianzhuang* otherwise connected to them when deciding what Chinese banks to offer loans to.[136] As a result, when the Sida qianzhuang the Xu family operated with the Ye family and the Shengda 升大 and Yanqing 衍慶 *qianzhuang* owned by the Ye family went bankrupt during the 1911 revolution, these six banks were in debt to the DAB for 397,800 Shanghai taels, more than to any other foreign bank.[137] This suggests that the Xus could use their connection to the DAB to channel the bank's money to those Chinese banks owned by or closely connected to the Xu family. Therefore, filling the position of comprador at the DAB provided the wider business network of the Xu family with access to cheap and abundant

---

[133] Sheng to Imperial Bank of China (Hankou) (4 December 1897), *Shanghai Municipal Archives, Shanghai, China*, Q281-1-1, p. 44. On foreign bankers' deficient knowledge of both the Chinese language and the inner workings of Chinese commerce and banking, also see Sano, *Shinkoku kahei mondai hakan kin'yū kikan chōsa hōkoku*, p. 80; Mizuno, *Kankō:chūō Shina jijō*, p. 270. Information asymmetries describe economic transactions or partnerships in which one party has better or more information than the others. See, for example, Greenwald and Stiglitz, 'Asymmetric Information', pp. 160–5.

[134] Tianjin Chamber of Commerce to Compradors of Foreign Banks (15 September 1908), TMA, J128-2-002449.

[135] This lack of alternatives to relying on a comprador is an old theme in writings on commerce in China that can already be found in contemporaneous accounts. See, for example, 'The "Middlemen" of China', pp. 2215–16; Dehn, 'Handel und Verkehr', pp. 399–400; Arnold, *Commercial Handbook of China*, pp. 254–8.

[136] McElderry also notes control over chop loans as a possible reason why some Chinese families engaged in banking or trade found it useful to have a family member serve as comprador; see McElderry, *Old-Style Banks*, pp. 50–1.

[137] *SHQZSL*, p. 90.

foreign capital. This gave them an advantage over those Chinese bankers with no connection to a foreign bank.

The Xu family could also profit from the margin between the interest rate it could offer to its own *qianzhuang* and the interest rate at which these *qianzhuang* loaned the money to Chinese merchants. For example, the former translator for the Chinese Maritime Customs Service, Joseph Edkins, noted in 1905 that 'native banks in Shanghai borrow foreign capital at seven per cent and lend it to shop-keepers on shop securities at ten per cent'.[138] In such a case, the Xus could not only profit from manipulating the market interest rate reported to the DAB, but also indirectly from the profits made by their own *qianzhuang* when they loaned the money on to Chinese customers.

As Wu Peichu later recalled, besides the regular chop loans, there also existed a specific practice among compradors of foreign banks called 'week bills' (libai piao 禮拜票). Unlike *qianzhuang*, foreign banks were closed on Sundays. As the daily clearing process for inter-bank loans took place late at night after the foreign banks had closed, loans that *qianzhuang* presented for repayment were normally only redeemed for cash on the following day. Thus, foreign banks only received the cash for loans due on a Saturday on the following Monday when they opened for business again. This enabled compradors to loan out the funds they received on Sunday morning for chop loans that had been due on Saturday and loan them out during the day. Some bank compradors loaned out these funds at no interest to *qianzhuang* connected to them. The Xu family was known for charging interest and loaning these funds to the Sida qianzhuang owned by them. As Wu remembered, at the time of the 1911 revolution, Xu Xingquan had lent over 200,000 Shanghai taels of the DAB as 'week bills' to the Sida qianzhuang.[139] As the files of the DAB and other foreign banks show no mention of this practice, it seems that, once more, the compradors could use the information asymmetry between themselves and the foreign banks to generate extra profits with the capital they received from foreign banks without letting the foreign bankers know. All the different ways just discussed by which Chinese bankers could use their position as compradors in foreign banks to access and use foreign capital to generate profits show that within the business partnership between foreign and Chinese banks, the latter had considerable control over the terms of this partnership and the ways in which capital provided by foreign banks was used.

Clearly, control over the loans granted by the DAB to Chinese banks gave the Xu family access to vast sums of foreign capital that they could use to generate extra profits and support their other businesses. It also gave them an

---

[138] Edkins, *Banking and Prices in China*, p. 34. The interest rate for loans made by *qianzhuang* could be even higher; see Pan, *Zhongguo qianzhuang*, p. 82.

[139] Wu, 'Shanghai waishang yinhang', pp. 269–70. For the clearing process of chop loans and the clearing house more generally, see McElderry, *Old-Style Banks*, pp. 40–1, 44–5.

advantage over those Chinese bankers and entrepreneurs with no connection to a foreign bank, especially given the growing importance of foreign banks and capital in the credit market of the China coast. Importantly, this also suggests that entrepreneurs like Xu could use their connection to foreign banks to access some of the funds rich Chinese individuals and government institutions were normally only willing to deposit with foreign banks, so that part of these deposits eventually found their way into the hands of Chinese banks. This has important risk implications that once more run counter to common views of the supposedly advantageous position of foreign banks in the Chinese banking sector. Essentially, when capital found its way from Chinese depositors into Chinese banks via the intermediation of foreign banks, risk was shifted from the depositors to the foreign banks. Chinese depositors not willing to deposit funds with Chinese banks could deposit their funds safely in foreign banks at low risk. At the same time, Chinese banks could then access these funds otherwise unavailable to them through their connection with foreign banks. Thus, in the end it were the foreign banks that carried the risk differential and accepted a higher risk when loaning the deposited funds to Chinese banks. Finally, situating the DAB within the wider business network of the Xu family also shows that rather than only focussing on the role bankers such as Xu Chunrong played as compradors in foreign banks, it is more useful to see foreign banks as institutions that were integrated into the wider business networks operated by those Chinese businesspeople who filled the position of comprador in these foreign banks.[140]

While the relationship between foreign banks and *qianzhuang* is normally perceived in terms of loans provided by the foreign to these Chinese banks, Nishimura Shizuya has recently shown that foreign banks occasionally borrowed from *qianzhuang* and suggested that there existed an important degree of interdependence between foreign and Chinese banks.[141] Kalb's report on the Shanghai banking sector supports this conclusion for the case of Shanghai, going so far as to suggest that foreign banks borrowed from Chinese banks even more often than described by Nishimura. Kalb reported that it was common for foreign banks to borrow from Chinese banks: 'Not only does a European bank lend money to the Chinese, but the bank might often find itself in a position where it borrows large sums from Chinese [banks]'. He continued that 'the Hongkong and Shanghai Banking Corporation often owes the Chinese [banks] large sums', which was not 'perceived as a weakness', so the DAB could do the same through their comprador.[142] Kalb noted that the

---

[140] For a more detailed account than can be presented here of how the DAB was connected to and integrated into the different layers of Xu's business network and risk sharing within such networks, see Moazzin, 'Sino-Foreign Business Networks'.

[141] Nishimura, 'Chop Loans'.

[142] Kalb, 'Bericht' (1 July 1890), PAAA, R9208/563, 149:13.

DAB already had 'acquired a splendid reputation' among the Chinese, so that it could borrow up to 500,000 Shanghai taels from Chinese banks if it wished to do so. He recommended that the bank should be as accommodating as possible to Chinese banks, never be late with the repayment of loans and always 'go hand in hand with the Chinese' to maintain the bank's reputation and its ability to borrow from Chinese banks.[143] This shows that it was common for foreign banks to borrow from Chinese banks, but also that inter-bank lending between foreign and Chinese banks involved a high degree of interdependence. At the same time, the lending of foreign banks from Chinese banks again shows how dependent foreign banks were on their comprador, who made borrowing from Chinese banks possible.

In sum, the relationship of foreign banks to Chinese banks was one of interdependence and interaction rather than one-sided control. Foreign banks occupied a strong position in the banking sector because of their large capital stock, perceived stability and the advantages of extraterritoriality. However, they depended on *qianzhuang* banks and their compradors if they wished to employ their working capital in the Chinese credit market. Given that they had no other options for accessing the banking sector, they had to rely on their comprador and Chinese banks to function as their intermediaries. Although they could withdraw their loans from the *qianzhuang* if they wished, they could never do so permanently, as they had no other way of employing their working capital in the Chinese banking sector. On the other hand, *qianzhuang* had multiple sources of credit and were not solely dependent on foreign banks. They could also borrow from other *qianzhuang* and from the *piaohao* banks. Owners of *qianzhuang*, such as Xu Chunrong, could use their position as compradors for foreign banks to generate extra profits and support their own businesses by manipulating interest rates and channelling cheap foreign capital into the *qianzhuang* connected to them. Using their connection to foreign banks, *qianzhuang* could take advantage of the superior legal position and capitalization of these banks and access and use the large working capital of these banks, particularly the capital that Chinese officials and the Chinese government deposited in foreign banks. Finally, the flows of capital between foreign and Chinese banks were not one-directional; foreign banks also often received loans from Chinese banks.

As foreign banks were barred from the Money Trade Guild of the *qianzhuang*, they had no direct influence on setting the interest rate for inter-bank lending and were mostly reduced to passive providers of capital that had to accept the conditions of the market and the information their compradors provided them with.[144] For foreign banks, this was acceptable, as such loans

---

[143] Kalb, 'Bericht' (1 July 1890), PAAA, R9208/563, 149:32.

[144] An exception to this passivity was the occasional role foreign banks played in stabilizing financial markets. See Moazzin, 'Sino-Foreign Business Networks'.

were only one part of their business besides trade finance, international remittances and the loan business and because the interest rate they received for these loans was still higher than what they were used to from home.[145] Foreign banks such as the DAB could not impose their practices on the Chinese banking sector, but were rather integrated into existing networks and market structures, such as the wider business network of their compradors or the inter-bank lending mechanism. They also had to adapt to the practices of Chinese banks. By providing loans to *qianzhuang*, they followed the previous practice of *piaohao* banks and also had to adapt to the riskier practices of Chinese banks and provide loans without any real collateral. Thus, the picture that emerges is one of interdependence between foreign banks and *qianzhuang* that required the DAB and other foreign banks to adapt to the new business environment. It was because of this interdependent relationship and the integration of foreign banks into the Chinese credit market that the growth of foreign banking in the economic hubs on the Chinese frontier not only facilitated China's foreign trade and capital flows between China and other economies, but also contributed to the internationalization of the wider banking sector of the treaty port economy.

2.5   The Internationalization of the Banking Sector

During the first decade of its existence, the DAB slowly but steadily developed into a healthy business. While little is known about the first few years of the bank's activities in China, they were later remembered as the most difficult period in its history up to the First World War.[146] During these years, the main obstacle the bank encountered was the fall in the price of silver, exacerbated in 1893 by the lifting of the American Sherman Silver Purchase Act, which had compelled the American government to purchase a certain yearly amount of silver, and the Indian stop of silver coinage.[147] The concern of Hermann Wallich before the establishment of the DAB regarding the danger of silver fluctuations was thus proven correct. The main incident that threatened the bank's existence during these early years was a failed attempt in silver speculation. In 1891, the bank hoarded 750,000 taels in silver to prepare for the tea season in Hankou. Then the price in silver dropped and the bank was left with losses amounting to 249,552 reichsmark. The bank would not have survived this crisis without the commitment of its founding banks, who covered these

---

[145] On the first point also see Nishimura, 'Chop Loans', pp. 121–2. In Germany, interest rates for short-term loans varied between 3 and 4 per cent per annum between 1890 and 1914. See Homer and Sylla, *A History of Interest Rates*, pp. 260, 513.

[146] Urbig, *Aus dem Leben*, p. 55; Urbig, Untitled Report (23 October 1933), HADB, P8401.

[147] Müller-Jabusch, *Deutsch-Asiatische Bank*, p. 66; 'Bericht der Direktion für das Geschäftsjahr 1893' (25 June 1894), PAAA, R9208/563, p. 225.

losses.[148] Because of these problems in the regular business of the DAB and with no large loan business forthcoming, the bank could not issue any dividend in 1891 and 1892 (see Figure 2.7).

Connected to these early problems of the DAB was the question of what strategy the bank was to follow in building up its business in China. Rinkel demanded more freedom for the bankers on the spot in China and, as we saw, also wanted to see a quick expansion of the branch network of the bank to London and other locations to support the regular business in trade finance. He was supported by German minister von Brandt, who believed that the close control and risk-averse business strategy of the supervisory board meant that the bank could not adequately support German commerce and would not be able to survive on its own. Rinkel petitioned the supervisory board in Berlin several times about these problems, culminating in his report from 1893 that the bank could not survive without additional branches.[149] Given the problems the banks had encountered and the still volatile business environment in China, the members of the supervisory board rejected Rinkel's proposal for expansion in favour of 'continued caution and [the accumulation of] reserves'. Consequently, Rinkel resigned from the bank.[150]

However, both Brandt and Rinkel were proven wrong. The bank would survive and generate growing profits, despite its cautious attitude towards business. As Franz Urbig, a DAB banker, later remembered, during these early years the bank lacked not funds 'but experience in the areas of East

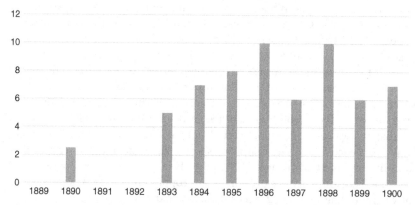

Figure 2.7 Dividend payments of the DAB, 1889–1900, in per cent. *Source*: Müller-Jabusch, *Deutsch-Asiatische Bank*, table opposite p. 326.

---

[148] Müller-Jabusch, *Deutsch-Asiatische Bank*, p. 62; Urbig, *Aus dem Leben*, p. 55.
[149] Brandt to Caprivi (11 December 1890), BArch, R901/12990, p. 124; Brandt to Caprivi (17 March 1891), BArch, R901/12990, p. 135; Rinkel, 'Bericht über die bisherige Geschäftstätigkeit' (February 1893), HSO, A VIII 114 Ostasiatische Geschäfte 1888–1914.
[150] Müller-Jabusch, *Deutsch-Asiatische Bank*, p. 66.

Asian trade and monetary transactions'.[151] As a remedy, the bank appointed Emil Rehders, who knew the China business well from his previous work as a China merchant, as the first director in China. Unlike Rinkel, Rehders was 'a cautious man guided by solid business principles', who 'restored the reputation of the bank and the trust in its right to exist' in the following years after the failed silver speculation, turning it into a profitable bank that created dividends for its shareholders (see Figure 2.7).[152] While critics of the bank were to continue to denounce the risk aversion of the bankers, the directors firmly believed that 'strictly staying away from speculative operations' was the best strategy to operate a bank in China given the fluctuations of silver.[153] This thinking was also reflected in the growth of the reserve funds of the bank from 46,821 Shanghai taels in 1893 to 735,883 Shanghai taels in 1900.[154]

By 1895, thanks to the positive development in China's foreign trade, the bank's turnover had risen to 137,348,571 taels, allowing for a dividend of 8 per cent.[155] This showed that even without the issuing and floating of large loans and involvement in railway development, the bank had learned to survive and create significant profits for its shareholders through its day-to-day business focused on trade finance.[156] The two indemnity loans the bank issued with the HSBC in 1896 and 1898, which will be discussed in Chapter 3, further increased the bank's turnover, so that the turnover of the Shanghai branch alone rose to 371,356,901 Shanghai taels in 1898, allowing dividend payments of 10 per cent.[157] While the branch network of the DAB so far had

---

[151] Urbig to Rust (26 February 1926), HADB, P8399.
[152] Quotes from Urbig, *Aus dem Leben*, p. 55; Müller-Jabusch, *Deutsch-Asiatische Bank*, p. 73.
[153] 'Bericht der Direktion für das Geschäftsjahr 1893' (25 June 1894), PAAA, R9208/563, p. 225.
[154] 'Bericht der Direktion für das Geschäftsjahr 1893' (25 June 1894), PAAA, R9208/563, p. 226; 'Bericht des Vorstandes für das Geschäftsjahr 1900' (28 June 1901), HADB, Geschäftsberichte, Deutsch-Asiatische Bank.
[155] 'Bericht der Direktion für das Geschäftsjahr 1895' (27 June 1896), BArch, R8024/283, pp. 1–2.
[156] The central importance of trade finance for the DAB's business can be seen in the yearly reports of the bank to its shareholders, which explicitly connected the development of China's foreign trade to the bank's performance and paid particular attention to the development of the turnover in bills of exchange. See 'Bericht der Direktion für das Geschäftsjahr 1894' (29 June 1895), HSO, A VIII 114 Ostasiatische Geschäfte 1888–1914; 'Bericht der Direktion für das Geschäftsjahr 1895' (27 June 1896), BArch, R8024/283, pp. 1–2; 'Bericht der Direktion für das Geschäftsjahr 1896' (28 June 1897), BArch, R8024/283, pp. 4–5; 'Bericht der Direction für das Geschäftsjahr 1897' (25 June 1898), HADB, Geschäftsberichte, Deutsch-Asiatische Bank. On the focus of the bank's business on trade finance, also see Strasser, *Die Deutschen Banken im Ausland*, p. 127. On the ability of the DAB to maintain itself through its day-to-day business alone, also see Müller-Jabusch, *Deutsch-Asiatische Bank*, p. 73.
[157] 'Bericht der Direktion für das Geschäftsjahr 1896' (28 June 1897), BArch, R8024/283, 4–5; 'Bericht der Direktion für das Geschäftsjahr 1898' (27 June 1899), HADB, Geschäftsberichte, Deutsch-Asiatische Bank.

only been made up of two branches, one in Shanghai and one in Tianjin, the positive development of the bank allowed the directors to start the first larger expansion of the bank's branch network between 1896 and 1900. First, in 1896 the bank opened a branch in Calcutta in India, which Wallich had early on described as 'the key to China's transactions in bills of exchange'. In the same year, the bankers also opened a branch in Berlin. This had become necessary for the administration of the growing business.[158] In 1898, agencies in Hankou and Qingdao were established and a branch in Hong Kong followed in 1900, which were all part of the bank's long-term plan to build up a branch network throughout East Asia.[159] To support this expansion of the branch network, the shareholders first paid up 62.5 per cent of the share capital in 1896 and then the full amount of the bank's capital of 5 million Shanghai taels by 1900.[160] Rehders returned to Germany to lead the new Berlin branch and remained on the executive board. He was replaced as first director and Shanghai manager first by Erich Karbe, and then, from 1899, by Johann Buse, who also had no banking background, but would lead the Shanghai branch until 1907.[161] As for the bank's head branch in Shanghai, which was also the DAB's most profitable branch, by 1895 it had been moved to a new, more central spot on the Bund. At No. 14, the Bund, it was now situated next to the buildings of the Chinese Maritime Customs Service and the HSBC (see Figures 2.8 and 2.9). Having rented it before, the bank purchased the building in 1898 and was to remain there until the First World War.[162]

---

[158] Quote from Wallich, 'Promemoria' (1887) GstA, I 109, 5363, p. 26; 'Bericht der Direktion für das Geschäftsjahr 1896' (28 June 1897), BArch, R8024/283, 4–5; 'Bericht der Direktion für das Geschäftsjahr 1897' (25 June 1898), HADB, Geschäftsberichte, Deutsch-Asiatische Bank. On the opening of the Tianjin branch in 1890, see Seckendorff to Caprivi (15 May 1891), BArch, R901/12991, p. 2.

[159] 'Bericht der Direktion für das Geschäftsjahr 1897' (25 June 1898), HADB, Geschäftsberichte, Deutsch-Asiatische Bank; 'Bericht der Direktion für das Geschäftsjahr 1898' (27 June 1899), HADB, Geschäftsberichte, Deutsch-Asiatische Bank; 'Bericht der Direktion für das Geschäftsjahr 1899' (30 June 1900), HADB, Geschäftsberichte, Deutsch-Asiatische Bank; 'Uebergabe des Neubaues der Deutsch-Asiatischen Bank in Hankou', Ostasiatischer Lloyd (10 July 1908).

[160] 'Bericht der Direktion für das Geschäftsjahr 1896' (28 June 1897), BArch, R8024/283, 4–5; 'Bericht der Direktion für das Geschäftsjahr 1899' (30 June 1900), HADB, Geschäftsberichte, Deutsch-Asiatische Bank.

[161] Erich to Schinckel (3 June 1905), HADB, K01/781, p. 128; Müller-Jabusch, Deutsch-Asiatische Bank, pp. 139, 142, 224, 318.

[162] According to contemporaneous directories, the DAB's Shanghai branch was initially situated at No. 26, the Bund. See Hongkong Daily Press, Chronicle & Directory 1890, p. 168. First evidence of its move to No. 14, the Bund can be found in 1895. See Hongkong Daily Press, Chronicle & Directory 1895, p. 123. On the HSBC and the Customs House being next to the DAB, apart from Figure 2.9, also see Tanioka, Saishin Shanhai chizu and Hibbard, The Bund Shanghai, pp. 135–67. On the purchase of the building by the DAB, see 'Bericht der Direktion für das Geschäftsjahr 1898' (27 June 1899), HADB, Geschäftsberichte, Deutsch-Asiatische Bank. On the Shanghai

Figure 2.8 Shanghai branch of the Deutsch-Asiatische Bank, early twentieth century. Image courtesy of Deutsche Bank AG, Historical Institute.

While the bank emerged successful from the first decade of its existence, problems also appeared on the horizon. In 1900, the directors complained about the growing competition from other foreign banks that had 'increased to a previously unknown degree'.[163] The banking sector in places like Shanghai had changed drastically since the DAB had arrived on the China coast in 1890. At that time, only the HSBC, a few other less significant British banks and the weakened Comptoir National D'Escompte had existed as competitors of the DAB. Before that year, except for one French bank, foreign banking in China had essentially been a British affair. Following the rapid increase of China's foreign trade and its opening to industrial investment after 1895, an increasing number of foreign banks settled in the economic hubs along the China coast (see Table 2.2). With

branch remaining at No. 14, the Bund until the First World War, see North-China Daily News and Herald, *North-China Desk Hong List 1917*, p. 73. On the Shanghai branch being the bank's most profitable branch in the period between 1895 and 1903, see Müller-Jabusch, *Deutsch-Asiatische Bank*, p. 141.

[163] 'Bericht der Direktion für das Geschäftsjahr 1899' (30 June 1900), HADB, Geschäftsberichte, Deutsch-Asiatische Bank. This growth in the competition among international banks due to the entrance of new banks also appeared in Asia more generally; see Nishimura, Suzuki and Akagawa, 'Jobun', p. x.

Figure 2.9 The Bund in Shanghai, from right to left: the Deutsch-Asiatische Bank, the Customs House, the Hong Kong and Shanghai Banking Corporation, early twentieth century. Image courtesy of Alamy.

Table 2.2 *Foreign banks in China, 1845–1903*

	Nationality	Entry into China (incl. HK and Macao)	Paid-up capital 1888 (in £000)	Balance sheet total 1888 (in £000)	Number of branches/ sub-branches/ agencies (incl. head branch) in 1888	Paid-up capital in 1903 (in £000)	Balance sheet total in 1903 (in £000)	Number of branches/ sub-branches/ agencies (incl. head branch) in 1903
(New) Oriental Bank Corporation	Britain	1845	500	?	30	Liquidated in 1892	/	/
Commercial Bank of India	Britain	1849	Went bankrupt in 1866			/	/	/	/
Chartered Mercantile Bank of India, London and China (from 1893: Mercantile Bank of India, Ltd.)	Britain	1854	750	8,270	14	562	4,122	?
The Agra Bank	Britain	1854	1,000	6,118	15	Liquidated in 1900	/	/
Chartered Bank of India, Australia and China	Britain	1858	800	11,813	17	800	16,218	25
Comptoir d'Escompte de Paris	France	1860	3,162	?	19	Chinese Branches transferred to Banque de L'Indochine and Russo-Chinese bank	/	/
Central Bank of Western India	Britain	1861	Went bankrupt in 1866			/	/	/

Table 2.2 Cont.

	Nationality	Entry into China (incl. HK and Macao)	Paid-up capital 1888 (in £000)	Balance sheet total 1888 (in £000)	Number of branches/ sub-branches/ agencies (incl. head branch) in 1888	Paid-up capital in 1903 (in £000)	Balance sheet total in 1903 (in £000)	Number of branches/ sub-branches/ agencies (incl. head branch) in 1903
Bank of Hindustan, China and Japan	Britain	1863	Went Bankrupt in 1866	/	/	/	/	/
Bank of India	Britain	1864	Went bankrupt in 1866			/	/	/
Asiatic Banking Corporation	Britain	1864	Went bankrupt in 1866			/	/	/
Hongkong and Shanghai Banking Corporation	Britain	1865	1,500	22,927	21	1,000	26,779	26
Deutsche Bank	German	1872	Left East Asia in 1875			/	/	/
National Bank of India	Britain	1875	Left China by 1885			/	/	/
Deutsch-Asiatische Bank	Germany	1890	/	/	/	585	2803	7
National Bank of China	Britain	1891	/	/	/	324	412	?
Yokohama Specie Bank	Japan	1893	/	/	/	1,800	22,120	15
Bank of China & Japan Ltd.	Britain	1894	/	/	/	?	?	?
Banque de L'Indochine	France	1894	/	/	/	238	?	13

Russo-Chinese Bank	Russia	1896	/	1,569[4]	?	50
Bank of Taiwan	Japan	1900	/	255	1843	?
International Banking Corporation	United States	1902	/	811	?	24
Sino-Belgian Bank[1]	Belgium	1902	/	39[5]	?	2
Banco Nacional Ultramarino	Portugal	1902	/	?	?	?
Guaranty Trust Co. of New York.	United States	1903[2]	/	414[5]	?	4
Netherlands Trading Society	Netherlands	1903	/	3,750	9,499	21
Societa Coloniale Italiana[3]	Italy	1903	/	?	?	8

Source: The Bankers' Magazine 27, No. 278 (May 1867), pp. 5, 455; Kalb, 'Bericht' (1 July 1890), PAAA, R9208/563, 149: 14; Müller-Jabusch, *Deutsch-Asiatische Bank*, table opposite p. 326; Brötel, *Frankreich im Fernen Osten*, pp. 234, 329–30, 427; *Economist* (20 February 1864, 18 May 1889, 19 October 1889, 19 May 1894, 7 November 1903, 21 May 1904); *The North-China Herald* (22 July 1865, 13 August 1864, 30 January 1889, 28 March 1900, 23 December 1903, 29 January 1904, 9 September 1904); *Le Figaro Supplément littéraire du dimanche* (4 May 1889); *The Far-Eastern Review* 1, No. 1 (June 1904), p. 36; Moreau and Monchicourt, *Rapport*, p. 48; Tatewaki, *Zainichi gaikoku ginkōshi*, p. 32; Hong, *Shanghai jinrong zhi*, pp. 205–6; Taiwan Ginkō, *Taiwan ginkō yonjunenshi*, pp. 20–1; Chen, *Aomen jingji*, p. 104; Hongkong Daily Press, *Directory & Chronicle 1903*, p. iii; Bank of Tokyo, *Yokohama shōkin ginkō zenshi*, p. 98; Netherlands Trading Society, *Brief History*, pp. 59, 83; Wang, 'Zai Hua waiguo yinhang gaishu', *Dagongbao (Jingji Zhoubao)* (7 August 1935). p. 547; Gonjō, *Furansu teikoku shugi*, p. 172; Wang, *Waiguo ziben zai jindai Zhongguo*, pp. 14, 94–5, 101, table between pp. 296 and 297, 439; Kanada, 'Chūgoku kaikō-go no gaikoku ginkō', pp. 1579–80. In the rare cases where a slight discrepancy exists between sources about a bank's year of entry into China, I have chosen the year with the most reliable evidence. Figures not available in £ were converted.

Notes:

[1] According to Tōa Dōbun Shoin Daigaku, *Shina Keizai zensho*, pp. 980–1000, the Sino-Belgian bank's only Chinese branch in 1903 was in Shanghai. I thus give the number of branches for the bank in 1903 as two (The Shanghai branch and the head branch in Brussels as stated in *The North-China Herald* from 23 December 1903).

[2] The earliest mention of a Chinese presence of the Guaranty Trust Co. of New York in China I could find is 1903 (see, for example, the *Desk Hong List* for that year).

[3] While the Societa Coloniale Italiana possibly also had a Guangzhou branch or agency (with an unknown establishment date), it seems to have only primarily operated as a bank in Shanghai (see Appendix 2). I have thus taken the Shanghai branch as my reference. The earliest mention of the Societa Coloniale Italiana in Shanghai I could find was in 1903. The Shanghai branch had ceased to exist by 1912. See *Desk Hong List* for 1903 and Hong, *Shanghai Jinrong zhi*, p. 205.

[4] Paid-up capital figure from Russo-Chinese bank's annual report for 1904 in *North-China Herald* (6 October 1905).

[5] For these two banks, the available sources only provide a figure for 'capital' without further specification, which I have thus taken as paid-up capital.

the DAB's establishment in 1890, a development had started that Frank Tamagna in 1942 described as the 'extensive expansion of foreign banking' in China during the two and a half decades before the First World War.[164]

This development naturally brought changes to the Chinese banking sector. As Table 2.2 shows, until the 1890s, the number of foreign banks in China had only grown slowly and foreign banking had been dominated by British banks. Moreover, the presence of foreign banks also remained limited as the presence of more than half of these banks in China, such as the Deutsche Bank or the Bank of India, remained short-lived. By the early twentieth century, the rapid influx of foreign banks had already led to the end of the British dominance in foreign banking in China and to a rapid increase in both the number of foreign banks in China and the amount and diversity of foreign banking capital invested in the banking sector of China's treaty ports. If we wish to gain a picture of the changing position of foreign banks in the banking sector of China's treaty port economy during this period, it is not possible to arrive at an absolute result of the growth of foreign banks relative to Chinese banks.[165] First, even for locations such as Shanghai, where the availability of data is

---

[164] Tamagna, *Banking and Finance*, pp. 25–8. Tamagna dates the start of this expansion period to 1890 in the relevant subheading, but then, by mistake it appears, in the text wrongly gives the date of the DAB's founding in China and correspondingly the start of this expansion period as 1891.

[165] In his work on modern Chinese banks, Cheng Linsun (程麟蓀) has asserted that foreign banks, *piaohao* and *qianzhuang* each occupied roughly a third of the whole Chinese banking sector in the 1890s. See Cheng, *Banking in Modern China*, p. 19. However, his calculations are problematic in several ways. First, he only looks at the year 1894 and bases his calculations for foreign banks on an article that assumes that the balance sheet totals of foreign banks represented their assets in China, although these banks also had branches in Europe and the rest of East Asia. Nishimura Shizuya also cast doubt on the data provided by Cheng, in particular on the data regarding the capital of foreign banks by correctly hypothecating that balance-sheet totals were used and by pointing to the fact that these banks had branches outside of China. However, Nishimura does not examine Cheng's sources or pursue the issue further besides providing his own estimates for the capital of foreign banks in Shanghai in 1894; see Nishimura, 'Chop Loans', pp. 112–13. For the article used by Cheng see Tang and Huang, 'Shilun 1927 nian yiqian de Zhongguo yinhang', pp. 57–89; data used by Cheng from pp. 58–9. Second, Cheng also uses this article to infer the total capital power of *qianzhuang*, even though the authors of the article only provide the total capital power of *qianzhuang* for the early republican period and a very rough estimate for the development of the capital power of *qianzhuang* in Shanghai between the period 'around the Sino-Japanese War' and the early republican period. The sources quoted by Tang and Huang are Nongshang Bu 農商部, *Zhonghua Minguo jiunian dijiuci nongshang tongjibiao*, p. 412 and *SHQZSL*. For the total capital power of *piaohao*, Cheng uses a source (p. 142 in the 1937 original version of Chen, *Shanxi piaozhuang kaoliie*; the corresponding passage in the 2008 reprint can be found on pp. 74–5) that only gives a rough attempted estimate of the assets of *piaohao* banks for their 'most prosperous period' without giving a specific year for this estimate. In general, the data and methodology used for estimates in the sources Cheng cites are questionable. Third, it is misleading to use data relating to foreign banks when discussing the whole 'Chinese financial market', as foreign banks only appeared on the China coast and were absent from

relatively good, information on the assets of the individual Shanghai branches of foreign banks is very difficult to obtain. Second, no reliable data exists about the assets of individual *qianzhuang* and *piaohao* branches in the treaty ports, so it is impossible to accurately assess the exact share foreign banks had in the banking sector of China's treaty ports relative to Chinese banks. Nevertheless, based on the advertisements, reports and publications of foreign banks, we can again use Shanghai as an example and estimate the absolute growth in the invested capital of foreign banks in the banking sector there. I used the paid-up capital of the foreign banks active in Shanghai in 1888 and 1903 and divided it by the total number of branches and agencies of each of these banks to estimate their capital power in Shanghai in these two years. The result is that the estimated invested capital of foreign banks in Shanghai rose from around £421,000 in 1888 to around £659,000 in 1903. The total number of foreign banks in Shanghai rose from six in 1888 to ten in 1903.[166] The growth in the number of foreign banks and invested foreign banking capital becomes even more significant if we consider that three of the six foreign banks with branches in Shanghai in 1888, the Comptoir D'Escompte de Paris, the New Oriental Banking Corporation and the Agra Bank, either gave up their branches in China or were liquidated before 1903.[167]

Thus, we see the significant degree to which the banking sector in Shanghai was internationalized during the 1890s, not only in terms of diversity of capital (as shown in Table 2.2), but also in terms of the number of foreign banks in Shanghai and the amount of invested foreign banking capital. While Shanghai can only act as an example, compared to the 1880s and before, foreign banks occupied a more important position in the banking sector of the treaty port economy at the beginning of the twentieth century. This growing internationalization was also reflected in the growth in the number of *qianzhuang*, who benefited from the increase in the number of foreign banks that provided them with capital. In Shanghai, the number of *qianzhuang* grew from sixty-two to

the banking sector in inner China. Therefore, Cheng's data is not reliable regarding the constitution of the whole Chinese banking sector.

[166] The estimate of the invested capital is calculated according to the sources and data listed in Table 2.2. Given that the Shanghai branch normally represented one of the largest branches of foreign banks, dividing the paid-up capital by the number of branches and agencies provides a very conservative estimate of the invested bank capital in Shanghai. I used the paid-up capital instead of the total assets of the banks, as total asset data is not available for all banks. The names and number of foreign banks in Shanghai are taken from: The Hongkong Daily Press, *Chronicle & Directory for China 1888*, pp. 432–3 and The North-China Herald, *Desk Hong List 1903*. As the Societa Coloniale Italiana seems to primarily have been a trading company that only focused on banking business with its Shanghai branch (see Appendix 2), I have not included it in my calculations here. The Mercantile Bank of India in 1903 is only represented in Shanghai through an agency agreement with Jardine, Matheson & Co. and therefore is not included in my calculation.

[167] On the three banks, see King, *HSBC History*, 1:404, 456.

eighty-three between 1888 and 1903.[168] Another important result of this influx of foreign banks was that more cheap foreign capital entered the Chinese credit market and the cost of money in the treaty ports further decreased. Between 1873 and 1889 the average yearly *yinchai* interest rate in Shanghai was 7.3 per cent, compared to only 5.4 per cent between 1890 and 1903.[169]

Besides the inflow of foreign banking capital into the banking sector of Shanghai and other economic hubs, the growth of China's foreign trade also accelerated the internationalization of the Chinese banking sector in the treaty ports by way of increasing flows of capital between China and other countries. As we have seen, during the 1890s China's foreign trade grew rapidly. In fact, it did so at an unprecedented scale. While China's foreign trade had only grown from 94 million Haiguan taels in 1864 to 207 million Haiguan taels in 1889, it more than doubled between 1890 and 1899 alone.[170] As this trade always involved transnational monetary transactions managed by foreign banks in the treaty ports, it also caused a hitherto unknown growth of monetary transactions and capital flows between China and its foreign trade partners. In turn, it was the growing number of foreign banks on the Chinese frontier and the financial infrastructure they provided that supplied the financial basis for the rapid growth of China's foreign trade.

Finally, as we will see in the next chapter, in addition to the growth of foreign trade, during the 1890s the floating of Chinese loans of unprecedented size on European capital markets, which was facilitated by foreign banks, also led to a sharp increase in the amount of capital flows between China and Europe. These monetary transactions carried out by foreign banks meant that the banking sector of Shanghai and other economic centres on the China coast saw a rapid increase of transnational in- and outflows of capital, which further accelerated the internationalization of the banking sector of China's treaty port economy. As China's trade with countries other than Britain, such as Germany, and its sovereign borrowing on markets other than London also gradually increased, the capital flows involved also grew more diverse.[171] Thus, the 1890s saw the acceleration of China's financial internationalization in the amount and diversity of both foreign banking capital invested in its treaty ports and the increasing transnational monetary transactions flowing through the economic hubs of the Chinese frontier.

[168] *SHQZSL*, pp. 32, 95.
[169] Calculated according to data in Kong, *Nankai jingji*, pp. 479–80. On this point also see Song, *Jindai Shanghai waishang yinhang*, pp. 267–9. For the beginning of the cheapening of money on the China coast in the nineteenth century, see Hao, *Commercial Revolution*, chapter 4.
[170] Hsiao, *China's Foreign Trade*, pp. 22–3. On the rapid growth of China's foreign trade during the last two decades of the Qing dynasty, also see van de Ven, 'Onrush', p. 176.
[171] On the growing diversity of China's foreign trade partners after 1890, see Ratenhof, *Chinapolitik*, pp. 564–5. On the growing diversity of China's sovereign borrowing, see Chapter 3 of this book.

2.6   Conclusion

The entry of the DAB into the frontier region of the China coast was an important step both for the outward internationalization of German banking and the inward internationalization of the banking sector of China's treaty port economy. After the failed attempt of the Deutsche Bank during the 1870s, there now finally existed a successfully operating German bank in China. Despite the problems the bank encountered during the first years of its operations, it survived and developed into a healthy business both because of the commitment and strength of the founding banks and the cautious attitude towards business adopted by the German bankers. During a period that also saw the failures or liquidation of foreign banks such as the Comptoir D'Escompte de Paris, the New Oriental Banking Corporation and the Agra bank, the DAB showed that a risk-averse business strategy could be successful, especially for a foreign bank that entered the market relatively late and with limited capital, even if it might have meant a certain limitation for the profitability and speed of expansion of the bank.

Like other foreign banks, the DAB could use its overseas branches and correspondents, comparatively large capitalization, stable business structure and the legal advantages of extraterritoriality to fill an institutional void in the banking sector of the China coast, monopolize the financing of China's foreign trade and attract large sums of deposits and profitably use them through its cooperation with Chinese banks. At the same time, being barred from access to guild organizations and market information, the DAB and other foreign banks had to rely on Chinese business partners and an interdependent relationship with *qianzhuang* banks to use their capital in the Chinese banking sector. While foreign banks played an important role as intermediary institutions that financially connected China to the global economy by filling an institutional void in the banking sector and setting foreign exchange rates, managing international remittances and financing China's foreign trade, their operation on China's frontier always depended on cooperation with Chinese actors.

As a consequence, the German bankers had to adapt their business practices to the Chinese environment, accepting the loan practices of their Chinese business partners and becoming part of existing credit networks. Thus, for German and other foreign bankers the internationalization and expansion of their business to China was also always accompanied by localization and adaptation.[172] At the same time, Chinese bankers used and benefited from their connections to foreign banks not only by exploiting information

---

[172] Jiang and Jiang also note that foreign banks showed signs of localization. However, they do so not from the perspective of the localization of business practices and adaptation to the local business environment but from the perspective of market and functional factors and the comprador system. See Jiang and Jiang, *Jindai Zhongguo waishang yinhang*, pp. 343–4.

asymmetries to their advantage, but also by integrating foreign banks into existing business networks to gain an advantage over their competitors. The interdependence between foreign banks and *qianzhuang* in the Chinese banking sector was one reason why the introduction of modern foreign banks and later modern Chinese banks that were modelled after foreign banks caused no Schumpeterian 'creative destruction' that might have eradicated the old and supposedly inferior structures of *qianzhuang* banks.[173] Rather, despite the differences, these banks continued to exist as foreign banks needed them for their operations in the Chinese banking sector. Even when modern Chinese banks, which were modelled after Western banks, rose in the republican period, they did not replace traditional Chinese financial institutions but followed the practice of foreign banks in working with them.[174] As the interdependent relationship between foreign banks and *qianzhuang* shows, on the Chinese frontier financial institutions that differed greatly in their business structure and practices and the management of risk interacted through transnational networks of cooperation. Within these networks on the frontier, Chinese actors possessed considerable agency. At the same time, by connecting foreign and Chinese financial actors, institutions and practices in China's treaty ports, such transnational networks played a key role both in China's financial internationalization and in the operation of the financial markets on China's frontier.[175]

Besides these new business structures, networks and practices that evolved, the most significant impact of the increasing influx of foreign banks after 1890 was the acceleration of the internationalization of the banking sector of China's treaty port economy. Before the 1890s, only a few foreign banks had gradually entered China over a time-span of several decades and initiated the internationalization of the banking sector of the China coast. However, only after 1890 did this process of internationalization reach unprecedented heights in terms of the number of foreign banks in China and the amounts and diversity of both foreign banking capital invested in the treaty port economy and flows of capital between China's economic hubs and other global financial centres. The consequence of this development was not only that foreign banks and capital became much more important for the banking sector of the treaty port economy. It also led to a decrease in the cost of credit and a drastic increase in China's financial connections to the global economy, which were mediated by foreign banks.

---

[173] Schumpeter, *Capitalism, Socialism and Democracy*, pp. 81–6.
[174] McElderry, *Old-Style Banks*, pp. 142–7; Nishimura, 'Chop Loans', p. 130.
[175] For a more detailed elaboration of the importance of transnational networks for the running of financial markets of the treaty ports, see Moazzin, 'Sino-Foreign Business Networks'. This article draws on the larger point made by Jeffrey Wasserstrom about the important role transnational networks played in the functioning of Shanghai. See Wasserstrom, 'Cosmopolitan Connections'.

Hao Yanping argued that China witnessed a 'commercial revolution' between the 1820s and the 1880s, which was mainly driven by the introduction of cheap foreign capital and new forms of credit and an increased participation in global trade.[176] However, from the perspective of financial internationalization, it seems more appropriate to see this period as an initial phase in the financial internationalization of China. During the period discussed by Hao, new forms of financial institutions, foreign capital and forms of credit were indeed introduced to China, leading, among other things, to the expansion of credit and a decrease in the cost of money. Moreover, this period certainly saw the establishment of new financial connections between China and the rest of the world.[177] However, these developments remained limited in extent because of the small number of specialized foreign banks in China and the comparatively slow growth of China's foreign trade and foreign borrowing. Only the increased influx of foreign banks that specialized in providing international financial services and the unprecedented growth of China's foreign trade and borrowing after the 1890s caused the acceleration of China's financial internationalization in the Chinese banking sector, the further expansion of credit and decrease in the cost of money, and the start of the full-scale financial integration of China into the global economy.

[176] Hao, *Commercial Revolution*.
[177] Wong, *Global Trade* also discusses such early financial connections.

3

Chinese Bonds for European Investors

The Indemnity Loans and the Internationalization of Chinese
Public Finance, 1895–1898

In May 1895, shortly after the end of the Sino-Japanese War, August Heinrich
Exner, a former member of the 1886 study mission to China, wrote an article
for the *Berliner Tageblatt* in which he answered the question of whether
German investors should buy Chinese bonds now that a large Chinese loan
for the payment of the Japanese war indemnity seemed imminent. Similar to
his earlier work on Chinese public finance, Exner painted a very positive
picture of China's large revenue, low foreign debt, the security and profitability
of Chinese bonds and China's potential for development. He asserted that 'for
China the war with Japan is the dawn of a new era' that would usher in 'an age
of transformations' and allow Chinese reformers to slowly modernize China.
He hoped that German capitalists would invest in Chinese loans, which would
also allow German industry and trade to partake in China's development:

> In the fight for new markets on the world market, China for a long time
> has given rise to great hope for the future. . . . Germany now already
> possesses a relatively large part of the trade and shipping traffic with
> China and for a decade preparations have eagerly been made so that it
> can play its due role in the economic development of the Middle Kingdom
> in railway construction, factories etc. etc. Only with the help of European
> credit can China utilise its precious natural resources and use them to the
> full extent in a relatively short time. Therefore, it is in the interest of our
> German trade and our German industry that we participate in future
> guaranteed Chinese government loans, in order to secure for German
> industry as big a part as possible in the future development of China.[1]

While Exner held very positive views of Chinese loans both as a safe and
profitable investment and as a means of securing a share in China's economic
development for German industry and trade, his views were representative of
the thinking of many German bankers. As we saw in the first chapter, the
floating of prospected large Chinese loans in Germany and the hope that such
loans would also bring business to German industry had been a major reason
for the establishment of the Deutsch-Asiatische Bank (DAB). This chapter tells
the story of the DAB's first successful participation in large Chinese loans in

---

[1] Exner, 'Soll Deutschland chinesische Anleihen kaufen?', *Berliner Tageblatt* (14/15 May 1895).

1896 and 1898 and the role these loans played in integrating China into the international financial system of sovereign borrowing and the international-ization of Chinese public finance.

Following China's defeat in the Sino-Japanese War of 1894/5, Japan had imposed a large indemnity of 200 million Kuping taels on China, a sum that far exceeded the annual revenue of the Chinese government, which had stood at around 81 million Kuping taels in 1894.[2] China decided to resort to foreign borrowing on an unprecedented scale to repay the indemnity and issued three loans each worth about £16 million in Europe between 1895 and 1898. While the first loan was issued by a Russo-French syndicate for the Chinese govern-ment in 1895, the Hongkong and Shanghai Banking Corporation (HSBC) and the DAB cooperated in issuing the second and third indemnity loans in 1896 and 1898. These loans were a watershed both in the history of the DAB and the history of Chinese foreign borrowing. As we will see, not only did they finally enable the DAB to gain equality with the HSBC and greatly increased the bank's reputation both in China and abroad, but these loans were also the first truly large Chinese loans issued in Europe, as the largest single Chinese foreign loan before had been for only £3 million.[3]

Previous scholarship has mainly discussed these loans in the context of the extension of foreign imperialism and control in China or has scrutinized the role the loans played in the transformation of the Chinese Maritime Customs Service into a debt collector for the Qing government.[4] In contrast, this chapter follows the loan negotiations between the Qing government, the German bankers and their partners and competitors, and foreign diplomats between 1895 and 1898, and looks at these loans from the viewpoint of China's integration into the international financial system of sovereign borrowing and the consequential acceleration of the internationalization of Chinese public finance in terms of both the increased diversity and amount of foreign borrowing by the Chinese state. To trace how China was further integrated into the international financial system through the negotiating and issuing of the indemnity loans, I draw on Susan Strange's distinction between 'structural power' and 'relational power' in the international political economy.

[2] For the Qing government's revenue in 1894, see Zhou, *Wan Qing caizheng jingji*, p. 154.
[3] For an overview of previous Chinese public loans, see Berliner Actionair, *Jahrbuch der Berliner Börse, 1890–1891*, p. 30 and Berliner Actionair, *Jahrbuch der Berliner Börse, 1897–1898*, p. 56. For an overview of previous smaller Chinese non-public loans, see Xu et al., *Cong bainian quru*, 1:517–21.
[4] See, for example, Barth, *Imperialismen*, pp. 139–59; Li, *Die Chinesische Politik*, pp. 89–102, 104–8; McLean, *British Banking and Government*, pp. 22–56; McLean, 'The Foreign Office and the First Chinese Indemnity Loan, 1895', *The Historical Journal* 16, No. 2 (1973): 303–21; Xu et al., *Qingdai waizhai shilun*, pp. 413–52; van de Ven, *Breaking with the Past*, pp. 138–44. For coverage of the loans in Frank King's institutional history of the HSBC, which, however, also tends to focus on the political side of the negotiations, see King, *HSBC History*, 2:264–90.

For Strange, relational power concerns the interaction between individual actors and represents the power of one party to make another party do something it would otherwise not do. Structural power is 'the power to shape and determine the structures of the global political economy' or, in other words, the framework under which individual actors act. For Strange, there exist four representations of structural power: 'control over security; control over production; control over credit; and control over knowledge, beliefs and ideas'.[5] In this chapter, I focus on the control over credit and the financial structure of the international system of sovereign borrowing, both represented by the foreign bankers.

I use the example of the indemnity loans to show that the integration of China into the international system of sovereign borrowing was not just a one-sided imposition of structural power, but a process of mutual negotiations and learning between the foreign bankers, who represented the Western financial structure of international sovereign borrowing and wanted to integrate China into this system, and Chinese officials, who wished to tap foreign capital markets and used their relational power to great effect in the negotiations to improve borrowing costs within the wider financial structure of international sovereign borrowing. In particular, this becomes clear once we depart from the view that the international financial structure of the late nineteenth century was largely uniform and notice that it comprised different foreign financial groups and diplomats, whose competition could be used by the Chinese negotiators to challenge the demands of specific financial groups and win better terms. Even though the Western bankers represented and controlled foreign credit, their structural power and the financial structure of sovereign borrowing during the late nineteenth century was constantly being renegotiated between foreign financiers and indigenous actors. Moreover, integrating China into the international system of sovereign borrowing was not only about fixing specific loan terms but also involved larger processes of learning and adaptation. While foreign bankers had to find ways to assess Chinese sovereign risk and identify streams of Chinese revenue that would be an acceptable security for European investors, Chinese officials had to learn how to use sovereign borrowing and test how far they could go in independently dealing

---

[5] Quote from Strange, *States and Markets*, pp. 27–37. Hopkins and Cain have recently started to use Strange's model to modify their original narrative of British imperial expansion and account for local agency on the 'periphery', mainly in settler colonies. (Their original study of British imperialism consisted of the following two volumes: Cain and Hopkins, *British Imperialism: Innovation and Expansion* and Cain and Hopkins, *British Imperialism: Crisis and Deconstruction*.) However, they remain sceptical of the ability of the 'periphery' to use relational power to challenge British structural power. See Hopkins and Cain, 'Afterword', pp. 196–220; Hopkins, 'Informal Empire in Argentina', pp. 469–84; Hopkins, 'Gentlemanly Capitalism', pp. 287–97.

with foreign capital markets.[6] It was through these negotiating processes that China was integrated into the international financial system and the internationalization of Chinese public finance was accelerated. While some of the actors we will meet operated in Western financial centres, it was the Chinese frontier that became the primary space where these processes of financial learning and negotiations between structural and relational power took place.

This chapter starts with a discussion of the first indemnity loan and focusses on the increased competition among foreign financiers and diplomats in China and the politicization of loan negotiations following the Sino-Japanese War. This increased competition allowed the German bankers to finally come to an agreement about issuing Chinese loans on the basis of equality with the HSBC. The chapter then turns to the second indemnity loan and shows how the Chinese government used the increasing competition among foreign financiers to attain favourable loan terms, even though the German bankers in particular felt this went against the established rules of foreign borrowing. The next section of the chapter then discusses how foreign bankers attempted to identify new securities for the third indemnity loan and Chinese officials unsuccessfully attempted to circumvent the demand of foreign bankers for further foreign control of Chinese revenues by trying to directly interact with the capital market in London. Eventually, again a compromise was struck. New revenues were put under foreign supervision to act as collateral for the third indemnity loan, but this foreign supervision eventually remained largely symbolic. Finally, the chapter concludes with a discussion of how the indemnity loans accelerated the internationalization of Chinese public finance.

3.1   The End of a Monopoly

When the DAB was established in 1889, the founding banks had hoped that the bank would be able to contract large loans with the Chinese government that could be floated in Germany. The bankers especially hoped that China would soon see the large-scale introduction of railways, which promised plenty of opportunities for German investment.[7] Kalb had explained early on that it was essential for the bank's loan business to establish a branch in Tianjin to have a 'reliable person near to Li Hongzhang and Beijing'.[8] Indeed, because of Tianjin's proximity to Beijing, the branches of foreign banks in the port city were often used for loan business with the Chinese government.[9] The DAB

---

[6] Sovereign risk means the probability that a government is able to repay its debt. For a good introduction to sovereign risk during the period in question, see Flandreau and Zumer, *The Making of Global Finance.*

[7] Rinkel, 'Bericht über die bisherige Geschäftstätigkeit' (February 1893), HSO, A VIII 114 Ostasiatische Geschäfte 1888–1914.

[8] Kalb, 'Bericht' (1 July 1890), PAAA, R9208/563, 149:6, 36.

[9] Tōa Dōbunkai, *Shina shōbetsu zenshi,* 18:1062.

established a branch in Tianjin in December 1890 and tried to establish good relations with Li, who at one point even expressed interest in acquiring shares of the DAB.[10] The bank also concluded a few smaller loan deals (see Appendix I). However, during the first years of the bank's existence the large-scale expansion of China's railways did not take place and the realities of the Chinese loan business fell short of the expectations of German bankers.[11] When the Sino-Japanese War ended in 1895, the imposition of an indemnity of 200 million Kuping taels on China by Japan meant that there were finally prospects for a large Chinese loan of unprecedented size to be floated in Europe. What made foreign borrowing for China especially attractive was that it allowed a fast repayment of the indemnity, which would save China additional interest payments.[12]

Robert Hart, Inspector General of the Chinese Maritime Customs Service, had already sensed in early April 1895 that China would require a large foreign loan to cover indemnity payments and other costs related to the end of the war. Therefore, he contacted the HSBC in London and asked whether the bank could raise £60 million for China. The HSBC responded positively, but explained that because of the large size of the required sum, it would need to contact bankers in other European financial centres.[13] This was a first sign that the HSBC's role as banker to China was coming to an end. While the HSBC had issued many of China's previous smaller loans on its own and had monopolized the business of issuing Chinese public loans, the British bankers now felt they needed the help of other foreign financiers to issue the prospected loan sum and for the first time took the initiative in proposing cooperation with other foreign bankers. The British bankers approached Adolph von Hansemann, now a member of the DAB's supervisory board, in Berlin through the HSBC's Hamburg manager, Julius Brüssel. Brüssel met with Hansemann in Berlin on 11 April. The German bankers were also convinced that the cooperation of London, Berlin and Paris was necessary to provide China with the necessary capital for the war indemnity. However, despite it having taken the initiative, the HSBC again refused to share its prerogative as banker to China. While it wanted to gain the financial help of other European financiers, it still wished to sign the loan agreement with China alone without the co-signature

---

[10] Seckendorff to Caprivi (15 May 1891), BArch, R901/12991, p. 2; Li to Seckendorff (6 December 1890), *LHZQJ*, 35:133; Brandt to Caprivi (11 December 1890), BArch, R901/12990, pp. 126–7. The bankers in Germany in fact agreed to offer Li participation, but there is no evidence that he eventually acquired DAB shares. See Auswärtiges Amt to Brandt (9 February 1890), BArch, R901/12990, pp. 128–9.

[11] Rinkel, 'Bericht über die bisherige Geschäftstätigkeit' (February 1893), HSO, A VIII 114 Ostasiatische Geschäfte 1888–1914.

[12] For the terms of the Treaty of Shimonoseki see MacMurray, *Treaties with and Concerning China 1894–1919*, pp. 18–23.

[13] Wright, *Hart and the Chinese Customs*, p. 657.

of the other participating banks. Thus the German bankers were again confronted with the unwillingness of the HSBC to grant them equality and Hansemann was compelled to refuse Brüssel's offer.[14]

So far the indemnity had primarily been discussed in banking circles. However, both the conclusion of the Treaty of Shimonoseki on 17 April 1895 and particularly the Triple Intervention of Russia, France and Germany against Japan's occupation of Liaodong on 23 April 1895 changed the situation and led to the politicization of the loan negotiations. Now the Russian, French and German governments became involved in the negotiations, each hoping to attain participation in the financing of the indemnity as part of what they viewed as their due reward for saving Liaodong. Each side tried to ensure that it was not excluded from the financing of the indemnity, which might be connected with political concessions made by China to the financing countries.[15]

As Hart pointed out to his London representative James Duncan Campbell, after the Triple Intervention, Germany, France and especially Russia were favoured by China and Britain had fallen into disfavour.[16] This also meant that the HSBC now for the first time was disadvantaged in Chinese loan negotiations.[17] The Zongli Yamen now explained to German Minister Gustav Adolf Schenck von Schweinsberg that it wished to split the loan between France, Russia and Germany.[18] In Berlin and London, Hansemann and Nathan Rothschild wanted a transnational solution and tried to unite Russian, French, British and German financial interests for the collective issuing of the indemnity loan.[19] Rothschild believed that the only politically and financially viable plan was that England, Germany, France and Russia must act together for the indemnity loan.[20] Hansemann felt that cooperation among the three financial capitals of Europe and Russia was the best solution for 'negotiating with China on a secure basis and maintaining the financial interests of these financial markets in every aspect'. For Hansemann, this solution avoided any political conflicts among the powers in China.[21] It also prevented unnecessary competition among European financiers that might

---

[14] Müller-Jabusch, *Deutsch-Asiatische Bank*, pp. 76–8, 311.

[15] Barth, *Imperialismen*, pp. 143–5; Brötel, *Frankreich im fernen Osten*, p. 400; Li, *Shimonoseki*, p. 93.

[16] Hart to Campbell (18 May 1895), *AMCS*, 8:867.

[17] King, *HSBC History*, 2:266.

[18] Schenck to Auswärtiges Amt (13 May 1895), PAAA, 17.772, p. 35.

[19] Rothschild to Hansemann (19 May 1895), PAAA, 17.772, pp. 131–3.

[20] Rothschild to Hansemann (22 May 1895), PAAA, 17.772, p. 127.

[21] Quote from Hansemann to Rothschild (23 May 1895), PAAA, 17.772, p. 136; Disconto-Gesellschaft, S. Bleichröder, Robert Warschauer & Co., Mendelssohn & Co and Berliner Handels-Gesellschaft to Rothstein (15 June 1895), PAAA, 17.775, p. 140; Barth, *Imperialismen*, p. 145.

entice the Chinese to pledge the Customs revenue for a smaller, insufficient loan.[22]

The HSBC at first still intended to stick to its traditional role as banker to China and carry out the management of the loan in China alone to maintain its pre-eminence among the foreign banks in China. After being rejected by the German bankers, the HSBC now wished to first provide China with £15 million, followed by two later loans to cover the costs of the remaining indemnity. The British bankers hoped that the British government would support it as the representative of British interests in China. The HSBC's confidence was not shared by the British Foreign Office, which favoured the plan of the Rothschilds to split the loan between Russia, Germany, France and Britain. This, the Foreign Office believed, would avoid any political conflicts and ensure that the Customs Service would continue to be managed by a British national. Eventually, the HSBC yielded to the pressure from the Foreign Office and joined the plan of the Rothschilds, thereby giving up opposition to equality among the different European financiers.[23] Unsurprisingly, Hansemann was pleased that the HSBC had finally accepted parity among the financiers and believed this arrangement meant an 'easement and improvement' of the loan negotiations.[24] In view of the British concern about the control over the Customs Service, it is important to point out that Hansemann was very content with Robert Hart's management of the Customs Service and valued the Customs revenue as a result of this.[25] Although the German Foreign Office pondered the possibility of placing a German citizen in a high position in the Customs Service,[26] there is no evidence that German bankers had any similar scheme.

Despite this agreement between financiers in Britain and Germany, they eventually emerged empty-handed from the competition for the first indemnity loan. This was mainly because the Russian government acted swiftly, while Hansemann and Rothschild still tried to unite European financial interests.[27] In the middle of May, Russian Finance Minister Witte offered China a loan of 100 million taels provided by the Russian Ministry of Finance to avoid China becoming the object of the speculation of bankers.[28] The Anglo-German group now followed with an offer to issue a £16 million loan at 5 per cent with a net price of 93 per cent, meaning the percentage of the nominal value of the loan

---

[22] Hansemann to Rothschild (14 May 1895), PAAA, 17.772, pp. 123–4.
[23] McLean, 'First Chinese Indemnity Loan', pp. 304–13; King, *HSBC History*, 2:266–70.
[24] Hansemann to Rothschild (23 May 1895), PAAA, 17.772, pp. 136–7.
[25] Hansemann to Rothschild (14 May 1895), PAAA, 17.772, p. 123.
[26] Marschall to Wilhelm II (12 May 1895), PAAA, 17.772, p. 172.
[27] Hansemann to Rothschild (28 May 1895), PAAA, 17.773, p. 37; Hansemann to Rothschild (27 May 1895), PAAA, 17.773, p. 34; Rothschild to Hansemann (27 May 1895), PAAA, 17.773, p. 35.
[28] Xu to Zongli Yamen (11 May 1895), in Yang, *Zhong-Ri zhanzheng*, 4:108.

sum China would receive. Unlike the Russian offer, which involved a Russian guarantee for the servicing of the loan that could potentially allow Russia to intervene in China's public finance, the Anglo-German syndicate only demanded Customs revenue as a guarantee.[29] However, the Anglo-German offer came too late to stop the Russian loan agreement with the Chinese government, which was urgently in need of money to repay the indemnity.[30] The loan agreement for a loan of 400 million Francs secured by Customs revenue and mainly backed by French banks was signed between China and Russia in St Petersburg on 6 July.[31] The loan was issued at a price of 99.2, thus almost at par.[32] The competition among foreign financiers had clearly reached a new level during the negotiations. After the Anglo-German syndicate had submitted its offer, Hansemann complained that 'the Chinese government continuously tries to play one [syndicate] off against the other'.[33] Robert Imelmann of the Bleichröder bank complained that 'as the negotiations proceeded at the moment, everyone is just working for the Chinese'.[34] Although the Russian guarantee probably also helped improve the loan terms, this competition among foreign financiers allowed China to reduce the interest rate of the loan to 4 per cent, as the participating French banks had initially demanded an interest rate of 5 per cent.[35] Unlike the majority of previous Chinese loans, the Chinese government did not receive the full nominal amount of the Franco-Russian loan. Nevertheless, the net price of the loan of 94 1/8 per cent still represented an improvement if compared to the 93 per cent initially offered by the Anglo-German group.[36] Importantly, the loan's interest rate was significantly lower than that of previous Chinese public loans. China's public loans issued during the two decades before were all significantly smaller in size. They were generally issued around or slightly above par, but, with the exception of the German loan of 1887, carried an interest rate of 6 per cent or, more

---

[29] 'Entwurf zu einem Telgramm nach Peking' (16 June 1895), PAAA, R17.775, p. 97; Hansemann to Rothschild (18 June 1895), PAAA, R17.775, p. 150.

[30] Imperial Edict (21 May 1895), *First Historical Archives of China, Beijing*, 1-01-12-021-0310.

[31] DAB (Shanghai) to DAB (Berlin) (24 June 1895), PAAA, R17.776, p. 108; Disconto-Gesellschaft, S. Bleichröder, Robert Warschauer & Co., Mendelssohn & Co. and Berliner Handels-Gesellschaft to Rothstein (15 June 1895), PAAA, R17.775, pp. 142–3; Brötel, *Frankreich im fernen Osten*, pp. 401–2. For the loan treaty see MacMurray, *Treaties*, 1:35–42.

[32] For the issue price of the loan, see Brötel, *Frankreich im fernen Osten*, p. 403.

[33] Hansemann to Rothschild (28 June 1895), PAAA, R17.777, p. 47.

[34] Imelmann to Rothstein (24 June 1896), PAAA, R17.776, p. 110.

[35] Brötel, *Frankreich im fernen Osten*, pp. 403–4.

[36] On previous loans and the issuing without a discount, see King, *HSBC History*, 1:535–62. For the net price and discount clause in the loan agreement, see MacMurray, *Treaties*, 1:38.

commonly, even 7 or 8 per cent per annum.[37] During the Sino-Japanese War, the HSBC had issued a public gold loan of £3 million in London for China with an interest rate of 6 per cent and in May the HSBC had offered Hart to float the indemnity loan at around 6 per cent per annum in London.[38] Even if we calculate in the discount of the loan, meaning the difference between the nominal value and issue price, the loan's effective interest rate of 4.03 per cent still represents an important improvement compared to previous loans. For example, the average effective interest rate of the five public gold loans issued by the HSBC for China between 1885 and 1895 was 6.66 per cent.[39] Thus, the Chinese negotiators had obtained an interest rate significantly lower than that of previous loans, which meant that, despite the discount, China managed to raise money in Europe much more cheaply than before.

Hansemann believed that the 'planned large Chinese loan [uniting all European financial interests] mainly failed because the participating markets did not unite in time to counter the Russian competition'. To avoid a similar situation in the future and block the 'tactic of the Chinese government to play off one against the other', the HSBC and the Konsortium für Asiatische Geschäfte (KfAG), represented by the DAB, signed an agreement on 27 July 1895 to share all future Chinese loans covered by 'Chinese Imperial or provincial Government guarantees'.[40] Importantly, the agreement was made 'on the principle of parity', meaning 'equal terms in every respect'. The agreement fixed the new equal relationship between the DAB and the HSBC, which had developed during the previous negotiations for the indemnity loan. Since the German bankers had tried to achieve a partnership with the HSBC and the British market on equal terms for a decade, the agreement represented a great success for the DAB. It acknowledged the increased importance of the DAB and the German capital market and the necessity for the HSBC to give up its prerogative as banker to China in order to gain the cooperation of the German capital markets necessary for securing and floating larger Chinese loans. Political reasons will have also played a role in the considerations of the HSBC. As we will see, China intended to give the second indemnity loan to

---

[37] King, *HSBC History*, 1:548, 557.

[38] Hart to Campbell (14 May 1895), *AMCS*, 8:864; King, *HSBC History*, 1:548.

[39] I calculate the effective interest rate I provide similar to a bond's current yield by dividing the interest rate by the issue price of the loan. On this also, see Chapter 5, pp. 203–204. The HSBC loans I have taken into account here can be found in King, *HSBC History*, 1:548.

[40] The first two quotes are from Hansemann to Rothschild (4 August 1895), BArch, R901/12991, pp. 46–7. The subsequent quote, the two quotes in the next sentence and the two quotes in the next paragraph are from the agreement. For the agreement see 'Vertrag zwischen der Hongkong and Shanghai Banking Corporation und der Deutsch-Asiatische Bank betr. chinesische Geschäfte vom 27. Juli 1895', HSO, A VIII 114 Ostasiatische Geschäfte 1888–1914.

German financiers, which made cooperation with the German bankers more attractive for the HSBC.[41]

While gaining an equal position with the HSBC in signing and managing the loan was important for the German bankers, they had no problem leaving the actual negotiations to the 'representative of the Hongkong and Shanghai Banking Corporation' as long as the course of the negotiations was 'subject to a mutual understanding' of the two groups. The DAB was willing to use the greater experience and standing of the HSBC in the negotiations as long as it was equal to the HSBC in every other respect.

The first indemnity loan also marked the end of the British monopoly for Chinese public loans.[42] While the 1887 loan of the Warschauer group and a second small German loan floated in Germany in 1895 by the Deutsche Nationalbank, which soon after joined the KfAG, had already shown that Chinese loans could be floated outside of London,[43] the large first indemnity loan showed that China was no longer dependent on the HSBC or other British financiers. The control over Western credit and the structural power of Western capital markets was no longer mainly represented in China by British financiers. This was an important step in the internationalization of Chinese public finance, as it opened up the spectrum of possible lenders for China and increased the competition among foreign financiers. Although the politicization of the loan business had played an important role in bringing in the French and Russian involvement into the Chinese loan business, the realization of the Rothschilds, Hansemann and eventually also the HSBC that the increased demands of the Chinese government for capital and the new competition necessitated new transnational alliances also showed that the field for Chinese borrowing was now being opened up. That the Chinese officials were adept at exploiting this new competition would become even clearer during the negotiations for the second indemnity loan.

3.2   Beating Down the Banks

While China had to act quickly in concluding the first indemnity loan to begin the repayment of the Japanese indemnity, the Franco-Russian loan completely covered the first two instalments of the Japanese indemnity loan due six and twelve months, respectively, after the exchange of ratifications of the Treaty of Shimonoseki in May 1895, and thus gave the Chinese government considerable

---

[41] King ignores other factors and seems to ascribe the HSBC's diminished position and need for cooperation with other financiers only to political factors. He explains that the HSBC 'had recognized its inability to operate alone on behalf of China in a politically competitive Europe'. See King, *HSBC History*, 2:281.

[42] On this point, also see Barth, *Imperialismen*, p. 149.

[43] King, *HSBC History*, 1:557; *BBZ* (11 July 1895, evening edition); Müller-Jabusch, *Deutsch-Asiatische Bank*, pp. 72–3.

breathing space before the next loan needed to be concluded.[44] This meant that China possessed the time and opportunity to use the new competition between the different syndicates, so that the question of how cheaply China could borrow in Europe became the central issue of the negotiations for the second indemnity loan. As it turned out, the Chinese officials proved able to exploit the new competition among financiers and borrow cheaply from Europe, this time even without a political guarantee given by a European state such as Russia had provided for the first indemnity loan.

After the Franco-Russian loan agreement, negotiations that had been started between the Anglo-German group and China came to a temporary end, as the Franco-Russian loan agreement stipulated that China could not issue any loans in Europe for six months. Nevertheless, the Zongli Yamen was still 'willing to allow [a loan of] fifty million taels [equal to £8 million] from the German bank'. The Chinese officials tried to leverage the improved loan terms of the Franco-Russian loan, whose loan terms they also wished to use for the next loan. Importantly, the Chinese negotiators showed a preference for giving the next loan for the payment of the indemnity to the DAB alone. They only spoke about a German loan and expressed that they did not wish to have British participation.[45] However, the Chinese still kept a back door open and promised to the British Foreign Office it would reserve at least a portion of the indemnity loans for Britain.[46] This suggests that the Chinese government wished to keep all of its options open and favoured an equal splitting up of the indemnity loans among different European financiers. In any case, Hansemann maintained the importance of cooperating with the HSBC. Both the HSBC and the DAB ordered their representatives in Beijing to halt the negotiations, as it was impossible to make a firm offer now for a loan only to be floated in six months.[47]

The negotiations only started moving again at the beginning of November. Although China still maintained that Germany had the prior claim to the next indemnity loan, the Zongli Yamen was also willing to accept an Anglo-German loan.[48] While Edward Guy Hillier (Figure 3.1), the representative of the HSBC, was to lead the loan negotiations, the British and German Foreign Office pledged that their ministers in Beijing would support them 'should the necessity for such

[44] Excluding interest payments, China was required to pay a total of 100 million taels in these two instalments by May 1896. For the payment schedule of the Treaty of Shimonoseki, see MacMurray, *Treaties*, 1:19–20. For the amount of the Franco-Russian loan in Chinese currency (ca.106 million taels), see Xu et al., *Cong bainian quru*, 1:521.

[45] Quote from Zongli Yamen to Schenck (6 July 1895), AIMH, 01–32–023–04–022; Franke, *Randglossen*, p. 79. Also see King, *HSBC History*, 2:277.

[46] Campbell to Hart (12 July 1895), AMCS, 6:323; Campbell to Hart (31 July 1895), AMCS, 8:878.

[47] Hansemann to Rothschild (7 July 1895), PAAA, R17.778, pp. 45–6.

[48] Schenck to Auswärtiges Amt (4 November 1895), PAAA, R17.780, p. 21.

Figure 3.1 Edward Guy Hillier (1857–1924), ca.1912. Image courtesy of Andrew Hillier and Special Collections, University of Bristol Library (www.hpcbristol.net).

action arise'.[49] Hillier had come to China in his early twenties and had first worked for Jardine, Matheson & Co. in Hong Kong in the early 1880s. There, he also learned the Chinese language and eventually was hired by the HSBC in 1883 – precisely because of his language skills. Hillier was posted first to Tianjin and later to Beijing to establish contacts with Chinese officials. He eventually became the HSBC's official Beijing agent in 1891. With few interruptions and despite an onset of blindness, he would stay in this position until his passing in 1924 and managed the negotiations for many loans the HSBC became involved in.[50]

The fact that, apart from Hillier, the British and German ministers in Beijing were also involved in the negotiations not only stemmed from the interest of the British and German government in the loans and their wish to support their respective banks. It was also due to the lack of an official channel of

[49] Gosselin to Marschall (12 November 1895), PAAA, R17.780, p. 53.
[50] On Edward Guy Hillier, see Hillier, *Mediating Empire*, pp. 140–6. For a contemporary, somewhat hagiographic account, see 'Death of Mr. Hillier of Peking', *The Times (London)* (15 April 1924).

communication between the Chinese government and the bankers, which meant that communication with the Chinese government had to be conducted through the Zongli Yamen and the foreign ministers. Moreover, the central government had promulgated that both the foreign ministers and the Zongli Yamen had to be involved in any case of foreign borrowing. Lastly, the Chinese government was used to issuing the imperial edict, which was used to confirm loan agreements and increase the trust of the lenders in repayment of the loans, to the banks through the foreign ministers.[51] These issues show that at the time of the indemnity loan negotiations, the Chinese government viewed national foreign borrowing as part of China's foreign relations and insisted that it was handled through official diplomatic channels. In this sense, what appears from the outside as one-sided meddling in the loan negotiations by foreign diplomats was also dictated by the rules China used to govern its foreign borrowing and official relations to foreigners.

The key question now was what terms the Anglo-German group could offer, especially regarding the interest rate and issue and net price of the loan. This was mainly a matter of how the bankers viewed Chinese credit and sovereign risk, meaning the probability that China could repay its debt. Here, an exchange between the bankers of the German consortium and Max von Brandt is instructive as to how the German bankers viewed China's creditworthiness. Regarding the security, they explained to Brandt that they still viewed China's Customs revenue as a sufficient security for the loan and demanded no additional security. They only insisted that the whole loan needed to be guaranteed by the remainder of the Customs revenue.[52]

In terms of the interest rate, Max von Brandt cautioned the bankers that 'after the conclusion of the Franco-Russian four percent loan, it is hardly to be expected that the conclusion of further loans will allow profits like the previous [loans issued before the first indemnity loan] and that it will be possible to conclude them at an interest rate similar [to previous loans of] 5 ½ – 7%'. He also warned the German bankers that it would be wrong to think that 'the Chinese will be forced to come to us' for the loan. Rather, it was important to immediately act once an opportunity to conclude a loan deal presented itself. The bankers, however, were of another opinion and believed that any loan agreement would most importantly need to be in accord with the rules and conditions of the market. For them, 'the main condition always remains that the price to be paid [by China] for the Chinese loan is commensurate to the conditions of the market here'. No concessions could be made to the Chinese

---

[51] Li, *Guo zhai zai jindai Zhongguo de mingyun*, p. 32; Imperial Edict (September/November 1891), in *LHZQJ*, 14:147–8. King also alludes to the need to go through diplomatic channels; see King, *HSBC History*, 1:536.

[52] DAB, Disconto-Gesellschaft, Deutsche Bank, S. Bleichröder, Berliner Handels-Gesellschaft and Robert Warschauer & Co. to Brandt (9 October 1895), PAAA, R17.780, p. 27.

that could 'cause the failure of the emission' of the loan in Europe. While the Chinese government wished to use the Franco-Russian loan as a basis for the negotiations, the German bankers believed that the low interest rate of the Franco-Russian loan had only been possible because of the Russian guarantee.[53]

Instead, the current notations of those Chinese gold bonds floated most recently during the Sino-Japanese War, which had been smaller in amount and secured on the then still less burdened Customs revenue but came with an interest rate higher than the Franco-Russian loan, were to be used to determine at what terms China could borrow. In addition, the emission costs of these loans and adequate profits for bond subscribers and the banks as underwriters also needed to be taken as a reference when determining the loan terms. Otherwise, success on European markets was not certain, as

> the Chinese loan is and will remain an exotic one and the world has not been turned upside down in such a way yet that China, who before the war borrowed for an interest rate of around 6 ¾ %, after the war can raise the funds for the payment to Japan with a loan without Russian guarantee at an interest rate of 5%, whilst the rich France, whose interest rates for loans before the war of 1870 was 4%, had to agree to an interest rate of 6% for the loans to repay the war indemnity.

From these remarks and particularly the comparison with France, it follows that the German bankers believed that China would need to pay at least around 6 per cent in interest, which had been the rate it had borrowed at during the war, or even more for coming loans, and that the interest rate of the Franco-Russian loan could not be seen as a new standard for Chinese loans.[54] While foreign bankers in China have often been blamed for

---

[53] DAB, Disconto-Gesellschaft, Deutsche Bank, S. Bleichröder, Berliner Handels-Gesellschaft and Robert Warschauer & Co. to Brandt (9 October 1895), PAAA, R17.780, pp. 28–9.

[54] DAB, Disconto-Gesellschaft, Deutsche Bank, S. Bleichröder, Berliner Handels-Gesellschaft and Robert Warschauer & Co. to Brandt (9 October 1895), PAAA, R17.780, pp. 28–30. For the 6% interest rate at which Chinese gold loans were issued during the Sino-Japanese War, see King, HSBC History, 1: 553. When the bankers speak about interest rates based on the Franco-Russian loan, previous Chinese loans and the French loans after the Franco-Prussian War in their correspondence with Brandt, they seem to speak of effective interest rates (see footnote 39), taking into account the discount of the bonds mentioned in this document. While the interest rate of 6¾ per cent fits the effective interest rate of the loans issued by China before the war (e.g. the four gold loans issued by the HSBC before 1894; see King, HSBC History, 1:548) and the 6 per cent interest given for the French indemnity loans fits the effective interest rate of these loans (see Monroe, 'The French Indemnity', p. 269), this is not the case for the Franco-Russian loan for China, which they give as 5% but whose effective interest rate was 4.03 per cent, as mentioned earlier. It is unclear why this is. But what is clear is that the German bankers were certain that China would not be able to continue to borrow at a similar interest rate as the Franco-Russian loan, which they attributed to the guarantee by the Russian state.

demanding overly high interest rates, their main income from loans was commission and underwriter's margin and, as their explanations to Brandt show, they were mainly concerned about the interest rate because it affected the reception of loans in Europe. A successful reception of the loan was not only important in terms of the profit the bankers could derive from issuing this individual loan. On European bond markets, where a hierarchy of underwriters existed, a failed bond emission could also damage the reputation and 'brand' of the foreign banks as issuers of foreign sovereign debt, with detrimental consequences for their overall business in floating foreign bonds.[55] Thus, it is not surprising that the bankers insisted on what they felt was a realistic rate of interest. Nevertheless, it would turn out that the bankers underestimated the impact of the increased competition of European financiers in China and the Chinese ability to use it to attain better loan terms.

On 22 November, the Zongli Yamen asked Hillier to submit a written offer with the loan terms proposed by the DAB and HSBC.[56] On 24 November, German minister Schenck sent over the written offer of the two banks to the Zongli Yamen. They offered a loan of £16 million with an interest rate that would not exceed 5 per cent. The banks proposed an issue price of not less than 95 per cent. However, what made the offer much more expensive for the Chinese was that the banks asked for a commission of 1.5 per cent and expenses of 4 per cent, which would have left China with only 89.5 per cent of the loan sum. The loan was to be secured on Customs revenue, the administration of which was to remain 'as at present' until the repayment of the loan after thirty-six years. Finally, 'should it be found that the loan can be floated on better terms than those named, the Chinese Government [is] to have the benefit of the difference', which indicates that in proposing these terms, the bankers were mainly concerned with the conditions investors in Europe were likely to accept.[57] As Hillier later related to HSBC London manager Ewen Cameron, the banks had 'giv[en] them [the] best terms' they felt the markets allowed for.[58]

Regarding the terms of the loan offer, the German bankers apparently had abandoned their demand for an interest rate like that of Chinese loans issued before the Franco-Russian loan. This might have been partly due to the influence of the HSBC, but the competition of other financial groups and the stance of the Zongli Yamen were also important factors. Not only were rumours floating around about a possible second loan with a Russian state guarantee, but the Zongli Yamen had also sent Schenck the Franco-Russian loan treaty as a reference, which again implied this was what they saw as the

---

[55] Flandreau and Flores, 'Bonds and Brands', pp. 646–84. In his institutional history of the HSBC, King also mentions the importance of the assessment of capital markets for the consideration of loan terms by the bankers. See King, *HSBC History*, 2:263.
[56] Schenck to Hohenlohe (23 November 1895), PAAA, R17.780, pp. 123–5.
[57] Schenck to Hohenlohe (25 November 1895), PAAA, R17.780, pp. 131–6.
[58] Hillier to Cameron (17 December 1895), PAAA, R17.781, p. 75.

basis for further negotiations.[59] The resolve of the Zongli Yamen to insist on a low interest rate must have been strengthened by an American loan offer with an interest rate of 5 per cent or lower they had received at the end of October.[60] In this atmosphere, it must have seemed impossible to succeed with an offer with an interest rate as high as suggested by the German bankers in their discussion with Brandt. The concerns of the German bankers, however, seem to have influenced the proposed issue price. While the latest notations for the Chinese gold loans floated during the Sino-Japanese War in Berlin and London, which the German bankers had named as a reference for assessing China's credit, showed an average of around 106 per cent, the bankers seem to have somewhat compensated for the potential risk of floating such a large loan amount with a low interest rate by only offering 95 per cent as the issue price.[61] At the same time, the proposed issue price was similar to that of the 6 per cent Sterling Loan issued by the HSBC at 96.5 per cent for the purposes of the Sino-Japanese War in 1895.[62] On 1 December the Chinese side sent back the offer with several points that needed to be changed. Most importantly, the Chinese negotiators demanded an interest rate of 4 per cent instead of 5 per cent and criticized the high charges asked for by the banks.[63]

Hillier then met with the minister of the Board of Revenue, Weng Tonghe 翁同龢 (Figure 3.2), and the deputy minister of the same ministry, Zhang Yinhuan 張蔭桓, at the Zongli Yamen. Weng, a prominent official who also held positions at the Zongli Yamen and Grand Council and acted as tutor to the Chinese emperor, was to play an important role in the loan negotiations. During the meeting, Weng and Zhang increased the pressure on the banks to lower the interest rate and charges. They insisted that 'interest must not exceed 4 ½ %, other terms (charges) should be reduced'. Hillier explained that the offer represented an estimate that could still be improved upon when the loan was issued, but for now it had to be 'based on the existing value of Chinese credit' according to the notations of China's former loans and considering the 'depreciated security' of the Customs revenue. He even asked Weng and Zhang to ask their ministers in Berlin and London to verify this. However, the Chinese negotiators were not willing to do this. Although Hillier had already done so once, Weng insisted that Hillier telegraph home again to ask for better

[59] DAB, Disconto-Gesellschaft, Deutsche Bank, S. Bleichröder, Berliner Handels-Gesellschaft and Robert Warschauer & Co. to Brandt (9 October 1895), PAAA, R17.780, p. 27; Zongli Yamen to Schenck (2 November 1895), AIMH, 01–32–024–06–013.

[60] Denby to Zongli Yamen (24 October 1895), AIMH, 01–32–024–06–001.

[61] For the bond notations, see *Investor's Monthly Manual* (31 October 1895); *BBZ* (31 October 1895, evening edition).

[62] King, *HSBC History*, 1:548.

[63] Zongli Yamen to Schenck (1 December 1895), AIMH, 01–32–024–07–005; Schenck to Hohenlohe (23 January 1896), PAAA, R17.781, pp. 168–9.

Figure 3.2 Weng Tonghe 翁同龢 (1830–1904). From Weng Tonghe, *Weng Wengong Gong riji*, vol. 1. Image courtesy of The University of Hong Kong Libraries.

terms. He even threatened that 'if you refuse to telegraph [home to demand better terms] there is nothing for it but to break off negotiations'. Hillier could do nothing but comply and wired the Chinese demands home under protest.[64] It became more and more unlikely that the Anglo-German group could maintain its demands given the pressure from the Chinese side, as more competition arrived on the scene in the form of a renewed American loan offer. American minister Charles Denby promised Weng that 100 million taels could be raised in the United States at a price cheaper than the Franco-Russian

---

[64] Hillier to Cameron (17 December 1895), PAAA, R17.781, pp. 74–6. On Weng Tonghe, see Hummel, *Eminent Chinese*, pp. 860–1.

loan.[65] Robert Hart also criticized the high expenses demanded by the banks.[66] While the discussions with Denby remained without result, negotiations with the Anglo-German group also did not progress during January 1896, as both sides stuck to their positions and the bankers maintained that they offered the best terms possible based on China's credit and the condition of the market.[67] On 23 January, the HSBC and DAB eventually went on the offensive to end the protracted negotiations that 'under the present conditions of the European markets [threaten] to endanger the prospects of the loan'. They issued an ultimatum to the Zongli Yamen to either accept or refuse the offer of the banks by 30 January. After this date, negotiations could be resumed only on the basis of new and less favourable terms'.[68]

Now it appeared that all the waiting would finally come to an end. The Chinese negotiators accepted the loan offer and only suggested a few small changes. They asked Hart to invite Hillier to the Zongli Yamen on 30 January to sign the preliminary loan agreement. However, on the day, the Zongli Yamen decided otherwise and let the banks' deadline pass. Thus, the agreement was not signed.[69] The reason for this was that Weng Tonghe received a last-minute telegram from Jiangnan *Daotai* Li Shengfeng 李盛鋒, who was negotiating with Americans in Shanghai and now reported that they could offer a lower interest rate. As a consequence, Weng intervened so that the loan agreement was not concluded.[70] The Zongli Yamen, still, as Hart had put it, 'trying everywhere for cheaper money', now told Schenck that China would only give the loan to the Anglo-German group if no other better offer could be found.[71]

The American promise to offer a lower interest rate than the Anglo-German group eventually did not materialize.[72] However, yet another challenge to the Anglo-German group now arose in the form of a possible French loan offer to China. After the Zongli Yamen had decided against signing the preliminary loan agreement with the Anglo-German group, Li Hongzhang suggested that France might be able to lend the money.[73] On 8 February Prince Gong

[65] Diary entry (30 November 1895), in Chen, *WTHRJ*, 5:2855; diary entry (16 December 1895), *WTHRJ*, 5:2859.

[66] Hart to Campbell (24 December 1896), *AMCS*, 8:886.

[67] Zongli Yamen to Denby (29 January 1896), AIMH, 01–32–025–03–031; Hillier, 'Memorandum for the Tsungli Yamen' (12 January 1896), PAAA, R17.781, pp. 180–1; Schenck to Zongli Yamen (13 January 1896), PAAA, R17.781, pp. 176–7; Schenck to Zongli Yamen (13 January 1896), PAAA, R17.781, pp. 177–8.

[68] Schenck to Zongli Yamen (23 January 1896), PAAA, R17.781, pp. 186–7.

[69] Schenck to Hohenlohe (6 February 1896), PAAA, R17.782, pp. 41–4.

[70] Weng Tonghe, 'Songchan ziding nianpu', *WTHJ*, 2:1063.

[71] Quote from Hart to Campbell (12 January 1896), *IGPK*, 2:1047; Schenck to Hohenlohe (6 February 1896), PAAA, R17.782, p. 47; diary entry (4 February 1896), *WTHRJ*, 5:2872.

[72] Zongli Yamen to Denby (19 February 1896), AIMH, 01–32–026–01–006.

[73] Weng, ' Songchan ziding nianpu', *WTHJ*, 2:1063.

contacted the French minister Auguste Gérard and asked about the possibilities of a French loan. Gérard replied that the loan would need to be strictly between the Chinese government and French bankers, but that he would be happy to mediate. He subsequently reported that a 5 per cent loan floated only slightly under par and with expenses significantly less than the Anglo-German offer could be offered by French banks.[74]

In reaction to the competition for the Anglo-German group, both Schenck and British minister William Beauclerk reminded the Zongli Yamen that it had agreed to issue the second indemnity loan through the Anglo-German group. Should other competitors be able to offer better loan terms, they insisted that China had to first inform the Anglo-German group of these terms to allow them to match the offer.[75] However, the Chinese informed Schenck that Gérard had promised to offer better loan terms. They also explained that they held on to their previous promise to borrow £8 million from German financiers, but also asked for an improvement of the German offer and insisted that after the breakdown of negotiations on 30 January they had no obligation to borrow from British bankers anymore.[76] Thus, the political influence of the German and British ministers on the Chinese government proved to be limited when it came to the competition for the loan.

On 17 February Gérard informed the Zongli Yamen that French banks were willing to float the loan with a 5 per cent interest rate at 98 per cent below par. However, he did not say what the expenses of the loan would be.[77] Driven by the competition and seeing the determination of the Chinese officials to go for the best price, the HSBC and DAB now felt compelled to improve their offer. They authorized Hillier to offer a net price of up to 91.5 per cent, although the HSBC felt that the 'British public would not be willing to subscribe freely over 96 % [which would have equalled a net price of 90.5 per cent]'.[78] While Hillier at the end of February reported to Schenck that these 'considerable [sic] better terms' were a 'consequence of the improved condition of the European markets', the increased competition was clearly the driving force that had led to the bankers offering better terms.[79] As Brüssel reported to the HSBC in London, the German bankers were 'willing to do everything in order to carry out business against the French'.[80]

Just like the American offer, the French proposal fell through and eventually Gérard could only offer a loan at 5 per cent with a net price of 90 per cent.

[74] Gérard to Zongli Yamen (20 February 1896), AIMH, 01–32–026–01–008.
[75] Schenck to Hohenlohe (21 February 1896), PAAA, R17.782, pp. 67–8; Beauclerk to Zongli Yamen (7 March 1896), AIMH, 01–32–026–01–026.
[76] Schenck to Hohenlohe (21 February 1896), PAAA, R17.782, pp. 66–76.
[77] Zongli Yamen to Gérard (7 March 1896), AIMH, 01–32–026–01–027.
[78] HSBC (London) to Disconto-Gesellschaft (24 February 1896), PAAA, R17.781, p. 99.
[79] Hillier to Schenck (29 February 1896), PAAA, R17.782, p. 107.
[80] Brüssel to HSBC (London) (6 March 1896), PAAA, R17.781, p. 137.

This was not only 'greatly different from what [Gérard] had said several times before', but also worse than what the Anglo-German group now offered.[81] As a result, the Zongli Yamen cancelled the negotiations with Gérard.[82] After the failure of the negotiations with Gérard, on the evening of 6 March the Zongli Yamen decided to let Hart handle the loan.[83] Hart insisted that the banks had to reduce the expenses they asked for and improve the loan terms. For Hart, it was mainly the HSBC that insisted on the 'big charges' by which it 'blocked and delayed business'.[84] These charges, he felt, were 'ridiculous and jeopardize everything'.[85] Hart warned Schenck that the French competition was still very much alive. He admonished him that 'the only idea the [Chinese] Ministers have is to search for the cheapest money [and] I believe they will find that in France', as he had just received word that the Russian government was once more backing a Russo-French loan.[86] Hart emphasized that the only way to 'win' against the 'Paris syndicate' was to issue the loan at 98 per cent with only 3 per cent in charges, coming to a net price of 95 per cent.[87]

The banks had once more increased their offer, but so far only up to a net price of 92 per cent.[88] Hart and Hillier met on the morning of 7 March and eventually agreed on a net price of 94 per cent.[89] Hillier had acted although the banks had not previously authorized these terms, but he felt this was necessary 'to save [the] situations' and secure the loan deal for the Anglo-German group against the competition.[90] Both banks agreed and Franz Urbig, the Tianjin manager of the DAB (Figure 3.3), was sent to Beijing to sign the formal preliminary treaty with Hillier on 11 March.[91] Urbig had joined the Disconto-Gesellschaft as a young man in 1884 and, after working in several positions within the bank, was sent to China in 1894 to fill in for DAB Shanghai director Rehders while the latter was on vacation in Europe during 1895. Eventually, Rehders decided that another DAB banker was to act as Shanghai director during his absence. Urbig was instead sent to Tianjin to lead the DAB's branch there. During his time working for the DAB in Asia, Urbig not only became

---

[81] Quote from diary entry (6 March 1896), *WTHRJ*, 5:2882; Zongli Yamen to Gérard (7 March 1896), AIMH, 01-32-026-01-027.

[82] Weng Tonghe, 'Songchan ziding nianpu', *WTHJ*, 2:1064; Zongli Yamen to Gérard (12 March 1896), AIMH, 01-32-026-01-035.

[83] Hart to Campbell (22 March 1896), *IGPK*, 2:1056; Schenck to Hohenlohe (7 March 1896), PAAA, R17.782, pp. 86-7.

[84] Hart to Campbell (8 March 1896), *IGPK*, 2:1054.

[85] HSBC (London) to Brüssel (5 March 1896), PAAA, R17.781, p. 138.

[86] Hart to Schenck (6 March 1896), PAAA, R17.782, p. 114.

[87] Hart to Schenck (5 March 1896), PAAA, R17.782, p. 118.

[88] Schenck to Hohenlohe (7 March 1896), PAAA, R17.782, pp. 93-4.

[89] Schenck to Hohenlohe (7 March 1896), PAAA, R17.782, p. 94.

[90] HSBC (London) to Brüssel (7 March 1896), PAAA, R17.781, p. 147.

[91] Schenck to Hohenlohe (10 March 1896), PAAA, R17.782, p. 129; Schenck to Auswärtiges Amt (11 March 1896), PAAA, R17.781, p. 152.

Figure 3.3 Franz Urbig (1864–1944) during his time in China. Image courtesy of Deutsche Bank AG, Historical Institute.

involved in Chinese loan negotiations, but also helped establish the bank's branches in Calcutta and Hong Kong. He would eventually return to Europe for good in 1900.[92] However, as we will see, Urbig would continue to play an important role within the DAB.

For the German bank, signing the loan agreement for the second indemnity loan in 1896 was a major success. As Urbig remembered, it 'greatly elevated' the position of the DAB, as it was now seen as the 'representative of [the] financial strength' of the German market 'which until then had been underestimated,

[92] Urbig, *Aus dem Leben*, pp. 43–80.

especially in England'.[93] Not only did the Prussian Seehandlungsgesellschaft act as a payment agent for the bonds, but the HSBC had also persuaded the Bank of England to inscribe the bonds. Partly because of this support by the two government banks, the loan was well received and could be floated in two series at 98.75 per cent and 99 per cent below par. For the German consortium, this meant a profit of almost 8 million reichsmark (~£391,840).[94]

In the end, the Chinese negotiators had successfully bargained down the Anglo-German loan offer. Within the new atmosphere of constantly appearing new loan offers, Weng, Robert Hart and the other Chinese negotiators had used these offers and the new competition among foreign financiers and diplomats to gain improved loan conditions from the Anglo-German group. Even though most offers eventually did not materialize, the Chinese determination to insist on gaining the best offer possible and play these offers out against the Anglo-German group still forced the DAB and HSBC to substantially improve their original loan offer by forgoing any fixed charges for expenses and commission (see Table 3.1). Although the Chinese negotiators did not succeed in decreasing the interest rate below 5 per cent, the forgoing of expenses and commission, which had been a common part of previous loans floated by the HSBC,[95] and the consequential increase in the net sum received by China meant that it received an additional £720,000 from the total loan sum. Importantly, the new atmosphere of competition and the agency of the Chinese negotiators meant that, despite the original assessment of China's creditworthiness by the German bankers, the world had indeed 'turned upside down' and China now borrowed more cheaply than before the war even

---

[93] Urbig, *Aus dem Leben*, p. 60.

[94] King, *History of the HSBC*, 2:280; McLean, *British Banking and Government*, pp. 34–5; Barth, *Imperialismen*, p. 153; Neueste Börsen–Nachrichten, *Jahrbuch der Berliner Börse, 1914/1915*, p. 236. King and Barth emphasize the importance of the support from the Bank of England and Seehandlungsgesellschaft for the successful issuing and high issue price, respectively. While this support was undoubtedly useful for the issuing of the loan, the conviction of the British Chancellor of the Exchequer Michael Hicks-Beach at the time that the banks would be able to issue the loan satisfactorily 'without the assistance of the Bank of England', and the fact that the Anglo-German loan of 1898, which, as we will see later, did not perform so well on bond markets, also had the Seehandlungsgesellschaft act as payment agent and was also inscribed by the Bank of England suggest that the effect of the support by the Bank of England and Seehandlungsgesellschaft should not be seen as an overly significant factor. Thus, I make the point here that this support was only in part responsible for the successful issuing. For Hicks-Beach's quote and opinion on the matter, see McLean, *British Banking and Government*, p. 34. On the Seehandlungsgesellschaft acting as payment agent for both Anglo-German loans, see Neueste Börsen–Nachrichten, *Jahrbuch der Berliner Börse, 1914/1915*, p. 236. On the inscription of the 1896 and 1898 Anglo-German indemnity loans by the Bank of England, see Kuhlmann, *China's Foreign Debt*, pp. 26, 28.

[95] See, for example, the 6% Sterling Loan of 1895, which included a payment of 6.5 per cent of the loan sum for expenses and commission: MacMurray, *Treaties*, 1:15–18.

Table 3.1 *Second indemnity loan comparison: original Anglo-German loan offer and final loan terms. Source: See text and MacMurray, Treaties, 1:57–59.*

	Interest rate	Expenses and commission	Issue price	Net price	Collateral
Nov. 1895 loan offer	5%	5.5 %	Not less than 95%	89.5%	Customs revenue
Final loan agreement	5%	No fixed commission/ expenses	98.75%/99%	94%	Customs revenue

without the guarantee of another government.[96] Thus, with the structural power of Western capital markets increasingly diffused among different competitors, the Chinese negotiators could use their relational power in the negotiations to great effect to challenge preconceived notions of Chinese credit and sovereign risk.

3.3 Accepting the Rules of the Market

The Chinese negotiators had used the increased competition among foreign financiers to their advantage. However, the negotiations for the third indemnity loan would show there were limits to what Chinese agency could achieve on the Chinese frontier and within the financial structure of Western capital markets, especially as China's Customs revenue was insufficient to act as collateral for yet another large loan. In the spring of 1897, China made preparations for raising the remaining funds for the repayment of the Japanese indemnity. As early as February 1897, Li Hongzhang had approached both the HSBC and the DAB about another loan.[97] On 16 March 1897, Weng Tonghe asked Li to approach the German and British minister about another Anglo-German loan for £16 million. Weng preferred an Anglo-German collaboration both because there was already a good precedent in the form of the second indemnity loan and because they believed that a collaboration between Britain and Germany would prevent the respective governments from attaching political demands to the loan.[98]

Hansemann entered into discussions with the HSBC about the terms of a possible Chinese loan after Li Hongzhang had notified the British and

---

[96] Even if the very minor discount of the second indemnity loan is taken into account, the effective interest rate was 5.05 per cent.

[97] King, *HSBC History*, 2:285; Heyking to Auswärtiges Amt (26 February 1897), PAAA, R17.784, p. 19; Heyking to Hohenlohe (24 March 1897), PAAA, R17.784, p. 86.

[98] Diary entry (16 March 1897), *WTHRJ*, 6:2981–2.

German ministers that China wished to borrow £16 million.[99] The negotiations between the two banks about the second indemnity loan had mainly centred on the interest rate and the issue and net prices of the loan. Now, however, the security of the loan became the focus of discussions, as the remaining Customs revenue was not seen as sufficient to cover the whole sum demanded by the Chinese. Both the bankers in Germany and the HSBC estimated that the remaining Customs revenue would only cover half of the prospected £16 million loan.[100] Therefore, a new security needed to be found for the third indemnity loan, which would be accepted by investors in Europe and would allow China to continue sovereign borrowing. Marc Flandreau and Frédéric Zumer have argued that during the late nineteenth century the primary determinant of a country's sovereign risk was a country's debt burden, meaning the annual amount necessary for the servicing of its debt, measured against its tax revenue. From this it followed that, especially after the Baring crisis of 1890, Western financiers and financial markets came to value a 'sound fiscal machinery' and the well-organized management of public finance in developing countries.[101]

If applied to China, these measures of assessing sovereign risk presented foreign financiers with several problems. While China's previous foreign loans and the annual amounts necessary for their servicing were of course known, there existed little knowledge among Western financiers about China's tax revenues. In 1887, Exner had already lamented that a difficulty of investing in China was that the Western investor was very 'desirous . . . of accurate statistical demonstration', but China published no official data about its revenue and expenditures.[102] The only exception to this were the publications of the Customs Service, which published regular reports on China's Customs revenue and accordingly had so far been the preferred security for foreign loans.[103] Further evidence is provided in the yearbook of the Berlin Bourse in 1897, which listed China's previous loans and their repayment periods but also wrote that 'little is known about the financial condition of China and reliable information about the parts of public finance managed by natives is difficult to obtain'.[104] Without such knowledge, assessing China's ability to service its debt and identifying a new stream of revenue that could act as

---

[99] HSBC (London) to Hansemann (17 March 1897), PAAA, R17.784, p. 77.

[100] 'Note Auswärtiges Amt' (16 March 1897), PAAA, R17.784, pp. 71–2.

[101] Quote from Flandreau and Zumer, Making of Global Finance, p. 54. Also see chapters 5, 6 and 9 in the same book.

[102] Exner, Einnahmequellen, p. 7. Instead of providing my own translation of the German original, I have drawn on the English translation of this text (Exner, 'Sources of Revenue') for direct quotations from this text in this paragraph and the next.

[103] Exner, Einnahmequellen, pp. 30–3. On the Customs revenue acting as collateral for previous foreign loans, also see van de Ven, Breaking with the Past, pp. 134–42.

[104] Berliner Actionair, Jahrbuch der Berliner Börse, 1897–1898, pp. 55–7.

collateral was difficult. A further complicating factor was that even if a sufficient stream of revenue could be identified, many Western bankers were sceptical of China's ability to efficiently manage its public finance and believed only Western supervision and fiscal management could guarantee the adequate servicing of debt. For example, Exner had described the 'Chinese system' of tax collection as being rife in 'mismanagement' and because of China's 'semi-civilized condition' only revenue collected 'according to the European system and administered under European control' could act as collateral for a large foreign loan.[105]

Because of such views and difficulties, the British and German bankers tried to first identify a potential new source of revenue that could be put under foreign supervision. Hansemann hoped that the collection of salt revenue could be put under the supervision of Robert Hart, so that it could act as collateral for the loan.[106] He saw European supervision of the salt tax as a means of reforming China's public finance and salt revenue in such a way that it could act as collateral for a foreign loan. In contrast, he was opposed to a simple guarantee by a Western state for the loan, as it did not advance or encourage Chinese financial reform.[107] The choice of the salt tax was not surprising as Exner had already explained it in detail in his work and suggested that under 'a more rational [foreign] system of fiscal administration' the salt revenue could easily be increased from 9.6 million to 20 million taels per year.[108] Accordingly, the DAB and HSBC ordered Hillier to ask Li whether the management of the salt revenue could be turned over to the Customs Service, so that it could act as collateral. Under this condition the banks were willing to offer a loan at a 5 per cent interest rate with a net price of 90 per cent and an issue price of 95 per cent.[109] While the Chinese government offered to pledge the salt or land tax as collateral, it was not willing to place any 'taxes under European control'.[110]

Because of the insufficient guarantees offered by China, the Anglo-German group cancelled the negotiations.[111] The Chinese government also tried to solicit help from France, but was confronted with similar demands for foreign control of revenues.[112] It seemed that Li Hongzhang and the Chinese

[105] Exner, *Einnahmequellen*, pp. 30–4.
[106] 'Note Auswärtiges Amt' (16 March 1897), PAAA, R17.784, pp. 71–2.
[107] Hansemann to HSBC (Hamburg) (24 December 1897), PAAA, R17.785, p. 218; Hansemann to HSBC (Hamburg) (25 December 1897), PAAA, R17.785, p. 221.
[108] Exner, *Einnahmequellen*, pp. 24–5.
[109] Heyking to Hohenlohe (4 April 1897), PAAA, R17.784, pp. 111–13.
[110] Quote from Heyking to Hohenlohe (4 April 1897), PAAA, R17.784, pp. 111–13; Cameron to Brüssel (28 May 1897), PAAA, R17.784, p. 172.
[111] Direktion der Disconto-Gesellschaft, Denkschrift (24 May 1897), PAAA, R17.784, p. 165.
[112] Brötel, *Frankreich im fernen Osten*, pp. 409–13.

government had reached a dead end. With the Customs revenue largely used up as a loan security, they either had to accept the rules of sovereign borrowing as advocated by the foreign financiers or be barred from contracting any further loans. However, Li did not give up yet. Rather, he changed his strategy for arranging for the next loan. As we have seen, the Chinese government had so far mainly tried to arrange larger loans through diplomatic channels in Beijing, the established foreign banks in China or with the help of Robert Hart. Li now attempted to circumvent the demands for further foreign control of Chinese revenues and directly find the money in London through independent agents in China and Chinese minister to Britain, Luo Fenglu 羅豐祿. Li first negotiated with George Wilson of the George Wilson Eastern Contract Company in London. Wilson was a friend of John Dudgeon, a Scottish physician who worked in China, was well connected within Chinese officialdom and was a long-time acquaintance of Li Hongzhang.[113] As early as November 1896, Campbell had described Wilson to Hart as a rather dubious character who 'has been going round to various financial houses, saying that he has got the promises of concessions for railways and gold mines' from China for which he only asked the payment of a deposit to him. According to Campbell, these concessions were only works of fiction based on 'empty promises obtained through the notorious Dr. Dudgeon'.[114] Wilson promised to Li and Luo that he represented Glyn Mills Currie & Co. and other banks, which were willing to arrange a loan of £16 million similar to the terms of the second indemnity loan without any extension of foreign control over other streams of revenue.[115] However, after initial negotiations, Luo had to discover in London that Wilson was no official representative of Glyn Mills Currie & Co., but only acquainted with two directors of the bank and the Imperial Ottoman Bank and had falsely used the names of these banks.[116] Li eventually realized that Wilson was unreliable.[117]

Following the failure of the Dudgeon–Wilson deal, Li turned to yet another syndicate in London. In August, Sheng Xuanhuai was in contact with the loan agent Frosell, who represented the Hooley-Jamieson syndicate of London. This syndicate offered a £16 million loan at a 5 per cent interest rate and a net price of 95 per cent, but insisted on the swift signing of a preliminary agreement. After discussing the matter with Weng Tonghe, Li ordered Sheng to sign the

---

[113] Li to Luo (19 April 1897), *LHZQJ*, 26:317; Luo to Li (21 April 1897), *LHZQJ*, 26:317. For a good biography of John Dudgeon, see Gao, *De Zhen zhuan*. On his relationship with Qing officials, see pp. 165–76 and 187–99.

[114] Campbell to Hart (13 November 1896), *AIMC*, 3:193.

[115] Li to Luo (19 April 1897), *LHZQJ*, 26:317; Li to Luo (16 May 1897), *LHZQJ*, 26:328; Luo to Li (21 May 1897), *LHZQJ*, 26:331; Li to Luo (21 May 1897), *LHZQJ*, 26:331; Li to Luo (23 May 1897), *LHZQJ*, 26:332.

[116] Luo to Li (23 April 1897), *LHZQJ*, 26:319; Luo to Li (29 April 1897), *LHZQJ*, 26:323.

[117] Li to Luo (2 June 1897), *LHZQJ*, 26:335; Li to Luo (7 June 1897), *LHZQJ*, 26:336.

preliminary agreement.[118] According to the agreement, the remaining Customs revenue and revenues from the salt tax were to act as guarantee for the loan. However, no new revenues were to be put under foreign supervision.[119] The Chinese negotiators also hoped that working with the Hooley-Jamieson syndicate would make it possible for Sheng's newly established Commercial Bank of China (Zhongguo tongshang yinhang 中國通商銀行) to act as intermediary bank.[120] However, the loan deal with the Hooley-Jamieson syndicate also soon evaporated. As Campbell reported, Jamieson was known in London as a 'projector of wild schemes and was quite discredited in the City' as someone 'whose money existed only on paper'. Jamieson turned out to be an 'impecunious M.P. to whom nobody in the City, who knew him, would be willing to lend a £10 note'. The consensus among financiers in London was that the Hooley-Jamieson syndicate 'could never float a Chinese Loan of £16,000,000'.[121]

It soon surfaced that the syndicate was mainly interested in using the indemnity loan to gain a railway concession from China.[122] Moreover, Hooley could not provide a £100,000 deposit that Li had demanded as a condition before signing the final agreement.[123] In October, Li eventually conceded that 'Hooley, Jamieson and Frosell are not trustworthy and have no shame' and broke off the loan negotiations.[124] This marked the end of Li's attempts to circumvent the demands of the established banks to find new ways of contracting the third indemnity loan for China without their help. While this initiative showed the increasing willingness of Chinese officials to directly and independently approach and engage with foreign capital markets, their failure also showed that their knowledge of these capital markets and the assessment of the market and the credibility of financiers there was limited. As a result, Li easily fell victim to the promises of the gamblers and speculators who wanted to profit from the growing Chinese loan business. As it turned out,

---

[118] Sheng to Li (13 August 1897), *LHZQJ*, 26:356; Li Hongzhang memorial (July/August 1897), *LHZQJ*, 16:90.

[119] 'Jiekuan caoyue' (July/August 1897), *LHZQJ*, 16:90–1. The preliminary agreement speaks of *yan lijin* or salt *lijin*, which was collected as part of the salt tax. Also see footnote 145. Brötel wrongly claims that the Hooley-Jamieson Syndicate also asked for foreign control of further revenues. See Brötel, *Frankreich im fernen Osten*, p. 413.

[120] Hamashita *Chūgoku kindai keizaishi kenkyū*, pp. 75–8.

[121] Campbell to Hart (21 August 1897), *AIMC*, 3:272–3.

[122] Li to Luo (8 September 1897), *LHZQJ*, 26:368; Hart to Campbell (5 September 1897), *AIMC*, 3:277.

[123] Li to Sheng (29 August 1897), *LHZQJ*, 26:364–5; Campbell to Hart (8 October 1897), *AIMC*, 3:285; Luo to Li (7 October 1897), *LHZQJ*, 26:376; Li to Sheng (9 October 1897), *LHZQJ*, 26:376.

[124] Quote from Li to Luo (10 October 1897), *LHZQJ*, 26:377; Li to Luo (16 October 1897), *LHZQJ*, 26:380.

only charlatans were willing to promise the floating of the loan without an acceptable security.

Li now had to return to his old method of negotiating loans. During the summer of 1897, he resumed negotiations with the Anglo-German group. Li now was only willing to provide the general income of the Board of Revenue besides the remaining Customs revenue as security for the loan.[125] However, for the banks, European control over some new stream of revenue remained an important condition for any loan. The HSBC believed that 'any additional revenue placed under [the] Chinese Customs [Service]' would be a sufficient security. As they projected that China's Customs revenue would soon increase sufficiently to cover the whole loan sum, they felt that 'even [the] land tax with nominal European control' would allow the floating of the loan at 92.5 per cent with a net price of 86 per cent and a 4.5 per cent interest rate. Hansemann agreed with this, but was hesitant about the specifics of the guarantee and wished to consult Hart as to whether he saw the 'native opium, likin, salt and or land tax to be collected at Treaty ports by Chinese Customs as [a] tangible security for [the] loan'.[126] This once more revealed the limited knowledge of the bankers about China's tax revenues and the problems they faced when trying to identify a solid security. As a consequence, the German bankers now brought in outside expertise to deal with their lack of understanding of Chinese finance. For this, Robert Hart and the Customs Service were the obvious choice.

Hart believed that it was 'practicable' for the Customs Service to take over the collection of either the *lijin* or salt tax, but that the former was most likely more acceptable to China. However, Hart contended that a special revenue designated for the service of the loan without any foreign control was a sufficient security for a loan.[127] Hansemann and the other members of the KfAG, however, maintained that 'tangible securities under Foreign Control' were 'absolutely required' to ensure the success of placing the loan on the German market.[128] In contrast, the HSBC now feared that China would continue to reject foreign supervision of additional revenue and simply pay the indemnity in smaller instalments with an additional interest payment of 5 per cent as allowed by the Treaty of Shimonoseki.[129] In Germany, Brüssel and DAB director Erich now sought more expertise on China's tax revenues and particularly on the *lijin* tax Hart had recommended. They consulted Friedrich Hirth, also an official of the Chinese Maritime Customs Service,

---

[125] Brüssel to Disconto-Gesellschaft (8 June 1897), PAAA, R17.784, p. 176; Li to Luo (9 June 1897), *LHZQJ*, 26:337.
[126] Brüssel to Disconto-Gesellschaft (8 June 1897), PAAA, R17.784, p. 175.
[127] HSBC (London) to Disconto-Gesellschaft (11 June 1897), PAAA, R17.784, p. 180.
[128] Brüssel to HSBC (London) (11 June 1897), PAAA, R17.784, p. 178.
[129] HSBC (London) to Disconto-Gesellschaft (11 June 1897), PAAA, R17.784, 180; Brüssel to Cameron (24 June 1897), PAAA, R17.784, pp. 211–12.

who had published a book that discussed Chinese public finance.[130] The three came up with a scheme by which China remained in control of *lijin* collection, but had to transfer the *lijin* income from several provincial *lijin* bureaus (lijin zongju 釐金總局) to the customs house in the nearest treaty port every month for the servicing of the loan. Only if there were irregularities in the payment would the Customs Service assume control over the collection of the *lijin* tax in these provinces.[131] Most likely to confirm their scheme, they also seem to have solicited a memorandum by a Mr Cartwright, judging from his expertise possibly also a member of the Customs Service, which outlined a similar scheme for the security of the loan.[132] Besides consulting Hirth, Erich and the other German bankers also consulted the estimates for China's salt and *lijin* revenue the British consul-general in Shanghai, George Jamieson, had published earlier during the year.[133] This once more shows how, in the absence of official Chinese publications on China's state revenue, foreign bankers had to draw on outside expertise, such as Customs officials or Jamieson's report, and produce their own knowledge about China's revenue to estimate its debt burden and sovereign risk.

Largely following the scheme developed with Hirth, the HSBC and German consortium agreed to accept the *lijin* and salt tax 'under Chinese administration' as an adequate security, but sufficient amounts had to be paid monthly to the Commissioner of Customs. In case of default, these tax revenues were, however, to be handed over to the control of the Customs Service. On this basis, on 24 June Cameron ordered Hillier to make an offer to the Chinese government for a 4.5 per cent loan with a net price of 85 per cent.[134] This compromise of forfeiting immediate foreign control was most likely struck because of the aforementioned fears of the HSBC that China might persist in its rejection of further foreign control of Chinese revenues and eventually decide to pay Japan directly in smaller instalments with interest. There were also once more rumours of a possible Russian-backed indemnity loan.[135] In any case, the new offer was a compromise between the demands of the Chinese

---

[130] Hirth, *Chinesische Studien*.
[131] 'Promemoria. Mit Prof. Hirth und J. Brussel aufgestellt am 19/6 1897' (19 June 1897), PAAA, R17.784, pp. 197–200.
[132] 'Memo. Proposed Security for Loans of Taels 100000000. Annual provision: Taels 6000000' (no date); Brüssel to Cameron (24 June 1897), PAAA, R17.784, pp. 211–12.
[133] Jamieson's report is cited as a source for the estimate of the salt and *lijin* revenue of several provinces in the following draft loan agreement: 'Entwurf eines Prospektes für eine in Unterhandlung befindliche chinesische Anleihe von £16,000,000, welche die Grundlagen für einen etwa abzuschliessenden Vertrag enthält' (1897), PAAA, R17.784, pp. 206–7. For the report, see Jamieson, *Revenue and Expenditure*, pp. 15–16, 18.
[134] Quote from Brüssel to Disconto-Gesellschaft (24 June 1897), PAAA, R17.784, pp. 209–10; Brüssel to Cameron (24 June 1897), PAAA, R17.784, pp. 211–12; Brüssel to HSBC (London) (29 June 1897), PAAA, R17.784, p. 216.
[135] Brüssel to Disconto-Gesellschaft (24 June 1897), PAAA, R17.784, p. 209.

and Western requirements for sovereign borrowing. The low net price showed, though, that the bankers were doubtful about the potential success of floating a loan with this new arrangement for its security in Europe at the time.

However, it was only in November that Li agreed to the scheme the bankers had developed and accepted the offer of the HSBC and DAB from June. He conceded that 'in case of default [the] Banks may appoint [the foreign] Inspector General [to] inspect [and] administer [the] security'. He asked the bankers to draw up a memorandum as a basis for a 'preliminary treaty'.[136] Although it now seemed as if a successful conclusion of the loan deal was finally possible, the negotiations were again disturbed, this time by the political developments in China. After the German occupation of Jiaozhou Bay in Shandong in November 1897, the loan question became more politicized. Both Britain and Russia now offered to provide a guarantee for the third indemnity loan, but demanded political concessions in exchange.[137] Pressured from both sides, the Chinese negotiators first planned to split the loan between Russia and Britain, but eventually cancelled all loan negotiations.[138]

Eventually, the Chinese government again asked Robert Hart to handle the loan negotiations. He mediated between Weng and the other Chinese negotiators and the HSBC.[139] Despite the previous compromise, the HSBC now told Hart that foreign investors would only accept the loan if the security was immediately put under Hart's control.[140] This reversion was most likely due to the political difficulties China found itself in after the occupation of Jiaozhou Bay and the growing demands of other Western governments.[141] Hart tried to persuade the Chinese government to entrust him with the administration of several *lijin* and salt tax bureaus sufficient to act as security for the loan. He argued that this measure was better than risking a delay of the repayment of the indemnity, which could lead to more intervention by the foreign powers. Also, according to the Treaty of Shimonoseki, China had to make the next indemnity payment by May 1898 already, especially if it wanted to pay back the loan in full within three years from the exchange of ratifications to save interest payments. Eventually, the Chinese negotiators concurred with Hart's request and agreed to hand over control of certain *lijin* and salt tax bureaus to him. Hart coordinated the signing of the preliminary treaty with the HSBC and signed the treaty with Hillier on 19 February 1898.[142]

---

[136] Quote from Hillier to HSBC (London) (13 November 1897), PAAA, R17.785, p. 163; Luo to Li (November 1897), PAAA, R17.785, pp. 163–4.
[137] HSBC (Hamburg) to Disconto-Gesellschaft (23 December 1897), PAAA, R17.785, 213; diary entry (15 January 1898), WTHRJ, 6:3081.
[138] Weng Tonghe, 'Songchan ziding nianpu', WTHJ, 2:1071.
[139] Zhang, 'He De yu Ying De xujie kuan', pp. 160–1; MacMurray, Treaties, 1:19–20.
[140] Diary entry (17 February 1898), WTHRJ, 6:3094.
[141] King, HSBC History, 2:288.
[142] Zhang, 'He De yu Ying De xujie kuan', pp. 161–2.

After the preliminary agreement for a 4.5 per cent interest rate loan at a net price between 82 per cent and 85 per cent was signed, the HSBC informed the DAB of the offer.[143] The German bankers immediately agreed to it.[144] According to the final loan agreement signed on 1 March 1898, seven provincial *lijin* and salt tax bureaus were placed under the control of the Customs Service and China pledged to place further revenues under the Inspector General of Customs' control if necessary for the repayment of the loan.[145] While this was a concession the Chinese negotiators eventually had to make, it was still a good deal for China. It only had to hand over a certain number of bureaus and could use the existing Customs Service for supervision without having to make any other large political concessions.

As we have seen, the insistence by the bankers on good securities under foreign supervision to ensure the repayment of the loan was mainly due to their mistrust of China's financial management. Nevertheless, before 1911 the securities pledged for the indemnity loans remained only a formality and China maintained its freedom to arrange the repayment of the loans as it saw fit.[146] Moreover, the banks could do little to actually ensure that the pledged provincial *lijin* and salt taxes were put under Hart's control and had to largely trust the Chinese government and Hart with this matter. As late as December 1898, the DAB complained that the pledged provincial *lijin* and salt taxes had still not been placed under the supervision of the Customs Service.[147] It would be several years until Hart really took control over the new revenues.[148] Therefore, the extension of foreign control over Chinese tax collection and the bowing of China to the structural power of foreign bankers remained limited, and financial reform, like elsewhere in the world, 'involved more symbols than content' and was carried out with an 'eye . . . on financial market perceptions'.[149] As we will see, such symbolic pledges of revenues without real substance became even more common during the last decade of the Qing.

---

[143] Brüssel to Hansemann (21 February 1898), PAAA, R17.787, p. 132; 'Aktennotiz übergeben am 21. Februar durch J. Brüssel' (21 February 1898), PAAA, R17.787, pp. 133–4.

[144] Deutsche Bank (Berlin) to Deutsche Bank (London) (23 February 1898), HADB, S2588; Disconto-Gesellschaft to Brüssel (22 February 1898), PAAA, R17.787, p. 137.

[145] For the loan agreement, see MacMurray, *Treaties*, 1:107–12. Also see van de Ven, *Breaking with the Past*, p. 142. While the other relevant sources all use the term 'salt taxes', the loan agreement actually uses the term 'salt lekin [*lijin*]' when discussing the pledged sources of revenue. The salt *lijin* was collected by salt officials and thus seen as part of the salt tax and not the general *lijin*. See Jamieson, *Revenue*, p. 13.

[146] Wright, *China's Customs Revenue*, pp. 108–9.

[147] DAB (Berlin) to HSBC (Hamburg) (1 December 1898), HADB, S2589.

[148] King, *HSBC History*, 2:288.

[149] Flandreau and Zumer, *Making of Global Finance*, p. 24.

Where China, however, had to accept the rules of financial markets was in the market's assessment of China's credit after using up the Customs revenue and, more importantly, the competition of foreign powers for political concessions had taken off after the German seizure of Jiaozhou Bay. As a result, the final net price of the third indemnity loan was set at 83 per cent, over 10 per cent lower than the second indemnity loan.[150] The low net price shows that the bankers anticipated a low issue price. This likely can be attributed in part to the remaining doubts of the bankers about how the investing public would receive the new security arrangement for the loan, even though the Chinese side had eventually accepted foreign control of the additional new revenues. More importantly, the low net price reflected the deterioration of both China's credit and the situation of European financial markets. In the spring of 1898, the markets had not only been exhausted by the Greek indemnity loan floated in Europe in 1897, but, as Campbell reported from London, the Spanish-American War and conflicts between France and Britain in West Africa also made investors nervous.[151] At the same time, China's credit had suffered from concern about the fluctuations in the silver price and the more immediate political crisis that had started after the German occupation of Jiaozhou Bay.[152] As a result, previous Chinese bonds issued in Britain and Germany had decreased in value and Hart had to explain to Weng Tonghe that China's credit was simply not as good as before.[153] Finally, the German bankers had pointed out that after the issuing of the second indemnity loan in Germany, there had been a decrease in demand for Chinese bonds there.[154] It was thus no surprise that the net price was set at only 83 per cent, even though an unforeseen upturn in the market eventually made it possible to issue the loan at 90 per cent, which, however, immediately dropped to 88 per cent and 89 per cent in London and Berlin, respectively.[155] Despite the fact that only this unforeseen market upturn allowed for the issue price of 90 per cent, it needs to be pointed out that this meant an effective interest rate of 5 per cent for the loan – in line with the larger development towards lower interest rates for Chinese bonds after the Sino-Japanese War.

[150] For the final net price, see MacMurray, Treaties, 1:110.
[151] Campbell to Hart (21 February 1898), AIMC, 3:1407; Campbell to Hart (25 February 1898), AIMC, 3:317. King also mentions the weakness of bond markets at the time. See King, HSBC History, 2:288.
[152] King, HSBC History, 2:288-90.
[153] Hansemann to HSBC (Hamburg) (24 December 1897), PAAA, R17.785, p. 218; Campbell to Hart (25 February 1898), AIMC, 3:1408; diary entry (28 February 1898), WTHRJ, 6:3097.
[154] 'Note Auswärtiges Amt' (27 February 1897), PAAA, R17.784, pp. 22-3; 'Note Auswärtiges Amt' (3 March 1897), PAAA, R17.784, pp. 35-7; Direktion der Disconto-Gesellschaft, 'Denkschrift' (24 May 1897), PAAA, R17.784, p. 165.
[155] Campbell to Hart (5 March 1898), AIMC, 3:1409; Campbell to Hart (11 March 1898), AIMC, 3:320; King, HSBC History, 2:289; Barth, Imperialismen, p. 158.

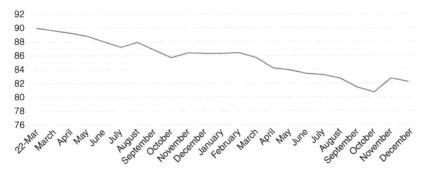

Figure 3.4 4.5% Chinese Imperial Government Gold Loan of 1898 bond notations in Berlin, 1898–9, in per cent. *Source: BBZ, 1898–9.*

However, if we look more generally and from a long-term perspective at the development of the 1898 loan bonds on the German market shown in Figure 3.4, we see that despite the good securities the bankers succeeded in including in the loan agreement, the German demand for Chinese loans and China's credit in Germany remained limited. By the end of 1898 the value of the bonds had already fallen to 86 per cent and by the end of 1899 to 82.2 per cent, which was less than the net price China had received. In London, the price also fell first to 86.5 per cent by the end of 1898 and then to 81 per cent by the close of the following year.[156] While this performance suggests that the bankers set the interest rate of the loan too low, their concern about the difficulties of floating the loan and the necessity for a good security had clearly not been unjustified. Not only were markets in Europe in a volatile position, but after two large Chinese loan issues, they also lacked demand for Chinese bonds. However, for the DAB, issuing the third indemnity loan was a success. It constituted the DAB's most important business operation of 1898 and boosted its net profit for the year to 846,479 Shanghai taels compared to only 273,042 Shanghai taels during 1897.[157] The issuing of the loan (Figure 3.5) also undoubtedly cemented the bank's rank as one of the premier foreign banks in China.

---

[156] *Investors' Monthly Manual* (31 December 1898); *Investors' Monthly Manual* (30 December 1899).

[157] 'Bericht der Direction für das Geschäftsjahr 1898' (27 June 1899), HADB, Geschäftsberichte, Deutsch-Asiatische Bank; 'Bericht der Direction für das Geschäftsjahr 1897' (25 June 1898), HADB, Geschäftsberichte, Deutsch-Asiatische Bank.

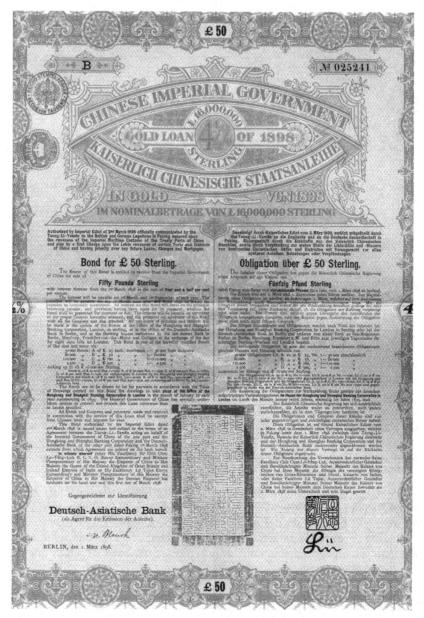

Figure 3.5 Bond of the 4.5% Chinese Imperial Government Gold Loan of 1898. Image courtesy of Deutsche Bank AG, Historical Institute.

3.4 Conclusion

With the conclusion of the indemnity loans of 1896 and 1898, the DAB finally succeeded in floating large Chinese loans on the German capital market, thereby gaining equality with the HSBC and a leading position as a financier of the Chinese government and as a foreign bank in China. The indemnity loans gave the bank and the German consortium the opportunity to play out its strength as the sole representative of the German capital market and turn itself into a major player in China's loan business. As the sums now required far exceeded previous sums the HSBC had raised in London and cooperation between European capital markets was necessary, the positions between the DAB and the HSBC were now to a certain extent reversed. While the HSBC was the premier foreign bank in East Asia, it was only a small player in Europe. It now not only had to cooperate with the Rothschild group in London, but also had to grant equal status to the German bankers in exchange for their cooperation. As explained in the second chapter, the participation of German bankers in the floating of the two indemnity loans allowed the DAB to issue high dividends. However, more importantly, it also greatly increased the reputation of the bank not only in Europe but also in China, where the DAB's participation in the indemnity loans was later remembered as the first important activity of the bank relating to Chinese foreign loans.[158] The financing of such a substantial part of China's indemnity loans in Germany also contributed to the growth of German foreign investment and was representative of Berlin's rise as the third financial centre in Europe after London and Paris.[159]

The loans were also an important turning point in China's integration into the international system of sovereign borrowing and the internationalization of Chinese finance. Before 1895, China had only borrowed relatively small sums abroad. With only the exceptions of two small German loans, its public loans had all been floated in London and had mostly been managed by the HSBC. The indemnity loans not only led to the emergence of China as a major borrower on foreign capital markets, but also rang in the end of the British monopoly as the main provider of Chinese loans. They accelerated the internationalization of China's public finance in terms of both the amount and the diversity of foreign capital that contributed to Chinese state income. While the total sum of foreign capital borrowed by China before 1895 was limited to 52,591,449 Kuping taels, it had increased almost ten-fold to 486,410,801 Kuping taels by the end of 1898.[160] This rapid increase in foreign borrowing was for now primarily the result of the Japanese indemnity forced upon China and imposed a great burden on the Chinese state, increasing the portion of the

---

[158] 'De Hua Yinhang zhi jinxi guan', *Yinhang Zhoubao* (24 July 1917).
[159] On the rise of Berlin as an international financial centre, see Cassis, *Capitals of Capital*, pp. 108–14.
[160] Calculated according to Xu et al., *Cong bainian quru*, 1:517–29.

annual state expenditures used to repay foreign debt from 3–6 per cent before the Sino-Japanese War to 23 per cent in 1900.[161] However, it was also accompanied by a greater diversification and competition of possible lenders (see Figure 3.6). Thus, Chinese public finance witnessed accelerated internationalization between 1895 and 1898 both in the amount and the diversity of foreign capital used by the Chinese state. As we will see, this trend was to continue during the following years.

This rapid internationalization and integration into the international system of sovereign borrowing also meant that for the first time China was confronted fully with the structural power of foreign financiers and capital markets and their demands and requirements for sovereign borrowing. At the same time, the Western financial structure as it manifested itself in China after 1895 was far from uniform but rather comprised many competing financial groups, who, at times backed by their home governments, vied for the concession to float Chinese loans. As we have seen, as long as the Customs revenues was still a sufficient collateral that met the demands of foreign financiers, Chinese officials could use this new diverse competition to gain improved loan terms better than those of any previous Chinese loans. This was especially remarkable if we remember that the German bankers had believed that only the Russian political guarantee had made the low interest rate of the first indemnity loan possible. This trend for cheap borrowing continued in the following years (see Figure 3.7) and saw China being able to borrow on foreign capital markets at an average yearly interest rate of 5 per cent between 1895 and 1911 compared to 7.4 per cent for public loans before 1895.[162] As Hassan Malik has shown in the case of Russia, such dynamics of a borrowing emerging market being able to leverage competition among international bankers for its own benefit were not limited to China.[163]

The decrease in the cost of Chinese borrowing shows that the Western financial structure was not simply imposed on China. Rather, Chinese local agents used their relational power in the negotiations and exploited the competition among foreign financiers to challenge foreign preconceptions about Chinese credit and the structural power of foreign financiers and gain better loan terms. Nevertheless, the third indemnity loan also showed that there were limits to the ability of Chinese agency and relational power to challenge the structural power of foreign financiers and markets. China not only had to concede to the demand for foreign control over the revenues pledged as security, but also had to accept that the changes in the state of foreign markets, the demand for Chinese bonds or the views of Chinese political stability abroad could all have a significant impact on China's foreign credit.

---

[161] Chen, *1895–1936 nian*, p. 72; Zhou, *Wan Qing caizheng jingji*, p. 157.
[162] Average yearly interest rates calculated according to the sources for Figure 3.7.
[163] Malik, *Bankers and Bolsheviks*, pp. 106–12.

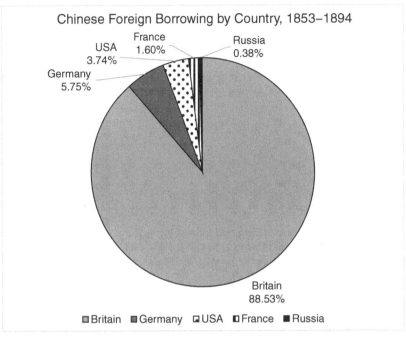

Chinese Foreign Borrowing by Country, 1853–1894

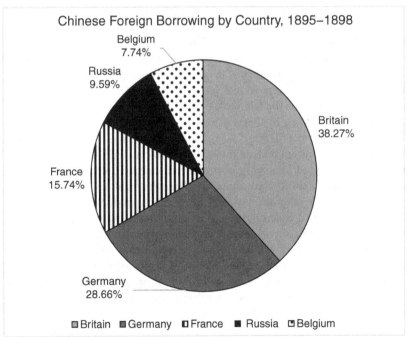

Chinese Foreign Borrowing by Country, 1895–1898

Figure 3.6 Chinese foreign borrowing by country, 1853–94/1895–8. *Source:* 1853–94: Xu et al., *Cong bainian quru*, 1:517–20; 1895–8: Xu, *Zhongguo jindai waizhai tongji*, p. 92 (in the rare cases where loans could not clearly be assigned to a country, these loans were left out of the calculation in the two pie charts).

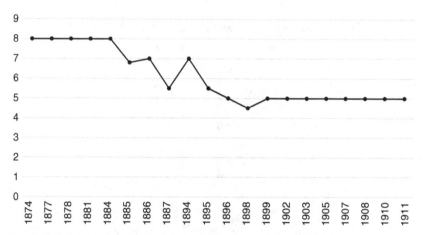

Figure 3.7 Average interest rate of issued Chinese public loans, 1874–1911, in per cent.
Source: 1874–93: King, *HSBC History*, 1:548, 557; 1894–1911: Verlag für Börsen- und Finanzliteratur AG, *Jahrbuch der Berliner Börse*, 1914/15, pp. 236–43.

As this chapter has shown, the Chinese frontier became the main stage for the growing integration of China into the international financial system of sovereign borrowing and the increased internationalization of Chinese public finance, with frontier banks such as the DAB playing a key role in making these processes possible. While events and actors on Western capital markets naturally also played an important role, it was the frontier where most of the loan negotiations took place and where the structural power of foreign financiers and capital markets met the relational power of Chinese actors most forcefully. Most clearly seen during the negotiations for the second indemnity loan, when there was sufficient competition among foreign financiers, the Chinese negotiators were under no immediate time pressure to conclude a loan and matters were not complicated by insufficient collateral sources, political instability or adverse conditions on foreign capital markets, the frontier afforded Chinese negotiators much agency and power. However, as seen during the loan negotiations for the third indemnity loan, in turn increasing time pressure, the drying up of sources of revenue acceptable to foreign financiers, political instability due to foreign military interference and changes in foreign capital markets could curtail the space for Chinese agency in loan negotiations on the Chinese frontier. We thus see what important factors contingency and timing could be for determining the power relations between foreign and Chinese actors on the frontier.

Besides these consequences for Chinese foreign borrowing, China's accelerated integration into global financial markets also involved new processes of
knowledge production and mutual learning for both foreign financiers and
Chinese officials. For the foreign bankers, it meant that they had to learn more
about China's tax revenue to assess its debt burden and sovereign risk and find
adequate securities for future loans. In the absence of information about
Chinese tax revenues and with the transparent Customs revenue used up,
foreign bankers had to produce their own knowledge about Chinese public
finance. They did so both by drawing on the scarce writing of foreigners who
had tried to estimate Chinese tax revenues and by seeking the help of foreign
experts of the Chinese Maritime Customs Service. This learning process made
it possible for the bankers to assess China's creditworthiness and sovereign
risk, situate it within the global system of sovereign borrowing and identify
adequate securities for Chinese loans. This was a key aspect of their function as
intermediaries between the Chinese state and foreign capital markets. As Dong
Yan has shown for the case of the Sino-foreign negotiations about the payment
mechanism for the Boxer indemnity imposed on China in 1901, and as will
also become clear in the following two chapters, the absence of Western
knowledge about Chinese finance and processes of foreign learning about
Chinese public finance, coupled with hopes for Chinese fiscal reform – hopes
already visible in calls for the reform of the salt tax during the negotiations for
the third indemnity loan – remained an important feature of Sino-foreign
financial interactions in the years to come.[164]

For China, its accelerated integration into global financial markets also
involved important learning processes. As the knowledge of Li Hongzhang
and other Chinese negotiators about foreign capital markets was limited, they
were constantly testing what borrowing terms they could attain. While they
were at first successful in exploiting the new competition among foreign
financiers to gain better loan terms, they also had to realize what their limitations were and eventually accept the rules of the markets. This became most
evident in Li's failed attempt to find cheap foreign capital in London and
circumvent the demands for adequate securities for the third indemnity. After
the failed attempt, China had to return to using established foreign banks as

---

[164] See Dong Yan, 'Boxer Indemnity'. Somewhat confirming my discussion of the earlier
indemnity loans in terms of structural and relational power dynamics in this chapter, in
his treatment of the Boxer Indemnity and its aftermath, Yan also highlights the ability of
Chinese actors to resist certain foreign demands for fiscal reform. He also points out the
Chinese central government's interest in (and provincial authorities' scepticism towards)
foreign-proposed reforms if they served the central government's aim of fiscal central-
ization – a phenomenon with some similarities to what we will see in Chapter 4 in the
case of the pledging of provincial revenues as collateral for foreign railway loans by the
central government. For the Boxer protocol that fixed the Boxer indemnity, see
MacMurray, 1:278–284.

intermediaries and had to concede foreign control over the securities pledged for the loan.

At the same time, the indemnity loans were also part of another kind of learning experience for Chinese officials, as they showed them what large sums of money China could cheaply borrow abroad. The openness of Chinese officials to using these new possibilities was reflected in China having used the opportunity of the indemnity loans to borrow significantly more foreign money than necessary for the repayment of the indemnity. China only ended up paying 201.5 million Kuping taels in principal and interest for the payment of the Japanese indemnity, but borrowed over 328 million Kuping taels with the indemnity loans.[165] A good example for the increased Chinese openness to foreign borrowing induced by the indemnity loans is Zhang Zhidong, an important Chinese reformer and official. Before 1894, Zhang had not advocated using foreign capital for purposes other than war. Now, after the conclusion of the first indemnity loan, he argued that foreign capital should be used to carry out reform projects and self-strengthening: 'Having already borrowed so much for [the repayment of] the indemnity today, it would be best to borrow ten or twenty percent more [for other purposes]. ...As a result, we would gain an opportunity for self-strengthening and naturally would not have to fear that there is no way of repaying the debt.'[166] It was this thinking among a growing number of Chinese officials that would further accelerate foreign borrowing during the last decade of the Qing dynasty. Although some of these processes of learning and knowledge production happened outside of China, they mostly focussed and took place on the Chinese frontier. Thus, we see the Chinese frontier emerge not only as a space for loan negotiations and the confluence of capital flows, but also as the locale for finance-related knowledge production.

Finally, the indemnity loans can tell us more about the reasons for the high level of global financial integration during the three decades before the First World War, which was marked by a convergence in interest rates for sovereign borrowing.[167] As Table 3.2 shows, with the indemnity loans China had become part of this convergence of interest rates. It could now borrow at similar interest rates to other developing countries, which was proof of China's increased integration with foreign financial markets. Historians studying financial globalization have largely explained the convergence of interest

---

[165] Calculated according to Chen, *1895–1936 nian*, p. 61 and Xu et al., *Cong bainian quru*, 1: 521. I have deducted the thirty million taels China paid for the return of Liaodong peninsula from Chen's figure, as it was not part of the indemnity. See MacMurray, *Treaties*, 1: 18–23, 50–53.

[166] Zhang Zhidong memorial (19 July 1895), in *ZZDQJ*, 2: 1001. On Zhang's changing views from opposition to support for the use of foreign debt, see Ma, *Views of Foreign Debt*, pp. 41–45.

[167] Flandreau and Zumer, *Making of Global Finance*, pp. 17–20.

Table 3.2 *Selected sovereign loans of developing countries, 1891–9*

Country	Year	Issue amount	Annual interest rate	Issue price	Years until maturity
Ottoman Empire	1891	£6,316,920	4%	93.5%	60
Chile	1892	£1,800,000	5%	95%	Not fixed
Brazil	1895	£7,422,000	5%	85%	Not fixed
Chile	1896	£4,000,000	5%	95.5%	Not fixed
China	1896	£16,000,000	5%	98.75%/99%	36
Ottoman Empire	1896	£2,975,200	5%	96%	49
China	1898	£16,000,000	4.5%	90%	45
Japan	1899	£10,000,000	5%	90%	55

Source: A. W. Kimber & Company, *Kimber's Record*

rates from the perspective of the suppliers of capital and have therefore focussed on the perceptions of investors in Europe. They explain that 'policies reducing the perception of risks by the market' were the main drivers for the reduction in borrowing costs and the increase in global financial integration. Accordingly, they see the increased global spread of fiscal and economic reforms and policies or foreign financial control that were perceived positively by European investors as the key factor for the global convergence of interest rates.[168] While the indemnity loans show that this is partially true, the ability of Chinese negotiators to exploit foreign financial competition and reduce borrowing costs suggests that local actors and their agency also played an important role in global financial integration. Therefore, shifting our view from the supply to the demand side of global capital flows might be helpful in further explaining financial globalization in the decades before the First World War.[169]

---

[168] Quote from Flandreau and Zumer, *Making of Global Finance*, pp. 55–8. Also see Obstfeld and Taylor, 'Globalization and Capital Markets', pp. 124–5; Tuncer, *Sovereign Debt*, p. 186.

[169] For a similar observation of the previous bias in the literature on the history of financial globalization on the supply side and the need to pay more attention to the demand side and the agency of borrowers, see Malik, *Bankers and Bolsheviks*, especially p. 16.

4

Railway Dreams

German Bankers and Chinese Railway Development, 1895–1910

In 1898, the prominent Chinese official and reformer Zhang Zhidong authored his famous reform tract *quanxue pian* (勸學篇; An Exhortation to Study). It was written as a reaction to China's defeat by Japan in the Sino-Japanese War of 1894/5 and laid out a detailed reform programme for the Chinese state. The *quanxue pian* represented a growing consensus among Chinese officials that far-reaching reforms were necessary after the Sino-Japanese War. It also foreshadowed many aspects of the reforms carried out by the Qing government during the *Xinzheng* (新政; New Policies) reforms between 1901 and 1911.[1] An important pillar of the reform programme Zhang put forward in the *quanxue pian* was railway construction:

> Is there any one power that will open the door of learning for the scholar, the farmer, the workman, the merchant, and the soldier? To this question we reply emphatically, there is, and it is the Railway. . . . The Railway is the source of the wealth and power of Western countries. . . . Let us build Railways and then the scholar can have easy communication with distant friends, the farmer can utilize much that is now waste, the merchant can readily meet the demand for supply, forwarding the heaviest material, the workman will soon find machinery everywhere, the abundant products of the mines will be beneficially distributed, and our China coast will be securely protected and guarded by myriads of efficient troops. . . . We have been looking into the Railway affairs of the world for thirty years. Every country considers Railways most urgently important. They have been introduced all over the globe, and even now are daily spreading. . . . If China does not introduce them, we will remain isolated from the rest of the world.[2]

It is not surprising that Zhang, writing at the end of the nineteenth century, accorded railways such an important place in his reform plan for strengthening and enriching China. During the nineteenth and early twentieth centuries, the railway became one of the most visible symbols of progress and modernity,

---

[1] Bays, *China Enters the Twentieth Century*, p. 56; Feng, *Zhang Zhidong pingzhuan*, pp. 267–8; Li, *Zhang Zhidong yu Qingmo xinzheng yanjiu*, p. 363.

[2] Zhang Zhidong, 'Quanxue pian' (1898), ZZDQJ, 12:9763–4. Translation from Zhang, *China's Only Hope*, pp. 125–7.

first spreading throughout Europe and then around the world. Railways transformed perceptions of space and time and allowed greater national and economic integration. Because of their sheer size, they also became the first truly big businesses that attracted large sums of capital and became one main driver of international capital flows.[3] As we saw in the first chapter, Chinese reformers had pondered the introduction of foreign railways with the help of foreign capital as early as the 1870s. At the same time, the large profits and industrial contracts promised by the financing of Chinese railway construction had been one major factor that had drawn German bankers towards China. Nevertheless, before 1895, most of these plans had remained visions for the future that yet had to be realized.[4]

This chapter continues the story of the connection between Chinese railway development and German banking and finance for the period between the end of the Sino-Japanese War and the last years of the Qing dynasty, which was the period of greatest progress in Chinese railway construction before 1949.[5] It will do so by focussing on the loan negotiations surrounding the financing of the Tianjin–Pukou railway (Jin-Pu Tielu, 津浦鐵路), an important trunk line connecting the port city of Tianjin in North China with the Yangzi valley in China's South, which was among China's most economically important regions. The financing and construction of this railway was not only the most important railway project the German bankers were involved in, but was also at the heart of the plans of many Chinese reformers for railway development, and it became an important part of China's railway system.[6] The negotiations for the financing of this important railway lasted from 1898 to 1908 and take us through the many changes Chinese railway development witnessed during this period, starting in the late 1890s with the first serious effort of the Chinese government to carry out railway development on a large scale and grant concessions to foreign financiers, through to the *Xinzheng* reforms and the rise of the provincial and anti-foreign railway rights recovery movement during the 1900s.

Previous scholarship on foreign involvement in Chinese railway development during this period has largely interpreted it as a conflict between foreign imperialism and Chinese nationalism,[7] or as collaboration between foreign imperialism and the Qing government.[8] While Ralph Huenemann's economic

---

[3] Osterhammel, *The Transformation of the World*, pp. 715–19; Cassis, 'Big Business', pp. 175–6; Jones, *Multinationals and Global Capitalism*, p. 116; Roth and Dinhobl, 'Introduction: Across the Borders', pp. xxiii–xxxviii.

[4] Huenemann, *The Dragon*, p. 47.

[5] Huenemann, *The Dragon*, pp. 37–97.

[6] On the history of the Tianjin-Pukou railway during the republican period see Köll, 'Chinese Railroads', pp. 123–48.

[7] See, for example, Li, *Railway-Rights Recovery Movement*; Mi, *Diguo zhuyi*.

[8] Sun, *Chinese Railways and British Interests*; Hopkins and Cain, *British Imperialism*, chapter 13.

analysis of modern Chinese railway development has cast doubt upon this narrative that sees foreign involvement in Chinese railway construction as predominantly negative and exploitative,[9] it remains largely unchallenged.[10] The scholarship on the Tianjin–Pukou railway loan negotiations is no exception.[11] This leaves us with a simplistic view of the foreign role in modern Chinese railway involvement that is limited by binary distinctions between foreign and Chinese interests, undervalues Chinese agency, sees Sino-foreign contact mainly in terms of state-to-state relations, ignores the specific roles played by different Chinese and foreign interest groups and state and non-state actors, and neglects the changing power relations between them.

This chapter uses the example of the Tianjin–Pukou railway loan negotiations to challenge this narrative by focussing on the transnational networks that developed between German, British and Chinese actors during the negotiations. I see these networks as a specific phenomenon of the Chinese frontier, where both Chinese and foreign dreams, visions and plans for Chinese railway construction could meet and transnational networks based on common objectives, interests and benefits could evolve. The chapter pays particular attention to the crucial role played during the negotiations by Chinese, German and British 'men in the middle', who were part of these networks of the frontier and possessed the cultural background and linguistic abilities that allowed them to act as mediators between the participants in the transnational network.[12] It was in the 'contact zone' of frontier cities such as Tianjin that these middle men interacted and, through both formal and informal contact, negotiated the interests of the different actors in the network on the local level, so that common objectives could be reached.[13] While

---

[9] Huenemann, *The Dragon*.

[10] See, for example, Yang, *Zhongguo jindai tielushi*. For recent exceptions that offer a more nuanced view of foreign involvement in Chinese railway development see Cui, 'Lun Qingmo tielu zhengce de yanbian', pp. 62–86; Hirata, 'The Sino-British Relations', pp. 130–47.

[11] Apart from the description of the negotiations in Li, *Railway-Rights Recovery Movement*, pp. 169–88, there exist several studies that use Western sources to depict the negotiations from the perspective of Western imperialism: Schmidt, *Deutsche Eisenbahnpolitik in Shantung*, pp. 110–35; Otte, 'The Baghdad Railway of the Far East', pp. 112–36; Barth, *Imperialismen*, pp. 159–65, 279–87.

[12] Such 'men in the middle' and their important role in transnational networks covering the West and China are discussed by Hans van de Ven in van de Ven, 'Robert Hart and Gustav Detring', pp. 631–62. Hirata also refers to the concept of 'men in the middle' in Hirata, 'Britain's Men on the Spot', pp. 895–934. Along somewhat similar lines, Wasserstrom highlights the importance of 'border-crossing' actors for transnational networks in Shanghai. See Wasserstrom, 'Cosmopolitan Connections', pp. 206–24.

[13] For the concept of the 'contact zone' see Pratt, *Imperial Eyes*. As pointed out in the Introduction, another concept for describing frontier spaces is Richard White's 'middle ground' (see White, *Middle Ground*). I prefer the use of the concept of the contact zone in this chapter because of Pratt's particular emphasis on the contact zones as 'social spaces'. See Pratt, *Imperial Eyes*, p. 4.

Chapter 2 showed the important role of transnational networks for the functioning of local financial markets on the frontier, this chapter's focus on transnational networks highlights their important role in facilitating transnational financial projects, such as Chinese railway development and foreign investment in China, on the local, granular level. It once more reveals that cooperation and interdependence were just as much part of Sino-foreign contact as were tensions and conflict. What we will see once more in this chapter is the frontier as a dynamic space of Sino-foreign contact and negotiations that connected China to global financial networks and flows of capital, thereby also contributing to China's accelerated financial internationalization. Transnational networks were not only themselves a product of the frontier but also played a key role in making Sino-foreign cooperation viable within the frontier space. This chapter also demonstrates that because of the cooperation in these networks, the continued interest of foreign financiers to invest in China, these financiers' lack of understanding of Chinese public finance and a diminishing willingness of foreign governments to apply diplomatic pressure, Chinese negotiators during the last years of the Qing dynasty were able to gain better loan terms than ever before.

The chapter starts by exploring the growing advocacy of Chinese officials like Zhang Zhidong for railway construction after the end of the Sino-Japanese War. I then explain how a combination of foreign and Chinese interest in constructing a railway line that would connect North and South China led to the signing of the preliminary Tianjin–Zhenjiang railway loan agreement in 1899. The chapter then turns to the loan negotiations between 1903 and 1906 that took place in the contact zone of Tianjin and focusses on the group of middlemen that negotiated between the different participants in the network. The last section will then show how all actors had to make final compromises and work together to win the eventual railway concession for the Sino- British-German transnational network. The chapter closes with a discussion of the final loan agreement and the reception of the bonds in Europe. The loan negotiations led to the evolution of a global financial network spanning from investors and bankers in Europe to Chinese officials and foreign bankers in China. Eventually, only cooperation and compromise between the different actors within this network made the financing of the Tianjin–Pukou railway possible.

4.1   The Aftermath of the Sino-Japanese War

Before the Sino-Japanese War, Chinese railway construction remained a limited enterprise with only 515 kilometres of railways constructed by 1895.[14] While the Sino-French War of 1884/5 had led to a shift in official opinion in favour of Li Hongzhang and other reformers that advocated railway

---

[14] Huenemann, *The Dragon*, p. 47.

construction, it was only in 1889 that the court officially acknowledged the importance of constructing railways. Even after 1889, financial constraints and Li's view that railways had to be introduced to China slowly and primarily to serve military purposes prevented the coordinated large-scale construction of railways.[15] This changed after China's defeat against Japan. In July 1895, the throne issued an imperial edict that – among other reform measures – stressed the importance of railways for self-strengthening and called upon officials to submit plans for carrying out these reforms.[16]

As the majority of China's high officials now supported the construction of railways, the edict was met with a very positive response.[17] After Li Hongzhang's fall from power following the Sino-Japanese War, Zhang Zhidong (Figure 4.1) now emerged as the leading figure in Chinese railway development.[18] Zhang was a prominent Chinese official and reformer who had served as governor of Shanxi and governor-general of Guangdong and Guangxi during the 1880s before being appointed as governor-general of Hubei and Hunan in 1889.[19] In his response to the imperial edict, Zhang explained that railways had played a key role in Japan's successful reforms and portrayed them as the cure to China's many problems. If railways were built throughout China's provinces, 'the state of the country will greatly change, the commodities of merchants will multiply tenfold and the revenue of the state will also increase tenfold. Because of the rapid deployment of troops [by railways], we will be able to greatly reduce the number of battalions. There will also be no impediment to the transportation of grain.'[20] This representation of railways as the ultimate remedy for many of China's ills reflects how they were seen as both symbols and means of achieving progress.

The question now was what railway line was to be constructed first. Official discussions soon focussed on two possible lines, one from Beijing to Qingjiang, a city located north of Nanjing in the Yangzi valley, and another from the Marco-Polo Bridge (Lugouqiao 盧溝橋) in Beijing to Hankou in South China. Both lines were to connect and integrate North and South China, a project that had been at the heart of plans for Chinese railway development since the 1870s.[21] While the plan for a Beijing–Qingjiang railway was supported by Li Hongzhang, it was criticized for being too close to the coast and therefore difficult to defend against enemies. In contrast, the Beijing–Hankou railway line was to be built further

---

[15] Yang, *Zhongguo jindai tielushi*, pp. 23–6; Zhu, *Wan Qing jingji zhengce*, p. 136; Li, *Zhongguo zaoqi de tielu*, pp. 24–32, 85.
[16] Imperial Edict (19 July 1895), *ZJTS*, pp. 199–200.
[17] Yang, *Zhongguo jindai tielushi*, pp. 26–7.
[18] Li, *Zhongguo zaoqi de tielu*, p. 117.
[19] Hummel, *Eminent Chinese*, pp. 27–31.
[20] Zhang Zhidong memorial (19 July 1895), *ZJTS*, 1:200.
[21] Li Hongzhang to Song Guotao (11 July 1877), *ZJTS*, 1:107; Li, *Zhongguo zaoqi de tielu*, pp. 55–62, 83, 87, 123, 127–8.

Figure 4.1 Zhang Zhidong 張之洞 (1837–1909). Image courtesy of Quentin Gregory Papers (#200) Box 2, Folder D. East Carolina Manuscript Collection, J. Y. Joyner Library, East Carolina University, Greenville, NC, USA (https://digital.lib.ecu.edu /21922).

inland, running through the provinces of Zhili, Henan and Hubei, and presented no similar problem.[22] Moreover, since 1889, Zhang Zhidong had advocated the construction of this railway as part of his larger scheme for railway development based on constructing trunk lines.[23] Besides Zhang, Hu Yufen 胡燏棻 (Figure 4.2), who played an important role in China's railway development because of his appointment as administrator-general of the Imperial Railways of North China (Guanneiwai tielu 關內外鐵路) in December 1895, also recommended the construction of the Beijing–Hankou railway.[24] The court soon agreed and ordered that Zhang Zhidong should manage the construction of the railway with Zhili governor-general Wang Wenshao 王文韶. As in the decades before,

---

[22] Li, *Zhongguo zaoqi de tielu*, p. 128.
[23] Zhang Zhidong memorial (1 April 1889), *ZJTS*, 1:167–70; Zhang Zhidong memorial (4 October 1889), *ZJTS*, 1:184–6; Li, *Zhang Zhidong yu Qingmo xinzheng*, pp. 206–10.
[24] Hu Yüfen memorial (June/July 1895), *ZJTS*, 1:201. On Hu, see 'A Loss for China', *North-China Herald* (7 December 1906).

Figure 4.2 Hu Yufen 胡燏棻 (1840–1906). Image courtesy of P. A. Crush Chinese Railway Collection.

the state lacked the necessary capital for large-scale railway construction, so the Qing government hoped that rich merchants could be encouraged to provide it.[25]

However, Zhang and Wang were sceptical about the possibilities of raising the construction funds in China. Instead, they believed that the state should take the lead in constructing the railway by first borrowing foreign capital to construct the railway. To avoid that the Chinese state, which was already short on money and pressed with indemnity payments, had to pledge state revenues like customs income as security for railway loans, Zhang wished to pledge the railways themselves as loan collateral. That it was Zhang who first proposed using railways as collateral is important to point out here, as this was later often criticized by Chinese nationalists, who viewed it as an attempt of foreign syndicates to gain control over the railways. Once the railway was constructed,

[25] Imperial Edict (6 December 1895), *ZJTS*, 1:205; Imperial Edict (24 April 1896), *ZJTS*, 1:225.

Zhang hoped that Chinese merchants would see the results and be more willing to contribute capital, which could then be used to repay the foreign loan. Wang and Zhang also hoped that Sheng Xuanhuai 盛宣懷, who had successfully managed the China Merchants' Steam Navigation Company (Lunchuan zhaoshangju 輪船招商局) and the Imperial Telegraph Administration (Dianbaoju 電報局), would be put in charge of constructing the railway. Sheng was to establish a railway company that would manage both foreign borrowing and the soliciting of capital from Chinese investors.[26] In October 1896, the Chinese Ministry of Foreign Affairs, the Zongli Yamen 總理衙門, followed their recommendation and ordered the establishment of the Chinese General Railway Company (Zhongguo tielu zonggongsi 中國鐵路總公司) under the directorship of Sheng. He was not only put in charge of constructing the Beijing–Hankou railway but was also to manage other railway projects. Therefore, Sheng, with Zhang Zhidong and Wang Wenshao, was now effectively in charge of Chinese railway development. Because of the difficulties of raising Chinese capital, their strategy for railway development from the start relied on foreign capital.[27]

In Germany, this new Chinese openness to railway construction did not go unnoticed. The German bankers sent former diplomat Max von Brandt to China in 1895 to negotiate railway loans with the Chinese government, as 'the Chinese central government has in recent months issued several decrees … that [it] wishes to bring the constructions of railways into flow'.[28] However, while Brandt entered into negotiations about a potential loan with Sheng Xuanhuai, the one-sided German attempt of proposing a railway loan agreement to the Chinese government failed because of differing Chinese and German views regarding the conditions of a possible railway loan, in particular the demands of the German bankers for a proper loan security and foreign control over the railway's construction and management.[29] After ending his mission with no tangible results, von Brandt stressed that the German capitalists had to 'adapt to Chinese views' of how railways were to be constructed in China and could not just impose their plans and demands on the Chinese. He also criticized how the networks and contacts of the Deutsch-Asiatische Bank (DAB) in 'Chinese

---

[26] Zhang, Wang memorial (2 September 1896), *ZJTS*, 1:252–5; Ma, *Qingmo minchu tielu waizhai guan*, pp. 41–55.

[27] Imperial Edict (20 October 1896), *ZJTS*, p. 261; Cui, 'Lun Qingmo tielu', p. 64; Yang, *Zhongguo jindai tielushi*, pp. 27–8; Li, *Zhongguo zaoqi de tielu*, pp. 133–47. On Sheng's control of Chinese railway development (with the exception of the Imperial Railways of North China), also see Feuerwerker, *China's Early Industrialization*, p. 270n50.

[28] DAB (Berlin), Direction der Disconto-Gesellschaft, Deutsche Bank, Bleichröder, Berliner-Handelsgesellschaft, Robert Warschauer & Co. to von Brandt (15 October 1895), PAAA, R17.780, pp. 32–41.

[29] DAB (Berlin), 'Denkschrift betreffend die Unternehmungen im Yangtse- und Huangho Thal' (3 September 1900), PAAA, R17.859, pp. 330–31; Direction der Disconto-Gesellschaft, Denkschrift (24 May 1897), PAAA, R17.784, pp. 167–9.

[government] circles' were insufficient, so that it was very difficult for them to obtain information about the plans and activities of governors-general and other Chinese political elites.[30] If the German financiers wanted to invest in China's railway development, they had to find Chinese officials with whom they could cooperate and agree on a plan for railway financing and construction.

Brandt had urged the bankers to pursue the negotiations with Sheng despite the bankers' misgivings about the loan conditions. However, as he complained to the Foreign Office, the German bankers in Berlin did not reply to his letters.[31] Brandt returned to Germany disappointed about the bank's reluctance to accept Sheng's loan conditions and be more open to investment in China. He complained to the Foreign Office that the German bankers had not only missed a profitable investment opportunity when they rejected Sheng's offer, but also permanently turned Sheng, who was now the all-powerful figure in Chinese railway development, against Germany.[32] Brandt's mission to China and his disappointment about the German bankers once more revealed the different attitudes towards investment in China held by German diplomats and bankers. While the diplomats wanted to see a readiness from German bankers to invest in China and support German industrial exports without shirking from risk, the bankers were mainly concerned with the safeness of their investment, protecting their investors and the modernization of China along rational Western lines. This discrepancy between the political objectives of German diplomats and the economically driven objectives of German bankers led to recurring and increasing conflicts between the DAB and the German Foreign Office in the following years.[33]

However, the German bankers continued to pursue railway investment in China and new opportunities for railway development continued to appear. After the German occupation of Jiaozhou Bay in 1897, the Sino-German treaty of 6 March 1898 allowed Germany to construct railway lines in Shandong province in North China. A railway that would connect these German railways in Shandong with Beijing in the north and the Yangzi valley in the south would have been beneficial to the development of the German Shandong railways. Therefore, both the German government and the DAB, who wanted to finance the Shandong railways, were interested in a Tianjin–Yangzi railway. Still, the first initiative to take up the plan to build a railway between Tianjin and the city of Zhenjiang in the Yangzi valley with foreign capital did not come from the DAB. It rather was Hu Yufen who in April 1898 approached the DAB through the German trading firm Carlowitz & Co. to plan for the construction of such

[30] Brandt to Direktion der Disconto-Gesellschaft (27 June 1896), PAAA, R17.783, pp. 129–30.
[31] See Brandt to Direktion der Disconto-Gesellschaft (24 May 1896), PAAA, R17.783, p. 96 and Brandt's nota bene to the Foreign Office at the end of the letter.
[32] Hallgarten, *Imperialismus vor 1914*, 1:411.
[33] On this point also see Barth, *Imperialismen*, especially p. 21.

a railway.[34] Although Hu played an important role in Chinese railway development as administrator-general of the Imperial Railways of North China and had initially supported the Beijing–Hankou railway, Zhang Zhidong, Wang Wenshao and the court had given the management of the new Chinese General Railway Company to Sheng Xuanhuai instead, so that Sheng and not Hu was now the leading figure in Chinese railway development. A rivalry between Sheng and Hu developed, and constructing a Tianjin–Zhenjiang railway under Hu's own control presented him with an opportunity to regain control over China's railway development for himself.[35] Thus, the German bankers had found a Chinese partner for financing railways.

Hu Yufen also had very good ties to the Hongkong and Shanghai Banking Corporation (HSBC), as his brother-in-law Wu Maoding 吳懋鼎 worked as comprador of the HSBC and as the Imperial Railways of North China had previously received advances from the British bank. He recommended cooperation between the DAB and HSBC in the financing of the railway.[36] The 1895 agreement between the banks also suggested a partnership in the matter of the railway. However, Germany's military occupation of Jiaozhou Bay sparked a dispute among the banks regarding the Shandong and Shanghai–Nanjing railways (Hu-Ning tielu 滬寧鐵路) that turned into a diplomatic conflict between the German and British governments over railway concessions and spheres of influence.[37] In September 1898, the German bankers eventually came to an agreement with the HSBC that fixed that the Yangzi valley was to become the sphere of interest for British finance, while Shandong and the Yellow River valley became the sphere of the German financiers. Accordingly, the northern part of the Tianjin–Zhenjiang railway was to be financed and built by the DAB, which left the southern part to the HSBC.[38] Although this agreement was mainly intended to solve the problem of the Tianjin–Zhenjiang railway, it led to the exclusion of German bankers from the Yangzi valley for over a decade.

Because of the agreement between the two groups, Hu could now finally go forward with his plan to unite German and British bankers for the financing of the Tianjin–Zhenjiang railway. The Sino-British-German network comprising the DAB, the HSBC and Hu Yufen now formally applied to the Chinese government for the railway concession. While they initially encountered

[34] Müller-Jabusch, *Deutsch-Asiatische Bank*, p. 123; Schmidt, *Eisenbahnpolitik*, pp. 110–11.
[35] For Hu's rivalry with Sheng Xuanhuai see Feuerwerker, *China's Early Industrialization*, p. 270n50. On this point, also see Schmidt, *Eisenbahnpolitik*, p. 208n540.
[36] King, *HSBC History*, 2:304; Mi, *Diguo zhuyi*, p. 662; Müller-Jabusch, *Deutsch Asiatische Bank*, p. 124.
[37] King, *HSBC History*, 2:306–9; Müller-Jabusch, *Deutsch Asiatische Bank*, pp. 101–21.
[38] 'Minutes of meetings held at New Court St. Swithins Lane, London on the 1st and 2nd September 1898' (2 September 1898), PAAA, R17.854, pp. 119–20.

resistance from Sheng Xuanhuai, who feared the possible competition of the Tianjin–Zhenjiang railway line for the Beijing–Hankou railway, the pressure from the British and German ministers in Beijing eventually led to the opening of negotiations in December 1898.[39] Hu Yufen, who had supported a German-British financing of the railway all along, was elected as director-general of the Tianjin–Zhenjiang railway and was to lead the negotiations.[40]

After several months of negotiations, the preliminary agreement to construct the Tianjin–Zhenjiang railway was signed between the British and German group and the Chinese government on 18 May 1899.[41] It gave the concession to the two groups to raise a £7.4 million loan for the Chinese government with an interest rate of 5 per cent. The loan was to be repaid over fifty years and could be redeemed early after thirty years. The issue price was not fixed and the net price for the loan was set at 90 per cent. The railway itself acted as collateral for the loan and the DAB and the British and Chinese Corporation (BCC), an associate company of the HSBC, were to purchase construction materials and construct the northern and southern parts of the railway, respectively.[42] Until the repayment of the loan, the two groups were also to operate the railway and receive 20 per cent of the railway's annual revenue for constructing and operating it. The two boards of commissioners that were to supervise the construction and operation of the northern and southern part of the railways each comprised five members, only two of whom were Chinese. Thus, the preliminary agreement not only guaranteed the DAB and BCC large profits but also gave the two groups far-reaching control over the construction and operation of the railway. However, the agreement also stated that modifications to the terms could still be made in the final agreement and, as it turned out later, the main part of the negotiations was yet to come before this final agreement could be signed in 1908.

4.2   The Contact Zone of Tianjin

After the conclusion of the preliminary treaty, disputes between the British and German groups about other railway concessions delayed the start of the negotiations for the final loan agreement. Only in March 1903 did the two groups agree to start the negotiations for the final loan agreement of the Tianjin–Zhenjiang railway on the basis of identical draft treaties.[43] Meanwhile, Chinese railway

---

[39] Heyking to German Foreign Office (27 October 1898), PAAA, R17.855, p. 61; MacDonald to Salisbury (20 December 1898), in Great Britain, House of Commons, *China No. 1*, p. 16.

[40] DAB (Shanghai) to DAB (Berlin) (9 December 1898), PAAA, R17.855, p. 184.

[41] 'Preliminary Agreement for Tientsin–Chinkiang Railway' (18 May 1899), in MacMurray, *Treaties*, 1:694–7. For the negotiations, see Schmidt, *Eisenbahnpolitik*, pp. 114–18.

[42] On the British and Chinese Corporation, see King, *HSBC History*, 2:295–302.

[43] Schmidt, *Eisenbahnpolitik*, pp. 118–23; Otte, 'The Baghdad Railway', pp. 121–4.

development had further increased its reliance on foreign capital. Because of the lack of both government funds and Chinese investment that could be used for railway construction, Sheng's Chinese General Railway Company now entirely relied on foreign loans and signed loan agreements for 4,543 kilometres of rail between 1897 and 1903.[44] As part of the *Xinzheng* reforms initiated by the Qing government after 1901, a new Board of Commerce (Shangbu 商部) was established in 1903 and nominally given central control over China's railway development. The Board of Commerce tried to centralize control over Chinese railway development and encourage Chinese private construction and operation of railways (*shangban* 商辦) instead of foreign investment. However, local governors-general retained great influence and control over Chinese railways and Zhili governor-general Yuan Shikai 袁世凱 (Figure 4.3) emerged as the Chinese official most influential in the management of Chinese railway development.[45]

Before rising to the governor-generalship of Zhili in 1901, Yuan had distinguished himself as a military reformer, Chinese diplomatic resident and commissioner of commerce in Korea and governor of Shandong. As governor-general, with a growing modern army under his command, he implemented a wide-ranging reform programme in North China.[46] In foreign accounts of the time, Yuan was often described as 'the most powerful man today in the [Chinese] Empire'.[47] Yuan had early on understood the potential economic power of railways, especially as a source of new income both for himself as a reformer in charge of operating railways and for the Chinese state. Therefore, in response to the 1901 imperial edict that started the *Xinzheng* reforms, Yuan had urged the court to continue its efforts to construct railways.[48] In August 1902, Yuan had been appointed imperial director-general of the Tianjin–Zhenjiang railway and had been ordered to negotiate the final agreement with the Anglo-German group.[49] He advocated a pragmatic form of Chinese nationalism and believed that China should use foreign capital and expertise in constructing railways as long as China's sovereignty was not compromised by this.[50] Therefore, he

---

[44] Cui, 'Lun Qingmo tielu', p. 65.

[45] Cui, 'Lun Qingmo tielu', pp. 69–74.

[46] Hummel, *Eminent Chinese*, pp. 950–2. For a good study of Yuan, particularly during his time in Zhili, see MacKinnon, *Power and Politics*.

[47] Foster, *Present Conditions in China*, p. 6. Also see, for example, Edmunds, 'The Passing of China's Ancient System', *The Popular Science Monthly* (February 1906), p. 110.

[48] Yuan Shikai memorial (25 April 1901), *YSKQJ*, 9:148; Chu, *Biange zhong de weiji*, pp. 29–30, 107.

[49] Li, *Railway-Rights Recovery Movement*, p. 172.

[50] MacKinnon, *Power and Politics*, p. 185. Li Enhan also sees Yuan – together with his subordinate Tang Shaoyi – as representing a 'realistic' approach to the development of Chinese railways that focussed on Chinese control rights over the railways. See Li, *Railway-Rights Recovery Movement*, pp. 273–4.

Figure 4.3 Yuan Shikai 袁世凱 (1859–1916). From the *Popular Science Monthly* (February 1906): 110. Courtesy of the Biodiversity Heritage Library.

supported a British-German loan for the railway throughout the negotiations, while trying to win as much control over the railway as possible for China.

During the following four years, the loan negotiations took place in the city of Tianjin, which was the seat of Yuan's provincial government and the central port city and commercial hub of North China. A city of roughly 1 million inhabitants, Tianjin was one of the most important cities of China's eastern frontier, connected to global trade through its port and to Beijing via railway and the Hai River (Haihe 海河). It was an international city with over 3,000 foreign inhabitants living in the nine foreign concessions. Contemporaries described it as the city 'where Chinese and foreigners appreciate each others' merits perhaps more highly than anywhere else in China'.[51] The hybrid character of the city with the foreign concessions in the southeast and the

[51] St. John, *The China Times Guide to Tientsin*, p. 9.

Chinese city and government offices situated in the west and north facilitated Sino-foreign contact in trade, finance and diplomacy. From the offices of the DAB at the Bund, one only had to walk up the river northwards to reach the Chinese part of the city, or go further north and cross the bridge across the North River to reach the Yamen (衙門) office of the Customs Daotai, where many negotiation meetings for the railway loan were to be held. Therefore, the Sino-foreign contact zone of Tianjin was the ideal place where foreign and Chinese capital, ideas, knowledge and plans could come together and where a project like the Tianjin–Pukou railway could be negotiated, developed and realized.[52]

Before we turn to the beginning of the negotiations, it is important to note who the foreign and Chinese negotiators in Tianjin were. Although the negotiations were formally conducted between the DAB, the British group and the Chinese government, the actual negotiations were mostly held on the individual interpersonal level between the foreign and Chinese negotiators in Tianjin. The Tianjin–Yangzi railway was not only a major railway project for the DAB, but also the first large project Heinrich Cordes (Figure 4.4), the DAB's newly hired Tianjin deputy-manager, negotiated. Cordes was one of the most extraordinary figures in the bank's history. He was born in 1866 in Lübbecke, a small town in western Germany. He was later drawn to the capital of the new German empire, Berlin, where he studied law at the University of Berlin and Chinese at the famous Seminar for Oriental Languages, which had been established by Bismarck in 1887 because of the increasing global connections and aspirations of Germany and the need to produce personnel able to communicate in Chinese and other Asian and African languages.[53] In 1892, Cordes entered the German foreign service and, aged twenty-six, left for Beijing to complete his language studies and work as a translator for the German legation there. In the following years he worked for the German legations and consulates in Beijing, Guangzhou and Hankou. During his time in Guangzhou, he began a relationship with a Chinese woman called Chou Yuksin. Cordes and Chou had nine children together and were later married in 1914.

During a stay in Germany in 1901, he was approached by Adolf von Hansemann and recruited as the deputy-manager of the DAB's Tianjin branch. However, he never worked as a regular banker, but was specifically hired to act as representative of the bank and the German Konsortium für Asiatische Geschäfte (KfAG) in loan negotiations and to maintain relations with Chinese official circles, filling a role very similar to that of Edward Guy Hillier at the HSBC. With Cordes and his great ability in the Chinese language, the DAB now had an agent that could directly speak to Chinese officials and solely devote his time to

---

[52] The description of Tianjin in this paragraph is based on Tientsin Press, Guide to Tientsin (Tianjin: Tientsin Press, 1904); St. John, The China Times Guide to Tientsin. For a good map of Tianjin see General Staff, Geographical Section, War Office, 'Plan of Tientsin, GSGS 3959' (1935), Map Collection, The British Library, London, United Kingdom.

[53] Sachau, Denkschrift über das Seminar für Orientalische Sprachen.

Figure 4.4 Heinrich Cordes (1866–1927). From Arthur Wright, *Twentieth-Century Impressions of Hong Kong, Shanghai, and Other Treaty Ports of China*, p. 759. Image courtesy of The University of Hong Kong Libraries.

the task of securing and negotiating government business for the bank. This obviously increased the independence of the bank, as it no longer needed to rely on Hillier in loan negotiations. In 1905, Cordes was made manager of the DAB's Beijing agency (Figure 4.5), which had been established in the same year to further the bank's relations to the Chinese government. What becomes clear is that Cordes' hiring and the establishment of the Beijing agency were further important steps to expand the bank's network in government circles and bolster its ability to act independently. Cordes became a leading figure in the foreign community and was well connected among Chinese officials like Zhang Zhidong, Yuan Shikai and many members of the Chinese court. His knowledge of the Chinese language, the long time he spent in China and his relationship to his wife and children seem to have created a deep affection for China and the Chinese.[54]

---

[54] My recounting of Cordes' life in these two paragraphs is based on Paul W. Wilm, *Rückblicke eines Neunzigjährigen: Erlebtes in der Heimat, in China und der Mongolei, in Brasilien und in Südostasien*, 3 vols (unpublished manuscript, 1990), Teil II a, Teil II b,

Figure 4.5 Deutsch-Asiatische Bank in Beijing, early twentieth century. Image courtesy of Deutsche Bank AG, Historical Institute.

The British syndicate had several other railway projects in China and paid less attention to the Tianjin–Yangzi railway.[55] Therefore, during the first few years after 1903, Cordes was the main representative of the Anglo-German group. This only changed in 1906 when John Otway Percy Bland (known as J. O. P. Bland) was sent as a new British negotiator by the Chinese Central Railways (CCR), which was formed in 1904 and thereafter represented the

StuDeO-Bibl., Nr. 0371c, Nr. 0372b; 'Heinrich Cordes: Eine deutsche Persönlichkeit in China' (July 1927), *Täglicher Dienst für nationale Zeitungen*, StuDeO-Archiv, *0716; Heiratsurkunde Heinrich Cordes, Juksin Chou, Beglaubigte Abschrift (27 December 1936), StuDeO-Archiv, *0715; DAB, 'Geschäfts-Bericht für das Jahr 1905', HADB, Geschäftsberichte, Deutsch-Asiatische Bank; Müller-Jabusch, *Deutsch-Asiatische Bank*, pp. 154, 206. Also see Wilhelm Matzat's excellent account of Cordes' life: Matzat, 'Cordes, Heinrich', www.tsingtau.org/cordes-heinrich-1866-1927-dolmetscher-und-bankdirektor. On the business of the DAB's Beijing office, also see Akagawa, 'Doitsu Ginkō – Du A Ginkō 1870–1913 nian', pp. 1141–2. He shows that apart from loan dealings with the Chinese government, the Beijing branch otherwise also focused its activities on providing capital to Qing nobles, officials and government institutions.
[55] On other British railway projects, see Sun, *Chinese Railways and British Interests*; King, *HSBC History*, 2:366. On the limited British interest in the railway, see Schmidt, *Eisenbahnpolitik*, p. 124.

interests of the HSBC and BCC in the railway.[56] Like Cordes, Bland had a very particular background. He had arrived in China in 1883 to join the Chinese Maritime Customs Service. He worked as a Chinese customs official in Beijing and several treaty ports. Later, apart from becoming involved in railway loan negotiations, he also worked for the Shanghai Municipal Council and as a *Times* correspondent. Like Cordes, Bland was proficient in Chinese.[57]

The negotiators Yuan Shikai first appointed were Tang Shaoyi 唐紹儀 (Figure 4.6) and Liang Ruhao 梁如浩.[58] They were later replaced by Liang Dunyan 梁敦彥 (Figure 4.7) and Zhou Changling 周長齡.[59] What is striking is that all these Chinese officials had been part of the Chinese Educational

Figure 4.6 Tang Shaoyi 唐紹儀 (1862–1938). From Merwin, *Drugging a Nation*. Image courtesy of Gullans-Espey Collection of American Trade Bindings, Library Special Collections, Charles E. Young Research Library, UCLA.

---

[56] The CCR later also included Belgian and French interests. On the CCR, see King, *HSBC History*, 2:331–6.

[57] Bickers, 'Bland, John Otway Percy', www.oxforddnb.com/view/article/31920; *The Times (London)* (25 June 1945). It is unclear when Bland gained his proficiency in Chinese, but as a customs official he was bound to study the Chinese language. See van de Ven, *Breaking with the Past*, p. 98. On his Chinese ability, see Beresford, *The Memoirs of Admiral Lord Charles Beresford*, p. 433 and Trevor-Roper, *Hermit of Peking*, p. 47.

[58] Yuan Shikai to Tang Shaoyi and others (13 May 1903), *TDS*, p. 47.

[59] Yuan to Liang Dunyan (29 November 1904), *TDS*, p. 70; Yuan to Tianjin Customs Daotai (26 April 1906), *TDS*, p. 71.

Figure 4.7 Liang Dunyan 梁敦彥 (1857–1924). From *The Far-Eastern Review* 11, no. 1 (1914). Image courtesy of The University of Hong Kong Libraries.

Mission of 1872–81, had been educated in the United States and thus were fluent in English.[60] Having studied at Columbia University, after his return to China Tang Shaoyi served first at the Korean Maritime Customs and then as a secretary under Yuan Shikai in the Chinese diplomatic service in Korea. He later followed Yuan first to Shandong and then to Zhili, where he was appointed Customs Daotai in 1902.[61] Liang Ruhao had studied engineering at the Stevens Institute of Technology in New Jersey. After his return to China in 1881, he worked as junior director and later managing director at the Beijing–Shanghaiguan railway line.[62] Liang Dunyan had been a student at Yale University in the United States and, after his return home, had served under Zhang Zhidong for several years and, among other duties, assisted him in foreign affairs. In 1904, he was appointed as Tang's successor as Customs Daotai of Tianjin.[63] Zhou Changling had studied at Columbia University and after his return from the United States also served first

---

[60] Wen, *Zuixian liu Mei tongxue lu*. For more on the Mission, see Rhoads, *Stepping Forth into the World*.
[61] Millard's Review, *Who's Who in China*, p. 3.
[62] The China Weekly Review, *Who's Who in China (Biographies of Chinese), Third Edition*, p. 500.
[63] 'The New Minister of Communications', *The Far Eastern Review* 11, No. 1 (1914), p. 16; China Mail, *Who's Who in the Far East*, p. 198.

in the Korean Maritime Customs and then in the Chinese consular service in Korea under Yuan Shikai. Later, he was first appointed to the managing direct-orship of the China Merchants Steam Navigation Company in Tianjin and then in 1904 as managing director of the Beijing–Fengtian Railway (Jing-Feng Tielu 京奉鐵路).[64] It was not surprising that Yuan chose the Customs Daotais of Tianjin (Jinhaiguandao 津海關道), first Tang Shaoyi and then Liang Dunyan, to deal with the railway negotiations, as the Customs Daotai was a position that had been established by Li Hongzhang in 1870 in response to the growing need for a government office that could specifically deal with external trade, foreign affairs and negotiations with foreigners.[65]

All these negotiators can be seen as representatives of a form of new trans-national elites that had emerged both in Europe and China during the late nineteenth century because of the new and increasing global entanglements of both regions. These men were all themselves products of Sino-Western contact zones and their unconventional backgrounds, experience abroad and language skills gave them the unique ability to act as middlemen and mediators between the different transnational actors in the railway loan negotiations. As the negoti-ators stayed in Tianjin for most of the time, they also met outside the formal negotiations and sometimes even visited each other's homes or discussed the current state of the negotiations when they ran into each other on the street.[66]

The negotiations for the final loan agreement began on 1 June 1903. Most likely as only the DAB had already finished its surveying works for the northern part of the railway, the British representative explained that Cordes would take the lead in the negotiations for now.[67] During the second half of 1903, the negotiations between Tang and Liang Ruhao and the bank represen-tatives only made slow progress as every clause of the preliminary agreement was repeatedly deliberated over.[68] Moreover, compared to the negotiations for the preliminary loan treaty, the Chinese negotiators now were more eager to protect Chinese control over the railway and put up much stronger resistance to the demands of the German and British group than before. Cordes seems to have realized this and the need to make compromises, which is shown in a draft for the final agreement that Tang and the foreign representatives agreed on in March 1904.[69] Tang and Liang persuaded the representatives to give in to Chinese demands for more control over the railway. It was agreed that the two

[64] Burt, Powell and Crow, Biographies of Prominent Chinese, p. 79; Kasumigaseki Kai and Gaimushō Ajiakyoku, Gendai Chūgoku jinmei jiten, p. 240.
[65] Leung, The Shanghai Taotai, p. 114; Li, 'Ming Qing liangdai difang xingzheng zhidu', p. 175.
[66] Cordes to Krebs (5 April 1907), PAAA, R17.866, pp. 192–4.
[67] Müller-Jabusch, Deutsch-Asiatische Bank, p. 156.
[68] Tang to Yuan (17 March 1904), TDS, p. 58; Yuan to Tang (25 July 1904), TDS, p. 67.
[69] For the draft agreement see Yuan to Tang (18 March 1904), TDS, pp. 58–66. Also see Yuan to Tang (21 April 1904), TDS, p. 66–67. On the changed stance of the Chinese negotiators, also see Schmidt, Eisenbahnpolitik, pp. 123–6.

boards of commissioners, which were to supervise the construction and administration of the northern and southern part of the railway by the groups, were to be made up of three members each, two of whom needed to be Chinese. Moreover, the Chinese negotiators – despite initial opposition from the German minister in Beijing – convinced the groups to allow an early redemption of the loan after twelve and a half years and also gained a reduction of the groups' share of the railway profits from 20 per cent to 10 per cent.[70] In return, Cordes gained a 5 per cent commission for the purchase of construction materials that the groups demanded. He also maintained the most important financial conditions of the agreement such as a 5 per cent interest rate and a net price of 90 per cent. This temporary agreement shows that the Chinese negotiators were generally willing to accept the financial demands of the groups as long as they gained better terms regarding Chinese control over the railway, which at least Cordes seems to have been willing to concede to them.

Despite the progress made, no final agreement was signed and the negotiations came to a halt in 1904. One reason for this was that, unlike Cordes, the DAB directors and board members in Berlin did not see the necessity of giving up any concessions gained in the preliminary agreement.[71] The other reason was that the British group still had not surveyed the route of the southern part of the railway and generally showed only limited interest in the negotiations because of the limited demand for Chinese bonds on the London capital market at the time.[72] The DAB tried to persuade the Chinese to first independently come to a separate agreement about the northern part of the line. The Chinese side, however, strictly opposed this and only wanted to conclude an agreement with both groups.[73]

It was only in March 1905 that the British group finished surveying the southern railway line, so that the groups could finally present their cost estimate to the Chinese negotiators and restart the negotiations. As a result of the surveying works, the British group moved the endpoint of the line from Zhenjiang to Pukou opposite Nanjing, as this suited other British railway plans and allowed for a direct connection of the Tianjin–Pukou and Shanghai–Nanjing railways. Because this change of the endpoint meant that the railway would lead through more populous regions, which promised more tax income from the railway, reduced related construction costs and decreased competition with water traffic on the Grand Canal, it was also welcomed by the Chinese.[74]

---

[70] For the opposition of the German minister to a possible early redemption of the loan, see Mumm to Bülow (10 December 1903) quoted in Barth, *Imperialisms*, p. 283.
[71] Mumm to Bülow (25 November 1905), PAAA, R17.865, p. 12.
[72] King, *HSBC History*, 2:365.
[73] Yuan to Tang (25 July 1904), *TDS*, pp. 67–9; Yuan to Tang (14 August 1904), *TDS*, pp. 69–70.
[74] Schmidt, *Eisenbahnpolitik*, pp. 119–20; King, *HSBC History*, 2:309–10.

Towards the end of 1905, another obstruction to the negotiations appeared in the form of the growing Chinese movement for the recovery of railway rights. This movement was part of a larger rise in Chinese nationalism after the Sino-Japanese War. It argued that any foreign involvement in the financing and construction of railways led to a loss of China's sovereignty and advocated that foreign railway concessions should be reclaimed and Chinese railways only built with Chinese capital.[75] Some officials in the capital demanded the cancellation of the preliminary agreement of the Tianjin–Pukou railway.[76] However, in Tianjin, the new Chinese negotiator Liang Dunyan and Yuan Shikai were eager to reassure the groups that they had no intention to cancel the loan. In a personal meeting between Cordes and Liang on 10 November 1905, Liang clarified that Yuan still wanted to borrow the necessary capital from the groups. However, Liang also used the popular opposition towards foreign railways in China to make further demands. He stated that 'under today's circumstances' the preliminary agreement could no longer be accepted as a basis for the negotiations. The groups should instead only act as financers of the railway and 'the railway [had to] be built by the Chinese'.[77] This showed the Chinese negotiators' intention to ensure Chinese control of the railway. Cordes realized that under these circumstances the preliminary agreement had to be abandoned and 'a new formula found' to continue the negotiations.[78] It again fell to Cordes to mediate and persuade the two groups to make further concessions.[79] He proposed that instead of holding on to the rights of the preliminary agreement, the groups should try to use the rejected agreement Cordes had struck with the Chinese negotiators in 1904, which allowed more Chinese administrative control, as a basis for further negotiations.[80] It is likely that Cordes made this suggestion in accordance with the Chinese negotiators in Tianjin, as they made a similar proposal at the end of 1905.[81]

However, the two bank groups could only be persuaded to make limited concessions. Partially following Cordes' agreement of 1904, in early December 1905 they allowed the redemption of the loan after twelve and a half years and also were willing to accept a reduction in their share of the profits of the railway from 20 per cent to 10 per cent. At the same time, they only agreed to allow that each board of commissioners be made up of two Chinese and two European officials and strictly opposed letting the Chinese

---

[75] Li, *Railway-Rights Recovery Movement*, p. 268.
[76] Li, *Railway-Rights Recovery Movement*, pp. 173–4.
[77] Cordes to Mumm (10 November 1905), PAAA, R17.865, p. 16.
[78] Mumm to Bülow (30 October 1905), PAAA, R17.865, p. 8.
[79] Mumm to Bülow (25 November 1905), PAAA, R17.865, p. 11.
[80] Cordes to Mumm (10 November 1905), PAAA, R17.865, p. 18.
[81] Report of the Deutsch-Chinesische Eisenbahn-Gesellschaft (9 July 1906), PAAA, R17.865, p. 166.

construct and operate the railway.[82] Cordes doubted that such limited concessions would be sufficient for a successful conclusion of a final agreement.[83]
Consequently, as both the bank groups in Berlin and London and the Chinese
negotiators were unwilling to make any further concessions, the negotiations
only recommenced in August 1906. Meanwhile, J. O. P. Bland had been sent to
act as the representative of the CCR in Tianjin and he took a more active stance
in the negotiations. After the recommencement of the negotiations, six meetings between Liang Dunyan, Zhang Zhouling and Cordes and Bland took place
at the office of the Customs Daotai in Tianjin between 11 August and
22 September 1906.[84] In these meetings Liang and Zhang again reasserted
that 'if China guarantees the interest on a Government railway loan, the final
control in construction and working of the line must rest with the Chinese
authorities'. Liang also tried to gain a reduction in the interest rate of the loan
from 5 per cent to 4 per cent and a reduction of the loan period from fifty to
thirty years. While Cordes and Bland suggested that the groups might be
prepared to agree to a loan period of thirty years, they persuaded the
Chinese negotiators to drop the demand for a lower interest rate.[85]
Moreover, although Yuan Shikai insisted on Chinese control during and
after construction, Bland and Cordes persuaded Liang and Zhang to agree to
'foreign supervision and joint control' during construction and to the appointment of an auditor to watch the 'Syndicate's financial interests' after
construction.[86]
After these meetings Cordes – this time together with Bland – again tried to
persuade the groups to make more concessions so that a conclusion of the
agreement could be reached. They explained that they assumed that the groups
were mainly interested in 'obtain[ing] satisfactory financial results under
conditions affording adequate security to the Bondholders'. Bland and
Cordes continued that the payments to the bondholders were secured by the
Chinese government guarantee, the railway that acted as collateral and the
financial supervision through the auditor. Furthermore, 'from the Syndicate's
point of view' the main financial gains in the form of the 'profit on floatation' of
the loan and the 'profit on construction' would still be maintained. They
advised the groups that the Chinese negotiators insisted on Chinese control

---

[82] Report of the Deutsch-Chinesische Eisenbahn-Gesellschaft (9 July 1906), PAAA,
R17.865, pp. 164–6. Also see the draft agreement (10 February 1906) in PAAA,
R17.865, pp. 40–51.
[83] Promemoria Cordes (21 November 1905), PAAA, R17.865, p. 23.
[84] Goltz to Bülow (18 October 1906), PAAA, R17.865, p. 172. See the respective minutes
contained in PAAA, R17.865 and TNA, FO 228/2590.
[85] 'Minutes of the Meeting Held at the Office of the Haikuan Tautai of Tientsin on Saturday
25th August at 3pm', attachment to Bland to CCR (29 August 1906), PAAA, R17.865,
pp. 180–4.
[86] Bland to CCR (26 September 1906), PAAA, R17.865, pp. 188–96.

of the railway after construction but had promised to grant 'reasonable financial terms' in return. Cordes and Bland stated that unless massive German and British diplomatic pressure could be used – which they did not see as forthcoming – the groups should 'meet the Chinese on the question of control after construction' to facilitate the negotiations of the loan.[87]

Because of this pressure from Cordes and Bland, but also because the German and British governments after the Russo-Japanese War had changed their stance to a more conciliatory attitude towards China and were no longer willing to apply diplomatic pressure, the groups finally agreed to give in to their representatives' demands.[88] During a conference between the German and the British group in Berlin on 1 December 1906 it was agreed to abandon the demand for direct control over the railway both during and after construction. It was only stated that the chief-engineer, accountant and auditor had to be appointed in agreement with the groups so that they could supervise Chinese control through these intermediaries.[89] In the end, the groups gave in to the demands of their representatives and made even more far-reaching concessions than they had asked for. After the chance to agree to better conditions in 1904 had already been missed, the two groups most likely felt that they had to make more far-reaching concessions if they wanted to at least secure the financial profits of the loan. It was the groups' forgoing of control over the railway that paved the way for the final conclusion of the loan agreement.

Although at the end of 1906 the final loan agreement between the different sides had still not been signed, the period between 1903 and 1906 was very important for the loan negotiations. Although a lot of friction occurred between the different members of the Sino-British-German transnational network, the network was still maintained and did not break up during the three-year period. On the one hand, this was because the groups still wanted to gain their profits from the loan and the Chinese negotiators and Yuan Shikai wanted to conclude the loan agreement with both the German and the British groups. In this way, the common interest of the actors to construct the railway with foreign capital held the network together. On the other hand, the contact zone of Tianjin was also very important in maintaining the network. It not only functioned as a channel of communication between the different actors of the network throughout the 1903–6 period. Mediators like Bland, Liang Dunyan and especially Cordes also acted as nodes within the transnational network that connected the different parties, mediated the interests and relationships between them and struck compromises that made an agreement between the higher-level authorities in Berlin, London and Beijing possible. China's

---

[87] Bland to CCR (26 September 1906), PAAA, R17.865, pp. 188–96.
[88] For the changed China policies of Germany and Britain see Otte, 'The Baghdad Railway of the Far East', pp. 128–9.
[89] Li, *Railway-Rights Recovery Movement*, p. 177.

position had become stronger with the rise of politicians like Yuan Shikai that stressed Chinese sovereignty and with the growth of the railway rights recovery movement. Cordes and Bland acknowledged this strengthened position and in their strategy consequently now focussed on the groups' role as financers of the railway on favourable financial terms, which the Chinese were willing to accept in return for better rights of control. Thereby, the Western and Chinese mediators prevented the failure of the negotiations and paved the way for the final agreement.

4.3 Final Compromises

On 23 February 1907 Cordes and Bland submitted a new draft agreement to the Chinese negotiators that reflected the concessions made by the German and British groups in December 1906.[90] Still, during the spring of 1907 Cordes and Bland felt that the negotiations were making no progress, as the Chinese negotiators lacked adequate instructions for bringing the negotiations to a conclusion.[91] The reason behind the delay and lack of adequate instructions most likely was the renewed popular protest against an Anglo-German loan for the Tianjin–Pukou railway. In early 1907, officials from Zhili, Shandong and Jiangsu province again petitioned the throne and asked for the cancellation of the preliminary treaty and the permission to raise Chinese capital and construct the railway themselves. They hoped that besides Yuan Shikai, Zhang Zhidong, who had 'before recovered the Guangzhou–Hankou railway' for the Chinese to construct and operate themselves in 1905, could be appointed to negotiate the cancellation of the preliminary agreement.[92] As a reaction to the recurring protest, the court on 1 April 1907 appointed both Yuan Shikai and Zhang Zhidong to handle the negotiations with the German and British groups.[93]

While Zhang had played an important role in the recovery of the Guangzhou–Hankou railway,[94] we have already seen that he was not opposed to using foreign capital for railway construction. Moreover, after the recovery of the Guangzhou–Hankou railway he had grown frustrated with the unsuccessful Chinese efforts to construct the railway with Chinese capital.[95] Thus,

---

[90] Li, *Railway-Rights Recovery Movement*, pp. 177–8.
[91] 'Minutes of Meeting (the 29th) held at the Office of the Haikuan Taotai March the 16th at 3 p.m. (1907)', PAAA, attachment to Bland to CCR (19 March 1907), PAAA, R17.866, pp. 175–8.
[92] Quote from petition by Beijing officials from Zhili, Shandong and Jiangsu (March 1907), *ZJTS*, pp. 795–6; petition by Beijing officials from Zhili, Shandong and Jiangsu (without date), *ZJTS*, p. 795.
[93] Rex to German Foreign Office (4 April 1907), PAAA, R17.866, p. 48.
[94] See Feng Tianyu *Zhang Zhidong pingzhuan*, pp. 268–88.
[95] Zhang to Li Sixiang 李嗣香 and other officials from the three provinces of Zhili, Shandong and Jiangsu (24 May 1907), *ZJTS*, p. 803.

although he had previously advocated a cancellation of the railway concession, he was now quickly in agreement with Yuan Shikai that borrowing Anglo-German capital and employing foreign personnel under Chinese control was the best option for constructing the railway. Zhang Zhidong was in accord with Yuan's scepticism about the ability of the three provinces to raise the necessary capital and provide expert Chinese staff to construct the railway on their own.[96] They agreed that their strategy would have to be to appease the gentry-merchants of the three provinces and, at the same time, to negotiate with the Anglo-German group to gain better loan terms.[97] Both appealed to the gentry-merchants of the three provinces and tried to persuade them that the best solution for constructing the railway was to first use foreign capital and let foreign personnel construct the railway, before later redeeming it with Chinese capital. As a further compromise, the railway was to become an official-merchant jointly managed enterprise after the final redemption of the loan.[98] Following their agreed strategy, during the negotiations Yuan and Zhang also tried to find loan terms acceptable by the provincial elites to protect the final loan agreement from further criticism of the gentry-merchants.

As the distance between Yuan in Tianjin and Zhang in Wuchang was considerable, the negotiations were moved to Beijing and Liang Dunyan was again appointed to negotiate with the foreign representatives.[99] Meanwhile, Liang Dunyan, Zhang Zhidong and Yuan Shikai had agreed on a strategy for the final phase of the negotiations. Based on a suggestion of Liang Dunyan, they adopted the strategy of 'making economic concessions to gain rights of control' (*rangli zhengquan* 讓利爭權).[100] This strategy was very similar to the direction that Bland and Cordes had already proposed to the two banking groups and therefore must be seen as a direct result of negotiations between Liang and Cordes and Bland in Tianjin. It also reflected the tendency of late Qing officials to make financial concessions in exchange for the regaining of

---

[96] On Zhang's initial advocacy of cancellation, see Zhang to Lu Zhuanlin (12 March 1907), *ZJTS*, pp. 796–7 and Li, *Railway-Rights Recovery Movement*, p. 178. On his agreement with Yuan, see Yuan to Zhang (4 May 1907), *ZJTS*, pp. 797–8; Yuan to Zhang (15 May 1907), *ZJTS*, pp. 798–9; Zhang to Yuan (20 May 1907), *ZJTS*, pp. 799–801; Yuan to Zhang (24 May 1907), *ZJTS*, p. 802; Zhang to Li Sixiang and other officials from the three provinces of Zhili, Shandong and Jiangsu (24 May 1907), *ZJTS*, p. 803; Zhang to Yuan and Liang (10 June 1907), *ZJTS*, pp. 804–5; Zhang to Yuan and Liang (13 June 1907), *ZJTS*, pp. 805–6; Li, *Railway-Rights Recovery Movement*, p. 178.

[97] Zhang to Yuan (14 May 1907), *ZJTS*, p. 803; Yuan to Zhang (27 May 1907), *YSKQJ*, 16:162; Yuan and Zhang to Waiwubu (27 May 1907), *YSKQJ*, 16:162.

[98] Zhang to Li Sixiang and other officials from the three provinces of Zhili, Shandong and Jiangsu (24 May 1907), *ZJTS*, p. 803; 'Yuan Shikai pi Shandong Shenshang ziban Jin Zhen tielu wen', *Shenbao* (18 July 1907), *ZJTS*, pp. 806–7; Li, *Railway-Rights Recovery Movement*, pp. 178–80.

[99] Rex to Bülow (12 July 1907), PAAA, R18.767, pp. 79–80.

[100] Zhang to Liang and Yuan (13 June 1907), *ZJTS*, p. 805.

sovereign rights.[101] After the Chinese negotiators had settled on their strategy, the negotiations moved forward again. The next step towards the loan agreement was again made on the interpersonal level in meetings between Cordes, Liang Dunyan and Zhang Zhidong.

In June, Bland temporarily returned to London, which left Cordes as the sole representative of the Anglo-German group.[102] After Cordes' negotiations with Liang had yielded no results by the beginning of July, Liang suggested that Cordes should go directly to Wuchang and negotiate with Zhang Zhidong.[103] Following this advice, Cordes visited Zhang in early July. During their meeting, Zhang expressed his great interest in bringing the negotiations to a conclusion, but also told Cordes he was worried about the 'literati of the three provinces' of Zhili, Shandong and Jiangsu. While he had no intention to fulfil their wish for the cancellation of the railway concession, he still felt it was 'necessary to steer a middle course between the foreign claims based on the Preliminary Agreement and the demands of the gentry' to induce at least the more reasonable factions among the gentry to accept the loan. After discussing possible conditions of the loan agreement with Cordes, he submitted a fifteen-point note to Cordes that explained his general view on possible terms for the agreement.

These fifteen points reflected the strategy of giving economic concessions in return for Chinese control over the railway. Most importantly, instead of the railway itself, revenues from the three provinces of Zhili, Shandong and Jiangsu were to act as collateral for the loan. While this ran contrary to the plan of using railways as collateral for loans Zhang and Sheng Xuanhuai had developed in the late 1890s, the opposition of the gentry-merchants to leaving any possibility that might lead to the foreign financiers taking control of the railway made this new form of loan security necessary. Zhang mentioned no control or supervision of the railway's finances through foreign auditors and also stressed that the foreign chief-engineers were to be under Chinese control. The initial loan sum was to be set at a relatively low £5 million to please the members of the gentry of the three provinces. The loan was to be redeemable after ten years, so that the gentry would have the opportunity to raise capital and redeem the loan with Chinese capital after only ten years. While Zhang asked for these concessions to appease the gentry, he himself remained sceptical about their feasibility. Therefore, he also proposed that in case of the reduced loan sum being insufficient for constructing the railway, the British and German groups were to issue a second loan to the Chinese government. In terms of the conditions of the loan, he suggested a net price of 94 per cent and

---

[101] Schrecker, *Imperialism and Chinese Nationalism*, p. 251.
[102] Jordan to Foreign Office (29 June 1907), TNA, FO 228/2591; CCR to Foreign Office (12 July 1907), TNA, FO 405/181, p. 30.
[103] Grey to Jordan (24 July 1907), TNA, FO 405/181, p. 52.

an interest rate of 5 per cent.[104] Cordes was generally pleased with these terms and telegrammed to the DAB in Berlin that the Chinese government had made a 'serious endeavour to settle [the loan] in a friendly manner'. He 'strongly urge[d]' the Anglo-German group to accept these terms as 'this is under [the] present circumstances the only possible way left'.[105]

Back in Berlin, the German directors were generally willing to agree with the changed terms proposed by Cordes, the most important of which was the replacement of the railway as loan security with provincial revenues. They had expected for some time that maintaining the demand that the railway had to act as collateral would not be possible. However, the key question now was what revenues the Chinese could offer as collateral.[106] Cordes again met with Liang Dunyan to discuss this problem. Their discussion revealed the tense fiscal relationship between the Chinese central government and the provinces and the government's limited control over provincial revenues. While Cordes enquired whether the salt or *lijin* revenues of the three provinces – both under the control of the provincial governments – could be used as collateral, Liang preferred to use the centrally administered maritime Customs revenue, so that dealings with the provincial governors, who were 'entirely in the hands of the unreasonable gentry', could be avoided. However, after Robert Bredon of the Maritime Customs Service informed Liang that all remaining Customs revenue had been pledged for the payment of the Boxer Indemnity, another source of revenue had to be found.[107]

Given that most larger previous Chinese loans had been hypothecated on the railways itself or the Customs revenue and other foreign-administered revenues,[108] the negotiators were very much entering new territory in trying to find a suitable security. If no such security could be found, Cordes was now even willing to contemplate the advice of Hillier of the HSBC, who had suggested forgoing the demand for a specified security, as 'it is becoming more and more difficult to think of any tangible and accessible security', so that in the future foreign bankers would have to look to 'the guarantee and the good faith of the Chinese government' for their security. For now, the Chinese Foreign Ministry, the Waiwubu 外務部, promised Liang it would ask the

---

[104] 'Notizen Über meine Unterredung mit Changchihtung im Yamen des Vizekönigs in Wuchang am 1. und 2. Juli 1907' (12 July 1907), PAAA, R17.867, pp. 82–4. On Zhang's views on the Tianjin–Pukou terms also see Fraser to Jordan (4 May 1907), TNA, FO 228/2591.

[105] DAB (Shanghai) to DAB (Berlin) (16 July 1907), PAAA, R17.867, p. 58–9; Bland to Jordan (9 September 1907), TNA, FO 228/2591.

[106] 'Protokoll, Konsortium für Asiatische Geschäfte' (17 July 1907), HADB, S2592; Deutsche Bank to Jacob S. H. Stern (17 July 1907), HADB, S2592.

[107] Cordes, 'Notiz' (12 July 1907), TNA, FO 228/2591.

[108] For an overview of relevant Chinese loans, see Xu, *Zhongguo jindai waizhai tongji*, pp. 28–40 and Baylin *Foreign Loan Obligations of China*, pp. 6–12, 27–40.

provincial governors of the provinces the railway would pass through for information about *lijin* revenue that could be pledged.[109] However, Hillier's suggestion once more reflected the reality that beyond China's Customs revenue the bankers had very little knowledge of China's revenue. Moreover, as the growing railway rights recovery movement made putting further Chinese streams of revenue under foreign control unrealistic and as China was under no pressure to conclude the loan agreement with the two groups, the bankers had to follow the Chinese government's suggestions and trust in its ability to repay its loans if they wished to conclude the loan deal. Thus, Hillier's suggestion also showed how willing the bankers were to strike compromises and how desperate they were to close the loan deal.

While the revenues of Zhili province were under Yuan's control, it was a much more difficult task of persuading the provincial governor of Shandong and governor-general of Liangjiang to pledge revenues as a guarantee for the loan. In early July, Yuan asked the two governors what revenues they were willing to pledge for the loan.[110] Through the Waiwubu, Liang Dunyan also appealed to the two governors and explained that the pledged revenues did not have to be paid to the central government. Instead, they could simply 'point out false funds, so that the trust of the foreigners is won'.[111] By early August, only Zhili, the province under Yuan's control, had pledged sufficient revenues and Shandong governor Yang Shixiang 楊士驤 had also promised that his province might pledge some revenues. But Liangjiang governor-general Duanfang 端方 claimed that he had no revenues available that could be pledged for the loan.[112] Now Yuan again had to implore Duanfang to pledge funds, explaining again that no real revenue had to be pledged, as the loan would be repaid from the revenues of the railway and, if these were not sufficient initially, from the loan sum itself.[113] By mid-August, Yuan had finally accumulated *lijin* revenues amounting to 2.6 million taels that could be pledged as a guarantee. However, Hillier, who now represented the CCR, demanded at least 4 million taels as a guarantee, so that Yuan and Liang had to ask the two governors for more revenues.[114] While all three provinces eventually increased their pledged revenues, Duanfang felt that 4 million taels was too high a sum, so the two parties settled for provincial *lijin* revenue amounting to 3.8 million taels as a security.[115]

[109] Cordes to Mayers (24 July 1907), TNA, FO 228/2591.
[110] Yuan to Yang and Duanfang (3 July 1907), *YSKQJ*, 16:256.
[111] Waiwubu to Yuan, Yang and Duanfang (30 July 1907), *YSKQJ*, 16:359.
[112] Zhang and Liang to Yuan (31 July 1907), *YSKQJ*, 16:353.
[113] Yuan to Duanfang (4 August 1907), *YSKQJ*, 16:365–6.
[114] Waiwubu to Yuan, Yang and Duanfang (20 August 1907), *YSKQJ*, 16:439; Yuan to Waiwubu (25 August 1907), *YSKQJ*, 16:451.
[115] Yuan to Duanfang (29 August 1907), *YSKQJ*, 16:469; Jordan to Grey (18 September 1907), TNA, FO 405/181, p. 92; Yuan, Zhang and Liang memorial (13 January 1908), *YSKQJ*, 17:232.

This process of finding the revenue for the loan reflected the deep divide between central and provincial public finance that marked the last years of the Qing dynasty. Control over large parts of China's revenue had fallen into the hands of the provincial governments.[116] As a result, the centre needed to beg provincial governors to give up funds for central government projects like railway construction. In turn, the central government could now use foreign loans contracted for government projects to take back control over some provincial revenues, even if it was just by pledging them as collateral, and provincial governors were cautious not to give up too much of their scarce revenues to the central government. At the same time, the negotiations between Yuan, Liang and the provincial governors also reveal that China was borrowing foreign money by providing essentially empty securities. Their correspondence with Duanfang and Yang shows that to gain the trust of foreign investors, they were willing to even pledge false revenues as security, which in the case of a default would be of little use. Instead, Yuan had to hope that the profits of the railway or the loan sum itself would be sufficient for the repayment of the loan. While these practices would most likely have not been condoned by the foreign financiers, the unavailability of information about China's revenues meant that they had to accept and trust the information supplied to them by the Chinese government.

After the problem of the guarantee had been solved, one last issue remained. When Cordes had urged the Anglo-German group to accept the Chinese terms after his meeting with Zhang Zhidong, the directors in Berlin and London had assumed that they would retain some control over the use of the loan funds and the purchases made for the railway through the foreign chief-engineers and the accountant, as a certain degree of such control had always been in place in former railway loan contracts. However, the new Chinese offer Cordes forwarded to Europe on 24 July contained no such clause. Both the DAB in Berlin and the CCR in London were at first not willing to give up such control over the use of the loan funds.[117] British minister to Beijing John Jordan and the British directors, who, unlike the German consortium, were also negotiating other railway projects now became suspicious that Cordes and the German bankers were too 'accommodating' towards the Chinese, which could lead to these terms being imposed by the Chinese on all other future Chinese railway loans. Thus, they sent Hillier to negotiate alongside Cordes. Hillier requested that a clause be included in the loan contract to the effect that 'Engineers-in-chief and a Chief Accountant acceptable to the Syndicate' were appointed, who had 'a share of responsibility in the application of loan funds'.[118]

---

[116] On this divide, see Wei, 'Qingdai houqi', pp. 207–30.
[117] Bland to Cordes (10 September 1907), TNA, FO 228/2591.
[118] First quote from Jordan to Grey (6 August 1907), TNA, FO 405/181, p. 38; second quote from Jordan to Grey (20 August 1907), TNA, FO 405/181, p. 78.

However, Liang maintained that he had instructions to be 'liberal in all purely financial matters, but to preserve strictly and fully the Chinese management of the line'. As a compromise, he suggested that the loan accounts could be kept in English and the groups be given the rights to inspect them at any time.[119] While Cordes all along seems to have realized that the trend in the negotiations and Chinese railway development was set to continue towards purely financial loans, as Cordes later reported, Hillier gave up foreign control over the loan funds only after 'a tough fight' when he had to realize that it could 'never have been obtained under the current circumstances'.[120] The financiers in Berlin and London also had to realize that they had to drop the demand for control over the spending of the loan funds.[121] With this last issue resolved, the parties could finally move towards the finalization of the agreement. The only financial condition of the loan that still needed some discussion was the net price of the loan: the Anglo-German group wished to fix it at 93 per cent instead of Zhang Zhidong's proposed 94 per cent.[122] The Chinese negotiators again followed their strategy of being generous regarding the financiers' financial compensation, so that the foreign negotiators eventually fixed the net price at 93 per cent, which guaranteed the DAB and British group an even more formidable profit from floating the loan.[123]

4.4 The Loan Agreement

After these details had been discussed, the final agreement for the Tianjin–Pukou railway loan was signed by Cordes, Bland and Liang Dunyan on 13 January 1908.[124] The final loan agreement undoubtedly was much more advantageous for the Chinese than the preliminary agreement of 1899 (see Table 4.1). They had gained the funds for constructing this important railway, which could not have been raised in China itself, and – similar to what had happened during the negotiations for the 1896 Anglo-German indemnity loan – had managed to increase the net price of the loan compared to the preliminary agreement. Moreover, they had acquired control over the construction and operation of the railway and won the option of an early

[119] Jordan to Grey (2 September 1907), TNA, FO 405/181, pp. 82–3.
[120] Cordes to Knappe (31 August 1908), PAAA, R17.868, p. 250. Also see Jordan to Grey (2 September 1907), TNA, FO 405/181, pp. 82–4.
[121] 'Protokoll, Konsortium für Asiatische Geschäfte' (31 August 1907), HADB, S2593; Bland to Jordan (9 September), TNA, FO 228/2591.
[122] DAB (Berlin) to Cordes (11 October 1907), TNA, FO 228/2591.
[123] Bland to CCR (16 October 1907), TNA, FO 228/2591; Rex to German Foreign Office (received on 24 October 1907), PAAA, R17.867, p. 139.
[124] For the agreement text see 'Agreement for the Imperial Chinese Government Five Percent Tientsin-Pukou Railway Loan' (13 January 1908), in MacMurray, *Treaties*, 1:684–93.

Table 4.1 Comparison of the preliminary and final agreements of the Tianjin–Pukou railway loan

	Loan sum	Interest rate	Net price	Loan period	Loan collateral	Construction and operation of the railway	Purchase of materials
Preliminary Agreement of 1899	£7.4 million	5%	90%	50 years (redemption possible after 30 years)	The railway line and equipment	Carried out by the Anglo-German Group	Carried out by the Anglo-German Group
Final Agreement of 1908	£5 million	5%	93% (94.5% for the second charge)	30 years (redemption possible after 10 years)	Lijin-taxes of the provinces Zhili, Shandong and Jiangsu	Carried out by the Chinese government	Carried out by the Anglo-German Group (5% commission)

Source: MacMurray, Treaties, 1:684–97

redemption after ten years, while even avoiding having the railway act as collateral for the loan or any stream of revenue put under foreign control as with previous loans. In their report to the throne, Yuan, Zhang and Liang also lauded the improved terms of the final loan agreement. They stressed that they had successfully divided 'constructing the railway and providing the loan into two different affairs' and emphasized that this railway loan agreement was better conceived than other railway loan agreements, so that China's sovereignty was not compromised in any way.[125] Many other officials shared these views and even the gentry of the three provinces were satisfied with the separation of the financing and construction of the railway.[126] Among foreigners, these new loan terms soon became known as the 'Tientsin-Pukow terms', as they marked a new phase in Chinese railway finance and gave China unprecedented control over the railway's construction and operation.[127] Unless one views any foreign involvement in Chinese railway development or the pledging of any revenue as collateral as problematic,[128] the terms attained by China must be seen as an important achievement of the Chinese negotiators and an important step in Chinese railway development. Constructing the Tianjin–Pukou railway was also a success and after four years of construction the complete line was opened for traffic in March 1913.[129]

At the same time, despite the fact that their role had been mostly reduced to financing the railway, the loan agreement with its favourable financial conditions was still very profitable for the foreign financiers. The first £3 million tranche of the £5 million loan was floated at 98.5 per cent in March 1908, while the second charge of £2 million was floated in June 1909 at par.[130] In addition, eventually the loan funds turned out to be insufficient and, in accordance with the 1908 loan agreement, an agreement for a supplementary loan of £4.8 million was concluded on the same loan terms in 1910. Of this supplementary loan, only £3 million was floated in November 1910 at 0.5 per cent

[125] Zhang, Yuan and Liang memorial (13 January 1908), *ZJTS*, p. 812.
[126] Ma, *Qingmo minchu tielu waizhai guan*, p. 137.
[127] Rhea, *Far Eastern Markets*, pp. 49–50; Morse, *The International Relations of the Chinese Empire*, 3:89–90. Morse calls them 'Pukow terms'. Since these writings, other Western-language scholarship has mostly also acknowledged the unprecedentedly favourable character of the loan conditions of the Tianjin–Pukou railway loan. See, for example, Schmidt, *Eisenbahnpolitik*, p. 132; Barth, *Imperialismen*, p. 287.
[128] Ma, *Qingmo minchu tielu waizhai guan*, p. 145; Sun, *Chinese Railways and British Interests*, p. 168.
[129] Schmidt, *Eisenbahnpolitik*, pp. 132–3.
[130] 'Consortium für Asiatische Geschäfte, Sitzung am 31. März 1908' (31 March 1908), HADB, S2593; Deutsche Bank (Berlin) to Deutsche Bank (London) (7 June 1909), HADB, S2595.

above par.[131] Despite the changed collateral, the railway bonds were very well received both in London and Berlin.[132] Following on from what we saw in Chapter 3, the high issue price and low interest rate of the loans showed that China continued to enjoy good credit on foreign bond markets and was able to borrow there cheaply. In accordance with the two loan agreements, the German consortium received an underwriter's margin of 5.5 per cent for the £5.04 million floated in Germany. While the expenses of floating the loans took up 2.95 per cent of the loan sum, this left about 2.55 per cent or £128,520 in profits for the German consortium banks.[133] In addition, materials worth 44 million reichsmark (~£2.1 million) were ordered from German industry, and, in accordance with the loan agreement, the German bankers earned 5 per cent or 2.2 million reichsmark in commissions.[134] Thus, the total profits of the consortium banks amounted to around £236,020.

The surviving subscription lists of the bonds show that a wide range of investors bought these Chinese bonds. Besides the consortium banks such as the Deutsche Bank, which kept some bonds for themselves, individual bankers like Deutsche Bank director Arthur von Gwinner also bought Tianjin–Pukou bonds. A significant number of bonds were also sold to smaller banks throughout Germany ranging from Lübeck in the north to Stuttgart in the south, which must have either kept these bonds or passed them on to their customers.[135] Thus investment in Chinese bonds was not simply a matter limited to a small group of Berlin investors interested in China. It became a national phenomenon that reached down to small investors often far away from Berlin.

   While German and British bankers could be satisfied with the reception of the bonds by the investing public, at times they were themselves surprised by the trust of foreign investors in Chinese bonds. This could make it 'difficult to give the Chinese [government] solemn warnings about its credit so long as

---

[131] 'Supplementary loan agreement for the Tientsin-Pukow Railway' (28 September 1910), in MacMurray, *Treaties*, 1:814–23; Deutsche Bank (Berlin), 'Vertraulich: 5% Tientsin-Pukow Eisenbahn-Ergänzungsanleihe von £ 4.800.000' (27 October 1910), HADB, S2597; Kuhlmann, *China's Foreign Debt*, p. 60.

[132] *BBC* (31 March 1908) in HADB, K07/002/I; *BBZ* (15 June 1909, evening edition); *BBZ* (3 November 1910, evening edition); King, *HSBC History*, 2:364–5; *Financial Times* (30 June 1909); *The Economist* (5 November 1910).

[133] 'Consortium für Asiatische Geschäfte, Sitzung am 31. März 1908' (31 March 1908), HADB, S2593. The exact percentage the consortium banks received is only known for the first charge of the Tianjin–Pukou loan. As the percentage for the second charge and the supplementary loan will most likely have been similar, it is assumed here that they earned the same profit margin for these two bond issues. 63 per cent or £5.04 million of the total floated loan sum of £8 million was floated by the DAB in Germany. See Kuhlmann, *China's Foreign Debt*, pp. 51, 60.

[134] Schmidt, *Eisenbahnpolitik*, p. 134.

[135] 'Tientsin-Pukow Eisenbahn Anleihe. Deutscher Anteil £1.890.000' (1908), HADB, S2594.

[investors continue] ... to proclaim [their] faith' in Chinese bonds.[136] The enthusiastic response of foreign investors to Chinese bonds and the only secondary importance they attached to the bonds' security did not go unnoticed in China. In 1908, the Board of Communications (Youchuanbu 郵傳部), which was now in charge of Chinese railway development, commented on the Tianjin–Pukou loan terms. It especially praised the fact that the revenues pledged as collateral were only 'an empty name' (xuming 虛名). It was also aware that Chinese bonds had been very well received on foreign markets in recent years and that the collateral pledged was 'empty and false and only existed in name to stir up investors, so that the market price [of the bonds] is comparatively high'. However, as the financiers received large profits from floating these bonds, they were content with this situation and did not even demand any real collateral. Despite pledging false collateral for railway loans, the Board was confident that China would be able to repay the loans with the high profits they expected from the railways.[137] While the assumption that the financiers were fully content with this situation was an overstatement, the Board of Communications certainly had an accurate view of how easy it now was for China to raise foreign capital abroad.

4.5 Conclusion

The Tianjin–Pukou railway loan agreement was a success for pragmatic reformers like Zhang Zhidong and Yuan Shikai, who believed that railways were of great importance for China's development but that for now foreign capital was needed for their construction.[138] It was also a victory for the central state, who in the last years of the Qing dynasty tried to bring railway construction back under its control from the local gentry.[139] For the moment, Yuan and Zhang had prevailed against the growing tide of nationalism, whose supporters saw railways as the symbol of foreign control over China and wished to oust foreigners from Chinese railway development. While it is true that foreigners

---

[136] Bland to Jordan (13 January 1909), TNA, FO 228/2592. On the general optimism of foreign investors in China's future and their willingness to new loan terms more favourable to the Chinese, also see King, History of the HSBC, 2:434, 504.

[137] Ye, Xia An huibian, pp. 15–16. The Board of Communications had been put in charge of Chinese railways in 1906. See Cui, 'Lun Qingmo tielu zhengce de yanbian', p. 75.

[138] Li sees the Tianjin–Pukou railway loan agreement together with other railway loan agreements as part of the 'triumph' of the 'realistic' approach to Chinese railway development of Yuan Shikai and Tang Shaoyi. However, he still views their actions mainly as a reaction of the central government to nationalist agitation by local elites, and subsumes them within the larger nationalist railway-rights recovery movement instead of seeing the approach of pragmatic officials such as Yuan as separate and essentially antagonistic to the nationalist railway-rights recovery movement. See Li, Railway-Rights Recovery Movement, especially pp. 273–4.

[139] Cui, 'Lun Qingmo tielu zhengce de yanbian', p. 75.

held a certain degree of control over Chinese railway construction, by the end
of the Qing period pragmatic Chinese reformers managed to limit such control
significantly and win more favourable terms for Chinese public loans than ever
before. What made attaining these favourable terms possible was the Chinese
negotiators' cooperation with foreign financiers, a new reluctance of foreign
governments to apply diplomatic pressure, the continued strong interest of
foreign financiers in investing in China and the Chinese exploitation of the
little knowledge foreign financiers possessed of Chinese public finance. Thus,
we once more see that, under the right conditions, the frontier was a space that
allowed for considerable Chinese agency in Sino-foreign interaction. In contrast, the railway rights recovery movement did a lot to inhibit the plans of
pragmatic reformers for railway construction, but, despite all their fervour,
they remained impractical in their critique and failed to propose or implement
a successful alternative scheme for Chinese railway development.[140] This
dichotomy between pragmatic reformers willing to use foreign capital and
their nationalist critics who resisted any foreign involvement in railway development, but were unable or unwilling to provide the necessary capital themselves, was one of the central problems of late Qing railway development.

This was also reflected in the fact that, despite all the intentions of the gentry
to raise capital, the Tianjin–Pukou railway was not redeemed early and
a supplementary loan was necessary to complete its construction.[141]
Nevertheless, despite their disagreement with the railway rights recovery
movement, Yuan and Zhang could use their agitation and the eagerness of
foreign financiers to gain better loan terms from the Anglo-German group.
Moreover, the negotiations showed that the information asymmetry that had
previously existed for both Chinese officials and foreign financiers had now
tilted in favour of China. While foreign financiers still knew little about
Chinese public finance, Chinese officials now had a much better understanding of how foreign financial markets worked compared to a decade or two
before.[142] They knew how popular Chinese bonds were on foreign markets and
that investors would buy them as long as some kind of security was provided.
As a result, the Chinese negotiators could exploit this information asymmetry
both to gain leverage in the negotiations and to gain favourable loan terms
without having to pledge any significant revenue stream as collateral. China's
growing financial internationalization during the last years of the Qing dynasty
thus also led to a greater familiarity of Chinese government elites with foreign

---

[140] Li, *Railway-Rights Recovery Movement*; Cui, 'Lun Qingmo tielu zhengce de yanbian',
pp. 74–5.

[141] In fact, it was not only not redeemed early after ten years, but China later defaulted on
the 1908 and 1910 Tianjin–Pukou loans. See Kuhlmann, *China's Foreign Debt*, pp. 51–6,
60–6.

[142] With regards to the Chinese negotiators, Barth also notes their increased understanding
of 'stock market and financial details'. See Barth, *Imperialismen*, p. 282.

bond markets and a growing ability of these elites to manipulate foreign investors.

For the German bankers, the loan agreement meant that they had finally realized their dream of financing railways for the Chinese state, which was supposed to generate high yields and large business for Germany's industry. They had pursued this dream since the 1880s and it had been a major reason for establishing the DAB. Their desire to finance Chinese railways went so far that they were eventually willing to give up many rights the preliminary treaty had given them, especially regarding control of the construction and operation of the railway and the use of the loan funds. Their willingness to grant favourable loan terms reached its peak in the negotiations for the Huguang railway loan between 1909 and 1911, the other major railway project the DAB was involved in. During the negotiations, the DAB used the 'Tientsin-Pukow terms' to outbid the British financiers, temporarily break out of the Anglo-German partnership and strike a deal with Zhang Zhidong to finally get a foothold in the Yangzi valley.[143]

As we have seen, these Chinese and foreign visions for Chinese railway development converged on the Chinese frontier in cities such as Beijing, Tianjin and Wuchang. Here, common interests and benefits and possibilities for cooperation could be discovered and led to the formation of transnational networks, which became essential for the realization of transnational projects like railway construction. In the case of the Tianjin–Pukou railway loan negotiations, this was reflected in the development of the Sino-British-German transnational network of government elites like Hu Yufen and Yuan Shikai, the HSBC, CCR and DAB, and the cooperation of these actors that eventually made the Tianjin–Pukou loan agreement possible. While there also existed diverging interests among the participants in this network, the foreign desire for gaining railway concessions from China and the Chinese need for foreign capital bound them together in a transnational network of inter-dependence and led to the necessity to cooperate and compromise to accomplish their common goal of constructing the railway. This cooperation was most evident in the exchange of favourable financial terms granted to the bankers in return for their giving up of control rights, which allowed the Chinese negotiators to appease the gentry-merchants. What was at the heart of such networks were the Sino-foreign 'contact zone', where actual decisions were reached on the local level, and middlemen like Heinrich Cordes or Liang Dunyan, who communicated and negotiated different interests and struck

---

[143] King, *HSBC History*, 2:395–417; Müller-Jabusch, *Deutsch-Asiatische Bank*, pp. 166–74. Eventually, the terms and securities of the final loan agreement for the Huguang railways loan were indeed similar to those of the Tianjin–Pukou railway loan. See 'Final Agreement for the Hukuang Imperial Government Railways', in MacMurray, *Treaties*, 1:866–79.

compromises. Within these networks, power relations were dynamic and the Chinese negotiators often had more leverage and could gain the upper hand. At the same time, these networks operated on a much larger scale. They connected people in far-flung places, such as Chinese officials sitting in the *Daotai*'s office in Tianjin negotiating loan terms and a private investor in a little German town using his savings to buy Chinese bonds. Thus, they showed the scale financial globalization had reached at the beginning of the twentieth century.

However, the dreams that both Chinese officials and German financiers had for Chinese railway development eventually evaporated. For China, the hopes that large-scale railway development could act as an antidote for China's ills and boost its economic development never materialized. By 1911, the departure from power of pragmatic officials like Yuan Shikai and Zhang Zhidong, who could reconcile central and local interests, and the emergence of the ineffective Zaifeng 載灃 government that tried to consolidate central control over railways against the will of local elites meant there was little chance for a continued reconciliation and compromise between pragmatists and nationalists regarding railway construction.[144] Instead, the question of whether China's railways should be centrally or locally controlled and built with foreign or Chinese capital became one of the factors that led to the 1911 revolution. After the revolution, political instability and the outbreak of the First World War soon made it increasingly difficult for China to attain the same favourable terms and scale of cooperation with foreign financiers to finance Chinese railway development with foreign money.[145] As the next chapter will show, while the years before the fall of the Qing dynasty had provided Chinese actors with a lot of leverage vis-à-vis their foreign interlocutors on the frontier, once conditions on the frontier changed – in particular once the relative political stability of Qing rule was gone and the new republican government needed to raise money quickly – the space for Chinese agency on the frontier shrank.

For German bankers, the dreams of filling the pockets of German investors and fuelling German industry by financing Chinese railways also were never fully realized. While the Tianjin–Pukou railway was a success, they had to make large concessions in terms of control and collateral to make it possible. Moreover, the Tianjin–Pukou railway loan and the 1911 agreement for the Huguang railway loan remained the only Chinese state railways the German bankers successfully financed before the First World War and the DAB's liquidation put an end to German involvement in Chinese railway

[144] Chang died in 1909 and Yuan temporarily fell from power in the same year. See Hummel, *Eminent Chinese*, pp. 27, 952. On Zaifeng's railway policy see Li, 'Zaifeng and late Qing Railway Policy', pp. 90–106.

[145] Yang, *Zhongguo jindai tielushi*, pp. 89–90; Ma, *Qingmo minchu tielu waizhai guan*, pp. 179–80; Schmidt, *Eisenbahnpolitik*, p. 132.

construction. The reason German bankers had only very limited success in financing Chinese railways can be partly attributed to the limitations imposed on the DAB because of the 1898 agreement with the HSBC. However, more broadly, China only enjoyed the combination of political stability and broad acceptance of using foreign capital for railway construction among Chinese officials that would have been necessary for large-scale railway development for some fifteen years before the fall of the Qing dynasty. This meant that foreign financed railway development in China never had the opportunity to truly take off like it did, for example, in the United States and the visions of late Qing reformers for large-scale railway construction were only to be fulfilled after 1949.[146]

Moreover, German investors who had bought Chinese railway bonds could not enjoy their high yields for long. They had to pay for the eagerness of German bankers to conclude railway loans, which had led them to accept questionable securities. Following China's political disintegration after 1911, the Chinese government defaulted on the Chinese railway loans floated in Germany during the 1920s and never fully repaid them.[147] Thus, in terms of railway development, for both Chinese officials and German bankers and investors the frontier largely remained a space for dreams and visions, but not for the actual realization of their plans.

---

[146] In 1949, only 21,810 kilometres of railway were in operation in China compared to 139,900 kilometres at the end of 2019. See Zhuang, *Zhongguo tielu jianshe*, p. 8 and National Bureau of Statistics of China, *China Statistical Yearbook 2020*, ch. 16.3. On the role of foreign investment in American railway development see Wilkins, *The History of Foreign Investment*, pp. 190–325.

[147] Kuhlmann, *China's Foreign Debt*, pp. 51–6, 60–6, 69–73; 'Gilt-Edged Weaken and Rally', *Financial Times* (5 November 1925); 'Chinese Loans Secured on Internal Revenues', *Financial Times* (11 December 1930). In 1987, a Sino-British agreement provided for a small partial payout to British bondholders of defaulted Chinese bonds. See Burns, 'China to Settle UK Debts', *Financial Times* (6 June 1987); Waibel, *Sovereign Defaults*, p. 200.

5

Global Markets, International Finance and the 1911 Revolution in China

In June 1912, the executive board of the Deutsch-Asiatische Bank (DAB) in Berlin reflected on the impact of the 1911 revolution on China and the Chinese economy:

> The year 1911 constitutes an important episode in the history of China. The Manchu Dynasty, which had ruled since 1644, was overthrown and a republican form of constitution proclaimed. The calm observer, who had seen how the work of reform in China had progressed slowly but inexorably, stands surprised before this sudden change and hesitates to answer in the affirmative the question whether the new government will hold together the different population groups of the large empire and bring to the country a long-lasting period of peaceful development. . . . The failure of important government functions, which was caused by the [revolutionary] movement and currently remains prominent as an unpleasant phenomenon, disturbs the order in the country, has led to the temporary drying up of regular sources of [government] revenue and has thrown capital and productive work into a state of caution, which we cannot necessarily hope will be overcome soon.[1]

This assessment by the executive board reflects the uncertainty the revolution had brought to China and the business of the bank. It shows that the bankers were hesitant to welcome the departure of the Qing dynasty, which had guaranteed relative stability in the decades before and had started a large-scale reform effort that the bankers had financed and supported. The outbreak of the 1911 revolution replaced this stability with unprecedented uncertainty and insecurity. This chapter traces how the German bankers tried to manage this insecurity and the political risk connected to it and what role they played in China's transition from empire to republic.

The Chinese revolution of 1911 was a turning point in modern Chinese history. It brought an end to imperial rule and ushered in the first Chinese republic. Much research both in English and Chinese has been produced that has interpreted the 1911 revolution and its causes and aftermath from different

---

[1] DAB, 'Geschäfts-Bericht für das Jahr 1911', HADB, Geschäftsberichte, Deutsch-Asiatische Bank.

perspectives.[2] However, so far the financial side of the revolution and the role international financial connections played in its outcome have been understudied.[3] The research that discusses foreign banks during the revolution and its aftermath at some length has been largely limited to investigating the negotiations of the Reorganisation Loan of 1913, mainly from the perspective of Western diplomacy and imperialism.[4] In contrast, this chapter attempts to look at the 1911 revolution from a financial perspective and shed light on both the impact the revolution had on international financial markets and the influence of foreign financiers and international financial connections on the outcome of the revolution and the establishment of the new Chinese republic. Moreover, while previous scholarship on the relationship between bond markets and political risk has mainly focussed on Europe and European government bonds,[5] this chapter also sheds light on how Western bond markets reacted to and Western financiers involved with these markets tried to manage political crises and sudden increases in political risk in non-European countries such as China.

This chapter will first sketch the dire financial situation the Chinese government found itself in on the eve of the revolution. It will then turn to the reaction of the financial markets in London and Berlin to the revolution and scrutinize how foreign bankers attempted to maintain China's credit abroad. The chapter then returns to China and describes how both the Qing government and the revolutionaries tried to use foreign financiers to gain financial support for their party. Finally, I explain the role foreign financiers played in

---

[2] See, for example, Wright, *China in Revolution*; Esherick, *Reform and Revolution in China*; Esherick, 'How the Qing Became China', pp. 229–59; Zheng, *The Politics of Rights*. See also Zhang, 'Xinhai Geming yanjiu', pp. 4–10; Zhang and Tian, 'Xin shiji zhi chu de Xinhai Geming shi yanjiu', pp. 89–98; Sun, 'Xinhai Geming bainian yanjiu zongshu', pp. 95–110.

[3] For a recent exception see van de Ven, *Breaking with the Past*, pp. 162–71.

[4] See, for example, Edwards, *Finance and Diplomacy*, pp. 158–75; Barth, *Imperialismen*, pp. 386–401; Hirata, 'Britain's Men on the Spot in China', pp. 895–934; Xia Liangcai, 'Guoji Yinhangtuan he Xinhai Geming', pp. 188–215; Xu et al., *Cong bainian quru*, 2:91–128. In his institutional history of the HSBC, Frank King also focusses on the loan negotiations and only mentions in passing the reaction of the London bond market and the role of the HSBC in maintaining China's credit. See King, *HSBC History*, 2:472–504. King overemphasizes the role of the HSBC in maintaining China's credit and only comments on the reaction of the London bond market at the end of 1911. See King, *HSBC History*, 2:475–6.

[5] Ferguson, 'Political Risk', pp. 70–112; Malik, *Bankers and Bolsheviks*. Goetzmann, Ukhov and Zhu only provide a short overview of the impact of political events on the long-term development of Chinese bond yields without exploring the specific reactions of bond markets or the actions of bankers. See Goetzmann, Ukhov and Zhu, 'China and the World Financial Markets', pp. 277–9. On their analysis, also see Section 5.5 of this chapter. Political risk is defined as the possible harm or negative impact on businesses, investments and financial markets caused by political actions, events or developments. See McKellar, *A Short Guide to Political Risk*, p. 3 and Ferguson, 'Political Risk', p. 70.

financing the new republican government and situate the role of foreign borrowing during the 1911 revolution and its aftermath within the long-term development of China's reliance on debt. This chapter shows that the measures taken by foreign bankers to maintain China's credit and their decision to support the new republic under Yuan Shikai exerted a crucial influence on the outcome of the revolution and the founding of the new republic. We will thus see how global financial connections and interactions could have a profound impact on turning points in Chinese history like the 1911 revolution. At the same time, the continuation of the policy of foreign borrowing by the new republican government meant that the Chinese state's reliance on government borrowing continued into the republican period.

5.1   Chinese Finance on the Eve of the Revolution

When a revolutionary uprising broke out in Wuchang upstream from Shanghai on 10 October 1911 and the Qing government faced the challenge of responding to this threat to its power, Chinese public finance was in a grave state. When the Qing government launched its *Xinzheng* reforms in 1901, both the central and most of the provincial governments were out of money. Indemnity payments, corruption, lavish spending by the court and increasing costs for the military and disaster relief had further worsened the critical condition of China's public finance. As a result, a large part of the costly *Xinzheng* reforms was paid for by foreign loans. Not only did the central government pay with foreign money for large reform projects like the Tianjin–Pukou railway and to make up for its growing financial deficit, but as the central government's financial control over the provinces continued to be weakened, provincial governors also increasingly did the same.[6] This growing demand for foreign loans combined with the willingness of foreign financiers and investors to lend to China with favourable conditions, as seen in the previous chapter, led to a continued increase in Chinese foreign borrowing and the further internationalization of Chinese public finance (see Figure 5.1). Overall, China's foreign borrowing rose from an annual average of 1,712,028 Kuping taels between 1867 and 1894 to an annual average of 47,604,003 Kuping taels between 1895 and 1911. While China had only borrowed 52 million Kuping taels before 1895, this figure rose to 809 million Kuping taels between 1895 and 1911.[7] Even if one subtracts the large sums China had to borrow for the repayment of the Japanese indemnity from this sum, it still borrowed around 480 million Kuping taels for

---

[6] Zhou, *Wan Qing caizheng yu shehui bianqian*, pp. 315–23, 379–401; Ma, *Waizhai yu wan Qing zhengju*, pp. 172–91.

[7] Calculated according to the data in Xu et al., *Cong bainian quru*, 1:517–29. I do not take into account the large Boxer Indemnity, as this was a direct advance given by the foreign governments involved and not a foreign loan.

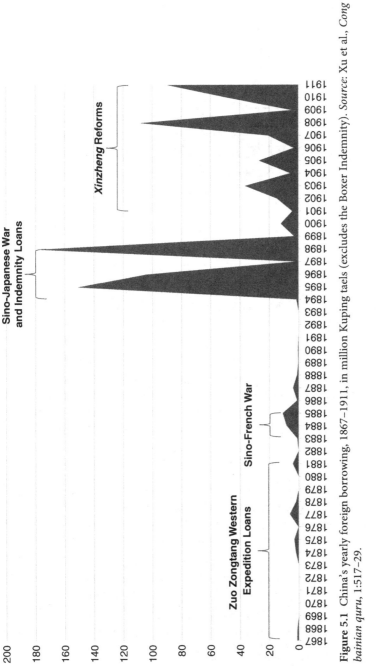

Figure 5.1 China's yearly foreign borrowing, 1867–1911, in million Kuping taels (excludes the Boxer Indemnity). *Source:* Xu et al., *Cong bainian quru*, 1:517–29.

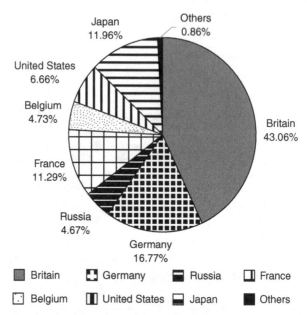

Figure 5.2 Chinese foreign borrowing by country, 1899–1911 (excludes the Boxer Indemnity). *Source*: Xu, *Zhongguo jindai waizhai tongji*, pp. 32, 34, 36, 92.

other purposes during this period. Moreover, as Figure 5.2 shows, the internationalization of Chinese public finance also continued to be reflected in the diversity of the sources of China's foreign borrowing. This also indicates that there continued to be significant foreign competition for Chinese loans Chinese officials could exploit.[8]

This increased borrowing meant that the central government and the provinces had to spend more and more of their revenues on the repayment of loans. Even though the Qing's revenue had almost tripled since 1900, in 1909 the Chinese government still had to spend 12 per cent of its total yearly income of 263 million Kuping taels on the servicing of foreign debt.[9] Most

---

[8] With regards to Chinese railway loans, Brötel also briefly notes that competition allowed Chinese diplomacy to attain 'a loosening of the control and binding clauses'. See Brötel, *Frankreich im Fernen Osten*, p. 580. A similar point about railway loan conditions, though neglecting the active role of Chinese agency in exploiting competition, is also briefly made in Nishimura, 'Honkon Shanhai Ginkō 1865–1913', p. 600.

[9] For the yearly income see Zhou, *Wan Qing caizheng jingji yanjiu*, pp. 157–60. For the expenses for the servicing of foreign debt see Chen, *1895–1936 nian*, p. 82. This does not include payments for the Boxer Indemnity.

provinces were in a similar situation. A good example is Hubei province, where Zhang Zhidong and his successors as governor-general had resorted to foreign borrowing to fund reform projects. The governor-general of Huguang Rui Zheng 瑞澂 in 1911 had to appeal to the court for permission to contract a foreign loan of 2 million taels for the repayment of old debt borrowed from Chinese and foreign merchants. He stated that 'Zhang Zhidong, when he was governor-general, bought warships and trained troops, and my predecessors carried out Xinzheng [reform] projects during the past years. All of this was paid for by loans.'[10] This need to borrow money just for the repayment of old loans showed the difficult financial situation some provinces found themselves in. The consequence of this trend of diminishing financial resources and increasing expenditures and borrowing due to the costs of reform and the repayment of debt was that the annual deficit of the Chinese central government grew from 30 million in 1903 to 41 million in 1910, and most provinces were also in deficit.[11] While the increased internationalization of Chinese public finance had opened Western capital markets as a new source of income for the Chinese state, by the end of the Qing, this had led to a strong reliance on foreign borrowing that had further increased and not solved the financial problems the Qing state had found itself in since the beginning of the nineteenth century. Thus, when the 1911 revolution broke out, Chinese public finance was in a grave state. Chinese officials had not only developed a reliance on using foreign borrowing to raise large sums of money, but because of the problematic financial situation of both the central and provincial governments, they were now hardly able to react to any emergencies that required large amounts of money without resorting to more foreign borrowing.

5.2 Maintaining China's Credit on Foreign Bond Markets

After the Chinese revolution erupted in October 1911, it quickly spread throughout China. Uprisings mushroomed and military conflict ensued between the revolutionary armies and the forces of the ruling Qing dynasty.[12] Foreign banks quickly felt the impact of these events. A financial crisis hit the banking sector that caused many Chinese banks to go bankrupt. Moreover, the revolution also had a negative effect on China's foreign trade, which in turn affected the business of foreign banks, who financed China's foreign trade. Only the restoration of a proper government and stability could

---

[10] Rui Zheng memorial (25 April 1911), *QWSL*, 3:224. On foreign loans used to pay for the reforms in Hubei also see Esherick, *Reform and Revolution*, pp. 114–15.

[11] Zhou, *Wan Qing caizheng yu shehui bianqian*, pp. 384–6.

[12] On the historical background of the revolution, see Gasster, 'The Republican Revolutionary Movement', pp. 463–534; Wright, *China in Revolution*.

resuscitate commerce.[13] However, despite the disastrous state of Chinese commerce after the revolution, the greatest concern of foreign bankers at that time was the performance of Chinese bonds in Europe and the mainten- ance of China's credit abroad. In 1911, London and Berlin were the main markets where Chinese bonds were traded.[14] In the years before the revolu- tion, Chinese bonds had performed well in London and Berlin – also compared to those of other developing countries – and were always traded either at a premium or only slightly below par.[15] It was this favourable credit China enjoyed abroad that had made it possible for the Chinese government to borrow such large amounts at a comparatively cheap price and favourable terms in the preceding years.

News of the uprising in Wuchang reached Britain on 12 October and 'brought a feeling of uncertainty over the [bond] market' in London.[16] In Berlin, investors also grew concerned about the situation in China and soon the topic that 'received most of the attention' at the bourse was 'the news about the uprising in China, which indicates that the danger of the revolutionary movement is in fact greater than previously expected'.[17] Newspapers in London and Berlin kept on informing investors about the course of events in China and increasingly reported on 'the progress made by the rebels' and 'the sympathy with which the rebellion is regarded throughout China'.[18] The Berliner Börsen-Zeitung, a newspaper specifically published for German invest- ors, reported on the situation in China and expressed worries that a 'civil war [between the government and the revolutionaries] appears to be becoming

---

[13] On the immediate impact of the revolution on Chinese financial markets and trade, see Moazzin, 'Investing in the New Republic', pp. 508–14.

[14] See the overview of China's outstanding debt in Heinemann et al., Saling's Börsen-Jahrbuch für 1912/1913, pp. 212–18. For only slightly different numbers, see Bell and Woodhead, The China Year Book, 1912, pp. 298–301. While Chinese bonds could be freely traded within Europe, this assessment is made according to the bonds' place of issue. According to Xu Yisheng, Britain and Germany were also China's greatest creditors overall for the period between the Sino-Japanese War and the 1911 revolution. See Xu, Zhongguo jindai waizhai tongji, p. 92. For details of individual public loans during this period, see Kuhlmann, China's Foreign Debt.

[15] Ernst Heinemann et al., Saling's Börsen-Jahrbuch, pp. 212–18; Investor's Monthly Manual (1905–1910). The only exception was a 7 per cent loan floated in London in 1894, which, unlike the other loans, was denominated in silver, which explains its lower price. For a comparison with other Asian sovereign bonds see Goetzmann, Ukhov and Zhu, 'China and the World Financial Markets', pp. 277–85.

[16] 'Money Market', The Times (London) (14 October 1911).

[17] BBZ (16 October 1911, evening edition).

[18] Quote from 'The Chinese Government and the Rebellion', The Times (London) (27 October 1911). Also see 'Die Revolution in China', Berliner Tageblatt (18 October 1911); 'The Manchu Dynasty and the Chinese Revolution', The Economist (21 October 1911).

more and more likely'.[19] While there were also more positive reports that 'the Chinese troubles will soon come to an end',[20] there existed a general anxiety about the political instability in China. The uncertainty on the bond markets led to a price fall of some 'Far Eastern stocks ... on account of the Revolution'.[21] This reaction on the bond markets in London and Berlin shows clearly that the Qing dynasty – despite its problems – at least to a certain extent had been seen as a regime that guaranteed stability in China. Once revolution broke out and the Qing government seemed at risk of falling, markets became nervous that the previous stability might be lost. Figure 5.3 shows the price development of China bonds in Britain and Germany immediately after the revolution using the example of the two large Chinese indemnity loans floated in 1896 and 1898. As we can see, between 7 October and 30 November the price average of these bonds decreased from 102.125 per cent to 97.75 per cent in Britain and from 100.4 per cent to 96.65 per cent in Germany.

This volatility in the price of Chinese bonds was a concern not only for bondholders, but also for banks like the DAB and the Hongkong and Shanghai Banking Corporation (HSBC), who had underwritten and floated many loans

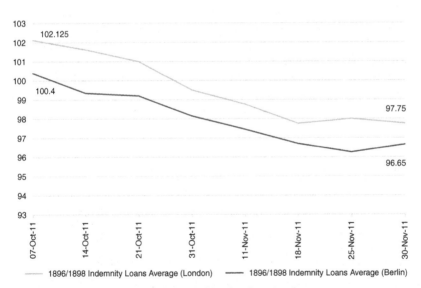

Figure 5.3 Price of British and German China bonds, 7 October 1911 to 30 November 1911, in per cent. *Source: The Economist, Investor's Monthly Manual, BBZ.*

---

[19] 'Die chinesischen Wirren', *BBZ* (25 October 1911, evening edition).
[20] *BBZ* (30 October 1911, evening edition).
[21] 'Money Markets', *The Economist* (21 October 1911).

for the Chinese government in Europe in the past. For these banks, a worsening of China's credit not only could hurt their reputation as under-writers of Chinese loans, but naturally could also threaten the floating of future Chinese loans, which represented an important part of the business of these banks. Given the reliance of the Chinese government on foreign borrowing, any new regime that could restore stability in China for Chinese commerce would most likely depend on the ability to continue to borrow foreign capital. As Frank King has argued for the HSBC and its loan business more generally, foreign bankers also had an interest in protecting China's credit because of a feeling of responsibility towards existing owners of bonds, the bankers' own investment in Chinese bonds and a long-term business interest in financially supporting Chinese economic growth.[22]

The greatest fear of these bankers was that China would default on its loans. Charles Addis, an experienced British banker that had worked in China for the HSBC for many years and from 1911 served as the British bank's senior manager in London, believed that 'even a temporary failure of the [Chinese] Government to meet its obligations' would have had a serious impact on China's credit.[23] Although these foreign banks still held limited funds to the credit of the Chinese government, at the end of 1911 the first payments of foreign loans fell due without payment having been arranged by the Chinese government.[24] Thus, there existed the serious threat of a full Chinese sovereign default. The concerns of the bankers grew further when news appeared in late October that the revenues of the Chinese government from the Yangzi provinces, which 'contributed the greater portion of money required for monthly remittances' for the servicing of loans, had stopped flowing.[25] Furthermore, in November 1911 some of the rebels abolished the *lijin* tax, which had been

[22] King, *History*, 2:482–4. King makes this argument not in specific reference to the situation immediately after the outbreak of the 1911 revolution when political instability threat-ened China's credit, but about the HSBC bankers and their loan business and opposition to 'ill-advised borrowing' in general. Thus, he also mentions that China would wish to tap foreign capital markets after a loan agreement was reached as a reason for the HSBC bankers to oppose such 'ill-advised borrowing' and preserve China's credit.

[23] Addis to Campbell (2 December 1911), TNA, FO 405/205, p. 324. On Addis, see Dayer, 'Addis, Sir Charles Stewart', *Oxford Dictionary of National Biography*, 23 September 2004, www.oxforddnb.com/view/10.1093/ref:odnb/9780198614128.001.0001/odnb-9780198614128-e-38334.

[24] King, *HSBC History*, 2:474–5. King explains that the funds held in the Shanghai branches of the banks could not be used for payments in the absence of instructions from the Chinese government. However, there is evidence that for a time money held in London to the credit of the Chinese government, possibly having already been transferred for that purpose before the revolution, was used for loan payments for the Shanghai–Hangzhou–Ningbo and Shanghai–Nanjing Railway Loans. See Jordan to Grey (16 November 1911), TNA, FO 405/205, pp. 335–6.

[25] Urbig to Townsend (27 October 1911), TNA, FO 405/205, p. 177.

pledged as a guarantee for several loans.[26] The political developments in China had not only affected the business of foreign banks on the spot in China, but had also increased the political risk of those multinational banks that had underwritten Chinese bonds and for those investors that owned Chinese government bonds. Clearly, this new situation had to be managed somehow in Europe until things calmed down in China and stability could be restored.

The first measure taken by foreign banks to mitigate the impact of the revolution on Chinese bonds was that they pledged to pay the interest payments on Chinese loans should there be delays in Chinese payments. This strategy was first fixed during an international banking conference held in Paris on 8 November 1911 with French and American bankers, with whom the HSBC and DAB had formed a consortium for issuing Chinese loans in 1910. This consortium was known as the Four Power Groups (or Four Groups) consortium (Figure 5.4) and constituted the most powerful foreign financial consortium in China. In May 1911 it had signed the Huguang railway loan with the Chinese government.[27] At the conference in Paris, the problem of 'coupons [of Chinese loans] falling due was discussed and there was no difference of opinion among the Groups that such coupons should be protected as far as possible and that all Groups should arrange the matter in the same way'.[28] As Addis later explained, the understanding of the groups was that the bankers would 'take common action for the protection of these coupons by paying the money themselves'.[29] Hence, the bankers were essentially pledging their own money to maintain China's credit.

As the 6 per cent 1895 Gold Loan floated by the HSBC in London was due first, the HSBC was the first bank to issue a statement that it would purchase the coupons for this loan.[30] The Nationalbank für Deutschland, which was a member of the Konsortium für Asiatische Geschäfte (KfAG) and had floated a Chinese loan in Germany in 1895, also soon pledged to pay for due coupons.[31] When payments for the 1898 indemnity loan were about to be due, the KfAG in

---

[26] 'Minutes of Meeting of the French, British, German & American Groups at the Offices of the Banque de l'Indo-Chine, Paris, on the 8th November, 1911' (8 November 1911), HADB, S2592.

[27] On the development of the consortium, see King, *HSBC History*, 2:406–15, 434–45. An old but still useful account is Field, *American Participation in the China Consortiums*, chapters 2–4.

[28] 'Minutes of Meeting of the French, British, German & American Groups at the Offices of the Banque de l'Indo-Chine, Paris, on the 8th November, 1911' (8 November 1911), HADB, S2592.

[29] Addis to Campbell (2 December 1911), TNA, FO 405/205, p. 324.

[30] 'Chinese Imperial Government 6% Gold Loan of 1895, £3,000,000 (Notice)' (21 December 1911), TNA, FO 371/1098, p. 351. Also see King, *HSBC History*, 2:475.

[31] 'Consortium für Asiatische Geschäfte, Protokoll der Sitzung vom 27. December 1911' (27 December 1911), S2592, HADB; DAB to Deutsche Bank (28 December 1911), HADB, S2592.

Figure 5.4 The Beijing representatives of the German, British, French and American groups of the Four Groups consortium. From left to right: Heinrich Cordes (Deutsch-Asiatische Bank), Edward Guy Hillier (HSBC), Maurice Casenave (Banque de l'Indochine), Willard D. Straight (J. P. Morgan & Co.). From *The Far Eastern Review* 8, no. 3 (1911). Image courtesy of P. A. Crush Chinese Railway Collection.

Berlin pledged to pay both the coupons and drawn bonds due, as the HSBC had now agreed to pay drawn bonds as well.[32] British banks and syndicates other than the HSBC, such as the Chartered Bank and the Peking Syndicate, also paid interest coupons for due bonds. As the secretary of the Peking Syndicate put it, this was done to avoid the 'disastrous effect [a Chinese default would have] on all Chinese Government securities'.[33] Thus, the foreign financiers used their own

---

[32] 'Consortium für Asiatische Geschäfte. Protokoll der Sitzung vom 19. Februar 1912' (19 February 1912), HADB, S2592.

[33] Quote from Peking Syndicate to Foreign Office (19 December 1911), TNA, FO 405/205, p. 417; 'Memorandum communicated to Wai-wu Pu' (4 January 1912), TNA, FO 405/208, p. 123. In the case of the Peking Syndicate, the sum for the payment of the interest coupons was included in a loan to the Imperial Chinese Railways.

money during the months following the revolution to avert a Chinese failure to service its debt and maintain China's credit, although it was yet unclear if and when a stable Chinese government that could repay them would be established.

While the banks were willing to put forward their own money for the time being, it soon became clear that a long-term solution for guaranteeing the payment of Chinese bonds needed to be found. As Hillier put it, the 'gravity and uncertainty of [the] situation have so increased since [the] Paris Conference' in November that the banks could not 'prolong indefinitely' their pledge of paying for interest.[34] For the time being, discussions of both British and German bankers focussed mainly on securing the Customs revenue under control of the British Inspector General Francis Aglen (Figure 5.5), who after Robert Hart's death in 1911 had succeeded the latter as head of the Chinese Maritime Customs Service. As we have seen, a significant number of Chinese loans were hypothecated on Customs revenue.[35] Therefore, the second measure that bankers took to maintain China's credit was to work with Aglen to secure the Customs revenue for the servicing of Chinese loans. As early as 14 October 1911, Aglen had started devising plans to deposit Customs revenue at the HSBC to secure them from the revolutionaries and ensure the repayment of foreign debt. In December 1911, he then ordered the customs commissioners, who until now had exercised no control over the revenue, to assume control over the revenue.[36] The Chinese government had at first planned to ask for 'deferring the payment' of the Boxer Indemnity, which in October had been the first payment due to be paid from the Customs revenue to a foreign party, but as this 'would have ruined [China's] credit', the Chinese officials decided to 'fulfil the payment as usual', and, agreeing to Aglen's plan, 'instructed [him] to place into foreign banks the whole amount of the Customs revenue, which will be used to pay the indemnity and foreign loans' hypothecated on Customs revenue.[37]

In November 1911, the foreign banks in Shanghai proposed that a commission was to be established consisting of those banks whose countries received parts of the Boxer Indemnity, which was not a loan, but also hypothecated on Customs revenue. This commission was to elect an executive commission consisting of the DAB, the HSBC and the Russo-Asiatic Bank. The Inspector General was to remit the Customs revenue to these three banks every

---

[34] HSBC (Beijing) to Addis (5 December 1911), TNA, FO 405/205, p. 347.
[35] HSBC (Beijing) to Addis (5 December 1911), TNA, FO 405/205, p. 347; DAB to Deutsche Bank (4 January 1912), HADB, S2592. On Francis Aglen, see Oxbury, 'Aglen, Sir Francis Arthur', *Oxford Dictionary of National Biography*, 23 September 2004, www .oxforddnb.com/view/10.1093/ref:odnb/9780198614128.001.0001/odnb-9780198614128- e-37097.
[36] Van de Ven, *Breaking with the Past*, pp. 162–3.
[37] Waiwubu to Liu Yulin (21 November 1911), TNA, FO 405/205, p. 281.

Figure 5.5   Francis Arthur Aglen (1869–1932). Sketch by Juel Madsen, early 1920s. From Juel Madsen, *Some China Personalities.*

week to repay those loans guaranteed by Customs revenue. The remaining surplus would then be used for the repayment of the Boxer Indemnity starting at the end of 1912.[38] Franz Urbig, now the head of the supervisory board of the DAB, agreed with this proposal and wrote to Addis that he considered it 'very reasonable' and especially stressed that not only was 'mak[ing] effective the security given by the maritime customs' the banks' 'duty towards the bond-holders', but safeguarding it was also necessary for the 'protection of [the banks'] issuing credit'.[39] By the end of December diplomatic support for this measure was also forthcoming.[40] In January 1912, an International Commission of Bankers was established. From now on, the Customs revenue was transferred in equal amounts to the HSBC, the DAB and the Russo-Asiatic Bank to ensure the repayment of China's foreign obligations.[41]

---

[38] DAB (Shanghai) to DAB (Berlin) (28 November 1911), HADB, S2592.
[39] Urbig to Addis (30 December 1911), TNA, FO 405/208, p. 22. On Urbig being the head of the supervisory board, see Müller-Jabusch, *Deutsch-Asiatische Bank*, p. 314.
[40] DAB to Deutsche Bank (4 January 1912), HADB, S2592.
[41] Van de Ven, *Breaking with the Past*, p. 167.

In London, Addis published a telegram by Aglen in the *Times*, which confirmed the establishment of the commission and the safety of the repayment of Chinese loans secured by Customs revenue. Addis was certain that this would 'hardly fail to have a reassuring effect upon the holders of Chinese bonds'.[42] He continued to publish reports on customs funds received by the foreign banks to reassure investors.[43] German bankers do not seem to have used newspapers in the same way to publicize the establishment of the commission, although news about the establishment certainly would have reached Berlin. This different approach was possibly because, unlike the HSBC, which was a relatively small bank, Chinese loans floated in Germany were guaranteed by the DAB and the members of the KfAG, which comprised all major German banks and whose reputation must have bolstered the trust of investors in Chinese bonds. For the German consortium, the main advantage of the establishment of the commission thus was that it could reduce its guarantees for the payment of loans floated by the DAB, as at least the servicing of those loans secured by Customs revenue was now ensured.[44] Both in the British and the German case the arrangement the foreign bankers concluded with the Customs Service and the foreign diplomats had a reassuring effect for investors and provided a long-term solution for the servicing of a large part of Chinese loans, thereby also maintaining China's credit.

Besides these two measures, the German bankers took a further step to deal with the increased political risk for investors and to maintain China's credit. They pooled money to actively intervene in the bond market in Berlin and buy up Chinese bonds to stabilize their price, especially for those bonds not secured by Customs revenue. It is unclear whether British banks took similar measures, but unlike the HSBC or the Chartered Bank, the German banks united in the KfAG possessed such a large capital power that they were able to pool enough money easily without putting any single member of the consortium at too much risk. After the outbreak of the 1911 revolution, German bankers started to buy up Chinese bonds on 14 October.[45] Two days later, bankers of the Disconto-Gesellschaft and Deutsche Bank met at the Berlin bourse and agreed that a consortium was to be established to purchase bonds for the purpose of 'price regulation' of Chinese bonds. The costs were split among the consortium banks.[46]

---

[42] Addis to Langley (1 February 1912), TNA, FO 405/208, p. 163. For the telegram from Aglen see Aglen to HSBC (London) (31 January 1912), TNA, FO 405/208, p. 163 and 'Chinese Customs Revenues: Early Resumption of Loan Service Payments', *The Times (London)* (2 February 1912).

[43] 'Chinese Customs Revenue. Recent Improvement Maintained', *The Times (London)* (5 February 1912); 'Chinese Loan Service. Payments Expected Shortly', *The Times (London)* (7 February 1912).

[44] DAB to Deutsche Bank (2 March 1912), HADB, S2592.

[45] 'Aufnahme-Consortium für Chinesische Anleihen' (30 December 1911), HADB, S2606.

[46] Disconto-Gesellschaft to Deutsche Bank (16 October 1911), HADB, S2606.

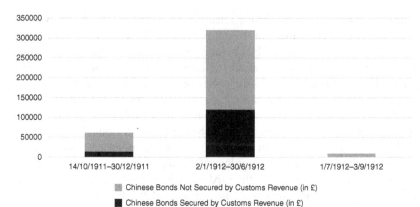

Figure 5.6 Chinese bonds purchased by German consortium, 14 October 1911 to 3 September 1912, in pound sterling. *Source*: Relevant tables in HADB, S2606.

On the following day, it was decided to extend the consortium to include all the members of the KfAG, as there was the possibility that the volume of the 'intervention purchases' could grow further.[47] As Figure 5.6 shows, during the following year the consortium bought up a large number of Chinese bonds to increase demand in the market and prop up the price for these bonds. It needs to be pointed out that the consortium not only purchased but also sold bonds at the same time.[48] Figure 5.6 shows the total volume of purchases rather than the consortium's balance of payments. While purchases remained limited to only £61,260 between October and December 1911, they rose sharply to a total of £320,375 in the first half of 1912. This sum eventually decreased to only £9,460 in the last months before the consortium decided in December 1912 that further purchases were unnecessary for the time being.[49] Importantly, the bankers spent more money on purchasing bonds not secured by Customs revenue. This becomes especially clear when we consider that the majority of Chinese bonds traded in Berlin were secured by Customs revenue. This suggests that the establishment of the bankers' commission in Shanghai reassured German investors of the security of bonds secured by Customs revenue and also reflects that members of the KfAG in December 1911 appeared more concerned

---

[47] Quote from Disconto-Gesellschaft to Deutsche-Bank (17 October 1911), HADB, S2606; Disconto-Gesellschaft to Deutsche Bank (20 October 1911), HADB, S2606.
[48] For the sales, see the relevant tables in HADB, S2606.
[49] Disconto-Gesellschaft to Deutsche Bank (4 December 1912), HADB, S2606.

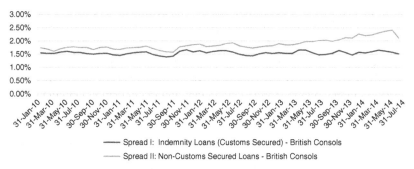

Figure 5.7 Spreads of British China bonds (current yield), January 1910 to July 1914. *Source: Investor's Monthly Manual, 1910–14.*

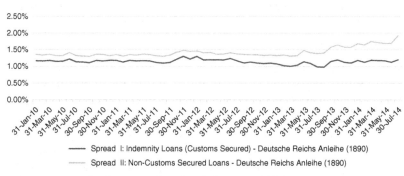

Figure 5.8 Spreads of German China bonds (current yield), January 1910 to July 1914. *Source: BBZ, 1910–14.*

with the servicing of those bonds not secured by Customs revenue.[50] While the correspondence of the consortium contains no specific information on the direct impact of the purchases on bond prices, the fact that the consortium continued to carry out large intervention purchases throughout the first half of 1912 suggests that they believed purchases were necessary to stabilize bond prices until then.

If we look at the overall performance of Chinese bonds on the London and Berlin markets from 1910 to 1914 provided in Figures 5.7 and 5.8, we can see how the measures taken by the bankers were reflected in the performance of Chinese bonds. The two figures use the current yield of these Chinese bonds, as this is the most common indicator used to compare bond prices and the performance of bonds. The current yield is calculated by dividing the annual interest payable by the bond price. Therefore, a decrease in the bond price

---

[50] 'Consortium für Asiatische Geschäfte, Protokoll der Sitzung vom 27. December 1911' (27 December 1911), HADB, S2592.

results in an increase of its current yield.[51] Chinese bonds are divided into two samples of bonds traded in both London and Berlin. One consists of the two Anglo-German indemnity loans of 1896 and 1898, both secured by revenues collected by the Maritime Customs Service ran by foreigners, and the other consists of three railway loans not secured by Customs revenue or any other revenues under foreign control.[52] The two graphs (Spread I and Spread II) show the spread between the two samples of Chinese bonds and British consols and German sovereign bonds, respectively, thereby demonstrating how the Chinese bonds performed compared to the overall development of the markets.[53]

From the two figures, we can see that overall yields for Chinese bonds remained stable throughout the 1911 revolution and its aftermath. Clearly, the measures taken by the bankers in London and Berlin were effective in limiting the impact of the increased political risk in China on European bond markets and in preventing any large-scale fluctuations in bond prices. The bankers succeeded in maintaining China's credit and mitigating the impact of the 1911 revolution and the increased political risk for investments in China on foreign bond markets. The two figures also show that Chinese bonds with and without foreign control of Chinese revenues performed similarly before 1911. There seems to have been a slight divergence in bond yields between the two groups of bonds only after the revolution, indicating that investors to a certain degree lost confidence in bonds secured by revenues without foreign control. As we will see, the overall stability of bond yields achieved by the foreign bankers allowed China to continue to raise capital on foreign markets and thereby keep the new republic afloat. However, we now must first turn to the role foreign capital played in the transition from the Qing empire to the new republic. Because of the destitute financial reserves of both the Qing government and the revolutionaries, foreign financiers came to play a decisive role in this process.

5.3   Foreign Capital and the Transition from Empire to Republic

In October 1911, both the Qing government and the revolutionary armies found themselves short of money and immediately approached foreign financiers for support. Because of its desperate financial situation and habit of

---

[51] See Fabozzi, Bond Markets, p. 48.

[52] The three railway loans are the Tianjin–Pukou railway loan (1908), Tianjin–Pukou supplementary railway loan (1910) and the Huguang railway loan. Because of their later issuing, the latter two loans are only included in the calculation after February and October 1911, respectively, for Britain and after January and November 1911, respectively, for Germany.

[53] The British consols used are 2.5 per cent British Consols Redeemable, 1923. The German sovereign bonds used are Deutsche Reichs-Anleihe (1890), 3 per cent.

relying on foreign borrowing, it soon became clear that the Qing could only pay for their military campaign against the revolutionaries if they were able to access foreign capital. In late October, Sheng Xuanhuai wrote to Yuan Shikai that he was confident that the government troops could win, but that all hinged on the contracting of new foreign loans as 'the treasury is completely empty. I am afraid that it will be difficult to endure without a loan.'[54] Emblematic of the dire financial situation of the Qing government was that in November the court even started to sell parts of the palace treasure to foreign banks.[55] As early as 14 October, Qing officials had approached the DAB in Beijing about a possible loan of 5 million reichsmark (~£244,315) to buy weaponries.[56] The German bankers were willing to provide the loan but hesitated when they received news that the banking groups in Britain, France and the United States and their governments had declined to issue any loans to the Chinese government.[57]

As early as October 1911, the Qing government asked the Four Groups for an advance of 12 million taels. The HSBC in Beijing felt hat the 'groups should entertain [the] proposal' if Yuan Shikai 'returns with full powers', as they believed that his return would mean that the 'government will be able to cope with [the] revolution'.[58] This sympathy for Yuan Shikai, who was brought back from retirement by the Qing as prime minister in November 1911 to fight the revolutionaries, was already indicative of the later support of foreign bankers for him. However, at the time, HSBC director Townsend in London was opposed to such a loan, deeming such a proposal 'undesirable and impolitic'.[59] In Germany, the KfAG agreed that the banks should remain neutral and not provide any loans to the Chinese government to fight the revolutionaries. However, they were open to providing the Chinese with loans that allowed China to continue previous loan payments, which again reflected the importance the bankers attached to maintaining China's ability to service its loans.[60] Nevertheless, the Four Groups eventually decided that they were 'not opposed to making [a] loan to a responsible Chinese Government', but given 'the present uncertainty of the situation... [were] not disposed at present to entertain application for financial assistance', thereby essentially declaring their neutrality in the conflict.[61]

[54] Sheng to Yuan (21 October 1911), YSKQJ, 19:21.
[55] 'The Palace Treasure in Peking', The Times (London) (11 December 1911).
[56] DAB to Deutsche Bank (14 October 1911), HADB, S2592.
[57] DAB to Deutsche Bank (17 October 1911), HADB, S2592.
[58] HSBC (Beijing) to HSBC (London) (24 October 1911), TNA, FO 405/205, p. 170.
[59] Townsend to Campbell (25 October 1911), TNA, FO 405/205, pp. 169–70.
[60] 'Consortium für Asiatische Geschäfte, Protokoll der Sitzung vom 28. Oktober 1911' (28 October 1911), HADB, S2592.
[61] 'Minutes of Meeting of the French, British, German & American Groups at the Offices of the Banque de l'Indo-Chine, Paris, on the 8th November, 1911' (8 November 1911), HADB, S2592.

Despite this declaration of neutrality, sympathy with the efforts of Yuan Shikai to unify the country and return it to stability remained among Cordes and the other representatives in Beijing. In December 1911, they even drafted and proposed to their directors a loan agreement for 3 million taels to be provided to Yuan.[62] However, a lack of diplomatic support for providing Yuan with a loan and the instability in China prevented any financial assistance rendered by the bankers to Yuan. At the end of November, the representatives of the Four Groups in Beijing asked their diplomatic representatives to 'accord your support to the conclusion of a loan to enable the Premier [Yuan Shikai] to conserve and extend his authority which we venture to believe constitutes the most promising nucleus for a responsible government of China'.[63] However, the involved foreign governments refrained from 'intervening in China's internal affairs' and, in accordance with 'the policy of strict neutrality . . . look[ed] with disfavour upon loans . . . unless assured that such loans would be of neutral effect'.[64] Moreover, despite his sympathies for Yuan and his hope that Yuan would 'remain alive and able to work' towards maintaining China's unity, Cordes had to admit the difficulty of manoeuvring through the chaotic political developments since the outbreak of the revolution and was unsure what the 'future central government' would look like.[65]

It was this instability and the desire not to be perceived as 'sid[ing] with a certain party' which could be 'taken amiss in China', before an agreement between Yuan and the revolutionaries had been struck, that led Urbig and Addis – despite their sympathies for Yuan – to reject any direct financial help for Yuan as proposed by their representatives in Beijing.[66] As Addis wrote to Urbig, the banks' neutrality had resulted in 'plac[ing] Yuan in a circle from which he finds it difficult to emerge. Without money he cannot form a stable government; without a stable government he cannot get money.' However, Addis was unwilling to pledge his support to Yuan's party before a peace agreement had been concluded and a new government formed that was recognized by the foreign governments, as such premature support for Yuan could make him 'uncompromising' and lead to 'anti-foreign feeling' among the revolutionaries. Addis also believed that 'the diminishing financial resources of the two contestants [due to no access to foreign borrowing] . . . in itself [might be] an incentive to a compromise being arrived between' Yuan

[62] Cordes to DAB (Berlin) (18 January 1912), PAAA, R9208/522, p. 23.
[63] Cordes to Haxthausen (29 November 1911), PAAA, R9208/521, p. 266.
[64] Quote from Bernstorff to Auswärtiges Amt (February 1912), in Lepsius et al., Große Politik, 32:257. Bernstorff quotes a note by the American government that is later endorsed by the other involved countries; see Bernstorff to Auswärtiges Amt (February 1912), in Lepsius et al., Große Politik, 32:257–8.
[65] Cordes to DAB (Berlin) (5 December 1911), PAAA, R9208/521, pp. 255–8.
[66] Quote from Urbig to Warburg (9 December 1911), PAAA, R17.799, p. 53; Addis to Urbig (7 December 1911), HADB, S2592.

Shikai and the revolutionaries.[67] This withholding of financial support from both the Qing government and the revolutionaries must also be seen as a method by which the bankers tried to mitigate the risk of long-term warfare and instability.[68]

Confronted with the opposition by the Four Groups, which had become the main suppliers of capital for the Chinese government before 1911, the Chinese government tried to go elsewhere to acquire funds. As the Ministry of Finance (Duzhibu 度支部) reported, military costs for conscripting soldiers and buying military equipment in Sichuan and Hubei were growing rapidly and as other provinces had to set up defences, most of them had not remitted the regular revenue (jingxiang 京餉) to the capital. As a result, the Ministry desperately needed money and the throne ordered the Ministry to arrange a foreign loan to raise the funds to cover the rising military expenses. The Ministry managed to sign a contract with the French syndicate of Baron Cottu for a loan of £3,600,000 at a 6 per cent annual interest rate, to be repaid within sixty years. The Ministry was not satisfied with the loan conditions but the urgency of the situation did not allow any delay in contracting the loan.[69]

Because of increasing requests by the provinces for more funds for the defence against the revolutionary armies and the necessity of continuing to repay China's foreign debt, the central government needed even more funds. This situation was exacerbated further by a crisis in the money markets of China's ports set off by the revolution. The head of the Ministry of Finance, Zaize 載澤, reported that 'the money market in each port is very tight and in an extremely dangerous situation, so that we also have to find a way to stabilise [the market]'. To pay for these expenses, the Ministry of Finance soon approached the Cottu syndicate again and contracted a second loan for £2,400,000.[70] However, the French government, in support of the neutrality of the Four Groups, did not allow Cottu to quote the loans in Paris and so both loan deals fell through.[71]

By the end of 1911, the Qing government's financial problems had still not been resolved and Yuan was worried that the inability of the government to

[67] Addis to Urbig (7 December 1911), HADB, S2592.

[68] I discuss the use of their control over the supply of foreign capital (both the withholding of foreign capital and its supply to the new republican government discussed later in this chapter) as part of the risk management strategy of foreign banks during the 1911 revolution and its aftermath in more depth in Moazzin, 'Investing in the New Republic'.

[69] Duzhibu to Waiwubu (30 October 1911), AIMH, 02–24–008–02–017.

[70] Quote from Zaize memorial (31 October 1911), QWSL, 3:275–6; Duzhibu to Waiwubu (2 December 1911), AIMH, 02–24–008–02–038; Waiwubu to Picors (2 December 1911), AIMH, 02–24–008–02–039.

[71] Haxthausen to Bethmann-Hollweg (8 December 1911), PAAA, R17/799, p. 78; Bastid, 'La Diplomatie Française et La Révolution Chinoise de 1911', pp. 235–6; King, HSBC History, 2:479. King provides a correct total loan sum, but incorrectly refers to one instead of two Cottu loans.

pay its troops might lead many of them to turn into bandits and cause further turmoil.[72] In a letter to the governor-general of the three northern provinces, Zhao Erxun 趙爾巽, he complained that no foreign loan was forthcoming and indicated that the court now wished to come to an agreement with the revolutionaries, as the military campaign against them could not be supported financially any longer.[73] This confirmed Addis' thinking that the withholding of financial support would quicken a compromise between the belligerent parties.

Just as the Qing government tried to raise funds through foreign borrowing, the revolutionaries also tried to win financial support. When revolutionary leader Sun Yat-sen (Sun Zhongshan 孫中山) heard of the outbreak of revolution, he did not immediately return to China, but first made stops in London and Paris to gain foreign support.[74] Besides seeking diplomatic support, Sun also tried to win over foreign financiers for his cause. While in Europe, he reassured investors that popular Chinese opposition to foreign loans was only due to the Chinese people mistrusting the Qing government. They were not opposed to foreign capital.[75] In London, he approached the HSBC about financial assistance, but the British bankers were not willing to help before a proper Chinese government was established.[76] After his arrival in Paris, Sun tried his luck with Stanislas Simon, the director of the French Banque de L'Indochine, but Simon could only explain to him that the Four Groups – of which his bank was a member – had decided to remain neutral.[77] Sun firmly believed that 'victory or defeat [against the Qing government] is decided by [foreign] loans'. Reflecting on his failed attempts to gain financial support in Europe, he recognized the main problem as the reluctance of foreign lenders to financially support the new republican government, as it was so far only a temporary government not recognized by other states. As a temporary solution, Sun proposed that the revolutionaries should use companies as collateral to borrow funds in a private capacity, which could then be used to support the government.[78]

Using the Jiangsu Railway Company (Jiangsu tielu gongsi 江蘇鐵路公司) and the Hanyeping Company (Hanyeping gongsi 漢冶萍公司), the Sun's Provisional Government in Nanjing was able to borrow 5,033,557 silver dollars from Japanese firms. In total, the Provisional Government received over 26 million silver dollars in foreign loans – including funds received from

---

[72] Ijūin to Uchida (17 December 1911), *YSKQJ*, 19:166.
[73] Yuan to Zhao (29 December 1911), *YSKQJ*, 19:219.
[74] Bergère, *Sun Yat-sen*, pp. 207–9.
[75] Sun Zhongshan, 'Zai Ouzhou de yanshuo' (1911), *SZSQJ*, 1:560.
[76] King, *HSBC History*, 2:477.
[77] 'Yu Ximeng de tanhua' (23 November 1911), *SZSQJ*, 1:563.
[78] Sun to Chen Jiongming 陳炯明, Provincial Assembly of Guangdong and the Guangdong Railway Company (26 January 1912), *SZSQJ*, 2:41–2.

loans contracted by the northern government – between its establishment in January 1912 and its dissolving at the end of the same year. While the government remained unable to contract any large loans, it still heavily depended on foreign capital. According to an official report by the Beiyang government, between the establishment of the Provisional Government and the end of April 1912, around 68 per cent of its total income of around 20 million silver dollars during this period came from foreign loans.[79] Thus, not only the Qing court, but also the revolutionaries had become dependent on foreign capital to run their government and continue fighting the other side. A consequence of this was that the struggle of both parties for sovereignty over China was not only fought militarily but also in the financial realm, as both the Qing government and the revolutionaries issued admonitions to the foreign representatives that they should prohibit any foreign lending to the other side in the conflict.[80] This financial struggle for sovereignty shows starkly the important role of international finance during the 1911 revolution. Eventually, both Yuan's admission that the Qing lacked the funds to continue fighting and Sun's realization that only a proper government recognized by other states would be able to borrow the needed foreign capital on a large scale suggest that the neutral position taken by foreign bankers was an important factor in bringing the two belligerents to the negotiating table, just as Addis had predicted.[81] After peace negotiations between the revolutionaries and Yuan, the Qing emperor abdicated in February 1912 and, after only a little over four months, the revolution ended and Yuan Shikai emerged as the provisional president of the new Chinese republic.

5.4   Financing the New Republican Government

After the abdication of the Qing ruling house and the transfer of power to Yuan Shikai (Figure 5.9) as provisional president, contracting a large foreign loan became an important element in Yuan's presidential programme.[82] He had the support of the foreign bankers, who early on had seen him as the person

---

[79] Xu, *Zhongguo jindai waizhai tongji*, pp. 95–105; Zhongguo di'er lishi danganguan, *Minguo waizhai dangan shiliao*, 4:18, 50; 'Nanjing caizhengbu shouzhi baogao', *Zhengfu gongbao*, No. 81 (20 July 1912). The total amount of foreign loans contracted by the Provisional Government is based on Xu's detailed list of foreign loans between January and November 1912. This does not include loans contracted by local governments. The percentage of the total income between January and April 1912 is based on a report from the *Zhengfu Gongbao* also cited by Xu.

[80] Sun Zhongshan, 'Tonggao ge guoshu' (October/November 1911), *SZSQJ*, 1:545; Waiwubu to Foreign Ministers (9 January 1912), AIMH, 02–24–008–02–061.

[81] On the effect of withholding financial support on the agreement, though from a diplomatic perspective, also see Edwards, *Finance and Diplomacy*, pp. 159–60.

[82] Young, *The Presidency of Yuan Shih-k'ai*, p. 123.

Figure 5.9   Yuan Shikai as president in 1912. Image courtesy of Bundesarchiv, Bild 183-R03613a.

capable of restoring stability.[83] In Berlin and London, newspapers welcomed the fact that Yuan was taking charge of the government and hoped that stability could now be restored.[84] Given the bleak financial situation the government found itself in, it was not surprising that foreign loans became the basis for any other plans the government might have. The *Far Eastern Review* reported at the time that when 'the [newly established] Republican Government assumed control' it had only 'sixty thousand taels in the treasury at Peking [Beijing], and thirty thousand at Nanking [Nanjing]'.[85] According to an estimate by Xiong Xiling 熊希齡, who briefly served as minister of finance in 1912, the annual deficit of the new government would be around 178 million taels because of the existing deficit of the Qing government and additional costs for the repayment of foreign debt, the upkeep and disbandment of troops,

[83] HSBC (Beijing) to HSBC (London) (24 October 1911), TNA, FO405/205, p. 170; HSBC (Beijing) to HSBC (London) (3 November 1911), TNA, FO 405/205, p. 218; Straight to J. P. Morgan (no date), attachment to Urbig to Zimmermann (21 November 1911), PAAA, R17.798, pp. 194–5; 'Auszug aus dem Protokoll No. 122 der Sitzung des Geschäftsausschusses der Deutsch-Asiatischen Bank vom 8. Dezember 1911' (8 December 1911), HADB, S2592.
[84] *BBZ* (13 February 1912, evening edition); 'The First President of China', *The Times (London)* (11 March 1912).
[85] 'Hsiung Hsi Ling', *The Far Eastern Review* 9, no. 1 (1912): 23.

the repayment of domestic debt that had been issued, and administrative and other expenses.[86]

While this growing financial burden meant that the new government almost certainly had to resort to further foreign borrowing, it would be wrong to think there existed only 'unhappiness with [foreign] borrowing', and 'public resignation [about] … its inevitability', as has been argued before.[87] Rather, continuing from the trend that had set in during the late Qing dynasty, the borrowing of foreign capital was again seen as a way of financing – often very idealistic – plans for modernizing and strengthening China. Most prominently, Sun Yat-sen advocated using foreign debt. Shortly before his arrival in Shanghai in December 1911, he explained to Deng Zeru 鄧澤如, a fellow member of the revolutionary Tongmenghui 同盟會party, that 'the borrowing of foreign money has unlimited benefits and will do no harm at all. Without five hundred million [taels] China today cannot effortlessly carry out constructions.'[88] Yuan Shikai also not only wished to borrow funds for covering debt repayments, the disbandment and upkeep of troops, and administrative costs. He also had larger plans for using foreign capital to modernize the Chinese state. Thus, he initially planned to borrow a sum of £60 million, which was much higher than the loan amount eventually required to cover the administrative costs of the government and the repayment of debt. He wished to use the additional money for purposes such as railway construction.[89]

Given the need to raise the funds for running the new government and servicing debt and to finance modernization projects like railway construction, it was not surprising that Yuan started to approach the Four Groups in February 1912 about a possible loan. He immediately required 7 million taels for the disbandment of troops and the costs of the retiring Nanjing government. Moreover, Yuan asked for 3.4 million taels a month for the requirements of the central government and for a further 3 million taels for the expenditures of the rest of China.[90] He hoped that such monthly payments could continue at least until August and that eventually a larger loan could be concluded to repay the advances made by the Four Groups and provide a financial basis for his government.[91] Regarding this larger loan, Tang Shaoyi, who had become premier of Yuan's government, inquired on behalf of the Chinese government about a £60 million loan spread over five years and secured by the salt revenue. This sum was to be used first for debt and indemnity payments and then the remainder 'in proportion [of]

---

[86] Xiong to Tang (March 1912), in Zhou, *Xiong Xiling ji*, 2:572–5.
[87] Young, *Presidency*, p. 123.
[88] 'Yu Deng Zeru deng de tanghua' (16 December 1911), *SZSQJ*, 1:567.
[89] Addis to DAB (Berlin) (27 February 1912), HADB, S2592; HSBC (Beijing) to HSBC (London) (15 May 1912), TNA, FO 405/208, p. 602.
[90] HSBC (Beijing) to HSBC (London) (15 February 1912), TNA, FO 405/208, pp. 241–2; HSBC (Beijing) to HSBC (London) (24 February 1912), TNA, FO 405/208, p. 262.
[91] Yuan to Four Groups (9 March 1912), *YSKQJ*, 19:626.

80 per cent [for] productive works [and] 20 per cent [for the] army, navy, and education'. The productive works the Chinese had in mind were land reclamation of regions that had suffered from floods and the construction of a railway from Nanjing to Wuhu.[92] This willingness to borrow a large sum of money far in excess of the sum needed for the regular expenses of the government and the repayment of loans once more reflected the confidence of Chinese officials that the government could repay its debt once it managed to modernize China. At the same time, these plans show that China's public finance and Chinese plans for development were essentially based on foreign debt right from the founding of the new republic.

Now that a united Chinese government was again in place, the Four Groups were willing to financially support it and extend the required advances. They proposed that the Chinese government should issue treasury bills to the Four Groups as collateral for the advances made. These could then be redeemed from the proceeds of a large Reorganisation Loan.[93] The foreign bankers were inclined to satisfy Yuan's request because they feared competition by other banks and were anxious not to 'lose such an opportunity as may not recur for being first to deal with [the] Provisional Government'.[94] This fear of possible competition continued during the following months.[95] However, the banks also attached conditions to their willingness to provide financial assistance. While they were ready to continue to pay for outstanding loan payments of the Chinese government before the large Reorganisation Loan was concluded, they demanded the preferential option for the conclusion of this loan.[96] More importantly, the bankers saw the loan as a chance to push China towards financial reform. British and German bankers hoped that a part of the proceeds from the large loan could be used for fiscal reform and the expansion of infrastructure, both of which were to be carried out with the help of foreign experts.[97] As we saw in Chapter 3, many bankers were sceptical of China's

---

[92] HSBC (Beijing) to HSBC (London) (1 March 1912), TNA, FO 405/208, p. 291.

[93] HSBC (Beijing) to HSBC (London) (15 February 1912), TNA, FO 405/208, pp. 241–2; 'Consortium für Asiatische Geschäfte. Protokoll der Sitzung vom 19. Februar 1912' (19 February 1912), HADB, S2592; 'Inter-Bank Conference: Minutes of Meeting at the office of the British and Chinese Corporation, Limited, London, on the 12th March, 1912' (12 March 1912), HADB, S2592.

[94] HSBC (London) to HSBC (Shanghai) and HSBC (Beijing) (23 February 1912), TNA, FO 405/208, p. 262.

[95] 'Konsortium für Asiatische Geschäfte. Protokoll der Sitzung vom 18. März 1912' (18 March 1912), HADB, S2592; Addis to French, German, American, Russian, and Japanese Groups (2 July 1912), TNA, FO 405/209, p. 10.

[96] 'Inter-Bank Conference: Minutes of Meeting at the office of the British and Chinese Corporation, Limited, London, on the 12th March, 1912' (12 March 1912), HADB, S2592.

[97] HSBC (Beijing) to HSBC (London) (15 February 1912), TNA, FO 405/208, pp. 241–2; 'Consortium für Asiatische Geschäfte. Protokoll der Sitzung vom 19. Februar 1912' (19 February 1912), HADB, S2592; Deutsche Bank to Jacob S. H. Stern (19 February 1912), HADB, S2592.

ability to collect taxes and believed that foreign guidance was necessary if China wished to carry out meaningful fiscal reform. The Chinese salt monopoly, which China now wished to pledge as a security, had early on been seen as a source of revenue that could easily be increased under European supervision. Writing in 1912, Charles Addis believed that the current estimated yearly revenue from the salt monopoly of 47 million taels 'could be doubled under [a] reformed administration and improved methods [of] salt manufacture by machinery'.[98]

Naturally, the bankers were also concerned with their future bondholders and only willing to provide funds if China could provide the 'necessary guarantees'.[99] The last years of the Qing dynasty had seen an increasing willingness of foreign bankers to accept streams of revenue not under foreign supervision as security for loans and to leave control over loan funds to the Chinese officials. However, this changed with the political instability that ensued after the revolution and the consequential increased political risk that investment in Chinese government bonds would carry. While the Four Groups accepted the salt revenue as security for the large loan, they demanded that '[t]he Chinese Government shall take immediate steps to reorganise the Salt Gabelle, with the assistance of foreign experts… [and] [a]dequate guarantees shall be obtained for the control and supervision of the expenditures of the Loan proceeds'.[100]

At the same time, it also showed the concerns of the bankers about the ability of European markets to absorb such a large loan, especially given that China had previously already used part of its salt revenue as a security for loans. Addis believed that 'the Chinese are opening the mouth wide. For a nation which has recently been in default with its loan coupons to propose a loan of £60,000,000 against a second mortgage security is enough to stagger, if not humanity, at least the European markets.'[101] The directors of the DAB were also convinced that 'we will not find new investors for [the] Chinese loan unless they can realise [the] efficiency of [the] guarantee given for such a loan'. Such an efficient guarantee could only be the 'salt gabelle, to be reorganised under foreign experts'.[102] These demands all reflected the bankers' awareness of the increased risk of investing in China and their intention of encouraging Chinese fiscal reform and responsible spending and ensuring the successful floating and repayment of the loan. Although these fiscal demands are often

---

[98] Addis to DAB (Berlin) (no date), HADB, S2592.
[99] Deutsche Bank to Jacob S. H. Stern (19 February 1912), HADB, S2592.
[100] 'Inter-Bank Conference: Minutes of Meeting at the Office of the British and Chinese Corporation, Limited, London, on the 12th March, 1912' (12 March 1912), HADB, S2592.
[101] Addis to Langley (1 March 1912), TNA, FO 405/208, p. 291.
[102] DAB (Berlin) to Addis (1 July 1912), TNA, FO 405/209, p. 9.

seen as part of the policies of Western governments,[103] they originated from the views of bankers and not government officials. For example, at the beginning of March, the German consul in Shanghai, Paul von Buri, still only knew that China wished to negotiate a large loan with the Four Groups, but had no information about the 'specific conditions of the hypothecated securities'.[104] In the British case, there is also no evidence that the government proposed any fiscal measures before Addis informed them of the demands of the banks.[105]

In principle, Yuan was willing to grant the banks the preferential option for the Reorganisation Loan as long as there were no better offers. He also agreed to the reorganization of the salt tax with the help of foreign experts and to foreign assistance 'in inaugurating [a] modern system of accounts and [the] framing [of a] budget', which would have ensured the appropriate expenditure of the loan funds.[106] This openness towards fiscal reform was also reflected in a speech before the national assembly, in which Yuan proposed the reform of the salt administration according to Western methods and promised that the salt revenue could thus be increased to 50 million taels a year.[107] Thus the banks agreed to fund the expenses of the Chinese government until the conclusion of the Reorganisation Loan. By the end of May, the banks had already advanced 6.1 million taels to the Chinese government and estimated that until October the Chinese government would require advances totalling £10 million.[108] While these advances increased China's financial burden, the fact that the bankers primarily advanced the money to Yuan Shikai and his Beijing government also gave Yuan important leverage over Sun Yat-sen and the revolutionary party in Nanjing, who now were in a position of having to plead to Beijing for money.[109] Therefore, the resumed flows of foreign capital not only sustained the new republic but also fortified Yuan's power and control over it.

While the directors in Europe and the United States were satisfied with these demands, their representatives in Beijing, who witnessed the turmoil China

---

[103] Most recently, Hirata, 'Britain's Men on the Spot in China', p. 909.
[104] Buri to Bethmann Hollweg (1 March 1912), PAAA, R17.800, p. 87. Addis first mentioned the reforming of the salt gabelle in communications with the DAB in Addis to DAB (Berlin) (no date), HADB, S2592. The document has no date but judging from the other documents in the file it is certain that it is from February 1912.
[105] Enclosures of Addis to Langley (24 February 1912), TNA, FO 405/208, pp. 261–3; Addis to Langley (11 March 1912) and enclosures, TNA, FO 405/408, pp. 339–40; Addis to Langley (16 March 1912), TNA, FO 405/208, pp. 363–4.
[106] 'Inter-Bank Conference: Minutes of Meeting at the office of the British and Chinese Corporation, Limited, London, on the 12th March, 1912' (12 March 1912), HADB, S2592.
[107] Yuan Shikai, 'Zai canyiyuan yanshuoci' (1 May 1912), YSKQJ, 20:2.
[108] 'Konsortium für Asiatische Geschäfte' (24 May 1912), HADB, S2592.
[109] Sun to National Assembly (Nanjing) (12 March 1912), SZSQJ, 2:226; Sun to Yuan (16 March 1912), SZSQJ, 2:241.

still found itself in, viewed the political risk of floating a Chinese loan as even higher than the directors at home and wanted to go even further in their demands for foreign supervision and control. Under the impression of instability in Beijing, they strongly urged their directors in Europe and the United States to insist on more foreign control in terms of the loan security and the expenditure of loan funds. They reported that China's public finance was in a very serious state and, except the Customs revenue, 'practically no revenue' was being collected. The bank representatives had 'no confidence in [the] ability of [the] present government to reorganize [its] financial administration without foreign assistance, as officials are extravagant, inefficient and ... corrupt'.[110] They feared that 'China will ruin herself unless she is taken in hand properly'.[111] Based on this grave assessment and 'in view of the magnitude' of the sums demanded by the Chinese, they felt it would be best if the Chinese government designated the foreign banks as 'its financial agents' for around ten years to issue bonds on its behalf, 'scrutinize [the] securities offered' by China, provide that, if necessary, the 'revenue to be pledged [as security] shall be administered under foreign experts' and exercise far-reaching control over the expenditure of loan funds through 'foreign technical executive[s] and foreign chief accountant[s] ... and a foreign audit department to be established by the Board of Finance [in] Peking'.[112] As it was foreseeable that China would need to continue to borrow foreign money, this proposal would have essentially meant that significant parts of Chinese public finance would have come under foreign control for a decade. That the bank representatives in China, who in the past had acted as the voice of conciliation towards their directors at home and had opposed imposing too stringent financial control on China, were now only willing to lend funds to China under such strict control was testimony to the state of instability and uncertainty prevalent in Beijing.

In London, Charles Addis doubted that the programme of the representatives in Beijing was 'capable of realization'. As China's credit had 'not broken down' yet and the 'Chinese are a proud people', they were unlikely to accept 'financial tutelage'. He believed that the goal was to 'build up and strengthen China from within rather than imposing on it a system of external supports'. He therefore suggested a compromise in response to the concerns of the Beijing representatives, whereby the bankers should try to 'secure a degree of foreign control considered necessary to provide for the proper application of loan funds and the maintenance of the bondholders' security in such a manner as not to prejudice the self-respect and initiative of the Chinese government'. Accordingly, Addis proposed that any foreigner put in charge of collecting

---

[110] HSBC (London) to DAB (Berlin) (25 April 1912), HADB, S2592.
[111] DAB (Berlin) to Addis, Simon and Warburg & Co. (18 April 1912), HADB, K07/010/I/01.
[112] Bank Representatives to Four Groups (27 March 1912), HADB, S2592.

revenue allocated as loan security should be employed as 'officials of the Chinese Government' similar to the model of the Customs Service. Furthermore, demands for control of the expenditure of the loan funds should be limited to a 'right of veto' through a foreign official employed by the Chinese government and the 'appointment of a foreign auditor and accountant' by China.[113] In contrast to Addis, the German bankers in Berlin were principally in agreement with the programme suggested by the representatives in Beijing, especially given the fact that the representatives in Beijing had previously always 'advocated for sparing the [Chinese] government [from foreign control] as much as possible', but now regarded it as necessary to insist on strict controls.

However, the German Foreign Office signalled that it would not regard the scheme of far-reaching financial control proposed by the Beijing representatives as feasible and other foreign governments were also unlikely to lend their support. Moreover, there now existed a deadlock in the Four Groups. While the German and French group supported the scheme of the Beijing representatives, the American and British groups supported Addis' approach.[114] Eventually, a compromise was reached. Addis largely prevailed and the proposal for far-reaching foreign control and financial agency was not adopted. However, after the intervention by the Beijing representatives, the Four Groups not only required that the administration and collection of the salt gabelle was to be carried out by foreign officials employed by China. They now also demanded that China employ a foreign official who would countersign any loan expenditures jointly with the foreign banks, a foreign auditor who would check the expenditures each quarter and foreign technical experts to supervise any industrial expenses undertaken with the loan funds.[115] While these demands fell short of the demands of the Beijing representatives, which would have bound China to the Four Groups for a decade and would have meant even more far-reaching control, they went further than those favourable loan terms China had enjoyed during the last years of the Qing. This resulted from the increasing political risk of lending to China after the revolution, which was especially perceived by their representatives in Beijing. It was only with a greater degree of foreign control that the bankers felt this political risk could be managed.

---

[113] Addis to Simon (2 April 1912), HADB, S2592.

[114] Quote from Deutsche Bank to Jacob S. H. Stern (10 April 1912), HADB, S2592; 'Consortium für Asiatische Geschäfte, Protokoll der Sitzung vom 10. April 1912' (10 April 1912), HADB, S2592; 'Konsortium für Asiatische Geschäfte, Protokoll der Sitzung vom 17. April 1912' (17 April 1912), HADB, S2592.

[115] HSBC (London) to HSBC (Beijing) (18 April 1912), HADB, S2592; 'Inter-Bank Conference. Minute of Meetings of the Four Groups Held at the Office of the British and Chinese Corporation, Limited, London, on the 14th and 15th May, 1912', HADB, S2592.

When demanding this increased control, the foreign banks were mainly interested in putting the new Chinese government on a sound fiscal basis, so that it could maintain the unity of China and restore stability, both important conditions for the continuation of the banks' business and the resumption of Chinese payments to foreign bondholders. They envisioned such control to be carried out by foreign bankers and other foreign experts, not by foreign government officials. While they have often been accused of using the Reorganisation Loan to further the political control of their home governments, foreign bankers were not driven by a desire to do so. On the contrary, they feared that further destabilization of China due to a financial collapse would invite foreign political encroachment and endanger China's unity and stability as a market. Despite the instability still prevailing in China, the Beijing representatives in March 1912 demanded 'immediate active support of Yuan Shih-kai' to avoid the 'consequences to trade of collapse, chaos and foreign intervention'.[116] They were especially afraid that Russia and Japan might take advantage of China's weakness to further their political control over parts of North China. As Cordes and the other representatives wrote, 'the four groups have owed their influence very largely to the Chinese belief that they desired to profit by the legitimate development of China for, and by, the Chinese themselves, rather than to cooperate in what was considered to be the Russo-Japanese policy of exploitation'.[117] Cordes reiterated to the Berlin directors that 'the basis for the existence of the Four Groups is a China-friendly policy'.[118]

Eventually, the Four Groups limited these Russo-Japanese attempts by incorporating Russian and Japanese banks into their syndicate and binding them to the inter-bank agreement. This happened despite concerns of the German bankers that this would further slow down the decision-making of the groups and would insert 'political elements' into what had so far been an inter-bank agreement 'resting exclusively on a financial basis'.[119] The Chinese government had also encouraged the inclusion of the Japanese and Russian banks in the inter-bank agreement to rein in any political demands from the Russian or Japanese governments. As Tang Shaoyi put it in a conversation with Cordes, 'they (the Russians and Japanese) can never be so nasty to you as they can be to us'.[120]

[116] Hillier to HSBC (London), PAAA, R9208/522, p. 140.
[117] Bank Representatives to Four Groups (January 1912), PAAA, R9208/522, 25–8. The document is not dated, but should be from January 1912 as it is an attachment to Cordes to DAB (Berlin) (18 January 1912), PAAA, R9208/522, pp. 22–4.
[118] Cordes to DAB (Berlin), PAAA, R9208/522, p. 57.
[119] Quote from 'Konsortium für Asiatische Geschäfte, Protokoll der Sitzung vom 28. Februar 1912' (28 February 1912), HADB, S2592; King, *HSBC History*, 2:484–8; Müller-Jabusch, *Deutsch-Asiatische Bank*, pp. 185–7; Barth, *Imperialismen*, p. 388.
[120] Quote from Cordes, 'Aus meinen Notizen' (4 March 1912), PAAA, R9208/522, p. 170; 'Consortium für Asiatische Geschäfte, Protokoll der Sitzung vom 10. April 1912' (10 April 1912), HADB, S2592.

The loan negotiations eventually dragged on until April 1913. This was mainly due to public and political opposition by Chinese nationalists to foreign supervision of the salt administration. The negotiations saw not only the entry of a Russian and Japanese group into the consortium in June 1912 but also the exit of the American group after the election of Woodrow Wilson. Eventually, the Reorganisation Loan Agreement was signed in Beijing on 26 April 1913 between the Chinese government and the bank representatives. The loan sum had been reduced to £25 million following demands of the Chinese negotiators. The loan came with an interest rate of 5 per cent.[121] The Minister of Finance, Zhou Xuexi 周學熙 (Figure 5.10), was the main negotiator on the Chinese side. Zhou was the son of the prominent Qing official Zhou Fu, who we met in Chapter 1. Like his father, he first pursued a career as an official, eventually serving in various positions in Zhili province under Yuan Shikai. During the early republic, he served twice as Chinese minister of finance in 1912–13 and 1915–16, before becoming a prominent entrepreneur later in life. During the loan negotiations, Zhou had the difficult task of working between the foreign bankers, the Chinese government, the provisional national assembly and the Chinese public. While he eventually succeeded in closing the loan deal, he was exhausted by the long negotiations, the tough stance of the foreign bankers, the increasing attacks against him in the press and his resentment about the political tensions that arose because of the loan, and resigned from his post in late 1913. Zhou had been caught up in the larger conflict between two opposing factions that continued to exist in China: on the one hand, the pragmatic people in charge of the government who faced the reality that China needed to continue to borrow foreign money, and, on the other, the people who represented the rising tide of nationalism and either opposed foreign borrowing or were not willing to accept that foreign loan contracts inevitably came with certain conditions demanded by foreign bankers and investors.[122]

---

[121] On the negotiations see Barth, *Imperialismen*, pp. 388–402; King, *HSBC History*, 2:488–505; Hirata, 'Britain's Men on the Spot in China', pp. 908–916. For the agreement, see MacMurray, *Treaties and Agreements*, 2:1007–20. Russian and Japanese participation in the issuing of the loan was of relatively little financial significance, as 'the whole of the Japanese share and a considerable part of the Russian were actually issued in the financial centers of western Europe'. Remer, *Foreign Investments in China*, p. 127. However, in the case of Japan, it foreshadowed a growing involvement in Chinese finance during the following years. On this involvement, see Chapter 6 and Schiltz, *The Money Doctors from Japan*, pp. 121–54.

[122] For Zhou's own reflections on the negotiations see Zhou Xuexi, *Zhou Zhi'an Xiansheng zixu nianpu* (1932), in *Zhou Xuexi ji*, comp. Yu and Xia, pp. 602–3. For examples of attacks against him in the press, see 'Zhou Xuexi wuguo zhi zhenxiang', *Yanzheng zazhi* 6 (1913); 'Hutu huangmiu zhi Zhou Xuexi', *Shibao* (4 March 1913). For a general account of Zhou's role during the loan negotiations see Hao, *Zhou Xuexi zhuan*, pp. 175–80. On Zhou's background and career, also see Kwan Man Bun, 'Zhou Xuexi', pp. 2646–7.

Figure 5.10   Zhou Xuexi 周學熙 (1866–1947). From *The Far Eastern Review* 9, no. 12 (May 1913). Courtesy of The University of Hong Kong Libraries.

Nevertheless, the Chinese negotiators had managed to limit foreign supervision over Chinese finance considerably. According to the loan agreement, a new Central Salt Administration (Yanwu zongju 鹽務總局) was to be established, which was fully under the control of the Chinese Ministry of Finance. The foreign Associate Chief Inspector was to manage the Salt Administration with a Chinese Chief Inspector. Demands for the establishment of an audit department were reduced to a vague suggestion that could be modified by the Chinese and most likely was only included in the agreement to make the loan more attractive for investors. The bankers succeeded in having the salt revenues for the servicing of the loan deposited in the DAB and other foreign banks and in fixing what purposes the raised funds could be used for in the loan contract (see Figure 5.13), which had been an additional requirement of the bankers. However, without the establishment of a proper audit department, the control of the foreign bankers over the expenditure of the loan funds remained limited.[123]

---

[123] MacMurray, *Treaties and Agreements*, 2:1007–21; 'Inter-Bank Conference: Minutes of the four groups held at the Office of the British and Chinese Corporation, Limited,

Figure 5.11   Silver dollars being carried through Beijing following the signing of the Reorganisation Loan agreement. From *The Far Eastern Review* 9, no. 12 (May 1913). Image courtesy of The University of Hong Kong Libraries.

Given the still large amount of money required by China and the near failure on its loan payments to bondholders China had witnessed, it was surprising that the bonds were at first successfully floated in Britain, Germany, France, Russia and Belgium.[124] However, in London the bonds at first fell to 54.5 below par by the end of July. While the London price recovered in August, both in Germany and Britain the bonds soon stagnated around the issue value of 90 below par and remained clearly below the average of the indemnity loans of 1896 and 1898, which had a security similar to that of the Reorganisation Loan

London, on the 14th and 15th May, 1912' (15 May 1912), HADB, K07/002II-12. On the inefficacy of the auditing system, also see Adshead, *Salt Administration*, p. 86.
[124] 'The Chinese Loan', *The Times (London)* (22 May 1913).

Figure 5.12 Silver dollars being loaded at the Russo-Asiatic Bank for delivery to the treasury of the republican government. From *The Far Eastern Review* 9, no. 12 (May 1913). Image courtesy of The University of Hong Kong Libraries.

(see Figure 5.14).[125] Given the divergence in the performance of bonds after the revolution observed above, the Reorganisation Loan would have most likely performed even more poorly without a foreign-controlled security. Thus, the bankers had not been wrong in insisting on a good security. The weak performance of the Reorganisation Loan bonds also showed that a bond issue of this size would most likely not have been possible had the bankers not maintained China's credit in Europe and thereby limited the impact of the heightened political risk on bond prices during the months following the revolution. Only the previous actions of the bankers made it possible for China to raise this large amount of money abroad and keep the new government afloat (Figures 5.11 and 5.12). The Reorganisation Loan played an

---

[125] For the issue price of the loan, see Kuhlmann, *China's Foreign Debt*, p. 84.

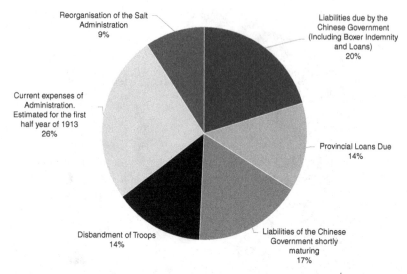

Figure 5.13 Purpose of proceeds from 1913 Reorganisation Loan according to the Reorganisation Loan agreement. *Source*: MacMurray, *Treaties*, 2:1007–21.

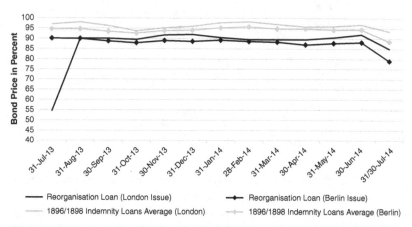

Figure 5.14 Reorganisation Loan bond prices (Berlin/London), July 1913 to July 1914, in per cent. *Source*: *Investor's Manual Monthly*, July 1913 to July 1914; *BBZ*, July 1913 to July 1914.

important role in Yuan's consolidation of power and his quick victory against an upheaval by several southern provinces in 1913.[126] Thereby, the actions of the bankers, this time in the form of financial support for the new government,

---

[126] Hirata, 'Men on the Spot', pp. 925–8.

once more prevented any prolonged interior conflict. The renewed stability also led to economic recovery, including foreign trade.[127]

From a fiscal perspective, the main problem of the loan was that only a small portion, the funds used for reforming the salt administration, were used in a productive manner.[128] Richard Dane, the foreign inspector put in charge of the reform of the salt gabelle, increased the annual salt revenue available to the central government from around 20 million silver dollars before 1911 to around 55 million silver dollars in the early 1920s.[129] However, most proceeds from the Reorganisation Loan were spent on the expenses of the government and the servicing of loans, without any further funds being used for productive purposes that could increase revenues. When at one point during the negotiations the Chinese negotiators had proposed to borrow only a minimal amount of £10 million to cover basic expenses without any commitment to reform, the bankers had criticized this 'hand-to-mouth policy of finance', which did not allow for a 'comprehensive scheme' for the reforming of Chinese finance.[130] Under these circumstances, the loan only increased China's debt without opening a real possibility for financial reform. With no new large stream of revenue available for the servicing of the debt, the funding of the expenses of the administration and large-scale fiscal reform, the new republic was bound to continue its reliance on deficit spending.

This reliance on foreign debt was not a new phenomenon. It needs to be seen as the continuation of the increasing reliance on foreign capital that had started during the last decades of the Qing dynasty. As we have seen in the preceding chapters, habits of relying on foreign borrowing had already developed before 1911; the Reorganisation Loan represented a new development in terms of the size of the individual loan, but was consistent with habits developed previously. Moreover, the Reorganisation Loan was not the only reflection of the new republic's increasing reliance on debt. While domestic borrowing had largely failed during the late Qing period,[131] during the revolution Sun Yat-sen's government had started to issue domestic debt to raise military funds.[132] Yuan also planned to use domestic debt to keep his government solvent. In one of his first speeches before the national assembly, he not only presented his plans for borrowing foreign money, but also proposed that domestic debt should be issued to keep the government afloat until the conclusion of the large foreign loan. The

---

[127] Moazzin, 'Investing in the New Republic', pp. 531–2.
[128] On the unproductive character of the loan more generally and an estimate of the actual sums available to the Chinese government, see King, *History of the HSBC*, 2:503–4.
[129] Adshead, *Salt Administration*, pp. 99–100.
[130] Quotes from Addis to French, German, American, Russian, and Japanese Groups (2 July 1912), TNA, FO 405/209, p. 10; HSBC (Beijing) to HSBC (London) (24 June 1912), TNA, FO 405/208, p. 731.
[131] Zhou, *Wan Qing caizheng jingji yanjiu*, pp. 193–4.
[132] Jiao, *Zhongguo caizheng tongshi*, pp. 92–7.

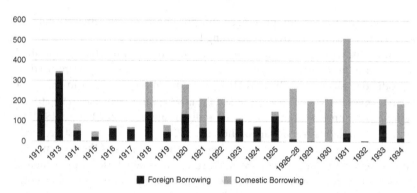

Figure 5.15 Chinese foreign and domestic borrowing, 1912–34, in million silver dollars. A small number of loans that do not have a clear year of issuance were not included. *Source*: Jiao, *Zhongguo caizheng tongshi*, pp. 289–90, 380–1, 693–701, 737–44.

proceeds from the foreign loan were then to be used to repay the domestic debt.[133] The republican government started to issue domestic bonds in 1912 and continued to do so in the following years, especially after the outbreak of the First World War made it impossible to access large sums of European capital.[134] Thus, even before the Reorganisation Loan, China was already well on its way into a spiral of debt. The use of foreign debt on a large scale was resumed after 1918, but domestic debt increasingly grew in importance and during the Nanjing decade came to make up most of government borrowing (see Figure 5.15).

However, the change from foreign to domestic borrowing did not change the larger pattern of relying on debt to maintain public finance. While issuing debt had already played an important role in maintaining the rising costs of the government before 1926, during the Nanjing decade the amount of issued debt reached new levels and the income derived from domestic debt alone on average made up 16.5 per cent of the total annual income of the government between 1927 and 1936.[135] Moreover, patterns of borrowing also remained similar. While China's Customs revenue had been used as security for foreign borrowing during the last years of the Qing dynasty, it was increasingly used as collateral for domestic bonds during the republican period.[136] Therefore, the 1911 revolution and the Reorganisation Loan only accelerated Chinese government borrowing, but were only part of a longer history of Chinese reliance on

---

[133] Yuan Shikai, 'Zai canyiyuan yanshuoci' (1 May 1912), *YSKQJ*, 20:2.
[134] Jiao, *Zhongguo caizheng tongshi*, pp. 379–400.
[135] Jiao, *Zhongguo caizheng tongshi*, pp. 204–7, 542–3.
[136] Van de Ven, *Breaking with the Past*, pp. 179–86; Qian, *Jiu Zhongguo gongzhaishi ziliao*, pp. 370–5.

debt that had started in the late Qing dynasty and continued and increased during the republican period.

5.5 Conclusion

This chapter has traced the interplay between foreign bankers and capital markets and political developments during and after the 1911 revolution in China. In the decades before 1911, China had increasingly used foreign capital markets to raise funds, and as a consequence many European investors owned Chinese bonds. When the revolution broke out in October 1911, it created uncertainty on European bond markets about a possible Chinese default, which could have seriously damaged China's credit and its ability to raise funds abroad. Driven by their responsibility as underwriters of Chinese bonds and by concerns about China's credit and the possibility of future investments in China, German and other foreign bankers took several measures to maintain China's credit abroad. While the 1911 revolution and its aftermath had an effect on Chinese bond prices, the bankers were largely successful in preventing any large-scale fluctuations in the price of Chinese bonds. At the same time, the 1911 revolution marked a turning point in the performance of Chinese bonds, as bonds secured by Customs revenue collected under foreign supervision and deposited in foreign banks remained stable in their price, while other Chinese bonds showed a decrease in their price following the revolution. It was the measures taken by foreign bankers to manage and maintain China's credit that made it possible for China to continue to raise capital on foreign bond markets and to keep the new republican government solvent. While the stability of Chinese bond yields during the late nineteenth and early twentieth centuries has been noted before and simply traced to risk being limited through continuous foreign control of Chinese revenues,[137] this chapter has shown the importance bankers played in maintaining this stability during and after the 1911 revolution.

Besides maintaining China's credit abroad, foreign financiers and foreign capital also played an important role in determining the outcome of the 1911 revolution in other ways. Given the problematic financial situation of both the Qing government and the revolutionaries, the decision of foreign bankers to stop any lending was undoubtedly an important factor in shortening the conflict between the two belligerents and bringing both parties to the negotiating table. As they were mainly interested in restoring stability, the bankers eventually supported Yuan Shikai. This support gave Yuan access to foreign capital and leverage over Sun Yat-sen and the revolutionary party. The advances extended by foreign bankers to the new republican government and the Reorganisation Loan issued in 1913 kept the new republican

---

[137] Goetzmann, Ukhov and Zhu, 'China and the World Financial Markets 1870–1939'.

government afloat, but as the borrowed capital was mainly spent for unproductive purposes these loans also perpetuated and increased the reliance of the Chinese state on borrowed money. All this shows that, following the rapid financial internationalization China had seen in the preceding two decades, Chinese public finance and the international financial connections of the Chinese state played an important role in determining the outcome of the 1911 revolution that should no longer be neglected.

At the same time, examination of the 1911 revolution from the perspective of international finance also reveals the problems that the rapid internationalization of Chinese public finance during the previous decades had created by 1911. While Chapter 4 showed how Chinese officials could use China's growing international financial connections to borrow money cheaply and at favourable terms in Europe to fund their modernization projects, this reliance on foreign debt and government borrowing had turned into an outright addiction by the end of the Qing dynasty. After the fall of the Qing, the frontier, where frontier banks like the DAB operated as intermediary institutions, remained the space that connected China to global financial markets and capital flows. However, once the Qing dynasty, which had been a guarantor for stability, had fallen, the new republican government found itself compelled to continue to borrow foreign capital, but, because of the new political instability and the increased political risk of investing in China, it was now only able to do so on terms that compared unfavourably with those enjoyed during the last years of the Qing. Moreover, in contrast to railway loans during the last years of the Qing dynasty, which could be negotiated without much immediate time pressure, the new republican government found itself in such a desperate fiscal situation that it needed to find foreign funding fast and thus was under greater pressure to give in to the foreign financiers' demands. Thus, we once again see how dependent power relations and the space for Chinese agency on the frontier were on contingency and timing.

Nevertheless, it would be wrong to think that this internationalization of Chinese public finance and the ensuing dependency on foreign capital had only worked in one direction. It was not only the Chinese state that had become increasingly connected to and dependent on foreign financiers and bond markets. The growing expansion of the bankers' business in China and the rapid increase of foreign investment in the Chinese market during the preceding decades meant that foreign bankers, and by extension the share- and bondholders they represented, were now closely connected to the political developments in China and could not simply stand by and let China collapse during the revolution and its aftermath. In other words, they had become bound to the Chinese frontier. The need to ensure the ongoing existence of a stable and unified Chinese state to protect their own business interests and those of the foreign investors they represented explains why the foreign bankers made such an effort to first stabilize China's credit abroad and then financially support the new republican government. Thus, the relationship between foreign bankers and investors and the Chinese state was not one of one-sided dependence but of interdependence between two interconnected parties.

Because of this interdependence, the foreign bankers had to act and manage the new and unprecedented situation and the increased political risk for investments in China after the 1911 revolution. The unstable political situation, the unclear future of the Chinese state, China's near-default on its foreign debt and the seeming inability of Chinese officials to quickly restore the state's fiscal operations – combined with long-existing views of many bankers that China required foreign help to develop a sound fiscal state – meant that foreign control and supervision by foreign bankers and experts seemed the only measure by which this new political risk could be managed. The bankers felt that only on the basis of foreign guidance and control could stability in China be restored, the Chinese state be provided with a sound fiscal basis and the rights of foreign bondholders be protected. Thus, the new demands for foreign control were not simply a means to increase foreign control over China and China's dependence on foreign creditors. They rather were the means foreign bankers chose to protect existing foreign bondholders and manage the increased political risk of investing in China after the 1911 revolution. Although these demands inevitably led to opposition in parts of Chinese society, the weak performance of the Reorganisation Loan on foreign markets proved that the foreign financiers would have most likely been unable to raise a similar loan if no measures of foreign control had been included in the loan agreement.

Previous scholarship has often criticized the issuing of the Reorganisation Loan by foreign bankers for sharply increasing China's dependence on foreign capital. However, this chapter has shown that the 1911 revolution and the Reorganisation Loan were only an episode in the long-term development of the growing reliance of the Chinese state on public debt. As the 1911 revolution happened when the Chinese deficit and its reliance on foreign debt had already been increasing for several decades, it was unlikely that the new republic could escape falling deeper into a spiral of debt, even if the Reorganisation Loan agreement had never been signed. As the visions of both Yuan Shikai and the revolutionaries for a new state were based on issuing foreign and domestic debt, the new republic was bound to continue and increase the state's reliance on debt. Without the large loan floated by the banking consortium, Yuan could have resorted to contracting small foreign loans that did not require securities under foreign control. He also could have issued domestic debt. However, the proceeds from such loans would have most likely been limited and would not have been sufficient to maintain his new government, let alone allow for the large-scale fiscal reforms necessary to increase revenues and reduce the reliance on foreign and domestic borrowing.

After all, the deeper cause of modern China's long-term reliance on foreign and domestic debt was not simply foreign intrusion or foreign loans supposedly imposed on China, but the late Qing state's failure to carry out large-scale fiscal reform and establish a modern fiscal state that could centrally collect revenues in an effective manner and use them to raise long-term resources on financial markets.[138] The question of how to establish such a centralized modern fiscal state stayed at the heart of Chinese economic reform throughout the republican period, especially under the Nanjing government, but was not sufficiently resolved.[139] As a result, China remained reliant on issuing debt, although a change from foreign to domestic borrowing occurred with the beginning of the Nanjing decade. While the 1911 revolution and the establishment of the new republic accelerated Chinese foreign borrowing, we should see the important role foreign capital played during the 1911 revolution and its immediate aftermath not as singular incidents, but as a consequence of the previously developed Chinese reliance on public debt that was to continue during the republican period.

[138] On China's failed attempt to establish a modern fiscal state during the late Qing period, see He, *Paths toward the Modern Fiscal State*.
[139] On attempts of fiscal reform under Yuan Shikai see van de Ven, 'Public Finance and the Rise of Warlordism', pp. 829–68. On fiscal reform under the Beiyang-government, see Jiao, *Zhongguo caizheng tongshi*, chapter 3. On fiscal reform during the Nanjing decade, see Young, *China's Nation-Building Effort*; and Strauss, *Strong Institutions in Weak Polities*, pp. 106–51.

6

Disentanglement and Liquidation

German Bankers and the First World War in China

In September 1934, the head of the supervisory board of the Deutsch-Asiatische Bank (DAB), Franz Urbig, reflected on the attempts of the German bankers to rebuild the bank's operation after the First World War. While the DAB had tried to revive its business after the war, 'the hopes associated with the re-opening of the bank have not been fulfilled'. As Urbig explained:

> The prospects of the bank [before the outbreak of the First World War] were . . . overall quite favourable. With a rough hand the war disrupted this state of affairs. The branches in Calcutta, Hongkong and Singapore were closed and liquidated by England. Japan closed the branches in Qingdao, Kobe and Yokohama. What in terms of damaging the bank had not been accomplished through the fate of these six branches was finished off by the Chinese government, which, when it joined the enemies in 1917, began to liquidate the branches in China that had remained open and by this measure – there is no more appropriate word – downright plundered the bank. What the bank was ultimately left with following these events were only the sad remains of what it had possessed before the war.

He continued that 'the shock suffered by [the bank] because of the events of the war was too severe' to allow for a proper recovery after the war. For Urbig, the First World War was the turning point in the bank's history that ushered in its fall from prominence as one of the leading foreign banks in China to its demise during the post-war period.[1] This chapter first completes the story of the DAB's business operations in China before 1914 by explaining the bank's growth during the decade before the outbreak of war and situating it within the ongoing broader international- ization of the banking sector on the Chinese frontier. It then follows the German bankers through the years of the First World War and describes the detrimental effect the war had on commerce and transnational connections and cooperation in China's treaty ports, the DAB's business and the previously diverse array of lenders facilitating Chinese sovereign borrowing. I show how the German bankers first tried to protect their business and keep China out of

[1] Urbig to Reichswirtschaftsministerium (19 September 1934), HADB, P08401.

the war during the period of Chinese neutrality before 1917 by supplying foreign capital to the Chinese government, but were eventually powerless when China joined the Allies and entered the war in 1917 and – under pressure from Britain and the other Allies – liquidated most of the bank's assets. Overall, we will see the grave rupture the First World War inflicted on the Chinese frontier, its globalized environment and functioning as a space for transnational cooperation and international flows of commodities and capital.

This chapter not only traces the DAB's demise during the First World War. While the previous chapter discussed political risk mainly from the perspective of international bond markets, this chapter looks at it more concretely from the perspective of the local operations of a foreign bank on the ground confronted with possible closure due to a potential declaration of war by its host country against its home government. It shows how the DAB tried to mitigate the risk a possible Chinese entry into the war posed to the survival of its business in China. Prominent studies by Osterhammel and van der Putten that specifically examine the management of political risk by foreign businesses in modern China focus on the time period after 1916 and largely view the treaty ports as 'sheltered enclaves' where foreign businesses could safely operate. In doing so, they neglect the impact of the First World War on foreign – and particularly German – businesses in China's treaty ports.[2] In contrast, this chapter provides a comprehensive account of the DAB's fate in China during the First World War to show that, once the transnational cooperation and power equilibrium of the treaty ports broke down, as it did after the outbreak of war and China's entry into the war, political events could have a grave impact on the very survival of foreign businesses in the treaty ports. The eventual liquidation of the DAB demonstrates the limitations in the ability of foreign businesses in China to manage the political risk caused by significant geo-political changes, such as the outbreak of war.

The fate of the DAB during the First World War also sheds new light on China's entry into First World War. So far, when discussing Chinese motivations for entering the war, the relevant scholarship has stressed that many Chinese were motivated to join the war as they saw it 'as an opportunity to join a fair international system' and become an equal member of a new world order.

---

[2] Quote from Osterhammel, 'Imperialism in Transition', p. 272. Also see van der Putten, *Corporate Behaviour*, especially pp. 5–9 and Osterhammel, *Britischer Imperialismus im Fernen Osten*. Two notable studies that touch upon the impact of the First World War on foreign businesses active in China are Cochran, *Big Business*, ch. 3 and Smith, 'A LBV Perspective', pp. 25–46. However, while Cochran's study of British-American tobacco only explains in passing that the First World War had little impact on the firm, Smith's article is primarily concerned with the HSBC's strategy for preserving its legitimacy in its British home country. For literature on the operations of multinational businesses and political risk in general, see, for example, Kobrin, 'Political Risk', pp. 67–80, and Kobrak, Hansen and Kopper, 'Business, Political Risk, and Historians', pp. 3–21.

However, we will see in this chapter that more pragmatic financial incentives, such as the larger financial aid promised to China by the Allies, likewise played an important role in motivating the Chinese decision to go to war.[3] This chapter uses the case of the German bankers to demonstrate the importance of public finance and economic factors in China's decision to join the Allies and reveals that the larger economic benefits China hoped to receive from the Allies if it entered the war on their side were a crucial factor leading to the Chinese decision to declare war against the Central Powers.

6.1 The Deutsch-Asiatische Bank in 1914

In 1914, the DAB celebrated the twenty-fifth anniversary of its founding in 1889. In the quarter-century the German bankers had spent on the China coast, the bank had become one of the most important foreign banks in China, with a branch network of fourteen branches and agencies employing 123 European bankers and spanning China's most important ports, but also Japan, India and Germany.[4] While the first years of the bank had been difficult, it thereafter grew steadily and, as we saw in Chapters 2 and 3, saw its first larger expansion during the second half of the 1890s, when its business in trade finance started to profit from the growth of China's foreign trade and it first became involved in floating large loans for the Chinese government. The growth of the bank continued after 1900, with the total assets of the DAB growing from 15 million taels in 1900 to 76 million taels in 1913.[5]

The bankers continued to provide government loans and, as we saw, finally became involved in the financing of railways for the Chinese state.[6] Nevertheless, the day-to-day business of the DAB centred on trade finance remained the main basis of the bank's business. As Franz Urbig, who had become the leading figure in the DAB after Adolph von Hansemann's death in 1903, wrote to Heinz Figge (Figure 6.1), a long-time DAB banker who became the bank's first director in China in 1907: 'You always have to assume of me that I value the day-to-day business more highly than anything else for the Deutsch-Asiatische Bank, because I see it as the source from which our regular profits come. . . . The consortium business [in Chinese loans] . . .only serves to

---

[3] Xu, *China and the Great War*, quote from pp. 164–5. Xu does discuss economic gains as one of China's war aims, but only in passing. See Xu, *China and the Great War*, pp. 171–4.

[4] For the number of employees, see 'Protokoll der Sitzung des Geschäfts-Ausschusses vom 16. Juni 1915' (16 June 1915), HADB, K07/010/I/01. For an overview of the branches and agencies of the DAB, see Table 6.2.

[5] 'Geschäft-Bericht für das Jahr 1900' (28 June 1901), HADB, Geschäftsberichte Deutsch-Asiatische Bank; 'Geschäft-Bericht für das Jahr 1913' (29 May 1914), HADB, Geschäftsberichte Deutsch-Asiatische Bank.

[6] For an overview of the loans of the DAB, see Appendix 1.

Figure 6.1 Heinz Figge (1865–1921). From Arthur Wright, *Twentieth-Century Impressions of Hong Kong, Shanghai, and Other Treaty Ports of China*, p. 442. Image courtesy of The University of Hong Kong Libraries.

improve our standing [in China] and, incidentally, our dividend.'[7] When they had planned the establishment of a German bank in China during the 1880s, the German bankers had at first mainly been interested in the Chinese loan business and, in particular, Chinese railway finance. However, as we saw in Chapter 2, during the early 1890s, when such business was not forthcoming, the bank learned to create profits through its day-to-day business. By the 1900s, this regular day-to-day business focussed on trade finance had become accepted as the main pillar of the bank's business.[8]

The bank profited from the continuous growth in China's foreign trade with Germany and other countries. While Germany's trade with China grew in value from 15 million Haiguan taels in 1900 to 101 million Haiguan taels in 1913, China's foreign trade overall more than doubled from 437 million to

[7] Quoted in Müller-Jabusch, *Deutsch-Asiatische Bank*, p. 205. On Urbig and Figge's position within the DAB, see Müller-Jabusch, *Deutsch-Asiatische Bank*, pp. 223–4, 239–40. On Figge, also see 'Funeral Services Held for Local German Banker', *The China Press* (21 November 1921).

[8] On the continued importance of the trade finance business as the main pillar for the bank's profits, also see Müller-Jabusch, *Deutsch-Asiatische Bank*, p. 233.

973 million Haiguan taels during the same period.[9] Although the DAB still did not finance all of Germany's trade with China, after the global economic crisis of 1907, German merchants increasingly relied on the services of the German bank.[10] At the same time, the bank continued to finance non-German trade. For example, in 1911 it signed an agreement with Sheng Xuanhuai's Pinghsiang Colliery (Pingxiang Meikuang 萍鄉煤礦) for the financing of the purchase of goods bought on behalf of the Colliery by their agent in Britain.[11] The DAB's business in trade finance grew in accordance with the overall growth of China's trade. This was reflected in the rise in the value of the bank's bills receivable from 6.4 million in 1900 to 19.4 million in 1913.[12]

From 1907, the DAB also started to issue its own bank notes in Qingdao, Tianjin, Hankou, Beijing and Shanghai.[13] By that time, the issuing of bank notes by foreign banks in Chinese ports had long been a common phenomenon.[14] In 1906, the DAB received permission from the German government to issue bank notes in these ports. The bank notes were denominated in the silver dollar and tael units common in the respective place of issue.[15] These bank notes proved popular among both Chinese merchants and foreign customers and the number of notes issued rose quickly from a total value of 447,774 taels in 1907 to 2,595,968 in 1913.[16] However, the bank's issuing of bank notes remained limited and, it seems, relatively insignificant in those ports

---

[9] For the trade statics of Sino-German trade, see Ratenhof, *Chinapolitik*, pp. 561–2. For China's foreign trade statistics see Hsiao, *China's Foreign Trade Statistics*, p. 23.

[10] Müller-Jabusch, *Deutsch-Asiatische Bank*, p. 234.

[11] 'Memorandum of Agreement Entered into Between the Deutsch-Asiatische Bank, Hankow and the Pinghsiang Colliery, Pinghsiang' (21 May 1911), *Shanghai Municipal Library, Sheng Xuanhuai Archives, Shanghai, China*, 065314–2.

[12] 'Geschäft-Bericht für das Jahr 1900' (28 June 1901), HADB, Geschäftsberichte Deutsch-Asiatische Bank; 'Geschäft-Bericht für das Jahr 1913' (29 May 1914), HADB, Geschäftsberichte Deutsch-Asiatische Bank; Müller-Jabusch, *Deutsch-Asiatische Bank*, p. 233.

[13] 'Geschäft-Bericht für das Jahr 1906' (26 June 1907), HADB, Geschäftsberichte Deutsch-Asiatische Bank; 'Geschäft-Bericht für das Jahr 1907' (25 June 1908), HADB, Geschäftsberichte Deutsch-Asiatische Bank; Müller-Jabusch, *Deutsch-Asiatische Bank*, p. 219.

[14] King, *Money and Monetary Policy*, p. 104; Hanna, Conant and Jenks, *Gold Standard in International Trade*, p. 48.

[15] Bernhard von Bülow, 'Konzession' (8 June 1906), BArch, R2/41689, pp. 75–7; 'Geschäft-Bericht für das Jahr 1906' (26 June 1907), HADB, Geschäftsberichte Deutsch-Asiatische Bank.

[16] 'Geschäft-Bericht für das Jahr 1907' (25 June 1908), HADB, Geschäftsberichte Deutsch-Asiatische Bank; 'Geschäft-Bericht für das Jahr 1909' (28 June 1910), HADB, Geschäftsberichte Deutsch-Asiatische Bank; 'Geschäft-Bericht für das Jahr 1913' (29 May 1914), HADB, Geschäftsberichte Deutsch-Asiatische Bank.

Table 6.1 *DAB bank notes in circulation in June 1914*

	Dollars	Taels
Qingdao	2,333,064	–
Shanghai	376,530	75,000
Tianjin	266,192	–
Beijing	237,643	23,690
Hankou	245,648	6,491
Total	3,459,077	105,181

Source: Müller-Jabusch, *Deutsch-Asiatische Bank*, p. 219

where other foreign banks were already present (see Table 6.1).[17] Only in Shandong, where the DAB remained the only foreign bank until 1912, did the note issuance reach levels similar to those of other foreign banks in China's ports, such as the Hongkong and Shanghai Banking Corporation (HSBC), whose notes issued in Shanghai in mid-1915 amounted to about 3.5 million silver dollars (~2.5 million Shanghai taels).[18] As suggested by Japanese and Chinese gazetteers, in the pre-war period the notes issued by the DAB in Shandong became an important means of payment in Qingdao, Jinan and Shandong more generally.[19] The issuing of bank notes, which had already been part of the business of several other foreign banks before 1907, undoubtedly increased the standing and influence of the DAB, especially in Shandong.

The growth of the bank was also reflected in the second larger expansion of the bank's branch network, which took place after 1904. To finance the expansion of the branch network and accommodate the 'further expansion of [the bank's] business', the DAB issued additional shares to increase its stock capital from 5 to 7.5 million Shanghai taels.[20] While the shares of the bank had

---

[17] For an overview of the presence of foreign banks in Shanghai, Tianjin and Hankou in 1902, see Yasuda, *Shinkoku kinyū kikan shoken*, pp. 30–2. On foreign banks in Beijing, see Beijing shi difangzhi bianzuan weiyuanhui, *Beijing zhi: jinrong zhi*, p. 89. For the presence of foreign banks in Beijing, Shanghai, Hankou and Tianjin in 1908 shortly after the DAB began to issue bank notes, see Appendix 2. On regional variations in foreign bank note issuing, also see Horesh, *Shanghai's Bund and Beyond*, p. 101.

[18] Betz to Bethmann-Hollweg (10 March 1913), BA/MA, RM3/6733, p. 22; Shandong sheng difang shizhi bianzuan weiyuanhui, *Shandong sheng zhi: jinrong zhi*, pp. 320–9; Horesh, *Shanghai's Bund and Beyond*, p. 100.

[19] Tōa Dōbunkai, *Shina shōbetsu zenshi*, 4:987–94, 1028; Tōa Dōbunkai, *Santō oyobi Kōshūwan*, pp. 127–9; Liang, *Laiyang xianzhi*, p. 532.

[20] 'Geschäft-Bericht für das Jahr 1904' (30 June 1905), HADB, Geschäftsberichte Deutsch-Asiatische Bank.

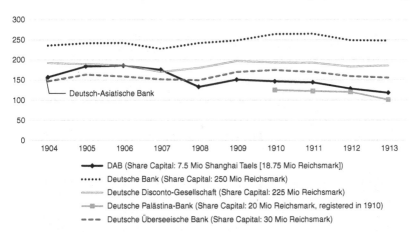

Figure 6.2 Share price of the DAB and other German banks, 1904–13, in Berlin, in per cent. Share capital in chart legend from 1914. *Source*: Verlag für Börsen- und Finanzliteratur A.-G., *Jahrbuch der Berliner Börse 1914/1915*; *BBZ*, 1904–13.

remained in the hands of the founding banks and had not been registered for trade on German stock markets before 1904, by 1906 the bank had registered all its shares (Figure 6.3) on the German stock market.[21] The delay in publicly issuing the shares seems to at least in part have been due to the bank's capital having been denominated and paid in by the founding banks in silver and the fall of silver in the years after the DAB's establishment.[22] Registering the shares of the bank at the stock market, where it could have potentially become subject to speculation, also shows that the German bankers now had sufficient trust in the bank's stability. As Figure 6.2 shows, they were not disappointed as the DAB's shares performed similar to the shares of other German banks, particularly those of other German overseas banks with a similar share capital, such as the Deutsche-Überseeische Bank and the Deutsche Palästina-Bank. At the same time, more than half of the shares remained in the hands of the founding banks and, as one German diplomat put it, 'business associates of the bank'

[21] DAB (Berlin) to Zulassungsstelle an der Börse zu Berlin (1 February 1934), BArch, R3118/ 379.

[22] Bernhard Dernburg, at different times a member of the DAB's supervisory board, explained that the founding banks had paid in the DAB's capital at a rate of 1 tael to 4.5 marks in 1890 and the public issue of the bank's shares was done at a rate of 1 tael to only 2.5 marks but at a premium that limited the loss of the founding banks' investment. See Bernhard Dernburg, 'Deutsch-Asiatische Bank' (17 January 1911), attachment to Dernburg to Bethmann Hollweg (27 January 1911), PAAA, R1.294. At the same time, the confidence that the shares could be issued at a premium shows the founding banks' confidence in the recent performance and potential of the bank.

Figure 6.3 Share of the DAB, 1906. Image courtesy of Deutsche Bank AG, Historical Institute.

also held a major portion of the shares, so that the founding banks remained in firm control of the DAB.[23]

The DAB extended its branch network between 1904 and 1906 from seven branches and agencies before 1904 to thirteen branches and agencies in 1906. A fourteenth office was added in Guangzhou in 1911 (see Table 6.2). This large-scale expansion of the branches between 1904 and 1906 was accompanied by a very positive development of the bank's profitability, as net profits rose from 623, 375 taels in 1903 to 876,662 taels in 1905, and dividends of 10 per cent (1903 and 1904) and 11 per cent (1905) were issued to the shareholders, before more difficult economic conditions arose in 1906 and throughout 1907 and 1908.[24] Situated at the heart of China's foreign trade, Shanghai (Figure 6.4) remained by far the most profitable branch of the bank

---

[23] Feindel to Bethmann Hollweg (26 May 1913), BArch, R901/4990, p. 51; 'Aufstellung der zur Generalversammlung vom 18. Juni 1909 hinterlegten Aktien der Deutsch-Asiatischen Bank' (18 June 1909), BArch, R901/4989, p. 136; 'Aufstellung der zu der ausserordentlichen General-Versammlung am 8. November 1928 hinterlegten Aktien der Deutsch-Asiatischen Bank' (8 November 1928), BArch, R3118/379, p. 79; 'Protokoll der Sitzung des Aufsichtsrats vom 8. Juni 1911' (8 June 1911), HADB, K07/010/I/01.

[24] Müller-Jabusch, *Deutsch-Asiatische Bank*, pp. 219–22.

Table 6.2 *Branches and agencies of the DAB, 1890–1914*

	Agency	Branch		Agency	Branch
Shanghai	–	1890	Jinan	1904	–
Tianjin	–	1890	Beijing	1905	1910
Calcutta	–	1896	Yokohama	–	1905
Berlin	–	1896	Singapore	–	1906
Hankou	1898	1910	Kobe	–	1906
Qingdao	1898	1899	Hamburg	–	1906
Hongkong	–	1900	Guangzhou	1911	1911

Source: HADB, Geschäftsberichte Deutsch-Asiatische Bank; BArch, R8024/ 283; BArch, R901/4990; *Ostasiatischer Lloyd* (10 July 1908); Müller-Jabusch, *Deutsch-Asiatische Bank*, pp. 54, 141, 225

Figure 6.4 The Shanghai Bund with the DAB on the left, early twentieth century. Postcard from author's collection.

in the decade before the First World War, but most of the other branches also generated regular profits.[25] The growth of the bank's business was representative of the continued internationalization of Chinese finance. While we have already seen how the internationalization of Chinese public finance progressed after 1900 in the previous

[25] Müller-Jabusch, *Deutsch-Asiatische Bank*, pp. 232–3.

chapters, the banking sector of the China coast also continued its trend towards further internationalization.[26] As Table 6.3 shows, during the decade before the First World War, foreign banks continued to enter China. However, in contrast to the 1890s and early 1900s, these foreign banks were less diverse, with half being Japanese banks mainly active in China's north, where Japan's economic influence was growing. This surge in the number of Japanese banks that established branches in China was to continue during the First World War.[27] If we once more take Shanghai as an example, we can also see that the internationalization of the banking sector continued in terms of the number of foreign banks and the amount of invested foreign bank capital in the banking sector. While the total number of foreign banks in Shanghai only rose from ten in 1903 to eleven in 1913, the estimated invested capital of these banks in Shanghai increased significantly from around £659,000 to around £772,000 during the same period (see Table 6.4).[28] Thus, the internationalization of Shanghai's banking sector continued between 1904 and 1913 and it still drew in new non-Chinese bank capital, even though it had already been home to several foreign banks at the beginning of the twentieth century. As a result, the cost of money also remained low in Shanghai, with the average yearly *yinchai* interest rate for inter-bank lending in Shanghai remaining stable at 5.4 per cent between 1904 and 1914, the same yearly average rate as during the period between 1890 and 1903.[29]

In considering the expansion of foreign banking along the China coast, it is also important to note that foreign banks did not only conduct business through their network of branches and agencies. They also often entered into agreements with foreign merchant firms, which acted as their agents in locations where these foreign banks did not have their own branch or agency. These firms would perform agreed-upon tasks for the bank in exchange for a fixed payment and commission. At times, an employee of the foreign bank would be sent to work under this agent.[30] While the DAB does not seem to have relied much on such agents, other foreign banks did. For example, in 1908 the HSBC had agent agreements with foreign firms in eight Chinese cities in addition to its own representations in seven Chinese cities. Some smaller foreign banks even mainly relied on such agent agreements for their business. A case in point is the Mercantile Bank of India. In 1908, this bank only operated one proper Chinese office in Hong Kong but had agent agreements with foreign firms in six other

---

[26] For an explanation of the indicators used here to assess the internationalization of the banking sector of the China coast, see Chapter 2.

[27] Tamagna, *Banking and Finance*, pp. 28–9.

[28] For the figures for 1903, see Chapter 2. As in Chapter 2, I divided the paid-up capital of the foreign banks in Shanghai by the number of their branches and agencies. Given that the Shanghai branch normally represented one of the largest branches of foreign banks, this provides a very conservative estimate of the invested bank capital in Shanghai.

[29] Calculated according to data in Kong, *Nankai jingji*, pp. 479–80.

[30] King, *HSBC History*, 1:123–5.

Table 6.3 Foreign banks established in China (asterisk marks Sino-foreign joint venture), 1904–13

	Nationality	Entry into China (incl. Hong Kong)	Stock capital in 1913 (£000)	Number of branches/sub-branches/agencies (incl. head branch) in 1913
Huaxing Bank*	France	1904	?	1
Nederlandsch-Indische Handelsbank	Netherlands	1906	2,474	16
Seiryu Bank*	Japan	1906	?	?
Société Franco-Belge de Tientsin (From 1910: Crédit foncier d'Extrême-Orient)	France/Belgium	1907	396	?
Banco-Italo-Chinese	Italy	1908[1]	?	?
Eastern Bank	Britain	1909	?	?
Bank of Chosen	Japan	1909	1,016	18
The Commercial Guarantee Bank of China*	Germany/Japan	1909	?	?
Antung Bank	Japan	1911	?	1
Manchuria Commercial Bank	Japan	1911	?	1
Antung Savings Bank	Japan	1911	?	?
International Saving Society	France	1912	?	?
Bank of Dalian	Japan	1912	?	?
Bank of Changchun	Japan	1912	?	1
Sino-French Savings Society*	France	ca.1912	?	?

Table 6.3 Cont.

	Nationality	Entry into China (incl. Hong Kong)	Stock capital in 1913 (£000)	Number of branches/sub-branches/agencies (incl. head branch) in 1913
Banque Industrielle de Chine*	France	1913	1,783	2
Industrial and Commercial Bank	Japan	1913	?	?
Southern Manchurian Bank	Japan	1913	?	1

Source: North-China Herald (9 August 1913), *Gil Blas* (20 January 1910), Nederlandsch-Indische Handelsbank, *Nederlandsch-Indische Handelsbank*; Chōsen Ginkō, *Chōsen Ginkō Nijugo Nen Shi*; Huang, *Wai Guo Zaihua Gongshang Qiye Cidian*, passim; Jiang and Jiang, *Jindai Zhongguo Waishang Yinhang*, pp. 356–8; Tōa Dōbunkai Chōsa Hensanbu, *Shina Kinyū Kikan*, passim; *Shenbao* (10 October 1918). In the rare cases where a slight discrepancy exists between sources about a bank's year of entry into China, I have chosen the year with the most reliable evidence. Jiang and Jiang, *Jindai Zhongguo Waishang Yinhang* also lists a Japanese bank called Baoxing Yinhang 寶興銀行 operating in Shanghai around 1897/1904. As I have not been able to find any other evidence for this (including the *Desk Hong List* for 1903 and 1904), I have not included it here. Figures not available in £ were converted.

[1] I was only able to find evidence for the existence of the Banco Italo-Chinese in Guangzhou in 1908. See Hongkong Daily Press, *Directory & Chronicle 1908*, p. 907.

Table 6.4 *Foreign banks in Shanghai, 1913*

	Nationality	Paid-up capital (£)	Branches/ sub-branches/ agencies	Estimated capital Shanghai branch/ sub-branch/agency (£)
Bank of Taiwan	Japan	762,643	29[1]	26,298
Banque Belge Pour L'Etranger (Formerly Sino-Belgian Bank)	Belgium	1,188,728	7	169,818
Banque de L'Indochine	France	475,491	19	25,025
Chartered Bank of India, Australia and China	Britain	1,200,000	37	32,432
Deutsch-Asiatische Bank	Germany	1,015,434	14	72,531
Hongkong and Shanghai Banking Corporation	Britain	1,500,000	33	45,454
International Banking Corporation	United States	650,000	18	36,111
Mercantile Bank of India	Britain	562,500	15	37,500
Russo-Asiatic Bank	Russian	4,745,000	56	84,732
Netherlands Trading Society	Netherlands	3,750,000	29	129,310
Yokohama Specie Bank	Japan	3,050,574	27	112,984

Source: This table includes those foreign banks that are listed in Bell and Woodhead, *The China Year Book, 1913*, p. 364 (this publication does not mention the Shanghai branches of the DAB and Yokohama Specie Bank. On these, see Table 6.2 and *The Economist* (18 October 1913)). The remaining data comes from: *The Economist* (12 October 1912, 4 January 1913, 22 February 1913, 18 October 1913, 8 November 1913, 21 February 1914, 23 May 1914, 24 October 1914 (as can be seen, in a few instances I had to rely on issues from slightly before or after 1913)); Hongkong Daily Press, *Directory & Chronicle 1913*, pp. 25, 28; Morriss and Maguire, *China Stock and Share Handbook*, pp. 17, 23; Huang, *Wai Guo zaihua gongshang qiye cidian*, passim; Manfred Pohl, ed., *Handbook on the History of European Banks* (Hants: Edward Elgar, 1994), p. 212. For the DAB, see Table 6.2 and Müller-Jabusch, *Deutsch-Asiatische Bank*, table opposite p. 326. Figures not available in £ were converted.

[1] The Bank of Taiwan always added '&c' at the end of listings of its offices in its advertisements. However, I have only taken into account those branches and agencies concretely named in their advertisement in *The Economist* (18 October 1913).

ports. Through such agent agreements, the business networks of foreign banks and the availability of their services extended much further than their branch and agency network would suggest. This will have been especially significant for smaller ports like Shantou or Zhenjiang, where no or only a limited direct presence of foreign banks existed, but local foreign firms acting as agents for foreign banks could provide some of the services of such banks.[31]

In addition to this expansion of foreign banking, as explained earlier, China's foreign trade continued to grow rapidly and more than doubled between 1900 and 1913. During this period, it also grew more diverse as countries like Germany and Japan continued to increase their share of China's foreign trade.[32] The monetary transactions connected to this trade, indemnity payments and China's continued foreign borrowing from diverse sources also meant that the transnational capital flows between China and other economies remained diverse and continued to grow at a rapid pace, contributing to the continuing fast-paced internationalization of the banking sector of China's treaty ports.

Despite the growth of the DAB's business, the criticism of the bank by the German government that had started with Max von Brandt more than two decades earlier continued. At the heart of this critique was that the bank maintained its risk-averse business strategy based on the principle that 'the basic condition of all conducted business is appropriate security for the bank'.[33] Consequently, the DAB remained unwilling to give preferential treatment to German firms or engage in any other business if it did not expect that such business would be safe and profitable. German diplomats continued to criticize the tight control of the Berlin directors and board members over the operations of the bank and the bank's lack of accommodation and support towards German firms, who as a consequence turned to other more obliging foreign banks for credit.[34] Connected to this criticism was the accusation that the bankers were purely driven by 'greed' and not willing to even 'risk a penny', in order to ensure that they received large profits. The criticism went so far as to suggest that Urbig would 'stop at nothing in matters of money, but has no sense for the national significance' of the DAB as a supporter for German commerce.[35] When the DAB partnered with non-German instead of German firms, it was even accused of

---

[31] The analysis in this paragraph is based on the overview of the branches/agencies and agents of foreign banks in major Chinese ports in 1908 found in Appendix 2.

[32] Ratenhof, *Chinapolitik*, pp. 564–5.

[33] Quote from 'Geschäfts-Anweisung für die Deutsch-Asiatische Bank in Shanghai und Berlin' (13 June 1900), BArch, R2/41689, pp. 32–3. For a later confirmation of the same guideline, see 'Geschäfts-Anweisung für die Filialen Calcutta, Hongkong, Tientsin und Tsingtau und die Agenturen Hankow und Tsinanfu' (24 February 1904), BArch, R2/41689, pp. 34–5.

[34] Auswärtiges Amt, Untitled Note (2 January 1913), BArch, R901/4990, p. 29.

[35] Feindel to Bethmann Hollweg (26 May 1913), BArch, R901/4990, p. 51.

having an 'un-German attitude'.[36] This ever-increasing resentment of German diplomats towards the bank led to plans in the Foreign Office to help establish a second German bank in China, but the First World War put an end to such schemes.[37]

The increasing estrangement between the bank and the Foreign Office reflected the larger conflict between the German bank, which was a globally operating business mainly interested in running a profitable business across national boundaries, and the German state that advocated economic nationalism and autarky in the form of a German commercial bloc and, if necessary, demanded from the bank that it make sacrifices and take additional risks for the larger cause of the growth and independence of German commerce in China.[38]

Despite this criticism, in 1914 the bankers could look back to over two decades of profitable business in China. As Figure 6.5 shows, after the difficulties of the early years of the bank's business in China had been overcome, it generated yearly dividends that were comparable to other German overseas banks and in some years even reached those of the large German joint-stock banks, such as the Deutsche Bank and the Disconto-Gesellschaft.[39] This is especially remarkable if we once more remember that the bank had originally been established by the founding banks primarily for the purpose of facilitating large government loans and German investment in infrastructure in China. The German bankers had indeed managed to challenge the British monopoly of supplying capital to China and had succeeded in making Germany the second largest investor in Chinese bonds, with 24.3 per cent of Chinese government obligations held by German investors in 1914.[40] Nevertheless, the high hopes held by German bankers for investment in the loan and railway business in China were on the whole not realized, so the bank had to learn to generate profits through its day-to-day business, which it had done successfully since the mid-1890s.

At the same time, the bank's performance always remained tied to the overall economic development of China. This is shown in the reduced dividends issued between 1907 and 1912 resulting from the impact of the global economic crisis

---

[36] Mechlenburg to Bethmann Hollweg (27 February 1911), BArch, R901/4990, p. 3.

[37] Deutsches Konsulat Hankou to Bethmann Hollweg (29 March 1916), BArch, R901/4990, pp. 150–1; Müller-Jabusch, *Deutsch-Asiatische Bank*, pp. 235–7.

[38] For the DAB's preference of economic over political goals also see Barth, *Imperialismen*, especially p. 409. Barth, however, in his work maintains that the bank remained subordinate to and part of the political development of Western imperialism in China in the years preceding the war.

[39] Akagawa argues that the DAB's business development was particularly profitable during the early twentieth century with trade finance at its centre. However, he does not compare the DAB's performance to other German banks. See Akagawa, 'Doitsu Ginkō – Du A Ginkō 1870–1913 nian', pp. 1085–7.

[40] Hou, *Foreign Investment*, p. 229.

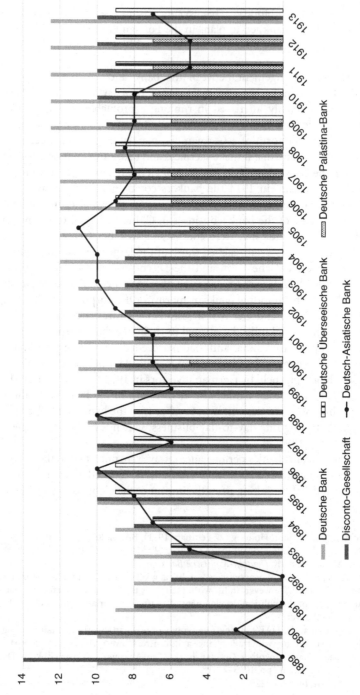

Figure 6.5 Dividends of the DAB and other German banks, 1889–1913, in per cent. *Source: BBZ* (1889–1914); Müller-Jabusch, *Deutsch-Asiatische Bank*, table opposite p. 326; Klaus Strasser, *Die Deutschen Banken im Ausland*, p. 195; Verlag Für Börsen- und Finanzliteratur a.-g., *Jahrbuch Der Berliner Börse 1914/1915*.

Legend:
- Deutsche Bank
- Disconto-Gesellschaft
- Deutsche Überseeische Bank
- Deutsch-Asiatische Bank
- Deutsche Palästina-Bank

of 1907 and the 1911 revolution on China's economy.[41] The DAB's business also still paled in comparison to China's leading foreign bank, the HSBC, whose total assets were worth £39.5 million at the end of 1913 compared to the DAB's mere £10.3 million.[42] The bankers acknowledged the superior position of the HSBC and explained it by the British bank's early establishment in China, its large reserves accumulated over many years of business and the fact that British merchants, who played such an important role in China's foreign trade, mainly favoured their own home institution.[43] Besides these explanations, an additional reason for the success of the HSBC was its magnanimity in business that contrasted with the DAB's risk-averseness.[44]

Even though this strategy of avoiding unnecessary risk might have prevented the bank from growing more quickly, the bank had shown that a successful business as a foreign bank in China, where the business environment remained volatile because of the political instability after the 1911 revolution and the continuing fluctuations in the price of silver, could be built based on this strategy that stressed the limiting of risk.[45] Moreover, the bank had successfully used what was arguably its biggest strength, the support of all major German banks and unrivalled control of the German financial market, to become one of the leading foreign banks in the Chinese loan business, which had also led to it becoming a member of several important Chinese loan consortia and one of the depositing banks for China's customs and salt revenue. As a result, the bank enjoyed a high standing in China, which was acknowledged by Chinese contemporaries like the famous Chinese banker Xu Jiqing 徐寄廎, who witnessed the last years before the DAB's liquidation and, despite the clear superiority of the HSBC in terms of the fundamentals of the banks' business, wrote that before the war the DAB's 'economic power was not inferior to that of the HSBC'.[46] The good standing of the DAB was also confirmed by Bernhard Dernburg, a German banker who had travelled in China and Japan in 1910. After his return, he reported that the DAB enjoyed a good reputation 'among the Chinese [people] and among [the bank's] foreign competitors' and, despite its relatively small working capital, ranked

---

[41] Müller-Jabusch, *Deutsch-Asiatische Bank*, pp. 220–32.
[42] 'Geschäft-Bericht für das Jahr 1913' (29 May 1914), HADB, Geschäftsberichte Deutsch-Asiatische Bank; King, *HSBC History*, 2:49.
[43] *BBZ* (28 June 1910, evening edition).
[44] Deutsches Konsulat Hankou to Bethmann Hollweg (29 March 1916), BArch, R901/4990, pp. 147–8.
[45] On the political instability and continued fluctuations of the silver price see the DAB's yearly reports between 1911 and 1913 in HADB, Geschäftsberichte, Deutsch-Asiatische Bank. For a similar positive assessment of the DAB's performance that takes into account the volatile business environment in China, also see Strasser, *Die Deutschen Banken im Ausland*, p. 128.
[46] Xu, *Shanghai jinrong shi*, p. 102. For a similar Chinese view from 1930, see Yang, *Shanghai jinrong zuzhi gaiyao*, p. 178.

'4th or perhaps 5th' among the foreign banks in terms of its 'importance as a commercial bank' for the business in China and second – presumably only to the HSBC – in terms of 'its importance in the international loan business' in China.[47] Based on this standing and its general performance, it seemed in 1914 as if the DAB could look to the future with hope and confidence. However, this all changed with the outbreak of the First World War.

6.2   The Outbreak of War

On 1 October 1914 the Shanghai newspaper Shenbao featured an article about the reaction of German businessmen to the outbreak of the First World War. The businessman the newspaper interviewed was Alfred Eggeling, deputy-manager of the DAB in Beijing. The article described how since the outbreak of the war Eggeling would spend his free time studying newspapers and other sources to keep himself updated on the progress of the European war. He had put up a big and detailed map of Europe in his office on which he stuck little flags representing the troop movements of the European armies, which he would update according to the newest developments in Europe.[48] The article vividly showed that after July 1914 the German bankers in China were closely following the events in Europe that increasingly also influenced and threatened their business and the position the bank had established for itself in China.

With the beginning of the First World War in Europe, the bank's business suffered a severe shock. The annual report of the DAB for 1914 describes the 'decisive impact' the outbreak of the war had on the bank's business. It disrupted 'the trade in and with East Asia'. Most of the maritime traffic with Europe 'was practically completely stopped and new business transactions were disturbed'.[49] According to one Chinese commentator, commerce in Shanghai was in a desolate state and 'the great impact [of the outbreak of the European war] on China's economy was even more severe than at the time of the conflict between North and South during the previous revolution [of 1911]'.[50] Only gradually did German and other merchants adapt to the new circumstances, partly by using new trade routes through America. Still, the fact that China's maritime customs income decreased by 11 per cent between 1913

---

[47] Bernhard Dernburg, 'Deutsch-Asiatische Bank' (17 January 1911), attachment to Dernburg to Bethmann Hollweg (27 January 1911), PAAA, R1.294. On Dernburg's travels, also see Bernhard Dernburg, *Japan und China: Eine wirtschaftspolitische Studienreise, Herbst 1910* (Berlin: Reichsdruckerei, 1911), attachment to Dernburg to Bethmann Hollweg (27 January 1911), PAAA, R1.294.

[48] *Shenbao* (1 October 1914).

[49] 'Geschäft-Bericht für das Jahr 1914' (29 April 1916), HADB, Geschäftsberichte, Deutsch-Asiatische Bank.

[50] Lu, 'Ouzhan ji yu Shanghai shangye zhi yingxiang', pp. 1–5.

and 1914 was proof of the negative impact the outbreak of the war had on China trade and consequently also on the bank's business in trade finance.[51] The outbreak of war also led to a severe crisis in the money market of the China coast. Importantly, for the first time it was the foreign banks that were the source of instability that caused the crisis. While they had previously been pillars of stability that at times would act as a quasi-central bank and lender of last resort and inject money into the market to stabilize the banking sector, people now feared that foreign banks might not be able to operate normally anymore because of the war in Europe.[52] Rumours that these banks might be compelled to close their business soon spread. For example, in Beijing news was going around that the DAB branch there did not operate and exchange currency as usual anymore.[53] As a result, runs on foreign banks occurred and the people that had previously trusted the bank notes issued by the foreign banks now frantically tried to exchange them for cash, which led to a tightening of the money market.[54] This sudden lack of trust in foreign banks was not limited to general Chinese customers, but extended to Chinese banks. For example, when news of the outbreak of war reached China, the Bank of China (Zhongguo yinhang 中國銀行) ordered branches to withdraw the money they had deposited with foreign banks.[55] Confronted with this sudden demand for cash, the foreign banks in Shanghai seem to have recalled loans and deposits, which led to a further shortage in the money supply.[56]

Given this unprecedented crisis in the trust of the public in foreign banks, the tables were now turned and the Chinese state and Chinese banks had to

---

[51] 'Geschäft-Bericht für das Jahr 1914' (29 April 1916), HADB, Geschäftsberichte, Deutsch-Asiatische Bank.

[52] *Shenbao* (12 August 1914); Shenbao (21 August 1914); 'China's Finances: Safety of Foreign Banks', *North-China Herald* (8 August 1914). For an example of how foreign banks had previously acted as a kind of central bank and lender of last resort and helped stabilize the Chinese money market, see Marie-Claire Bergère, *Crise Financière*, pp. 1–12. Also see Moazzin, 'Sino-Foreign Business Networks', p. 999. Cheng also points to the First World War as the beginning of a loss of trust in foreign banks, but only gives the DAB's demise as a proper example. See Cheng, *Banking in Modern China*, p. 76.

[53] *Shenbao* (12 August 1914).

[54] *Shenbao* (21 August 1914); 'China's Finances: Safety of Foreign Banks', *North-China Herald* (8 August 1914). Cheng gives an example of Chinese depositors in Hankou actually shifting their deposits to the American International Banking Corporation (Huaqi yinhang 花旗銀行) after the outbreak of the First World War. See Cheng, *Banking in Modern China*, p. 76. However, it is unclear where these depositors shifted their money from to the American bank. Moreover, this might have simply been the case because the United States only entered the war late and because the war was generally known in China as the 'European war' (*Ouzhan* 歐戰), thus not implicating the American bank as much.

[55] Bank of China (Tianjin) to Bank of China (Beijing) (7 August 1914), TMA, J0161-3-19, pp. 13–14; Bank of China (Beijing) to Bank of China (Tianjin) (8 August 1914), TMA, J161-3-19, pp. 15–16.

[56] 'Ouzhan yu shangye zhi yingxiang', *Ouzhou zhanji* 7 (1914), pp. 152–3.

come to the rescue of the foreign banks and the banking sector of the China coast. As evidence from Shanghai and Tianjin shows, to stabilize the money market and prevent speculators from making use of the volatile situation, the Chinese government ordered the additional minting of currency, instructed the Customs Service to prohibit the export of silver currency to avoid its outflow, punished merchants that demanded extra fees for the discount of foreign bank notes or otherwise obstructed the functioning of the market and asked merchants to continue to accept the notes of foreign banks as usual.[57] However, the market seems to have only been stabilized again when the Bank of Communications (Jiaotong yinhang 交通銀行) and the Bank of China – two large, recently established Chinese banks that represented the new type of modern Chinese financial institutions that followed Western models – pledged that they would accept and exchange the bank notes of all foreign banks.[58] It now was the Chinese state and Chinese banks that had to help stabilize the market. This also showed that the weakening of foreign banks due to the outbreak of the war opened up an even wider space for agency in the banking sector of the Chinese frontier for Chinese actors to assume than before. At the same time, the impact of the outbreak of war in Europe on the banking sector was also proof of the high degree of internationalization and global interdependence of the banking sector on the China coast in 1914.

Besides the impact of the downturn in Chinese commerce on the DAB's business, a more direct consequence of the outbreak of the war was that the bank's branches under British authority in Singapore, Hong Kong and Calcutta were closed and their liquidation started. After the occupation of Qingdao by the Japanese in November 1914, the Qingdao branch of the DAB was also closed. The branches in Yokohama and Kobe were allowed to continue their operations under strict regulations and limitations until being forced to close in 1916.[59] Thus, by the middle of 1915, the number of branches and agencies fully under the DAB's control had been decimated from fourteen to only eight. Its European staff had shrunk from 123 to only 57, as many bankers had been called up for military service or had been captured or interned in Asia.[60] The immediate result of these events was that the bank's

---

[57] *Shenbao* (12 August 1914); Tianjin Municipal Police to Tianjin Chamber of Commerce (28 August 1914), TMA, J128-2-3014.

[58] *Shenbao* (21 August 1914). On the Bank of China and Bank of Communications, see Cheng, *Banking in Modern China*, pp. 29–32, 53–4.

[59] 'Geschäft-Bericht für das Jahr 1914' (29 April 1916), HADB, Geschäftsberichte Deutsch-Asiatische Bank; 'Geschäft-Bericht über die Jahre 1915–1927' (21 September 1928), HADB, Geschäftsberichte, Deutsch-Asiatische Bank; 'Dokua Ginkō eigyō teishi', *Yomiuri Shimbun* (29 September 1916).

[60] 'Protokoll der Sitzung des Geschäfts-Ausschusses vom 16. Juni 1915' (16 June 1915), HADB, K07/010/I/01.

total assets shrank from 76,237,473 Shanghai taels at the end of 1913 to only 47,270,927 Shanghai taels at the end of 1914.[61]

As long as China remained neutral, the political stability in the treaty ports was maintained and allowed the DAB and other foreign enterprises to continue to operate their businesses. However, after the beginning of the war, foreign businesses like the DAB were not safe from the impact of the political events in Europe, which now was also felt in China's treaty ports. Besides its negative impact on commerce, the outbreak of war also led to the disentanglement of the cooperation among foreign banks in China that had not only been important for providing the Chinese government with loans, but also crucial for the functioning of the banking sector in the treaty ports. The German bankers first experienced the new complications this created for the operations of the DAB right after the outbreak of war, when the foreign banks of the Allied countries were suddenly not allowed to fulfil their agreements with the DAB anymore for the buying and selling of currency.[62] The exclusion of the bank from the community of foreign banks was taken a step further in 1916. When the foreign banks devised plans to assist the Bank of China during a crisis, the DAB was not allowed to attend the relevant meeting of the Foreign Bankers' Association in Shanghai and, eventually, the foreign bankers established a new association for foreign banks without the German bank.[63] These new complications also manifested themselves in the Chinese loan consortium, as the war saw the end of what was called 'cosmopolitan finance' before 1914, the cooperation of foreign banks to provide the Chinese state with loans.[64] While the members of the Five Group Consortium, which had supplied China with the Reorganisation Loan, were formally still bound by the consortium agreement to share all Chinese government loans, both the fact that the German group was now the enemy of the other consortium members and Europe's diminished financial resources largely rendered the consortium defunct during the war. This gap was filled by American and, more importantly, Japanese loans as Japan came to monopolize the financing of the Chinese government during the war.[65]

---

[61] 'Geschäft-Bericht für das Jahr 1913' (29 May 1914), HADB, Geschäftsberichte Deutsch-Asiatische Bank; 'Geschäft-Bericht für das Jahr 1914' (29 April 1916), HADB, Geschäftsberichte Deutsch-Asiatische Bank.

[62] 'Geschäft-Bericht für das Jahr 1914' (29 April 1916), HADB, Geschäftsberichte Deutsch-Asiatische Bank.

[63] Knipping to Bethmann Hollweg (30 May 1916), PAAA, R17.813, p. 259; Hintze to Bethmann Hollweg (October 1916), PAAA, R17.814, pp. 147–8; Müller-Jabusch, *Deutsch-Asiatische Bank*, pp. 251–2.

[64] 'Cosmopolitan Finance in China', *The Times (London)* (26 September 1913).

[65] 'The Powers and Chinese Finance', *The Times (London)* (5 January 1916); Dayer, *Finance and Empire*, pp. 85–7; Dayer, *Bankers and Diplomats*, pp. 39–73; King, *HSBC History*, 2:578–82. While Japan had only held 1.8 per cent of Chinese government obligations in 1914, it held 31.5 per cent by 1930. This was far more than any other country except Britain.

Finally, the First World War also marked the end of the cosmopolitan atmosphere in Chinese finance and China's treaty ports, which now gave way to more nationalistic sentiments.[66] People like HSBC London manager Charles Addis, who were in favour of transnational collaboration and at first hoped that cooperation between German and British bankers could be resumed after the end of hostilities, were soon side-lined by more nationalist voices bolstering anti-German sentiments.[67] Longstanding personal friendships across national lines, like the friendship that had developed between Hillier and Cordes, now also became the subject of scrutiny and criticism.[68] Probably no other individual illustrates the new atmosphere in China's treaty port more clearly than DAB deputy-manager Alfred Eggeling, who truly was a product of pre-war globalization, but now was forced to take sides. While Eggeling's family was originally from Germany, Eggeling was a British citizen born in Edinburgh as the son of Hans Julius Eggeling, professor of Sanskrit at the University of Edinburgh. After schooling in Scotland, Eggeling worked for several businesses first in Paris and Brussels and then in Qingdao, where he eventually joined the DAB. Before the war, Eggeling had been welcome among both the British and German communities in China. This changed after the outbreak of war. At first, British minister to China John Jordan tried to persuade Eggeling to leave the DAB, but when this failed Eggeling was marked as a traitor and had to defend himself, stating that, despite his loyalty to the DAB, he still was 'as good a Britisher' as others.[69] There were also those who viewed the effects of this atmosphere positively. German diplomats welcomed the fact that German firms – because of the war – now exclusively relied on the DAB and hoped that this could be continued after the war.[70] Such nationalistic feelings were also common on the side of the Allies, where people like the Beijing correspondent of the London *Times* George E. Morrison, who long had viewed the growth of German commerce and finance and Anglo-German cooperation in China with suspicion, came to see the war as an opportunity to eliminate the German presence in China.[71]

See Hou, *Foreign Investment*, p. 229. On Japan's growing role in providing capital to China, also see Schiltz, *The Money Doctors from Japan*, ch. 3.

[66] On the rise of nationalist sentiment in the treaty ports during the war also see Bickers, *Getting Stuck in for Shanghai*.

[67] Dayer, *Finance and Empire*, pp. 85–7; King, *HSBC History*, 2:604–6.

[68] King, *HSBC History*, 2:607–9.

[69] Quote from 'The Peking Gazette', *North-China Herald* (28 November 1914); Paul W. Wilm, *Rückblicke eines Neunzigjährigen; Erlebtes in der Heimat, in China und der Mongolei, in Brasilien und in Südostasien* (unpublished manuscript, ca.1990), Teil II a: 31–8, StuDeO-Bibl., Nr. 371c.

[70] Deutsches Konsulat Hankou to Bethmann Hollweg (29 March 1916), BArch, R901/4990, p. 146.

[71] G. E. Morrison to McCall (4 October 1916), in Lo, *The Correspondence of G.E. Morrison II*, pp. 557–8; Moazzin, 'From Globalization to Liquidation', pp. 60–1. On Morrison's

6.3 Keeping China Out of the War

With the great impact that the outbreak of the war had on the bank's business and the wider realm of trade and finance in China, it is understandable why bankers like Eggeling paid such close attention to the events in distant Europe. Despite the problems the DAB faced, the bankers tried to maintain their business in China, but also took precautions for the possibility of a worsening of the situation in China. First of all, to continue its operations, the bank had to find alternative ways of maintaining communication between Berlin and the branches in China and of transferring money between China and Germany, as this was becoming more and more difficult as the war proceeded. The bank ordered two DAB directors, Richard Timmermann and Adolf Koehn, who were in the United States at the time, to establish a small office for the bank in New York.[72] This measure not only made it possible for the bankers in China to maintain communications with Berlin, but also made the remittance of funds through the New York office possible. Because of the decline in China's foreign trade and the limitations imposed on the bank's business by the war, a high amount of capital remained unemployed in the Chinese branches. As there was no use for these funds in China, but, it seems, also as a response to the increased risk of storing this capital in the Chinese branches after the outbreak of war, the branches in China remitted consider-able sums of money back to the German branches through the New York office. As a result, by September 1917, the DAB held 41 million reichsmark (~£2 million) in Germany, which accounted for about a third of its total assets at the end of 1914.[73] Thus, the New York office was used not only to maintain communications between Germany and China, but also to remit part of the bank's assets back to Berlin, where they could be shielded from the increased political risk in China.

---

anti-German sentiments also see King, *HSBC History*, 2:531, 613; G. E. Morrison to Hillier (27 July 1909), in Lo, *The Correspondence of G.E. Morrison I*, pp. 507–8.

[72] 'Protokoll der Sitzung des Aufsichtsrates vom 5. Januar 1915' (5 January 1915), HADB, K07/010/I/01; Müller-Jabusch, *Deutsch-Asiatische Bank*, p. 243. The difficulties in com-municating with the Chinese branches were most likely mainly due to the Allied disrup-tion of German global communications after the outbreak of war. On this, see Headrick, *The Invisible Weapon*, ch. 8.

[73] Müller-Jabusch, *Deutsch-Asiatische Bank*, p. 243; 'Bericht über die Besprechung vom 6. September 1917 betreffs Auszahlung chinesischer Kupons in der Deutsch-Asiatischen Bank, vormittags 11 Uhr' (6 September 1917), HADB, S2583. In this meeting on 6 September 1917, Urbig responds to the worries of the banker Georg von Simson about possible confiscations in China by saying that the DAB directors in Berlin had pressured the branches to shift funds to Berlin after the outbreak of war. As no exchange rates for reichsmark and Shanghai taels are available during the First World War, the exchange rate for 1913 was used (including for the estimate in British pounds), so that we can only arrive at a rough estimate that the funds held in Germany amounted to a third of the total assets the bank had possessed at the end of 1914.

Another problem the bank faced was that it had to continue its payments for the Boxer Indemnity and for previous Chinese loans to the German government and bondholders in Germany. In order to continue these payments after the outbreak of the war, the bank used the indemnity and loan payments of the Chinese government worth £6,000 a day to buy bills of exchange and high amounts of gold on the Chinese market, thereby becoming the largest purchaser of gold in China at the time. The indemnity payments seem to have been paid directly to the German legation in China to be used by German diplomats for the expenses of the German legation and consulates and for the purposes of war. To pay bondholders in Germany, the bank shipped purchased bills of exchange and gold to the United States, where the bank used most of these assets to purchase German reichsmark, which were then transferred to Germany. In this way, in 1915 alone between 20 and 25 million reichsmark (~£976,965 and ~£1.2 million) was transferred to Germany and used to pay bondholders.[74]

While the bank tried to maintain its China business and protect its assets, its survival in China hinged on the question of whether or not China would remain neutral in the war. The German bankers in China dealt with the political risk of a possible Chinese declaration of war by trying to use the bank's limited financial resources to provide loans to the Chinese government to keep China out of the war. Given the still destitute state of China's public finance, the Chinese government proved receptive to the DAB's offers. The DAB not only continued its pre-war practice of providing the Chinese government with financial help, issuing loans worth around 4 million silver dollars between December 1914 and December 1916, but also tried to conclude a separate larger loan agreement with China, which was to stipulate that China was to remain neutral.[75] The opportunity for such a loan appeared in the spring of 1916, when the Chinese minister of finance approached the bank for a loan of 6 million silver dollars. Beijing manager Heinrich Cordes, who, together with German minister Paul von Hintze, was the driving force behind the plan of using financial means to keep China out of the war, immediately started negotiations with the Chinese minister.[76] When Cordes raised the

---

[74] 'Germans Still Trading in China', *Manchester Guardian* (15 November 1915), PAAA, R17.813, p. 190; DAB (Berlin) to Auswärtiges Amt (11 March 1916), PAAA, R17.813, p. 201; Reichenau to Auswärtiges Amt (13 October 1914), PAAA, R17.813, p. 162; Lucius to Auswärtiges Amt (16 November 1914), PAAA, R17.813, pp. 163–4. For the estimate in British pounds, I have again used the exchange rate from 1913.

[75] For the mentioned loans between December 1914 and December 1916 see Xu et al., *Cong bainian quru*, 2:605–10. The sum does not include the 10 million silver dollar advance agreement discussed later.

[76] Müller-Jabusch, *Deutsch-Asiatische Bank*, pp. 245–6; Hintze to Auswärtiges Amt (29 August 1916), *PVH*, pp. 378–9; Bernstorff to Auswärtiges Amt (2 September 1916), PAAA R17.813, pp. 262–3; Urbig, 'Memorandum' (4 October 1916), PAAA, R17.814,

point of China's commitment to neutrality, the Chinese government agreed to issue a declaration guaranteeing that it would remain neutral if the loan sum could be raised to 10 million silver dollars.[77]

When Cordes asked the German consortium about the possibility of providing such a loan, the bankers in Berlin were reluctant, as they felt that the loan was not feasible from a 'purely commercial perspective'. The main obstacle was that because of the demands imposed by the war on Germany's capital market and the unstable political situation in China, the consortium did not believe that such an amount of money could be raised on the German financial market. Therefore, the only alternative would have been that the banks of the German consortium connected to the DAB provided the money for the loan themselves. However, the consortium banks were not willing to use their own funds to provide the loan, unless the German government felt that it wished to financially support China 'for political purposes' and would guarantee the repayment of principal and interest of the loan.[78] For the members of the German consortium in Berlin, who would have been busy with the demands of the war in Europe, China had become a matter of only secondary importance. The German government proved unwilling to commit to any guarantee at first, as the Foreign Office believed that any change in China's neutrality was unlikely at the moment.[79] While he supported the loan deal itself, von Hintze also counselled the Foreign Office that the increasing weakness of the Beijing government made a political guarantee for a loan not advisable.[80] Therefore, at least in Berlin, the issue of a major loan to the Chinese government was not further pursued for now.

In Beijing, Cordes saw things differently and continued the negotiations on his own, supported by German minister von Hintze. He was determined that this was the only way of safeguarding the bank's business in China and decided to take things into his own hands. In August 1916, Cordes communicated to the DAB in Berlin that he had advanced 3 million silver dollars to the Beijing government for six months and had offered to increase the advance to 10 million silver dollars. The 7 million silver dollars difference was to be provided by the DAB as the reichsmark equivalent of the payments for the Boxer Indemnity and Tianjin–Pukou loan due to be paid by the Chinese government to the DAB between September 1916 and June 1917. This would have effectively meant that the DAB would make these payments to the

p. 17. While Urbig dates the beginning of the negotiations to February 1916, Müller-Jabusch states that they started in March.

[77] Urbig, 'Memorandum' (4 October 1916), PAAA, R17.814, p. 17.
[78] Quotes from DAB, Untitled Memorandum, attachment to DAB (Berlin) to Norddeutsche Bank in Hamburg (24 May 1916), HADB, K01/969; Urbig, 'Aktennotiz' (16 May 1916), PAAA, R17.813, p. 241.
[79] Müller-Jabusch, *Deutsch-Asiatische Bank*, p. 246.
[80] Hintze to Auswärtiges Amt (28 July 1916), PAAA, R17.813, p. 250.

German bondholders and the German government when they became due and each payment would take the form of an advance to the Chinese government.[81] Cordes believed these advances were 'the only feasible guarantee for the defense of our whole position in China'.[82]

In Berlin, Urbig was taken aback by Cordes' independent actions and still viewed the loan deal as primarily political. Nevertheless, he again started negotiations with the German government about a guarantee for the loan. The consortium banks now were willing to forgo a government guarantee for the 3 million silver dollar advance already issued by Cordes and only demanded a guarantee for the remaining 7 million silver dollars.[83] As von Hintze reported that the Allied countries were also trying to offer a large loan to China with the condition that China take measures against German commerce, the German Foreign Office now favoured a German government guarantee for the loan, which the German government eventually agreed to provide.[84] Urbig immediately notified Cordes and the agreement for the total advance of 10 million silver dollars with the Chinese government was signed in December 1916.[85]

Although the loan agreement had finally been concluded, eventually it came as too little too late. Most importantly, the bankers failed to obtain any guarantee for China's neutrality. Cordes later related that the Chinese government had been inclined to issue a letter of guarantee to the German government pledging its neutrality, but eventually such a guarantee did not materialize.[86] It seems that, if there had ever been a serious intention at all, the willingness of the Chinese government to guarantee its neutrality in exchange for a major German loan had already vanished by the time the loan was concluded. Thus, all the bank could hope for was that these advances might induce China not to sever relations and declare war against Germany. However, the Allies were already offering much more than the German bankers could. While the German bankers with difficulty had been able to offer a limited advance of 10 million silver dollars against the German share of the Boxer Indemnity and Tianjin–Pukou loan payments, the Allies promised China the complete postponement of the payment of their share of the Boxer Indemnity until the end of the war if China severed relations with Germany.[87]

---

[81] Urbig, 'Memorandum' (4 October 1916), PAAA, R17.814, pp. 17–19; DAB (Berlin) to Norddeutsche Bank in Hamburg (18 November 1916), HADB, K01/969.

[82] Quoted in Müller-Jabusch, *Deutsch-Asiatische Bank*, p. 247.

[83] Urbig, 'Memorandum' (4 October 1916), PAAA, R17.814, p. 18; Auswärtiges Amt to Roedern (25 October 1916), PAAA, R17.814, p. 53.

[84] Auswärtiges Amt to Roedern (8 October 1916), PAAA, R17.814, pp. 22–5; DAB (Berlin) to Auswärtiges Amt (20 November 1916), PAAA, R17.814, p. 73.

[85] DAB (Berlin) to Auswärtiges Amt (4 December 1916), PAAA, R17.814, p. 81.

[86] Müller-Jabusch, *Deutsch-Asiatische Bank*, pp. 247–8.

[87] Mumm to Auswärtiges Amt (10 March 1917), PAAA, R17.814, pp. 168–9.

Not only did their share of the indemnity far exceed that of the Central Powers, but a severing of relations would also have allowed China to stop payment of the Central Powers' share of the indemnity. Moreover, by the end of 1916, the Chinese government had already started to look to the United States for money and contracted a loan of 5 million US dollars with the Continental and Commercial Bank of Chicago.[88] In January, the Japanese government offered a loan of 10 million silver dollars to China and the Allies promised further 'outright financial support' if China joined the war on their side, with the United States pledging to provide a loan of 200 million US dollars to the Chinese government.[89] Thus, in the early months of 1917, it was obvious that the Allies had more to offer financially than Germany.

While other factors like international status were certainly important reasons for China's decision to enter the war, these financial advantages China gained by severing relations and declaring war against Germany were a far more important incentive for China's entry into the war than has been previously noted. Prime Minister Duan Qirui 段祺瑞 (Figure 6.6), a Chinese military leader who had been closely associated with Yuan Shikai and held the Chinese prime ministership several times after Yuan's death in 1916, was in desperate need of money and recognized that Allied financial could be of great help.[90] Recognizing the utmost gravity of China's financial problems, in early 1917 he was already busy planning what to do with the money he would receive from the Allies. As Zhang Guogan, Chief Secretary of the Cabinet, later recalled, Duan explained that China's 'greatest problem is its public finance. After we join the war, the [Allied] countries will provide us with financial help. Only then will our government be able to work smoothly.' He also seemed open to Zhang's suggestion that the financial help from the Allies and the funds gained from 'ceasing of German and Austria-Hungarian indemnity payments' could be used for modernization projects, such as currency reform.[91] While Eggeling later claimed that Cordes' strategy of financial aid helped keep China out of the war before 1917, eventually Cordes' plan was bound to fail.[92]

---

[88] 'Dalu Shangye Yinhang jiekuan hetong' (16 November 1916), in Caizheng kexue yanjiu-suo and Zhongguo di'er lishi danganguan, *Minguo waizhai dangan shiliao*, 5:654–9; 'Claim Former Group of Banks Dissolved', *The China Press* (5 December 1916), PAAA, R17.814, p. 133. For the share of the different countries in the Boxer indemnity, see MacMurray, *Treaties*, 1: 311.

[89] Quote from Xu, *China and the Great War*, pp. 171–2; Bernstorff to Bethmann Hollweg (26 January 1917), PAAA, R17.814, pp. 156–7; Hintze to Auswärtiges Amt (16 February 1917), PAAA, R17.814, p. 159.

[90] On the grave fiscal situation in the years after Yuan Shikai's fall from power, see Yang, *Minguo caizheng shi*, pp. 1–4; Jiao, *Zhongguo minguo caizheng shi*, pp. 178–9. On Duan, see Burt, Powell and Crow, *Biographies of Prominent Chinese*, p. 5; Ji, *Duan Qirui zhuan*, pp. 445–52.

[91] Zhang Guogan, 'Dui De-Ou canzhan', in Du, *Zhang Guogan wenji*, p. 158.

[92] For Eggeling's claim, see Paul W. Wilm, *Rückblicke eines Neunzigjährigen; Erlebtes in der Heimat, in China und der Mongolei, in Brasilien und in Südostasien* (unpublished manuscript, ca.1990), Teil IIa: 38, StuDeO-Bibl., Nr. 371c.

Figure 6.6 Duan Qirui 段祺瑞 (1865–1936). From Weale, *The Fight for the Republic*, between pp. 354 and 355.

Given their scarce financial resources and the limited willingness of the directors and the German government in Berlin to provide and sanction further financial help for China, the German bankers had no realistic chance of winning the bidding contest for China's favour against the more financially powerful United States and Japan and prevent China's entry into the war. This became clear once more when German minister von Hintze made a last effort and offered 1 million US dollars directly to Duan in early March to defer the severing of relations. Duan 'replied with a smile that the offer had already been outbid' and on the next day concluded a contract for 40 million US dollars for the construction of arsenals with Japan.[93]

6.4   The Liquidation of the Deutsch-Asiatische Bank

When China severed its relations with Germany on 14 March 1917, it ceased all loan and indemnity payments to Germany and the DAB. According to the new regulations for the non-repayment of loans issued by the Chinese government, China not only ceased to deposit part of its customs and salt revenues for

[93] Hintze to Auswärtiges Amt (3 July 1917), *PVH*, p. 386.

loan and Boxer Indemnity payments in the DAB, but also terminated all loan payments to the DAB for other public loans. Moreover, loans that the DAB and other German businesses had provided directly to the Chinese government were also not repaid anymore.[94] While this undoubtedly was a great relief for Chinese public finance, it meant that the DAB was now not only deprived of one of its last assets in China in the form of the regular Chinese loan and indemnity payments, but also had lost its last leverage for negotiations with the Chinese government. Given that no diplomatic relations existed anymore between China and Germany and China no longer needed to repay its German debt, there was no realistic possibility anymore that the German bankers could offer loans to the Chinese government or continue their strategy to offer advances to China against future loan payments to keep China out of the war.

When on 14 August 1917 China entered the war and joined the Allies, it first treated the DAB mildly, as goodwill towards Germany still existed among parts of China's elites. The Chinese government at first only sequestrated the bank's assets (Figure 6.7) with a view to returning them to the German bankers after the war, so that they would then be able to resume their business in China.[95]

Figure 6.7 Closure of the Beijing branch of the DAB in 1917. Image courtesy of Deutsche Bank AG, Historical Institute.

[94] For the regulations see Zhang Jiasen 張嘉森 to Waijiaobu (7 April 1917), AIMH, 03–21–012–03–005. Also see Wright, *China's Customs Revenue*, p. 27.
[95] Moazzin, 'From Globalization to Liquidation', pp. 54–62.

The German bankers also received mild treatment from the Chinese authorities. While the Allies pressed China early on to 'intern and expel enemy subjects', most German subjects who were in China in August 1917 were able to stay there until the end of the war without being interned or deported.[96] However, the Chinese government did issue a 'Black List' of important enemy subjects who were to be monitored.[97] The list was headed by Cordes and Eggeling.[98]

While Cordes was arrested, Eggeling fled Beijing and a manhunt for him began. He 'disguised [himself] as a monk and took the night train to Shanhaikwan (Shanhaiguan, 山海關)'. From there he ascended into the mountains and hid in temples and villages. Hidden and secluded like this, he remained in North China and avoided arrest until the end of the war.[99] Although Cordes was put under arrest, Eggeling later remembered that Cordes 'received princely treatment as an old friend of China'.[100] Cordes, together with other Germans deemed important, was interned at Xiyu Monastery (Xiyusi, 西峪寺) near Beijing at the end of 1918. However, here the German inmates were also treated very well and living conditions were more similar to a hotel than a prison or internment camp.[101] Cordes was even able to send money and letters from the monastery to Eggeling with the help of one of his Chinese servants.[102] Compared to China, conditions for German bankers in other countries could be much less favourable. In New York, DAB banker Richard Timmerscheidt came under great pressure from the American authorities. Eventually, he feared being arrested as a German agent so much that he committed suicide by 'jump[ing] from a window of his apartment'.[103]

Despite this relatively mild treatment, the nationalist tensions that originated in Europe now came to fully manifest themselves in China. The Allies pressured the Chinese government to completely liquidate and sell off the

---

[96] Quote from Xu, *China and the Great War*, pp. 192–8; Zhang, '1918 nian zaihua deqiao chuzhi an yinfa de zhongwai jiaoshe', pp. 80–9.

[97] 'German Intrigues – Herr Cordes Arrested', *The Shanghai Times* (11 September 1917).

[98] 'German Intrigue: Eggeling at Large', *The Shanghai Times* (15 September 1917); 'German Intrigues – Herr Cordes Arrested', *The Shanghai Times* (11 September 1917).

[99] Quote from Paul W. Wilm, *Rückblicke eines Neunzigjährigen; Erlebtes in der Heimat, in China und der Mongolei, in Brasilien und in Südostasien* (unpublished manuscript, ca.1990), Teil IIa: 38–9, StuDeO-Bibl., Nr. 371c; Müller-Jabusch, *Deutsch-Asiatische Bank*, p. 253.

[100] Paul W. Wilm, *Rückblicke eines Neunzigjährigen; Erlebtes in der Heimat, in China und der Mongolei, in Brasilien und in Südostasien* (unpublished manuscript, ca.1990), Teil IIa: 38, StuDeO-Bibl., Nr. 371c.

[101] Zhang, 'Zai Hua Deqiao chuzhi', p. 87.

[102] Paul W. Wilm, *Rückblicke eines Neunzigjährigen; Erlebtes in der Heimat, in China und der Mongolei, in Brasilien und in Südostasien* (unpublished manuscript, ca.1990), Teil IIa: 39, StuDeO-Bibl., Nr. 371c.

[103] Quote from 'Say Timmerscheidt Had German Secrets', *New York Times* (7 July 1917); 'Selbstmord des früheren Bankdirektors der D.A.B. Timmerscheidt', tr., *China Press* (16 August 1917), PAAA, R17.815, p. 13.

property of the DAB. British diplomats and interest groups in particular, such as the British Chamber of Commerce and the British China Association, saw the war as an opportunity to eliminate German influence and economic competition in China. They felt that it was China's duty as an ally to ensure that German businesses would not be able to go back to their business after the war. The DAB was seen as the 'keystone of the German commercial system in China', whose full liquidation would also enable the Allies to reach and hurt many of the German businesses that were the DAB's customers and owed the bank money.[104]

In case China did not comply, the Allies threatened that China would receive no Allied support at the post-war peace conference or might even be excluded from it, although the attendance of the conference had been a major reason why China had entered the war. With German political influence in China vanished after the severing of Sino-German relations, the German bankers were only left with a weak Chinese state to defend them against Allied demands. Eventually, China yielded to Allied pressure and on 1 January 1919 the liquidation of the DAB's main branch in Shanghai was handed over to British control. With that, the DAB was doomed. The British liquidators sold the DAB's main branch in Shanghai and several of its branch buildings elsewhere. They also pursued and filed legal proceedings against many of the DAB's customers before the Mixed Court in Shanghai. Within six months of the British takeover of the liquidation, much enemy property had been sold off and, in the words of one of the liquidators, the German bank's 'organisation at Shanghai [had been] completely broken up'.[105]

The liquidation of the DAB had grave consequences for the bank. It never received full compensation for the liquidation. It was only after the conclusion of a Sino-German treaty regarding the settlement of reparations between Germany and China in 1924 that the bank received 6 million silver dollars in compensation from the German government and regained its account books and remaining real estate.[106] This meant that the bank's competitors in China gained a head start when the China trade took off again after the war. As a consequence, many former customers of the bank moved to other British, Japanese or Dutch banks.[107] Moreover, the bank was not reinstated as one of the banks servicing loans for the Chinese government, which took important working capital away from it.[108] The only branches the bank had left after the

[104] Moazzin, 'From Globalization to Liquidation', pp. 54–62.
[105] Moazzin, 'From Globalization to Liquidation', pp. 60–71.
[106] Müller-Jabusch, Deutsch-Asiatische Bank, pp. 254–81.
[107] Van der Putten, Corporate Behaviour, p. 38; King, HSBC History, 2:81; Ratenhof, Chinapolitik, p. 283.
[108] Wright, China's Customs Revenue, p. 159.

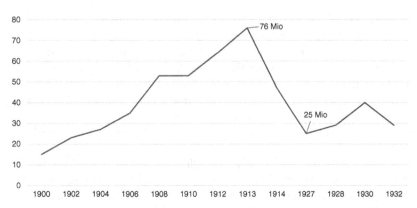

Figure 6.8 Total assets, DAB, 1900–32, in million Shanghai taels. *Source*: Müller-Jabusch, *Deutsch-Asiatische Bank*, table opposite p. 326.

war were those in Beijing and Hankou.[109] As contemporary observers noted, after the war the DAB was no longer one of the leading foreign banks, but had to start its business again on a much smaller scale.[110]

When the executive board of the DAB was finally able to issue a new yearly report to its shareholders in 1928, they estimated the loss caused by the liquidation at over 10 million Shanghai taels, which even the compensation from the German government and the business of the post-war years had not been able to compensate for.[111] Although the bank resumed operations in China after the war, its business never reached pre-war levels again. Rather, it became a matter of 'constant concern' for the members of the supervisory board in Berlin, who at times even considered liquidating the bank.[112] Figure 6.8 shows the development of the total assets of the bank between 1900 and 1932 and demonstrates the extent to which the bank's post-war business lagged behind the heights it had reached before the war. The main causes of this were the great losses the bank had suffered because of the bank's liquidation in China. Eventually, the Second World War put an end to the DAB's business in China.[113] For many of the German bankers, who had often spent long periods

---

[109] 'Geschäft-Bericht über die Jahre 1915–1927' (21 September 1928), HADB, Geschäftsberichte, Deutsch-Asiatische Bank.

[110] See, for example, the comparison of the pre- and post-war business of the DAB in Shanghai in Yoshida, *Shanhai ni okeru gaikoku kawase kinyū*, pp. 20–1.

[111] 'Geschäft-Bericht über die Jahre 1915–1927' (21 September 1928), HADB, Geschäftsberichte, Deutsch-Asiatische Bank.

[112] Dernburg to Urbig (5 October 1933), HADB, P8401.

[113] 'Bericht für die Jahre 1940–1952', HADB, Geschäftsberichte, Deutsch-Asiatische Bank. The DAB did open a branch in the then British colony of Hong Kong again in 1958.

of time in China, the First World War also meant the end of their stay in China, as most of them were deported in 1919 after the armistice.[114] The liquidation of the DAB also had a profoundly negative impact on German businesses. By June 1919, the British liquidators in Shanghai had sold property worth 660,000 Shanghai taels belonging to German individuals and businesses in debt to the DAB. The long list of debtors whose property had been liquidated also shows that the liquidation mostly hit small businesses and must have had a decisive impact on the ability of these small firms to resume their China business after the war. One such case was that of the soap manufacturer Gustav Boehm, who had an overdraft of 148,795.37 Shanghai taels and whose manufactured goods were seized and sold after a judgment by the International Mixed Court on 9 January 1919.[115] Thus the liquidation added to the damage already done to German trade and commerce in China by the confiscation of the assets of German businesses in Hong Kong and the Chinese ban on trading with Germany after August 1917.[116] William Kirby has rightly pointed out that German businesses managed to re-establish themselves in the early 1920s in China 'in an unexpectedly rapid fashion'.[117] However, we should not forget the profoundly negative impact the First World War and China's entry into the war generally and the liquidation of the DAB specifically had on German commerce in China. After the war, German imports to China only reached pre-war levels again in 1925 and German exports to China only did so in 1926. Even during the Nanjing decade, direct German business investments in China never again reached the pre-war amount of 136 million US dollars.[118]

6.5 Conclusion

The decade before the outbreak of the First World War saw the continued internationalization of the banking sector of China's treaty port economy and the expansion of the DAB's business. The bank consolidated its position as one of the most important foreign banks in China. However, during the war, the DAB and the economy of China's treaty ports witnessed a period of change, volatility and, in the case of the German bank, demise. When the impact of the

However, being largely unsuccessful in the post-war era, the bank was eventually merged into the new European Asian Bank, which in turn became part of the branch structure of the Deutsche Bank in 1987/8. See Pohl, *Handbook on the History of European Banks*, p. 384; Plumpe, Nützenadel and Schenck, *Deutsche Bank: The Global Hausbank*, pp. 365–7, 433–4.

[114] Müller-Jabusch, *Deutsch-Asiatische Bank*, p. 253.
[115] 'List of Debtors to the Deutsch-Asiatische Bank, Shanghai Outstanding 14th August 1917 with Balances Still Unpaid' (22 April 1919), TNA, FO228/2842, vol. 1, p. 134.
[116] Ratenhof, *Chinapolitik*, pp. 261, 268.
[117] Kirby, *Germany and Republican China*, p. 17.
[118] Ratenhof, *Chinapolitik*, pp. 561–2; Hou, *Foreign Investment*, p. 225.

outbreak of war hit the Chinese treaty port economy in 1914, it led to a decline in China's foreign trade and had a detrimental effect on Chinese commerce and finance. This was unsurprising given the global economic entanglements of the treaty port economy and the internationalization of the banking sector on the China coast. The war also caused an unprecedented loss of trust of the money market in the stability of foreign banks. For the first time, it was the Chinese government and Chinese banks that had to come to the rescue of foreign banks and stabilized the banking sector. Moreover, because of the end of cooperation among foreign banks and their joint provision of capital to China, Chinese foreign borrowing became dominated by Japan. The outbreak of the war also brought an end to the transnationalism of the treaty ports and led to a rise of those in favour of nationalism and national competition, whether in the economic realm or elsewhere.

The German bankers had to deal with this changed situation and tried to manage and limit the political risk of a possible Chinese entry into the war. To do so, they attempted to transform the bank's financial resources into political influence with the Chinese government to keep China out of the war. However, this attempt was eventually unsuccessful and the fate of the bank during the war reveals the limitations of the ability of foreign businesses in China to deal with increased political risk caused by the impact of large geo-political shifts on their host country. The DAB had become an important supplier of capital for the Chinese government during the pre-war period and continued to provide loans to China after the outbreak of war. Nevertheless, at a time when the question of who could offer China the largest financial support became an important factor in determining Chinese decision-making with regards to its position in the war, the bank's financial capacities were not sufficient to compete with the superior financial offers, promises and capabilities of the Allies, and thus the bankers' strategy of using loans and advances to keep China out of the war eventually was bound to fail. Here, we also once again see how international finance played a key role during a turning point in modern Chinese history. The liquidation of the DAB that followed China's siding with the Allies and the eventual Allied takeover of the liquidation not only prevented the bank from regaining its former position as a leading bank in China, but also contributed to the difficulties that German businesses faced when they tried to re-establish themselves after the war.

The fate of the DAB also reveals the vulnerability of the globalized treaty port economy on the Chinese frontier to political crises and global shifts of power. It shows that treaty ports were not always the safe havens from political tensions, instability and risk that they have been made out to be. An important characteristic of the treaty port economy was its 'politically and legally stable environment' that made the international flows of capital and commodities passing through these ports possible.[119] Because of the weakness of the Chinese state, an important element in the structure of the treaty ports was the relative equality of power among the different foreign powers contending for influence there.[120] Finally, treaty ports like Shanghai were based on the principle of transnational cooperation, co-existence and, in the case of Shanghai, shared governance among the foreign powers.[121] For foreign businesses, this relative power equilibrium among the powers and the consensus of transnational cooperation protected them from arbitrary actions by foreign powers against their businesses and guaranteed free competition and cooperation in business. Consequently, the treaty port economy of the China coast was tied not only to the development of the global economy but also to the willingness for transnational cooperation and the global balance of power of the pre-war era that was reflected in the treaty ports.

While the DAB remained safe from liquidation while China remained neutral, after the beginning of war in 1914, foreign businesses in the treaty ports quickly began to feel the negative impact of political events and developments in Europe. The decline of the China trade and the end of transnational cooperation in the treaty ports that followed the outbreak of war presented the DAB with significant new obstacles. The liquidation or closing of the DAB branches under British and Japanese control and the demise of China's foreign trade decimated the bank's branch network and curtailed its business activities. Moreover, the rise of nationalist sentiments and the end of cosmopolitanism in Chinese finance meant that the DAB could no longer cooperate with other foreign banks in its regular business and in the provision of loans to the Chinese government. However, while the impact of political events on the bank's business had at least still been manageable before 1917, it ultimately was China's declaration of war that completely upset the balance of power in the treaty ports and brought the shift in global power relations to China. It meant the end of the political and legal stability of the treaty ports based on the power equilibrium among the foreign powers. After the severing of Sino-German relations and China's declaration of war, the DAB and other German businesses could no longer rely on their home government for protection and were left at the mercy of the Allies and a weak Chinese government. Because of its dependence on the goodwill of the other Allies, China was eventually compelled to allow the full liquidation of the DAB by Britain, which represented the ultimate manifestation of the turn from pre-1914 cosmopolitan cooperation in the treaty ports to the rise and triumph of nationalist sentiment during the war. Thus, as was the case elsewhere in the world, the end of the pre-war

[119] So, 'Modern China's Treaty Port Economy', pp. 2–3.
[120] Taylor, 'The Bund', *Social History* 27, No. 2 (2011): 125–42.
[121] Bickers and Jackson, 'Introduction: Law, Land and Power', pp. 1–10; Jackson, 'Who Ran the Treaty Ports', pp. 43–60.

order of power and the conflict between the Allies and the Central Powers ultimately proved detrimental for global business and economic globalization in China.[122]

In general, the First World War represented a deep blow to the Chinese frontier and to frontier banks like the DAB. While the frontier normally acted as a space for transnational cooperation and mediation and the global flow of commodities and capital, these processes were disrupted by the war and foreign banks were no longer able to operate as intermediary institutions of the frontier to the same extent as before the war. Moreover, they became a source of instability and consequently lost standing in the Chinese banking sector. The weakening of foreign banks was partly compensated for by Chinese banks, who helped stabilize the money market after the outbreak of war. On the other hand, this rupture to the frontier also provided an opening for Japan to monopolize the previously diversified supply of foreign capital to China. Thus, the demise of the DAB was reflective of a larger shock to the Chinese frontier during the First World War.

---

[122] On the disintegration of the global economy and its impact on global business following the outbreak of the First World War, see Jones, *Multinationals and Global Capitalism*, pp. 27–9, 40–1.

~

Conclusion

In May 1926, Heinrich Cordes set out from Beijing on a trip to Germany. It was to be his last goodbye to China, where he had spent such a large part of his life. Shortly after his return to Germany, he died of cancer on 5 July 1927 at only sixty-one years of age.[1] Cordes' death marked not only the conclusion of a life closely entangled with China, but, more immediately, also the end of Cordes' failed attempts to find a role for himself in China after the First World War. Having been deported to Germany in 1919, Cordes had first returned to China in 1920 and unsuccessfully tried to negotiate with the Chinese government to enable the DAB to restore its activities.[2] More broadly, it seems that there was simply no space for Cordes at the Deutsch-Asiatische Bank (DAB) anymore. As Franz Urbig wrote already in February 1920, it was unlikely that Cordes would be able to return to his previous activities in negotiating Chinese loans anytime soon, as 'the bag of cash he used to be able to sit on has unfortunately turned into a beggar's bag'.[3] The time when German finance and Cordes as its representative played an important role in China was clearly over. It was unsurprising, then, that Cordes left the DAB in 1923.[4] Cordes thereafter seems to have tried to become involved in German industrial activities in China, but his premature death ended these endeavours.[5] The trajectory of Cordes' life after the First World War not only again evinces the demise of the DAB in the post-war period, but also shows how this was reflected in the personal lives and fortunes of German bankers. However, as we will see, the fate of Heinrich Cordes and the DAB also more broadly foreshadowed the decline of the role of foreign banks in modern China after the First World War.

[1] 'Heinrich Cordes: Eine deutsche Persönlichkeit in China' (July 1927), *Täglicher Dienst für nationale Zeitungen*, Studeo-Archiv, *0716; Paul W. Wilm, *Rückblicke eines Neunzigjährigen; Erlebtes in der Heimat, in China und der Mongolei, in Brasilien und in Südostasien* (unpublished manuscript, ca.1990), Teil II b: 167, StuDeO-Bibl., Nr. 372b.
[2] 'Heinrich Cordes: Eine deutsche Persönlichkeit in China' (July 1927), *Täglicher Dienst für Nationale Zeitungen*, Studeo-Archiv, *0716; Müller-Jabusch, *Deutsch-Asiatische Bank*, pp. 257–66.
[3] Urbig to Hintze (14 February 1920), *BA/MA*, N536/158.
[4] Müller-Jabusch, *Deutsch-Asiatische Bank*, pp. 266, 319.
[5] 'Heinrich Cordes: Eine deutsche Persönlichkeit in China' (July 1927), *Täglicher Dienst für Nationale Zeitungen*, Studeo-Archiv, *0716.

In this book, I have tried to complicate long-standing simplistic views that mainly see foreign banks in modern China as manifestations and agents of foreign imperialism that occupied a position of power and dominance vis-à-vis Chinese actors. Instead, I have proposed the conceptual framework of the frontier bank operating on the Chinese frontier – a dynamic and complex space of Sino-foreign interaction that presented foreign banks with both opportunities and limitations – to provide a more nuanced way of thinking about the activities of foreign banks in modern China. In tracing the operations of the DAB on the Chinese frontier, we have not only seen that the interests and motivations of the German government could often differ greatly from those of the German bankers, but also that the operations of foreign banks in China and the internationalization of Chinese finance were not one-sided impositions by foreign financiers. Rather, the operations of foreign banks as frontier banks on the Chinese frontier and China's financial international-ization rested on common interests and the cooperation of foreign and Chinese actors in financially connecting China to the global economy, and providing Chinese actors with access to foreign financial institutions and capital. These common interests led to the development of Sino-foreign partnerships and networks of cooperation and interdependence. Importantly, within these networks and partnerships, power relations were not as clear as previous scholarship has suggested. Rather, Chinese actors could often use foreign competition resulting from financial internationalization and informa-tion asymmetries to gain the upper hand in business transactions or loan negotiations.

At the same time, we saw that the space for Chinese agency and the complex power relations between foreign and Chinese actors on the frontier during the late nineteenth and early twentieth centuries were dependent on timing and contingency, particularly when it came to the conclusion of loan agreements. Here, the most important factors seem to have been political stability and time pressure. Under politically stable conditions and without any immediate time pressure, Chinese actors had considerable agency and often much leverage over their foreign interlocutors. That was certainly the case in the foreign banks' daily business in the Chinese banking sector of China's treaty port economy, which was highly dependent on their cooper-ation with Chinese banks throughout. However, we also saw such high degrees of Chinese agency and leverage in loan negotiations such as those for the second indemnity loan or the Tianjin–Pukou railway loan, when Chinese negotiators benefited from political stability and were under no immediate time pressure to conclude a loan agreement. In contrast, in times with little political stability and much time pressure to conclude a loan agreement, such as in the cases of the third indemnity loan or, even more so, the aftermath of the 1911 revolution, the space for Chinese agency on the Chinese frontier shrank.

Looking at the role of foreign banks in the modern Chinese economy and modern economic globalization in China, this book has followed the DAB through the heyday of foreign banking in modern China between the 1890s and the First World War, when foreign banks played a crucial role and occupied a monopoly in many areas of Chinese finance. During this period, foreign banks became an important element of the Chinese economy and rose to a position of unprecedented prominence in both the banking sector of China's treaty ports and Chinese public finance. While a few foreign banks had operated in China before the 1890s and, with Western merchants, had introduced new forms of credit, cheap capital and sovereign borrowing to China, it was only in the 1890s that this development witnessed a rapid acceleration and China saw a hitherto unknown growth in the number, diversity and invested capital of foreign banks in China and in the importance of these foreign banks and foreign capital for Chinese banking and public finance. As a result, Chinese finance went through a process of full-fledged internationalization during the two and a half decades before the First World War.

In the banking sector of China's treaty port economy, this financial internationalization manifested itself in the influx of a growing number of foreign banks, which now were of different origins and no longer predominantly British, and in the increase of the invested foreign banking capital. Subsequently, the importance of foreign banks as capital providers in the banking sector increased, and they formed business partnerships with Chinese banks and were integrated into institutional structures like the interbank lending system. A direct consequence of this growth of foreign banks was the decrease in the price of credit in the banking sector. Moreover, the accelerated internationalization of the banking sector was also reflected in the greater diversity and rapid increase of transnational capital flows between China's treaty ports and other economies due to both the unprecedented growth of China's foreign trade and the growing loan and indemnity payments between Europe and China. These transnational flows of capital were facilitated by foreign banks, who used their capital and branch networks to finance China's foreign trade, supply credit to Chinese banks that extended it to Chinese merchants and manage remittances between China and Western economies.

In Chinese public finance, this process of internationalization was reflected in an unprecedented growth in Chinese sovereign borrowing, the increasing diversity of the sources of Chinese loans and the integration of China into the international system of sovereign borrowing. Because of the negotiation skills of Chinese officials, their use of the increased competition among foreign financiers in China and the continued eagerness of foreign bankers to invest and lend to China on good terms during the last decade of the Qing, the Chinese government could borrow foreign capital at increasingly low costs and on favourable terms. This allowed China not only to repay the Japanese war indemnity of 1895, but also to fund infrastructure and other reform projects during the *Xinzheng* reforms and keep both the central and provincial governments afloat. The DAB and other foreign banks made Chinese sovereign borrowing possible not only by acting as intermediary institutions that mediated between foreign investors and Chinese officials, but also by guaranteeing Chinese loans with their reputation and assessing Chinese sovereign risk. However, the downside of this internationalization of Chinese public finance was that China developed a dependency on foreign debt. This dependency became especially decisive during and after the 1911 revolution, which was a turning point in Chinese foreign borrowing. After the fall of the Qing dynasty, the new government remained dependent on foreign loans, but the ensuing instability and increased political risk of investing in China meant that China was no longer able to borrow on terms as favourable as before.

The rise of foreign banks in China and the internationalization of Chinese finance also led to a further integration of China with the first global economy. By financially connecting China to Western capital markets and global flows of capital, foreign banks acted as intermediary institutions that made China's financial integration into the first global economy possible. As we saw in our discussion of the 1911 revolution and the impact of the First World War on the Chinese money market, this financial integration was reflected in the growing interdependence between the banking sector of China's treaty ports and Chinese public finance and actors, developments and events outside of China. A further indicator of China's financial integration with the global economy was the growing convergence of interest rates between China and Europe both in terms of the cost of capital in China's treaty ports and the cost of sovereign borrowing between the 1890s and the First World War.[6]

Furthermore, the influx of foreign banks, the internationalization of Chinese finance and the financial integration of China into the global economy also led to knowledge transfers between Europe and China and a growing uniformity in financial institutions and practices between China and Western economies. This growing uniformity, which was an important feature of modern globalization, was most prominently reflected in the development of Chinese banking and the Chinese adoption of Western tools of public finance.[7] In 1890, there still existed no modern Chinese banks and China also had no experience in issuing public debt. By 1914, not only had both government-sponsored and private modern Chinese banks started to emerge, but China had also begun to adopt the issuing of domestic bonds to raise money. Both

---

[6] For a similar argument about the global convergence of commodity prices as an indicator for greater global economic integration during the first global economy, see O'Rourke and Williamson, *History and Globalization*.

[7] For a discussion of growing uniformity as a feature of modern globalization, see Bayly, *Birth of the Modern World*, especially pp. 12–18.

modern Chinese banks and the issuing of bonds were modelled after Western examples, whose most prominent representations in China were foreign banks and the foreign loans they had provided to the Chinese government before 1914.[8] While these new financial tools and institutions would go on to play a crucial role in both the Chinese economy and Chinese public finance, their origin lay in the two and a half decades before the First World War, when the rise of foreign financial institutions and practices in China had provided Chinese officials and entrepreneurs with a model for financial reform and innovation. Finally, and more generally, tracing the history of foreign banks and global financial connections in late nineteenth- and early twentieth-century China also shows the important role international finance played at key moments in modern China's history.

Following the history of the DAB between its establishment in 1889 and its liquidation during the First World War has also been instructive with regards to the operations of German and other foreign banks as multinational enterprises in China and their limitations. First, the specific case of the DAB shows the unifying and accelerating influence the developmental state could have on the formation of multinational enterprises in the global economy, especially in late-comer nations such as Germany. The DAB especially benefited from the unifying influence of the German state, which led to it becoming the sole representative of German finance in China. It also lived up to the German government's hope that it would represent and further German financial interests in China and contribute to the global expansion of German finance. At the same time, differences between the economic nationalism of the German state and the cosmopolitan openness of the German bankers meant that the hopes of German government officials and diplomats for the formation of an independent German commercial bloc in China were disappointed. Moreover, the German bankers' adoption of a risk-averse business strategy proved successful for operating a multinational bank in China, but caused further grievances from the German state, who wished to see more active support by the bankers for German commerce.

Second, while the DAB and other foreign banks acted as frontier banks that used their position in the frontier region of the China coast and their global branch network to financially connect China to the global economy, their position as international banks on the frontier had its limitations and could prove volatile. Not only were foreign banks dependent on cooperation with Chinese actors both in the realm of public finance and banking, but they were also integrated into existing business networks and market structures by their Chinese business partners and had to localize and adapt their business

---

[8] On the development of modern Chinese banks, see Cheng, *Banking in Modern China*, pp. 20–52. On the development of the Chinese issuing of domestic debt, see Li, *Guozhai zai jindai Zhongguo* and van de Ven, *Breaking with the Past*, chapter 5.

practices. Moreover, the First World War showed that the position of multi-national enterprises in China depended on a power equilibrium and a consensus about transnational cooperation in the treaty ports. While multi-national enterprises both benefited from and contributed to economic global-ization in China's treaty port economy, they could do little to protect themselves once the cosmopolitan order of the treaty ports broke down and nationalist tensions came to the fore.

My findings also contribute to our understanding of modern Chinese economic development and the reasons for the origins of the Great Divergence and its persistence during the nineteenth and into the twentieth century. As I have shown, foreign banks occupied an important position in the Chinese economy. They set foreign exchange rates, managed international remittances, financed China's foreign trade, attracted large deposits, supplied the Chinese banking sector with capital and raised large sums for the Chinese government on international capital markets. They were able to play such an important role in the Chinese economy not simply because of the support and collaboration with Western imperialism, as previous historiography largely suggests, but because there existed no Chinese financial institution that could provide the same stable business structure, protection by property rights, large sums of cheap capital, tools of finance and global branch network. As Chinese demand for the services and financial tools of foreign banks nevertheless existed, foreign banks could fill this institutional void in the Chinese economy and rise to such prominence in the two and a half decades before the First World War.

Thus, just when Chinese reformers tried to economically develop China during the late nineteenth and early twentieth centuries, no financial institu-tions in China could effectively meet these existing economic demands for modern financial services and tools except foreign banks, which, however, were always limited in their operations to the small enclaves of the treaty port economy. This suggests that the lack of modern Chinese financial institutions and the institutional environment that contributed to the success of foreign banks, such as effective property rights and a functioning market for public debt in Europe, were important factors inhibiting economic growth and development and contributing to the origins and, more importantly, the persistence of the Great Divergence. The example of Japan provides a good comparison here. In the 1870s and 1880s, the Meiji government swiftly moved to establish both effective property law and a national banking system, includ-ing an international exchange bank and a central bank. As a result, foreign banks played a much more limited role in the Japanese economy.[9] More

---

[9] Okazaki and Okuno, 'Evolution of Economic Systems', pp. 492–7; Allen and Donnithorne, *Western Enterprise*, chapter 13; Davenport-Hines and Jones, 'British Business in Japan', pp. 222–4.

importantly, the faster and more effective development of economic institutions in Japan most likely contributed to Japan's ability to achieve more rapid economic development than China.

Finally, the conclusion that the success of foreign banks in China was made possible by an institutional void in the Chinese economy also helps explain the relative decline of foreign banks and the slowing down of financial internationalization in China after 1914. In the banking sector, the period between 1914 and 1937 saw the rapid expansion of modern Chinese banks that far exceeded that of the limited number of new foreign banks that entered China.[10] As Chapter 6 showed, the First World War dented the public's trust in foreign banks and provided space for agency for newly established modern Chinese banks like the Bank of China. In this sense, the First World War arguably had an effect in the Chinese banking sector somewhat comparable to the effect it had on modern Chinese manufacturing in the Chinese industrial sector.[11] This loss of trust in foreign banks continued after the war with a series of bankruptcies of foreign banks. Consequently, many Chinese customers of foreign banks shifted their deposits to modern Chinese banks. These quickly growing modern Chinese banks also took over many functions that foreign banks had carried out before, such as supplying *qianzhuang* banks with capital.[12] The establishment of the Central Bank of China in 1924, which under the nationalist government started to act as custodian bank of most of the salt and Customs revenue and began to set official foreign exchange rates, further eroded the previous privileges and monopolies of foreign banks.[13]

[10] Rawski, *Economic Growth in Prewar China*, p. 134; Tamagna, *Banking and Finance*, table between pp. 97 and 98.

[11] Marie-Claire Bergère famously argued that decreased foreign competition and imports and increased demand for Chinese exports during the First World War provided modern Chinese capitalists with a 'magnificent opportunity' for growth. See Bergère, *Golden Age*, pp. 63–98.

[12] Cheng, *Banking in Modern China*, pp. 37–77. While Cheng does not make a functional argument about the institutional void foreign banks previously filled being closed, he also sees the rise of modern Chinese banks as a key factor in the decline of foreign banks, which he, however, measures and views only from the perspective of capital power and foreign banks' supposed previous 'dominance over the Chinese financial market'. On the general problems with using capital power as a measure of comparison with the late nineteenth and early twentieth centuries, see Chapter 2, pp. 103–104 (and particularly footnote 165). Donnithorne and Allen also note briefly that foreign banks first benefited from and were able to extend their financial activities and functions broadly because of the absence of modern Chinese financial institutions, but later 'ceased to dominate the financing of the modern sector of the Chinese economy, except in the field of foreign trade' because of the rivalry from new modern Chinese financial institutions and Chinese monetary reform. See Donnithorne and Allen, *Western Enterprise*, pp. 102, 117–19, 249.

[13] Tamagna, *Banking and Finance*, pp. 100, 113–15; Song, *Jindai Shanghai waishang yinhang*, pp. 188, 191–4; Cheng, *Banking in Modern China*, pp. 75–6.

In the years preceding the Second World War, modern Chinese banks even started to compete with foreign banks in the areas of international remittances and foreign trade.[14] Moreover, the growth of China's foreign trade and China's foreign borrowing slowed down considerably compared to the period before the First World War.[15] This meant that the growth of global capital flows between China and Western economies slowed down. Thus, the diminished importance of foreign banks for the Chinese economy, their limited growth in numbers compared to modern Chinese banks and the deceleration of the increase of global capital flows between China and other economies meant that the overall internationalization of the banking sector of China's treaty port economy continued at a slower rate after the First World War. In Chinese public finance, the decline in internationalization and the importance of foreign banks was even clearer. As we have seen, the Nanjing government almost completely switched from using foreign to domestic loans. As previous Chinese loan defaults had made foreign borrowing impossible, the Nationalists successfully created a market for domestic debt and were no longer dependent on foreign banks or capital markets.[16] Thus, in a sense, the foreign bankers had been the makers of their own demise.[17] Many of the financial tools and institutions they had introduced and made successful in China were adopted by Chinese bankers and officials, so that on the eve of the outbreak of the Second World War in East Asia in 1937, the institutional void foreign banks had filled before 1914 had considerably shrunk. It would not be until the Communist revolution of 1949 that foreign banks were virtually evicted from China.[18] However, by 1949, the heyday of foreign banking in the decades before the First World War was already long gone.[19]

---

[14] Tamagna, *Banking and Finance*, pp. 111–12, 114; Song, *Jindai Shanghai waishang yinhang*, pp. 187–9.

[15] Between 1890 and 1913 China's foreign trade had more than quadrupled, but did not even double between 1914 and 1937. See Hsiao, *China's Foreign Trade Statistics*, pp. 22–3. For the switch from foreign to domestic government borrowing, see Chapter 5.

[16] Cheng, *Banking in Modern China*, pp. 114–16.

[17] This can also be said more generally about many countries where multinational banks did business. See Jones, *British Multinational Banking*, p. 390.

[18] After 1949, the Chinese government took over most foreign bank branches in mainland China. Before 1978, only the Hongkong and Shanghai Banking Corporation (HSBC), Standard Chartered Bank, Bank of East Asia and Oversea-Chinese Banking Corporation received permission to maintain a small representation in Shanghai. See Stent, *China's Banking Transformation*, p. 191.

[19] Despite his usual generous and positive assessment of the HSBC's performance, Frank King in his commissioned history of the HSBC also generally comes to the conclusion that the HSBC was not able to restore the 'grandeur' of the pre-First World War period after the war. See King, *HSBC History*, vol. 3.

*

After the beginning of China's Reform and Opening policies in 1978, foreign banks made a comeback in China. In 1979, the Export-Import Bank of Japan became the first foreign bank that opened a representative office in Beijing. By 1981, thirty-one foreign financial institutions had established representative offices in China. While these representative offices enabled foreign banks to establish bases in China, they were only allowed to engage in a very limited range of activities and were strictly 'not commercial' (*fei yingyexing* 非營業性). In 1981, the Chinese government also started to allow foreign banks to open proper 'commercial' (*yingyexing* 營業性) offices in the new special economic zones, which were permitted to engage in foreign exchange business. From 1990, foreign banks were also allowed to operate branches in Shanghai.[20] The 1980s also saw China's return to international capital markets. Between 1982 and 1985, China tapped bond markets in Hong Kong, Japan and West Germany twelve times to raise a total of around 1.1 billion US dollars, and continued to issue bonds abroad during the 1980s and 1990s.[21]

In 1985, when the Bank of China reached an agreement with Deutsche Bank to issue bonds worth 150 million marks (~£39 million) on the German capital market, criticisms were made by American and British financiers. They insisted that China had still not repaid part of the previous debt it had issued before 1949 and should thus not be allowed to re-enter Western capital markets. The German bankers, who by then had already cooperated with the Bank of China since the 1970s, obviously were less concerned about the issue.[22] So far, only British bondholders have received a very small amount of compensation for claims on old Chinese bonds through a Sino-British agreement signed in 1987 that allowed China to re-enter the London bond market.[23] More recently, this criticism of non-repayment has even resurfaced during the trade war between the United States and China. The American Bondholders Foundation has been trying to present the demand for repayment as possible 'political leverage' the United States could use against China, even though China does not recognize the old debt incurred by previous Chinese governments and thus actual repayment is not very likely.[24] However, overall, the issue of China's previous debt did not stop either China's re-entry into

---

[20] Liu, *Zhongguo yinhangye gaige kaifang*, pp. 12–13, 26.
[21] Zhang, *China's Emerging Global Businesses*, pp. 32–3.
[22] 'Unfair verhalten', *Der Spiegel* (3 June 1985), pp. 47–50; 'Deutsche Bank AG Geschäftsbericht für das Jahr 1985' (18 March 1986), Geschäftsberichte, Deutsche Bank, DBA; Friederike Sattler, *Herrhausen: Banker, Querdenker, Global Player: Ein deutsches Leben* (Munich: Siedler Verlag, 2019), chapter 3.
[23] Burns, 'China to Settle UK Debts', *Financial Times* (6 June 1987); Waibel, *Sovereign Defaults*, p. 200.
[24] 'Trump's New Trade War Tool Might Just Be Antique China Debt', *Bloomberg Businessweek* (29 August 2019).

Western bond markets or, more generally, the large-scale inflow of foreign investment into China during the past few decades.[25]

In 1986, Bu Ming 卜明, the chairman of the board of directors of the Bank of China, lauded the entry of foreign banks as 'a major break through in China's foreign financial relations which play an active role in China's carrying out of the open[ing up] policy and expanding foreign economic financial cooperation'.[26] Nevertheless, throughout the 1980s and 1990s China adopted protectionist policies in its treatment of foreign banks. Most importantly, foreign banks were – certain exceptions aside – limited to doing business in foreign currency, which made it largely impossible for them to engage in business with Chinese companies and effectively compete with Chinese financial institutions.[27] At the same time, the amount of capital raised through the issuing of bonds remained small compared to foreign direct investment, and China's inclination to tap foreign bond markets appears to have waned at the end of the 1990s.[28] While the Chinese central government's sovereign debt has been continually rising in recent decades, it is now overwhelmingly of domestic origin.[29] China's joining of the World Trade Organization (WTO) in 2001 was a turning point in the recent history of foreign banking in China. As part of its accession to the WTO, China agreed to level the regulatory playing field between Chinese and foreign banks operating in China by 2006. Foreign banks were to be given proper access to the Chinese market.[30]

Nevertheless, foreign banks have failed to make much of a foray into the Chinese banking sector since. Between 2003 and 2020, according to Chinese official statistics, the assets of foreign banks in China remained below 3 per cent of total banking assets, reaching a high of 2.36 per cent in 2007 and since declining to only 1.18 per cent in 2020.[31] In 2020, only forty-one locally incorporated foreign banking institutions operated in China compared to 4,552 Chinese incorporated financial institutions.[32] While the Chinese government has made efforts to widen market access to foreign banks over the last two decades,[33] foreign banks and observers have blamed Chinese government regulations and restrictions for foreign banks' limited

---

[25] On foreign direct investment in China (as opposed to the tapping of foreign bond markets), see Huang *Selling China*.

[26] Bu, 'New Development in Sino-Foreign Financial Relations', p. 10.

[27] Yabuki and Harner, *China's New Political Economy*, pp. 195–6.

[28] Zhang, *China's Emerging Global Businesses*, chapter 2.

[29] Zhu et al., *A Study of the Turning Point of China's Debt*, p. 24; Lin, 'China to Curtail Local Government Debt', p. 73.

[30] Stent, *Banking Transformation*, p. 191; Nolan, *China and the Global Economy*, p. 205.

[31] Calculated from data in Zhongguo yinhangye jiandu guanli weiyuanhui xuanchuan gongzuobu, *2017 nianbao*, p. 172; Zhongguo yinhang baoxian jiandu guanli weiyuanhui, 'Yinhangye zhuanti'.

[32] Zhongguo yinhang baoxian jiandu guanli weiyuanhui, 'Yinhangye zhuanti'.

[33] KPMG, *Mainland China Banking Survey 2017*, p. 40.

development in the Chinese market.[34] Even though Chinese efforts to liberal-
ize market access for foreign banks have been stepped up further by the
Chinese government since 2018, such criticism persists with, for instance,
the European Union Chamber of Commerce in China lamenting that even
most recent efforts at liberalizing market access were 'too little, too late' and
recommending further deregulation.[35]

However, it seems that, rather than current regulations, sophisticated
Chinese competition now is the main obstacle that makes further forays of
foreign banks into the Chinese banking sector difficult. According to James
Stent – a banker who successively worked for China Minsheng Bank
(Zhongguo minsheng yinhang 中國民生銀行) and China Everbright Bank
(Zhongguo daguang yinhang 中國光大銀行) between 2003 and 2016 – 'the
major problem for foreign banks now is not regulatory restriction, but rather
the difficulty that banks in any foreign market face competing with the local
connections, knowledge, and loyalties of domestic banks'. As Stent explains,
foreign banks in China are 'niche players', only ahead of Chinese banks in a few
specialist areas of business and not featuring as significant competitors of
Chinese banks for the general market of retail or corporate clients.[36] Indeed,
given how well developed Chinese financial institutions and their services are,
it seems unlikely that foreign banks will be able to properly compete with them
outside of certain specialized services.[37] Today, the position of foreign banks in
the Chinese banking sector is thus clearly very different compared to more
than a century ago. Not only are they now subject to Chinese regulations, but,
continuing the development of the republican period, Chinese banks have
largely taken over the institutional functions of modern banking, which had
initially been introduced to China by foreign banks.

Another important difference between the historical developments this
book has focussed on and the development of Chinese banking today is that
Chinese banks themselves now play a major role in China's financial links to
the rest of the world and global finance more broadly. While modern Chinese
banks started to make their first steps in expanding abroad as early as the
republican period, it was following China's Reform and Opening Up in the

[34] Stent, *Banking Transformation*, p. 193; European Union Chamber of Commerce in
China, *Business in China Position Paper 2018/2019*, p. 337.
[35] Quote from European Union Chamber of Commerce in China, *Business in China
Position Paper 2020/2021*, pp. 365–7. On recent market access liberalization see also
Wang, 'China's Economic Slowdown Prompts Beijing to Reaffirm Commitment to
Opening Up Financial Markets', *South China Morning Post* (22 July 2021); United
States Trade Representative, *2020 Report*, p. 56.
[36] Stent, *Banking Transformation*, pp. vii–viii, 193–4.
[37] European Union Chamber of Commerce in China, *Business Confidence Survey 2019*,
p. 13; Somasundaram, 'China Scraps Almost All Foreign Ownership Limits for Financial
Sector', *Nikkei Asia* (23 July 2020).

1970s and the start of the Chinese 'Going Out' (*zouchuqu* 走出去) policy aimed at supporting the international expansion of Chinese enterprise in 2001 that we have really seen an increasing overseas expansion of Chinese banking. While the international expansion of European, American and Japanese banks proceeded slowly between 2006 and 2012, Chinese financial institutions witnessed rapid global expansion during the same period with a growth of their assets outside mainland China from 227 billion to more than a trillion US dollars.[38] China's Big Four Banks – the Bank of China, the Industrial and Commercial Bank of China (Zhongguo gongshang yinhang 中國工商銀行), the China Construction Bank (Zhongguo jianshe yinhang 中國建設銀行) and the Agricultural Bank of China (Zhongguo nongye yinhang 中國農業銀行) – now operate 618 branches abroad.[39] Indeed, 'long term, a major Chinese presence in the money centers of the world will become routine'.[40] While Chinese banks so far are only responsible for 7 per cent of all transnational lending, they are particularly strong in the developing world, executing more than 60 per cent of transnational lending among emerging markets. Unsurprisingly, Chinese banks have benefited from China's One-Belt-One-Road (OBOR) project, channelling loans worth almost 600 billion US dollars into OBOR projects since 2013, according to consulting firm RWR.[41] Thus, it seems, we may well be coming full circle: while European, American and Japanese banks dominated global finance for much of the nineteenth and twentieth centuries and first brought modern multinational banking to China before the First World War,[42] it might now be the turn of Chinese banks to play a dominant role in the global financial system.

---

[38] Zhang and Li, *Zhongguo jinrong ye*, pp. 33–4; Stent, *Banking Transformation*, pp. 199–203.

[39] 'As China Goes Global, Its Banks Are Coming Out Too', *The Economist* (7 May 2020).

[40] Stent, *Banking Transformation*, p. 202.

[41] 'As China Goes Global, Its Banks Are Coming Out Too', *The Economist* (7 May 2020).

[42] On this dominance, see Jones, 'Banks as Multinationals'; Jones, *British Multinational Banking*, p. 321.

APPENDIX 1 DEUTSCH-ASIATISCHE BANK LOANS TO THE CHINESE CENTRAL AND PROVINCIAL GOVERNMENTS, 1890–1916

Year	Loan	Issued together with	Borrower	Loan sum	Annual interest rate in %	Repayment period	Collateral or guarantee
1890	Shandong Provincial Loan (1)		Shandong Provincial Government (Shandong Governor Zhang Yao 張曜)	400,000 Shanghai taels	6.5	4 years	
1890	Shandong Provincial Loan (2)		Shandong Provincial Government (Shandong Governor Zhang Yao)	200,000 reichsmark	6.5	1 year	
1891	Fujian Provincial Loan (1)		Fujian Provincial Government (Banner General of Fujian Xi Yuan 希元)	£48,500	6.75	10 years	Customs bonds of the Customs bank in Fuzhou
1891	Chinese Engineering and Minging Company Loan		Tang Jingxing 唐景星 on behalf of the Chinese Engineering and Mining Company	200,000 Tianjin taels	7.5	8 years and 1 month	Property of the company
1894	Fujian Provincial Loan (2)		Fujian Provincial Government (Banner General of Fujian Xi Yuan)	500,000 Shanghai taels	8	5 years	Bills (*piao*) issued by the Regional Office (Fansi)
1894	Fujian Provincial Loan (3)		Fujian Provincial Government (Banner General of Fujian Xi Yuan)	£75,000	7	5 years	Maritime Customs income of Fuzhou
1894	Jinlu-Railway Loan (1)	HSBC, Jardine, Matheson & Co.	Jinlu-Railway	1,000,000 Kuping taels	?	?	
1896	Jinlu-Railway Loan (2)	HSBC	Jinlu-Railway (Director Hu Yufen)	£400,000	5	10 years	
1896	Chinese Imperial Government 5% Sterling loan of 1896	HSBC	Chinese Central Government	£16,000,000	5	36 years	Chinese Customs revenues

Year	Loan	Lender	Borrower	Amount	Interest	Term	Security
1898	Chinese Imperial Government 4.5% Gold Loan of 1898	HSBC	Chinese Central Government	£16,000,000	4.5	45 years	Chinese Customs revenues and Lijin revenues
1905	Imperial Chinese Government 5% Gold Loan	HSBC	Chinese Central Government	£1,000,000	5	20 years	General Lijin and Tobacco and Wine Lijin of Shanxi province
1908	Imperial Chinese Government 5% Tientsin–Pukou Railway Loan	Chinese Central Railways	Chinese Central Government	£5,000,000	5	30 years	Lijin revenues of Zhili, Shandong and Jiangsu provinces
1908	Board of Communications Loan	HSBC, Banque de l'Indochine, Yokohama Specie Bank	Chinese Central Government (Board of Communications)	6,900,000 Beijing taels	8.4	3 months	
1908	Hanyeping Company Loan	Banque de L'Indochine, Carlowitz & Co., Jebsen & Co.	Hanyeping Company	702,000 Hankou taels	?		Company property

Cont.

Year	Loan	Issued together with	Borrower	Loan sum	Annual interest rate in %	Repayment period	Collateral or guarantee
1910	Loan for the Stabilisation of the Shanghai Financial Market	HSBC, Chartered Bank, Russo-Asiatic Bank, Yokohama Specie Bank, Banque de L'Indochine, International Banking Corporation, Nederlandsche Handel-Maatschappij, Sino-Belgian Bank	Shanghai Daotai	3,500,000 Shanghai taels	4	6 years	
1910	Imperial Chinese Government 5% Tientsin–Pukou Railway Supplementary Loan	Chinese Central Railways	Chinese Central Government	£3,000,000	5	30 years	Lijin revenues of Zhili, Shandong and Jiangsu provinces
1910	Shandong Provincial Loan (3)		Shandong Provincial Government (Governor Sun Baoqi 孫寶琦)	400,000 Shanghai taels	8.4	?	

1910	Liangjiang Provincial Loan for Financial Market Stabilisation	HSBC, Banque de l'Indochine	Liangjiang Provincial Government (Governor-General Zhang Renjun 張人駿)	3,000,000 Shanghai taels	7	6 years	Jiangsu province salt Lijin
1910	Shandong Provincial Loan (4)		Shandong Provincial Government (Governor Sun Baoqi)	150,000 Shanghai taels	8.4	?	
1911	Advance on Imperial Chinese Government 5 per cent Currency Reform and Industrial Development Sinking Fund Gold Loan	Four Groups Consortium	Chinese Central Government (Board of Finance)	£400,000	6	18 months	Salt surtax of all provinces and certain provincial revenues of Liaoning, Jilin and Heilongjiang provinces
1911	Imperial Chinese Government 5% Hukuang Railways Sinking Fund Gold Loan of 1911	Four Groups Consortium	Chinese Central Government	£6,000,000	5	45 years	Certain provincial revenues of Hunan and Hubei provinces
1911	Hubei Provincial Loan	Four Groups Consortium	Huguang Provincial Government (Governor-General Rui Zheng)	2,000,000 Hankou taels	7	10 years	Certain provincial revenues and military funds of Hubei province

Cont.

Year	Loan	Issued together with	Borrower	Loan sum	Annual interest rate in %	Repayment period	Collateral or guarantee
1911	Guangdong Provincial Loan	Four Groups Consortium	Liangguang Provincial Government (Governor-General Zhang Mingqi 張鳴歧)	5,000,000 Hong Kong dollars	5	25 years	
1911	Shandong Provincial Loan (5)		Shandong Provincial Government (Governor Sun Baoqi)	100,000 Jiping taels	8.4	?	
1912	Five Reorganisation Loan Advances	Four Groups Consortium	Chinese Central Government	12,100,000 Shanghai taels	7.5		
1912	Tianjin–Pukou Railway Loan Advance		Chinese Central Government (Tianjin–Pukou Railway)	£900,424	7		Unissued Tianjin–Pukou Supplementary Railway Loan bonds
1913	Chinese Government 5% Reorganisation Gold Loan	Five Groups Consortium	Chinese Central Government	£25,000,000	5	47 years	Salt and Customs revenues
1913	Ministry of Finance Loan (1)		Chinese Central Government (Ministry of Finance on behalf of Shandong Provincial Government)	650,000 Shanghai taels	6	1 year	Tianjin–Pukou Railway bonds, Jinan–Qingdao Railway shares
1914	Ministry of Finance Five Groups Loan	Five Groups Consortium	Chinese Central Government (Ministry of Finance)	750,000 Beijing taels	7	3 months	Salt revenues

Year	Loan	Lender	Borrower	Amount	Interest rate (%)	Term	Security
1914	Hulan Sugar Factory (Harbin) Loan		Chinese Central Government (Ministry of Finance)	100,000 rubles	8	4 months 24 days	
1914	Guangdong Paper Currency Consolidation Advance	Five Groups Consortium	Chinese Central Government (Ministry of Finance)	2,500,000 silver dollars	?	?	
1914	Ministry of Finance Loan (2)		Chinese Central Government (Ministry of Finance)	2,439,571 silver dollars	9.5	6 months 2 days	Parts of proceeds from Reorganisation Loan held in Berlin
1916	Audit Department Loan (1)		Chinese Central Government (Audit Department)	25,000 silver dollars	10	3 months	
1916	Audit Department Loan (2)		Chinese Central Government (Audit Department)	30,000 silver dollars	10	3 months	
1916	Ministry of Finance Loan (3)		Chinese Central Government (Ministry of Finance)	648,000 silver dollars	1.2	4 months 28 days	Salt revenues already deposited with DAB
1916	Ministry of Finance Loan (4)		Chinese Central Government (Ministry of Finance)	447,552 silver dollars	1.2	3 months 8 days	Salt revenues already deposited with DAB and certain other tax revenues
1916	Ministry of Finance Loan (5)		Chinese Central Government (Ministry of Finance)	530,150 silver dollars	1.2	3 months 27 days	Salt revenues already deposited with DAB and certain other tax revenues

Cont.

Year	Loan	Issued together with	Borrower	Loan sum	Annual interest rate in %	Repayment period	Collateral or guarantee
1916	Chinese Government Loan		Chinese Central Government	10,000,000 silver dollars	Unclear for initial 3,000,000 silver dollars advance/ 8% for remaining 7,000,000 silver dollars	Individual advances of 6 months	Unclear for initial 3,000,000 silver dollars advance. For remaining 7,000,000 silver dollars: salt revenues already deposited with DAB and German government guarantee

Notes

1. Sources:
1890–8: Xu, *Zhongguo jindai waizhai tongji*, pp. 30–1; PAAA, R17.777, pp. 15–18; BArch R901/12990, pp. 50–2, 60–1, 143–9; BArch R901/12991, pp. 11–16; Xu et al., *Cong bainian quru*, 1:520; Wei, *Zhong-Ri zhanzheng*, 1:60.
1899–1916: R17.791, pp. 139–43, 160–7; MacMurray, *Treaties*, 1:684–93, 814–23, 841–55, 866–79; Xu, *Zhongguo jindai waizhai tongji*, pp. 42–53, 98–9, 114–21; Caizheng kexue yanjiusuo and Zhong guo dier lishi danganguan, *Minguo waizhai dangan shiliao*, 4:559, 5:135, 184–6, 436, 485, 679–82; Xu et al, *Cong bainian quru*, 2:605–10; PAAA, R17.814, pp. 17–21, 59–61, 73–4, 81, 95.
2. This table includes loans made by the DAB to Chinese companies controlled by the Chinese government.

APPENDIX 2 FOREIGN BANK BRANCHES/ AGENCIES AND AGENTS IN MAJOR CHINESE PORTS WITH NUMBER OF EMPLOYEES, 1908

Country	Bank	Beijing*	Dalian	Fengtian (Mukden)	Fuzhou	Guangzhou (Canton)	Hankou	Hong Kong	Jiaozhou (Qingdao)	Jinan	Lushun kou (Port Arthur)	Macao*	Niuzhuang (Newchwang)	Shanghai	Shantou (Swatow)	Tianjin	Weihaiwei	Xiamen (Amoy)	Yantai	Zhenjiang
Belgium	Banque Sino-Belge													12		2				
Britain	HSBC	3*	A (Cornabé, Eckford & Co.)*		2	A (Deacon & Co.)*	3	79	A (Arnhold & Karberg & Co.)				A (Bush Brothers, Merchants & Commission Agents)	75	A (Bradley & Co.)	7	A (Lavers & Clark)	2	A (Butterfield & Swire)	A (Jardine, Matheson & Co.)
Britain	Chartered Bank of India, Australia and China				1	A (Dent & Co.)*	2	29	A (Siemssen & Co.)					30	A (Butterfield & Butterfield & Swire)	8	A (Cornabé, Eckford & Co.)	A (Tait & Co.)	A (Cornabé, Eckford & Co.)	
Britain	Mercantile Bank of India				A (Gilman & Co.)		A (Jardine, Matheson & Co.)	8						A (Jardine, Matheson & Co.)	A (Bradley & Co.)			A (Boyd & Co.)	A (Cornabé, Eckford & Co.)	
Britain	National Bank of China					A (Shewan, Tomes & Co.)	A (Geddes & Co.)	4					A (Bandinel & Co.)	A (Barlow & Co.)*	A (Bradley & Co.)		A (Cornabé, Eckford & Co.)	A (Pasedag & Co.)		
France	Banque de l'Indochine					3	2	9						12		3			A (Cornabé, Eckford & Co.)	
Germany	Deutsch-Asiatische Bank	2*				A (Carlowitz & Co.)	2	12	7					19		6			A (Diederichsen, Jebsen & Co.)*	
Italy	Società Coloniale Italiana					(3)	(3)*			1				9						
Italy*	Banco-Italo-Chinese*					2*														
Japan	Yokohama Specie Bank	8*	3	10*	A (Butterfield & Swire)	A (Carlowitz & Co.)	5	8	A (Carlowitz & Co.)		1		15	18		15	A (Cornabé, Eckford & Co.)	A (Butterfield & Swire)	4	
Japan	Bank of Taiwan				3			4*							3			4		
Netherlands	Nederlandsche Handel-Maatschappij							3*						5				A (Pasedag & Co.)*		

Portugal	Handelsbank* Banco Nacional Ultramarino*						6*					
Russia	Russo-Chinese Bank	6*	A (Holme, Ringer & Co.)*	A (Butterfield & Swire)	3	8		47	6*	A (Butterfield & Swire)	A (L.H. Smith & Co.)*	A (Butterfield & Swire)
										A (Butterfield & Swire)*		A (Butterfield & Swire)
United States	International Banking Corporation	A (Jardine, Matheson & Co.)*	A (Butterfield & Swire)	A 2*	21	A (Siemssen & Co.)	17	A (Armhold & Karberg & Co.)	8	A (Bradley & Co.)	A (Fait & Co.)*	A (Aruz & Co.)

Notes

1. Sources: The table is adapted from Tōa Dōbun Shoin Daigaku, *Shina Keizai zensho*, pp. 811–14. I have supplemented the information therein with information from Hong Kong Daily Press, *Directory & Chronicle 1908* (including adding Beijing and Macao). This supplemented information is marked with an asterisk. In the rare cases of conflicting information (where I did not just add information from the *Directory & Chronicle*), I have generally given preference to the Japanese source (with the exception noted below).

2. The numbers indicate the number of foreign employees employed by each bank in their branch or agency in the different locations (both sources do not differentiate between branches and agencies). An 'A' indicates that while the particular bank did not have its own branch or agency in that particular port, there was a foreign firm (provided in brackets) that acted as its agent in that particular locality. I have not included any banks that did not have at least one branch or agency of their own in China.

3. Tōa Dōbun Shoin Daigaku, *Shina Keizai zensho* also lists the 'Guaranty Trust Co., of New York' in its description of foreign banks (Meiguo baoxing yinhang [should correctly be Meiguo baoxin yinhang], English translation in the Japanese Tōa Dōbun Shoin Daigaku, *Shina Keizai zensho*, p. 805), but the table in Tōa Dōbun Shoin Daigaku, *Shina Keizai zensho* does not list any branches for the bank. On the preceding pages (pp. 805, 810) it is indicated that the bank had a branch in Shanghai. However, the *Directory & Chronicle* does not confirm this. Therefore, I have not listed the bank in this table.

4. The Italian Società Coloniale Italiana seems to have mainly been a trading company that only in Shanghai principally operated as a bank (see Cyclopedia Publishing Company, *Cyclopedia of India*, p. 382). Therefore, I have placed its employee numbers in brackets for other locations. It is also unclear whether the Società Coloniale Italiana had a branch or agency of its own in Guangzhou (sources are conflicting, with the *Shina Keizai zensho* (p. 808), Hong, *Shanghai jinrong zhi* (p. 205) and *Cyclopedia of India* (p. 382) confirming this, but the *Directory & Chronicle* not showing a presence in Guangzhou).

5. Several northern locations listed in the *Shina Keizai zensho* were not included in this table as only the Russo-Chinese Bank and Yokohama Specie Bank had representations there and there is no detailed information available on these. These locations are Tieling, Harbin, Jilin, Kulun and Changchun.

6. A name of a foreign firm corresponding to the Chinese Hong name indicated as agent for the HSBC in Guangzhou in Tōa Dōbun Shoin Daigaku, *Shina Keizai zensho* could not be found. Therefore, I have used the information from the *Directory & Chronicle* here.

BIBLIOGRAPHY

Consulted Archives (Unpublished Primary Sources)

Archiv – Studienwerk Deutsches Leben in Ostasien (Archives – Study Association for German Life in East Asia), Munich.

Archives, Institute of Modern History, Academia Sinica, Taibei:

- 外交部門 (Waijiao bumen; Archives of the Foreign Office)

    01: 總理各國事務衙門 (Zongli geguo shiwu yamen; Archives of the Zongli Yamen, 1858–1901).

    02: 外務部 (Waiwubu; Archives of the Foreign Office of the Qing Dynasty, 1901–11).

    03: 北洋政府外交部 (Beiyang zhengfu waijiaobu; Archives of the Foreign Office of the Beiyang Government, 1912–27).

Bibliothek – Studienwerk Deutsches Leben in Ostasien (Library – Study Association for German Life in East Asia), Munich.

Bundesarchiv Lichterfelde (Federal Archives of Germany, Lichterfelde), Berlin:

- R1501: Reichsministerium des Innern (Interior Ministry).
- R2: Reichsfinanzministerium (Ministry of Finance).
- R3118: Zulassungsstelle an der Berliner Börse (Registration Office of the Berlin Bourse).
- R8024: Kolonialwirtschaftliches Komitee (Committee for Colonial Economic Affairs).
- R901: Auswärtiges Amt (Foreign Office).

Bundesarchiv/Militärarchiv (Federal Military Archives of Germany), Freiburg:

- RM3: Reichsmarineamt (Imperial Naval Office).

First Historical Archives of China, Beijing:

- 軍機處電報電旨檔 (Junjichu dianbao dianzhi dang; Archives of the Telegrams and Edicts Transmitted by Telegram of the Grand Council).

Geheimes Staatsarchiv, Preussischer Kulturbesitz (Secret State Archives, Prussian Cultural Heritage Foundation), Berlin:

288

• I HA Rep. 109, No. 5363: Gründung einer Deutsch-Asiatischen Bank (Establishment of a German-Asiatic Bank).

Hausarchiv Sal. Oppenheim Bank (Archives of the Bank Sal. Oppenheim), Cologne:

• A VIII 114 Ostasiatische Geschäfte 1888–1914 (East Asian Business 1888–1914).

Historical Archive of Deutsche Bank, Frankfurt am Main:

• Bild-Archiv (Picture Archive).
• Geschäftsberichte, Deutsch-Asiatische Bank (Annual Reports, Deutsch-Asiatische Bank).
• Geschäftsberichte, Deutsche Bank (Annual Reports, Deutsche Bank).
• K01: Briefwechsel Max Schinckel mit den Geschäftsinhabern der Disconto-Gesellschaft (Correspondence between Max Schinkel and the Proprietors of the Disconto-Gesellschaft).
• K01/969: Konsortium für Asiatische Geschäfte – Mex Dollar 7,000,000 Vorschuss an Chines. Regierung, 1916–24 (Consortium for Asiatic Business – Mexican Dollar 7,000,000 Advance to Chinese Government, 1916–24).
• K07/002/I: Anleihen: Zeitungsausschnitte und Prospekte (Loans: Newspaper clippings and prospectuses).
• K07/002II-12: Inter-Bank Conferences 1912 und 1913 in London wegen chinesischer Anleihen (Inter-Bank Conferences of 1912 and 1913 Held in London about Chinese Loans).
• K07/010/I/01: Aufsichtsratssitzungen 1890–1915 (Meetings of the Supervisory Board 1890–1915).
• P08401: Deutsch-Asiatische Bank, Stützungsverhandlungen (Deutsch-Asiatische Bank, Subsidy Negotiations).
• P8399: Deutsch-Asiatische Bank, Berlin, Personalia (Deutsch-Asiatische Bank, Personnel Files).
• S2585: China, Chinesische Anleihen Vol. 1 (China, Chinese Loans Vol. 1).
• S2586: China, Chinesische Anleihen Vol. 2 (China, Chinese Loans Vol. 2).
• S2589: China, 4 ½ % Anleihe von 1898 – Konsortium für asiatische Geschäfte (China, 4.5% Loan of 1898, Consortium for Asiatic Business).
• S2592: China – Konsortium für Asiatische Geschäfte, 1905–14 (Consortium for Asiatic Business, 1905–14).
• S2593: Sekretariat – Chinesische Tientsin–Pukow Anleihe 1908, Vol. 1 (Secretariat – Chinese Tianjin–Pukou Loan 1908, Vol. 1).
• S2594: Sekretariat – Chinesische Tientsin–Pukow Anleihe 1908, Vol. 2 (Secretariat – Chinese Tianjin–Pukou Loan 1908, Vol. 2).

- S2595: Sekretariat – Chinesische Tientsin–Pukow Anleihe Übernahme Restbetrag 1909 (Secretariat – Chinese Tianjin–Pukou Loan Subscription Rest Amount 1909).
- S2597: Sekretariat – Chinesische Tientsin–Pukow Ergänzungs-Anleihe 1910 Beteiligte (Secretariat – Chinese Tianjin–Pukou Supplementary Loan 1910 Subscribers).
- S2606: China – Anleihen – Aufnahme-Konsortium (China – Loans – Acquisition Consortium).
- S3918: Deutsche Bank, Filiale Shanghai und Filiale Yokohama (Deutsche Bank, Shanghai Branch and Yokohama Branch).

HSBC Group Archives, London:

- HQ HSBCK 0008–0001: David McLean Private Letter Books.

Politisches Archiv des Auswärtigen Amtes (Political Archives of the Foreign Office), Berlin.

- R1.294: Akten betreffend Reichsbeamte, Bd. 3 (Files Related to Civil Servants, Vol. 3)
- R17.771–R17.814: China 3: Finanzen Chinas (China 3: The Finances of China).
- R17.854–R17.868: China 4 Nr. 1: Deutsche Eisenbahn-Unternehmungen in China (China 4 No. 1: German Railway Endeavours in China).
- R9208: Peking II: Akten der Botschaft in China (Peking II: Files of the German Legation in China).

Shanghai Municipal Archives, Shanghai:

- Q281: 中國通商銀行 (Zhongguo tongshang yinhang; Commercial Bank of China).

Shanghai Municipal Library, Shanghai:

- 盛宣懷檔案 (Sheng Xuanhuai dangan; Sheng Xuanhuai Archives).

Special Collections & Archives, Queen's University Belfast:

- MS 15.1: Hart Collection – Sir Robert Hart Diaries.

The British Library, London:

- Map Collection.

The National Archives, Kew:

- FO 228: Foreign Office: Consulates and Legation, China: General Correspondence, Series I, 1834–1930.
- FO 371: Foreign Office: Political Departments: General Correspondence from 1906 to 1966.

- FO 405: Foreign Office: China and Taiwan Confidential Print, 1833–1970.

Tianjin Municipal Archives, Tianjin:

- J128: 天津商會 (Tianjin shanghui; Tianjin Chamber of Commerce).
- J161: 中國銀行天津分行 (Zhongguo yinhang Tianjin fenhang; Bank of China, Tianjin Branch).

Published Primary Sources

Chinese

Caizheng kexue yanjiusuo 財政科學研究所 and Zhongguo dier lishi danganguan 中國第二歷史檔案館, comp. *Minguo waizhai dangan shiliao* 民國外債檔案史料 (Historical Archival Materials on Foreign Debt during the Republican Period), 12 vols. Beijing: Dangan chubanshe, 1990.

Chen Xiafei 陳霞飛, comp. *Zhongguo haiguan mi dang* 中國海關密檔 (The Secret Archives of the Chinese Imperial Maritime Customs Service), 9 vols. Beijing: Zhonghua shuju, 1990–5.

Chen Yijie 陳義杰, comp. *Weng Tonghe riji* 翁同龢日記 (The Diary of Weng Tonghe), 6 vols. Beijing: Zhonghua shuju, 1989–98.

'De Hua Yinhang zhi jin xi guan (zai xu) 德華銀行之今昔觀 (再續) (The Past and Present of the Deutsch-Asiatische Bank, Part Three)'. *Yinhang Zhoubao* (24 July 1917).

Ding Fenglin 丁凤麟, and Wang Xinzhi 王欣之, comp. *Xue Fucheng xuanji* 薛福成選集 (Selected Works of Xue Fucheng). Shanghai: Shanghai renmin chubanshe, 1987.

Du Chunhe 杜春和, comp. *Zhang Guogan wenji* 張國淦文集 (The Collected Works of Zhang Guogan). Beijing: Beijing Yanshan chubanshe, 2000.

Gu Tinglong 顧廷龍, and Daiyi 戴逸, comp. *Li Hongzhang quanji* 李鴻章全集 (The Complete Works of Li Hongzhang), 39 vols. Hefei: Anhui jiaoyu chubanshe, 2008.

Guangdong sheng shehui kexue yuan lishi yanjiushi 廣東省社會科學院歷史研究室, comp. *Sun Zhongshan quanji* 孫中山全集 (The Complete Works of Sun Yatsen), 11 vols. Beijing: Zhonghua shuju, 1981–6.

Huang Jianhui, ed. *Shanxi piaohao shiliao* 山西票號史料 (Historical Materials on Shanxi Piaohao). Taiyuan: Shanxi jingji chubanshe, 2002.

'Hutu huangmiu zhi Zhou Xuexi 糊塗荒謬之周學熙 (The Blindness and Absurdity of Zhou Xuexi)'. *Shibao* 時報 (4 March 1913).

Liang Bingkun 梁秉錕. *Laiyang xianzhi* 萊陽縣志 (*Laiyang County Gazetteer*). 1935.

Lu Shoujian 盧壽籛. 'Ou zhan ji yu Shanghai shangye zhi yingxiang 歐戰及於上海商業之影響 (The Impact of the European War on Shanghai's Commerce)'. *Zhonghua Shiyejie* 中華實業界 11 (1914): 1–5.

Luo Baoshan 駱寶善, and Liu Lusheng 劉路生. *Yuan Shikai quanji* 袁世凱全集 (The Collected Works of Yuan Shikai), 36 vols. Zhengzhou: Henan daxue chubanshe, 2013.

Ma Jianzhong 馬建忠. *Ma Jianzhong quanji* 馬建忠全集 (The Collected Works of Ma Jianzhong). Beijing: Zhonghua shuju, 2013.

Ma Yinchu 馬寅初. *Ma Yinchu quanji* 馬寅初全集 (The Complete Works of Ma Yinchu), 15 vols. Hangzhou: Zhejiang renmin chubanshe, 1999.

Mi Rucheng 宓如成, comp. *Zhongguo jindai tielushi ziliao* 中國近代鐵路史資料 (1863–1911) (Materials on the History of Modern Chinese Railways (1863–1911)), 3 vols. Beijing: Zhonghua shuju, 1963.

'Nanjing caizhengbu shouzhi baogao 南京財政部收支報告 (The Income and Expenses Report of the Nanjing Ministry of Finance)'. *Zhengfu gongbao*, No. 81 (20 July 1912).

Nongshang Bu 農商部. *Zhonghua Minguo jiunian dijiuci nongshang tongjibiao* 中華民國九年第九次農商統計表 (Statistical Tables Relating to Agriculture and Commerce Vol. 9, 1920). Beijing: Nongshang bu, 1924.

'Ou zhan yu shangye zhi yingxiang 歐戰與商業之影響 (The Impact of the European War on Commerce)'. *Ouzhou zhanji* 7 (1914): 152–3.

Qian Jiajun 千家駒. *Jiu Zhongguo gongzhaishi ziliao* 舊中國公債史資料 (Materials on the History of Public Debt in Old China, 1894–1949). Beijing: Zhonghua shuju, 1984.

Shanghai Commercial and Savings Bank, comp. *Chen Guangfu xiansheng yanlun ji* 陳光甫先生言論集 (The Collected Speeches of Mr Chen Guangfu). Shanghai: Shanghai Commercial and Savings Bank, 1949.

Tianjin shi dangangguan 天津市檔案館, comp. *Yuan Shikai Tianjin dangan shiliao xuanbian* 袁世凱天津檔案史料選編 (Selected Sources from the Tianjin Municipal Archives about Yuan Shikai). Tianjin: Tianjin dangan chubanshe, 1990.

Wang Jiecheng, comp. *Zeng Jize: Chushi Ying-Fa-E guo riji* 曾紀澤: 出使英法俄國日記 (Zeng Jize: The Diary from His Time as Ambassador to Britain, France and Russia). Changsha: Yuelushe, 1985.

Wang Wenjun 王文鈞. 'Zai Hua waiguo yinhang gaishu 在華外國銀行概述 (A Summary of Foreign Banks in China)', *Dagongbao (Jingji zhoubao)* 大公報 (經濟週報) (7 August 1935).

Wei Qizhang 戚其章, comp. *Zhong-Ri zhanzheng* 中日戰爭 (The Sino-Japanese War), 12 vols. Beijing: Zhonghua shuju, 1989.

Weng Tonghe 翁同龢. *Weng Wengong riji* 翁文恭日記 (Diary of Weng Tonghe), 40 vols. Shanghai: Shangwu yinshuguan, 1925).

Wu Peichu 吳培初. 'Shanghai waishang yinhang maiban qunxiang 上海外商銀行買辦群像 (A Portrait of the Compradors of Foreign Banks in Shanghai)'. In *Waishang yinhang zai Zhongguo* 外商銀行在中國 (Foreign Banks in China), edited by Shou Tongyi 壽統一 and Shou Leying 壽樂英, 260–94. Beijing: Zhongguo wenshi chubanshe, 1996.

Xiao Liang 驍良. 'Guoren ji yinggai bian xinli 國人急應該變心裡 (Our Fellow Countrymen Should Urgently Change Their Mind)'. *Shenbao* (11 June 1935).

Xie Junmei 謝俊美, comp. *Weng Tonghe ji* 翁同龢集 (The Collected Works of Weng Tonghe), 2 vols. Beijing: Zhonghua shuju, 2005.

Yang Jialu 楊家駱, comp. *Zhong-Ri zhanzheng wenxian huibian* 中日戰爭文獻彙編 (Collected Materials on the Sino-Japanese War), 8 vols. Taibei: Dingwen shuju, 1973.

Ye Gongchuo 葉恭綽. *Xia An huibian* 遐庵匯編 (The Collected Manuscripts of Ye Gongchuo (Xia An)), 2nd ed. Shanghai: Shanghai shudian, 1946.

Yu Heping 虞和平, and Xia Liangcai 夏良才, comp. *Zhou Xuexi ji* 周學熙集 (The Collected Works of Zhou Xuexi). Wuhan: Huazhong shifan daxue, 2011.

Yuan Shuyi 苑書義, Sun Huafeng 孫華峰 and Li Bingxin 李秉新, comp. *Zhang Zhidong quanji* 張之洞全集 (The Complete Works of Zhang Zhidong), 12 vols. Shijiazhuang: Hebei renmin chubanshe, 1998.

Zhang Gongquan 張公權. *Ge sheng jinrong gailüe* 各省金融概略 (A Summary of Finance in the Different Provinces). 1915.

Zhongguo Renmin Gongheguo Caizheng Bu 中國人民共和國財政部, and Zhongguo Renmin Yinhang zonghang 中國人民銀行總行, comp. *Qingdai waizhai shi ziliao (1853–1911)* 清代外債史資料 (1853–1911) (Materials on the History of Foreign Debt in the Qing Dynasty (1853–1911)), 3 vols. Beijing: Zhongguo renmin gonghe guo caizheng bu, Zhongguo renmin yinhang zonghang, 1988.

Zhongguo Renmin Yinhang Shanghai shi fenhang 中國人民銀行上海市分行, comp. *Shanghai qianzhuang shiliao* 上海錢莊史料 (Historical Materials on *Qianzhuang* Banks in Shanghai). Shanghai: Shanghai renmin chubanshe, 1960, reprint 1978.

Zhongguo shehui kexueyuan jingji yanjiu suo 中國社會科學院經濟研究所, comp. *Shanghaishi mianbu shangye* 上海市棉布商業 (Shanghai's Cloth Business). Beijing: Zhonghua shuju, 1979.

Zhongguo yinhang baoxian jiandu guanli weiyuanhui 中國銀行保險監督管理委員會. '"Shushuo shisanwu fazhan chengjiu" yinhangye zhuanti "數說十三五發展成就"銀行業專題 (Explaining the Development and Achievements of the 13th Five-Year Plan with Numbers: Specific Report about the Banking Sector)' (12 March 2021). www.cbirc.gov.cn/cn/view/pages/ItemDetail.html?docId=970583&itemId=954&generaltype=0.

Zhongguo yinhangye jiandu guanli weiyuanhui xuanchuan gongzuobu 中國銀行業監督管理委員會宣傳工作部. *Zhongguo yinhangye jiandu guanli weiyuanhui 2017 nianbao* 中國銀行業監督管理委員會 2017 年報 (Annual Report of the Committee for the Supervision and Management of the Chinese Banking Sector for the Year 2017). Beijing: Zhongguo jinrong chubanshe, 2018).

Zhou Qiuguang 周秋光, comp. *Xiong Xiling ji* 熊希齡集 (A Collection of the Works of Xiong Xiling), 8 vols. Changsha: Hunan renmin chubanshe, 2008.

'Zhou Xuexi wuguo zhi zhenxiang 周學熙誤國之真相 (The Truth about Zhou Xuexi's Betrayal of the Country)'. *Yanzheng zazhi* 6 (1913).
Zuo Zongtang 左宗棠. *Zuo Zongtang quanji* 左宗棠全集 (Collected Writings of Zuo Zongtang), 15 vols. Changsha: Yuelushe, 2009.

English

'A Loss for China'. *North-China Herald* (7 December 1906).
'Abstract of Assets and Liabilities, Hongkong and Shanghai Banking Corporation, 31 December 1900'. *The Economist* (16 March 1901).
Arnold, Julean Herbert. *Commercial Handbook of China, Vol. 2*. Washington, DC: Government Printing Office, 1920.
'As China Goes Global, Its Banks Are Coming Out Too'. *The Economist* (7 May 2020). www.economist.com/special-report/2020/05/07/as-china-goes-global-its-banks-are-coming-out-too.
A. W. Kimber & Company. *Kimber's Record of Government Debts*. New York: A. W. Kimber, 1920.
Baylin, J. R. *Foreign Loan Obligations of China: A Compendium of Such Secured External Loan Obligations of China as Are Provided with Regular Amortization Tables*. Tianjin: La Librairie française, 1925.
Bell, H. T. Montague, and H. G. W. Woodhead. *The China Year Book, 1912*. London: George Routledge & Sons, 1912.
Bell, H. T. Montague, and H. G. W. Woodhead. *The China Year Book, 1913*. London: George Routledge & Sons, 1913.
Beresford, Charles. *The Memoirs of Admiral Lord Charles Beresford*. Toronto: S. B. Gundy, 1914.
Bu Ming 卜明. 'New Development in Sino-Foreign Financial Relations'. In *Foreign Bankers in China Vol. 1*, compiled by the Bank of China, 7–13. Hong Kong: Kong Yuen Publishing Co., 1986.
Burns, Nick. 'China to Settle UK Debts'. *Financial Times* (6 June 1987).
Burt, A. R., J. B. Powell and Carl Crow. *Biographies of Prominent Chinese*. Shanghai: Biographical Publishing Company, 1925.
Chen Xiafei 陳霞飛 and Han Rongfang 韓榮芳, eds. *Archives of China's Imperial Maritime Customs Confidential Correspondence between Robert Hart and James Duncan Campbell 1874–1907*, 3 vols. Beijing: Foreign Language Press, 1990–3.
China Mail. *Who's Who in the Far East (1906–1907)*. Hong Kong: China Mail, 1906.
China Weekly Review. *Who's Who in China (Biographies of Chinese)*. 3rd ed. Shanghai: The China Weekly Review, 1925.
'China's Finances: Safety of Foreign Banks'. *North-China Herald* (8 August 1914).
'Chinese Customs Revenue: Recent Improvement Maintained'. *The Times (London)* (5 February 1912).

'Chinese Customs Revenues: Early Resumption of Loan Service Payments'. *The Times (London)* (2 February 1912).

'Chinese Government and the Rebellion'. *The Times (London)* (27 October 1911).

'Chinese Loan'. *The Times (London)* (22 May 1913).

'Chinese Loan Service: Payments Expected Shortly'. *The Times (London)* (7 February 1912).

'Chinese Loans Secured on Internal Revenues'. *Financial Times* (11 December 1930).

'Cosmopolitan Finance in China'. *The Times (London)* (26 September 1913).

Cyclopedia Publishing Company, *The Cyclopedia of India: Biographical, Historical, Administrative, Commercial*, Vol. 1. Calcutta: Cyclopedia Pub. Co., 1907.

'Death of Mr. Hillier of Peking'. *The Times (London)* (15 April 1924).

Edkins, Joseph. *Banking and Prices in China*. Shanghai: Presbyterian Mission Press, 1905.

Edmunds, Charles Keyser. 'The Passing of China's Ancient System of Literary Examinations'. *The Popular Science Monthly* (February 1906).

European Union Chamber of Commerce in China. *European Business in China Business Confidence Survey 2019* (20 May 2019). www.europeanchamber.com .cn/en/publications-archive/663/European_Business_in_China_ Business_Confidence_Survey_2019.

European Business in China Position Paper 2018/2019 (18 September 2018). www.europeanchamber.com.cn/en/publications-archive/646/European_ Business_in_China_Position_Paper_2018_2019.

European Business in China Position Paper 2020/2021 (10 September 2020). www.europeanchamber.com.cn/en/publications-archive/864/European_ Business_in_China_Position_Paper_2020_2021.

Exner, Heinrich August. 'The Sources of Revenue and the Credit of China'. *The China Review* 17, No. 5 (1887): 276–91.

Fairbank, John King, Katherine Frost Bruner and Elizabeth Macleod Matheson, comp. *The I.G. in Peking: Letters of Robert Hart, Chinese Maritime Customs, 1868–1907*, 2 vols. Cambridge, MA: Harvard University Press, 1975.

'First President of China'. *The Times (London)* (11 March 1912).

Foster, John W. *Present Conditions in China*. New York: Student Volunteer Movement, 1906.

'Funeral Services Held for Local German Banker'. *The China Press* (21 November 1921).

'German Intrigue – Eggeling at Large'. *The Shanghai Times* (15 September 1917).

'German Intrigues – Herr Cordes Arrested'. *The Shanghai Times* (11 September 1917).

'Gilt-Edged Weaken and Rally'. *Financial Times* (5 November 1925).

Great Britain, House of Commons, comp. *China No. 1 (1900): Further Correspondence Respecting the Affairs of China*. London: Harrison and Sons, 1900.

Hanna, Hugh H., Charles A. Conant and Jeremiah W. Jenks. *Gold Standard in International Trade: Report on the Introduction of the Gold-exchange Standard into China, the Philippine Islands, Panama, and Other Silver-*

using Countries, and on the Stability of Exchange. Washington, DC: Government Printing Office, 1904.

Hongkong Daily Press. *The Chronicle & Directory for China, Corea, Japan, the Philippines, Cochin-China, Annam, Tonquin, Siam, Borneo, Straits Settlements, Malay States, & C., for the Year 1888.* Hong Kong: The Hongkong Daily Press, 1888.

The Chronicle & Directory for China, Corea, Japan, the Philippines, Indo-China, Straits Settlements, Siam, Borneo, Malay States, &c., for the Year 1890. Hong Kong: The Hongkong Daily Press, 1890.

The Chronicle & Directory for China, Corea, Japan, the Philippines, Indo-China, Straits Settlements, Siam, Borneo, Malay States, &c., for the Year 1895. Hong Kong: The Hongkong Daily Press, 1895.

The Directory & Chronicle for China, Corea, Japan, the Philippines, Indo-China, Straits Settlements, Malay States, Siam, Netherlands India, Borneo, The Philippines, &c., for the Year 1903. Hong Kong: *The Hongkong Daily Press,* 1903.

The Directory & Chronicle for China, Japan, Corea, Indo-China, Straits Settlements, Malay States, Siam, Netherlands India, Borneo, the Philippines, &c. for the Year 1908. Hong Kong: *The Hongkong Daily Press,* 1908.

The Directory & Chronicle for China, Japan, Corea, Indo-China, Straits Settlements, Malay States, Siam, Netherlands India, Borneo, the Philippines, &c. for the Year 1913. Hong Kong: *The Hongkong Daily Press,* 1913.

'Hsiung Hsi Ling'. *The Far Eastern Review* 9, No. 1 (1912): 23.

Jamieson, George. *The Revenue and Expenditure of the Chinese Empire.* Shanghai: Shanghai Mercury, 1897.

KPMG. *Mainland China Banking Survey 2017.* Amstelveen, the Netherlands: KPMG, 2017.

Lo Hui-Min, comp. *The Correspondence of G.E. Morrison I, 1895–1912.* Cambridge: Cambridge University Press, 1976.

Lo Hui-Min, comp. *The Correspondence of G.E. Morrison II, 1912–1920.* Cambridge: Cambridge University Press, 1978.

MacMurray, John Van Antwerp, comp. *Treaties With and Concerning China 1894–1919,* 2 vols. New York: Oxford University Press, 1921.

Madsen, Juel. *Some China Personalities. Sketched by Juel Madsen.* n.p., n.d.

Merwin, Samuel. *Drugging a Nation: The Story of China and the Opium Curse; a Personal Investigation, During an Extended Tour, of the Present Conditions of the Opium Trade in China and Its Effects Upon the Nation.* New York and Chicago: F.H Revell Company, 1908.

Millard's Review. *Who's Who in China: Containing the Pictures and Biographies of Some of China's Political, Financial, Business and Professional Leaders, Vol. 1.* Shanghai: *Millard's Review,* 1919.

'Money Market'. *The Times (London)* (14 October 1911).

'Money Markets'. *The Economist* (21 October 1911).

Morris, H. E., and C. R. Maguire. *China Stock & Share Handbook 1913.* Shanghai: North-China Daily News and Herald, 1913.

Morse, Hosea Ballou. *The Trade and Administration of China*, 2nd ed. London: Longmans, Green & Co, 1913.

Morse, Hosea Ballou. *The International Relations of the Chinese Empire*, 3 vols. London; New York: Longmans, Green, and Co., 1910–18.

National Bureau of Statistics of China. *China Statistical Yearbook 2020*, ch. 16.3. www.stats.gov.cn/tjsj/ndsj/2020/indexeh.htm.

Nederlandsch Indische Handelsbank. *Nederlandsch Indische Handelsbank*. Amsterdam: Nederlandsch Indische Handelsbank, 1913.

Netherlands Trading Society. *A Brief History of the Netherlands Trading Society, 1824–1924*. The Hague: Mouton, 1924.

North-China Daily News & Herald. *The North-China Desk Hong List 1917, City Supplementary Edition, Revised and Corrected to July 1917*. Shanghai: North-China Daily News & Herald, 1917.

North-China Herald. *Desk Hong List: A General and Business Directory for Shanghai and the Northern and River Ports, &c, 1903*. Shanghai: North-China Herald, 1903.

Desk Hong List: A General and Business Directory for Shanghai and the Northern and River Ports, &c, 1904. Shanghai: North-China Herald, 1904.

Rhea, Frank. *Far Eastern Markets for Railway Materials, Equipment, and Supplies*. Washington, DC: Government Printing Office, 1919.

'Say Timmerscheidt Had German Secrets'. *New York Times* (7 July 1917).

Somasundaram, Narayanan. 'China Scraps Almost All Foreign Ownership Limits for Financial Sector'. *Nikkei Asia* (23 July 2020). https://asia.nikkei.com /Business/Finance/China-scraps-almost-all-foreign-ownership-limits-for-financial-sector.

St. John, Burton. *The China Times Guide to Tientsin and Its Neighbourhood*. Tianjin: The China Times, 1908.

'The Manchu Dynasty and the Chinese Revolution'. *The Economist* (21 October 1911).

'The "Middlemen" of China'. *British Board of Trade Review* (August 1898). In *Commercial China in 1899*, by United States Treasury Department, 2215–2216. Washington DC: United States Treasury Department, 1899.

'The New Minister of Communications'. *The Far Eastern Review* 11, No. 1 (1914): 16.

'The Palace Treasure in Peking'. *The Times (London)* (11 December 1911).

'The Powers and Chinese Finance'. *The Times (London)* (5 January 1916).

Tientsin Press. *Guide to Tientsin*. Tianjin: Tientsin Press, 1904.

'Trump's New Trade War Tool Might Just Be Antique China Debt'. *Bloomberg Businessweek* (29 August 2019). www.bloomberg.com/news/articles/2019-08-29/trump-s-new-trade-war-weapon-might-just-be-antique-china-debt.

United States Trade Representative. *2020 Report to Congress on China's WTO Compliance* (January 2021). https://ustr.gov/sites/default/files/files/reports/2020/2020USTRReportCongressChinaWTOCompliance.pdf.

Vissering, Gerard. *On Chinese currency: preliminary remarks about the monetary reform in China*. Amsterdam: J.H. De Bussy, 1912.

Wagel, Srinivas R. *Finance in China*. Shanghai: North-China Daily News and Herald, Ltd., 1914.

Wang, Orange. 'China's Economic Slowdown Prompts Beijing to Reaffirm Commitment to Opening Up Financial Markets'. *South China Morning Post* (22 July 2021). www.scmp.com/economy/china-economy/article/3142103/chinas-economic-slowdown-prompts-beijing-reaffirm-commitment.

Weal, B. L. Putnam. *The Fight for the Republic in China*. London: Hurst and Blackett, 1918.

Wright, Arthur. *Twentieth Century Impressions of Hong Kong, Shanghai, and other Treaty Ports of China: Their History, People, Commerce, Industries, and Resources* London: Lloyds Greater Britain Publishing Company, 1908.

Zhang Zhidong 張之洞. *China's Only Hope: An Appeal*. Translated by Samuel I. Woodbridge. Edinburgh and London: Oliphant, Anderson & Ferrier, 1901.

French

Moreau, Edmond, and Paul Monchicourt. *Rapport à l'assemblée générale des actionnaires du Comptoir d'escompte du 29 avril 1889*. Paris: Impr. de Dubuisson, 1889.

German

Berliner Actionair, *Jahrbuch der Berliner Börse, 1890–1891: Ein Nachschlagbuch für Banquiers und Capitalisten*. Berlin: Ernst Siegfried Mittler und Sohn, 1890.

Berliner Actionair, *Jahrbuch der Berliner Börse, 1897–1898: Ein Nachschlagbuch für Banquiers und Capitalisten*. Berlin: Verlag des Berliner Actionair, 1897.

Dernburg, Bernhard. *Japan und China: Eine wirtschaftspolitische Studienreise, Herbst 1910*. Berlin: Reichsdruckerei, 1911.

Dehn, Paul. 'Handel und Verkehr'. In *China: Schilderungen aus Leben und Geschichte, Krieg und Sieg. Ein Denkmal den Streitern und der Weltpolitik*, edited by Joseph Kürschner, 1:383–99. Leipzig: Verlag von Hermann Bieger, 1902.

'Die chinesischen Wirren'. *Berliner Börsen-Zeitung* (25 October 1911, evening edition).

'Die Revolution in China'. *Berliner Tageblatt* (18 October 1911).

Exner, August Heinrich. *China: Skizzen von Land und Leuten mit besonderer Berücksichtigung kommerzieller Verhältnisse*. Leipzig: Weigel, 1889.

Die Einnahmequellen und der Credit Chinas nebst Aphorismen über die Deutsch-Ostasiatischen Handelsbeziehungen. Berlin: Asher, 1887.

'Soll Deutschland chinesische Anleihen kaufen?' *Berliner Tageblatt* (14/15 May 1895).

Franke, Otto. *Erinnerungen aus Zwei Welten: Randglossen zur Eigenen Lebensgeschichte*. Berlin: Walter de Gruyter & Co., 1954.

Heinemann, Ernst. *Saling's Börsen-Jahrbuch*. Berlin: Verlag für Börsen-und Finanzliteratur, 1912.

Hirth, Friedrich. *Chinesische Studien. Erster Band.* München; Leipzig: G. Hirth's Verlag, 1890.

Hürter, Johannes, comp. *Paul von Hintze: Marineoffizier, Diplomat, Staatssekretär. Dokumente einer Karriere zwischen Militär und Politik, 1903–1918.* München: Harald Boldt Verlag im R. Oldenbourg Verlag, 1998.

Lepsius, Johannes, Albrecht Mendelssohn Bartholdy and Friedrich Thimme, comp. *Die Große Politik der europäischen Kabinette 1871–1914. Sammlung der diplomatischen Akten des Auswärtigen Amtes,* 40 vols. Berlin: Deutsche Verlagsgesellschaft für Politik und Geschichte, 1922–7.

Reiß, August. 'Das Bankwesen in China'. In *China: Wirtschaft und Wirtschaftsgrundlagen,* edited by Josef Hellauer, 168–84. Berlin: Walter de Gruyter & Co., 1921.

'Die Innere Organisation Fremder Firmen in China'. In *China: Wirtschaft und Wirtschaftsgrundlagen,* edited by Josef Hellauer, 159–67. Berlin: Walter de Gruyter & Co., 1921.

Sachau, Eduard. *Denkschrift über das Seminar für Orientalische Sprachen an der Königlichen Friedrich-Wilhelms-Universität zu Berlin 1887 bis 1912.* Berlin: Reichsdruckerei, 1912.

'Uebergabe des Neubaues der Deutsch-Asiatischen Bank in Hankou', *Ostasiatischer Lloyd* (10 July 1908).

'Unfair Verhalten'. *Der Spiegel* (3 June 1985): 47–50.

Urbig, Franz. *Aus dem Leben eines deutschen Bankiers.* Frankfurt am Main: Historische Gesellschaft der Deutschen Bank e.V., 2014.

Verlag für Börsen- und Finanzliteratur AG, *Jahrbuch der Berliner Börse, 1914/ 1915: Ein Nachschlagbuch für Bankiers und Kapitalisten.* Berlin: Verlag Leipzig Verlag Für Börsen- und Finanzliteratur A.-G., 1914.

von Brandt, Max. *Die Zukunft Ostasiens: Ein Beitrag zur Geschichte und zum Verständnis der ostaisiatischen Frage.* Stuttgart: Verlag von Strecker & Moser, 1895.

von Hänisch, Adolf. *Jebsen & Co. Hongkong: China-Handel im Wechsel der Zeiten 1895–1945.* Apenrade: Selbstverlag, 1970.

Wallich, Hermann. 'Aus der Frühgeschichte der Deutschen Bank'. In *Beiträge zu Wirtschafts- und Währungsfragen und zur Bankgeschichte. Nr. 1–20,* edited by Deutsche Bank, 401–17. Mainz: Hase & Koehler, 1984.

Wallich, Hermann, and Paul Wallich. *Zwei Generationen im deutschen Bankwesen, 1833–1914.* Frankfurt am Main: Minerva, 1978.

Wolff, Hermann. *40 Jahre Bankmann: Oldenbourg, London, Berlin, Schanghai, Hankau, Hongkong, London, Elberfeld, Gladbach-Rheydt, Köln.* Köln: DuMont Schauberg, 1932.

Japanese

Chōsen Ginkō 朝鮮銀行. *Chōsen Ginkō nijugo nen shi* 朝鮮銀行二十五年史 (The Twenty-Five Year History of the Bank of Chosen). Seoul: Chōsen Ginkō, 1934.

'Dokua Ginkō eigyō teishi 独亜銀行営業停止 (The Cessation of the Deutsch-Asiatische Bank's Business)'. *Yomiuri Shimbun* (29 September 1916).

Gaimushō Tsūshōkyoku 外務省通商局. *Honkon jijō*. 香港事情 (Hong Kong's Situation).Tōkyō: Keiseisha, 1917.

Kasumigaseki Kai 霞関会 and Gaimushō Ajiakyoku 外務省アジア局. *Gendai Chūgoku jinmei jiten* 現代中國人名辞典 (A Name Dictionary of Modern Chinese Persons). Tōkyō: Kōnan Shoin, 1957.

Mitsui Ginkō Shinkoku Shutchōin 三井銀行清国出張員. *Mitsui Ginkō Shinkoku shutchoin hōkokusho* 三井銀行清国出張員報告書 (Report by a Mitsui Bank Employee Sent to China on Business). Tōkyō: Mitsui Ginkō, 1912.

Mizuno Kōkichi 水野幸吉. *Hankou: Chūō Shina jijō* 漢口: 中央支那事情 (Hankou: The Situation in Central China). Tōkyō: Fuzanbō, 1907.

Sano Zensaku 佐野善作. *Shinkoku kahei mondai hakan kinyū kikan chōsa hōkoku* 清國貨幣問題滬漢金融機關調査報告 (An Investigative Report on the Currency Problem of China and the Financial Institutions of Shanghai and Hankou). Tōkyō: Tōkyō Kōtō Shōgyō Gakkō, 1905.

Shinkoku Chūtongun Shireibu 清國駐屯軍司令部. *Pekin shi* 北京誌 (Beijing Gazetteer). Tōkyō: Hakubunkan, 1908.

Taiwan Ginkō 台湾銀行. *Taiwan Ginkō yonjunenshi* 台湾銀行四十年誌 (The Bank of Taiwan's Forty-Year Record). Tōkyō: Dai Nihon Insatsu Kabushiki Kaisha, 1939.

Tanioka Shigeru 谷岡繁. *Saishin Shanhai chizu* 最新上海地圖 (A New Map of Shanghai City). Shanghai: Shosuido Shoten, 1908.

Tōa Dōbun Shoin Daigaku 東亜同文書院調査, comp. *Shina keizai zensho*支那経済全書 (Compendium about the Chinese Economy), Vol. 6, 3rd ed. Tōkyō: Tōa Dōbunkai, 1908.

Tōa Dōbunkai 東亜同文会. *Santō oyobi Kōshūwan* 山東及膠州灣 (Shandong and Jiaozhou-Bay). Tōkyō: Tōa Dōbunkai, 1914.

  Shina shōbetsu zenshi 支那省別全誌 (A Complete Record of China's Provinces), 18 vols. Tōkyō: Tōa Dōbunkai, 1917–20.

Tōa Dōbunkai Chōsa Hensanbu 東亞同文會調査編纂部, comp. *Shina kinyū kikan* 支那金融機關 (The Financial Institutions of China). Tōkyō: Tōa Dōbunkai Chōsa Hensanbu, 1919.

Uchida Katsushi 内田勝司. *Shina kawase ron* 支那為替論 (A Discussion of Exchange in China). Tōkyō: Ganshōdōshoten, 1923.

Yasuda Zensuke 安田善助. *Shinkoku kinyū kikan shoken* 清国金融機関所見 (A View of the Financial Institutions of the Qing Empire). Tōkyō: Fukuda Kumasaburo, 1902.

Yoshida Masaji 吉田政治. *Shanhai ni okeru gaikoku kawase kinyū* 上海に於ける外国為替及金融 (The Foreign Exchange and Finance of Shanghai). Osaka: Osaka Yago Shoten, 1925.

Newspapers

Berliner Börsen-Courier
Berliner Börsen-Zeitung
Berliner Tageblatt
Bloomberg Business
Dagongbao (Jingji zhoubao) 大公報 (經濟週報)
Der Spiegel
Deutscher Reichs-Anzeiger
Gil Blas
Investors' Monthly Manual
Journal des Débats
Le Figaro Supplément littéraire du dimanche
New York Times
Nikkei Asia
Ostasiatischer Lloyd
Ouzhou zhanji 歐洲戰紀
Popular Science Monthly
Shenbao 申報
Shibao 時報
South China Morning Post
The Bankers' Magazine
The China Press
The Economist
The Far Eastern Review
The North-China Herald
The Times (London)
Yanzheng zazhi 鹽政雜誌
Yinhang Zhoubao 銀行週報
Yomiuri Shimbun 読売新聞
Zhonghua Shiyejie 中華實業界

Secondary Sources

Abe, Kaori. *Chinese Middlemen in Hong Kong's Colonial Economy, 1830–1890.* London: Routledge, 2018.
Adelman, Jeremy. 'What Is Global History Now?' *Aeon* (2 March 2017). https://aeon.co/essays/is-global-history-still-possible-or-has-it-had-its-moment.
Adshead, Samuel Adrian Miles. *The Modernization of the Chinese Salt Administration, 1900–1920.* Cambridge, MA: Harvard University Press, 1970.
Akagawa Motoaki 赤川元章. 'Doitsu Ginkō – Dokua Ginkō 1870–1913 nen ド イ ツ銀行・独亜銀行 1870–1913 年 (The Deutsche Bank and the Deutsch-Asiatische Bank, 1870–1913)'. In *Kokusai ginkō to Ajia* 国際銀行と ア ジ ア:

1870–1913 (International Banks and Asia: 1870–1913), edited by Nishimura Shizuya 西村閑也, Suzuki Toshio 鈴木俊夫 and Akagawa Motoaki 赤川元章, 999–1209. Tokyo: Keiō Gijuku Daigaku Shuppankai, 2014.

'German Banks in East Asia – The Deutsche Bank (1870–75) and the Deutsch-Asiatische Bank (1889–1913)'. *Keio Business Review* 45 (2009): 1–20.

Allen, G. C., and Audrey G. Donnithorne. *Western Enterprise in Far Eastern Economic Development: China and Japan*. London: Allen & Unwin, 1954, reprint, London: Routledge, 2003.

Austin, Gareth, Carlos Dávila and Geoffrey Jones. 'The Alternative Business History: Business in Emerging Markets'. *Business History Review* 91, No. 3 (2017): 537–69.

Axelrod, Robert. *The Evolution of Cooperation*. New York: Basic Books, 1984.

Bank of Tokyo. *Yokohama shōkin ginkō zenshi, dai yi kan: Sōritsu kara kaiso ni itaru gaikan* 横浜正金銀行全史 第 1 巻: 創立から改組に至る概観 (Complete History of the Yokohama Specie Bank Vol. 1: Overview from the Founding to the Reorganization). Tokyo: Bank of Tokyo, 1980.

Barth, Boris. *Die deutsche Hochfinanz und die Imperialismen*. Stuttgart: Franz Steiner Verlag, 1995.

Bastid, Marianne. 'La Diplomatie Française et La Révolution Chinoise de 1911'. *Revue d'histoire Moderne et Contemporaine* 16, No. 2 (1969): 221–45.

Bayly, Christopher A. *The Birth of the Modern World 1780–1914: Global Connections and Comparisons*. Oxford: Blackwell, 2004.

Bays, Daniel. *China Enters the Twentieth Century: Chang Chih-tung and the Issues of a New Age, 1895–1909*. Ann Arbor: The University of Michigan Press, 1978.

Beijing shi difangzhi bianzuan weiyuanhui 北京市地方志編纂委員會, comp. *Beijing zhi: jinrong zhi* 北京志:金融志 (Beijing Gazetteer: Financial Gazetteer). Beijing: Beijing chubanshe, 2001.

Bergère, Marie-Claire. *Shanghai: China's Gateway to Modernity*. Janet Lloyd (trans.). Stanford, CA: Stanford University Press, 2009.

Sun Yat-sen. Translated by Janet Lloyd. Stanford, CA: Stanford University Press, 1998.

Une Crise Financière à Shanghai à la Fin de l'Ancien Régime. Paris: Mouton, 1964.

Bersch, Julia. *Financial Globalization and the Implications for Monetary and Exchange Rate Policy*. PhD Diss., Ludwig-Maximilians-Universität München, 2008.

Bickers, Robert. 'Bland, John Otway Percy (1863–1945), writer and journalist'. In *Oxford Dictionary of National Biography*, edited by H. C. G. Matthew and Brian Harrison. Oxford: Oxford University Press, 2004. www.oxforddnb.com/view/article/31920.

Getting Stuck in for Shanghai: Putting the Kibosh on the Kaiser from the Bund. London: Penguin, 2014.

Bickers, Robert, and Isabella Jackson. 'Introduction: Law, Land and Power – Treaty Ports and Concessions in Modern China'. In *Treaty Ports in Modern China: Law, Land and Power*, edited by Robert Bickers and Isabella Jackson, 1–22. London and New York: Routledge, 2016.

Blue, Gregory, and Timothy Brook. 'Introduction'. In *China and Historical Capitalism: Genealogies of Sinological Knowledge*, edited by Gregory Blue and Timothy Brook, 1–9. Cambridge: Cambridge University Press, 1999.

Bonin, Hubert. 'Introduction: Issues Regarding Asian Imperial Banking'. In *Asian Imperial Banking History*, edited by Hubert Bonin, Nuno Valério and Kazuhiko Yago, 1–20. London: Pickering & Chatto, 2015.

'Le Comptoir National D'escompte de Paris, Une Banque Impériale (1848–1940)'. *Revue Française D'histoire D'outre-mer* 78, No. 293 (1991): 477–97.

Brandt, Loren, Ma Debin 馬德斌 and Thomas G. Rawski. 'From Divergence to Convergence: Re-evaluating the History Behind China's Economic Boom'. *Journal of Economic Literature* 52, No. 1 (2014): 45–123.

Brötel, Dieter. *Frankfreich im Fernen Osten: Imperialistische Expansion und Aspiration in Siam und Malaya, Laos und China, 1880-1904*. Stuttgart: Franz Steiner Verlag, 1996.

Cain, Peter J., and Antony Gerald. Hopkins. 'Afterword: The Theory and Practice of British Imperialism'. In *Gentlemanly Capitalism and British Imperialism: The New Debate on Empire*, edited by Raymond E. Dumett, 196–220, 2nd ed. London and New York: Routledge, 2014.

British Imperialism: Crisis and Deconstruction, 1914-1990. New York: Longman, 1993.

British Imperialism: Innovation and Expansion, 1688-1914. New York: Longman, 1993.

British Imperialism 1688-2000, 2nd ed. London: Longman, 2002.

Canis, Konrad. *Bismarcks Aussenpolitik 1870 bis 1890: Aufstieg und Gefährdung*. Paderborn: Schöningh, 2004.

Cassis, Youssef. 'Big Business'. In *The Oxford Handbook of Business History*, edited by Geoffrey Jones and Jonathan Zeitlin, 171–93. Oxford: Oxford University Press, 2008.

Capitals of Capital: The Rise and Fall of International Financial Centres 1780-2009, 2nd ed. Cambridge: Cambridge University Press, 2012.

Casson, Mark. *Entrepreneurship: Theory, Networks, History*. Cheltenham: Edward Elgar, 2010.

Chan Kai Yiu. *Business Expansion and Structural Change in Pre-War China: Liu Hongsheng and His Enterprises, 1920-1937*. Hong Kong: Hong Kong University Press, 2006.

Chen Guodong 陳國棟. *The Insolvency of the Chinese Hong Merchants, 1760-1843*. Taibei: Institute of Economics, Academia Sinica, 1990.

Chen Lijun 陳麗君. *Aomen jingji* 澳門經濟 (The Economy of Macao). Beijing: Zhongguo minzhu fazhi chubanshe, 2010.

Chen Qitian 陳其田. *Shanxi piaozhuang kaolüe* 山西票裝考略 (A Short Study of Shanxi Banks). Shanghai: Shanghai yinshuguan, 1937; reprint, Beijing: Jingji guanli chubanshe, 2008.

Chen Zhengping 陳爭平. *1895–1936 nian Zhongguo guoji shouzhi yanjiu 1895–1936* 年中國國際收支研究 (A Study of China's International Income and Expenditure between 1895 and 1936). Beijing: Zhongguo shehui kexue chubanshe, 1995.

Cheng Linsun 程麟蓀. *Banking in Modern China: Entrepreneurs, Professional Managers and the Development of Chinese Banks, 1897–1937*. Cambridge: Cambridge University Press, 2003.

Chu Shuangzhi 楚雙志. *Biange zhong de weiji: Yuan Shikai jituan yu Qingmo xinzheng* 變革中的違紀:袁世凱集團與清末新政 (A Crisis within Change: The Yuan Shikai Group and the Xinzheng Reforms). Beijing: Jiuzhou chubanshe, 2008.

Cochran, Sherman. *Big Business in China: Sino-Foreign Rivalry in the Cigarette Industry 1890–1930*. Cambridge, MA: Harvard University Press, 1980.

Cohen, Paul. *Discovering History in China: American Historical Writing on the Recent Chinese Past*. New York: Columbia University Press, 1984.

Crisp, Olga. 'The Russo-Chinese Bank: An Episode in Franco-Russian Relations'. *The Slavonic and East European Review* 52, No. 127 (1974): 197–212.

Cui Zhihai 催志海. 'Lun Qingmo tielu zhengce de yanbian 論清末鐵路政策的演變 (A Discussion of the Changes in Railway Policy during the Late Qing Dynasty)'. *Jindaishi yanjiu*, No. 3 (1993): 62–86.

Davenport-Hines, R. P. T., and Geoffrey Jones. 'British Business in Japan since 1868'. In *British Business in Asia since 1860*, edited by R. P. T. Davenport-Hines and Geoffrey Jones, 217–44. Cambridge: Cambridge University Press, 1989.

Dayer, Roberta Allbert. 'Addis, Sir Charles Stewart (1861–1945), Banker and Government Adviser'. *Oxford Dictionary of National Biography*, 23 September 2004. www.oxforddnb.com/view/10.1093/ref:odnb/9780198614128.001.0001/odnb-9780198614128-e-38334.

Bankers and Diplomats in China 1917–1925: The Anglo-American Relationship. London: Frank Cass, 1981.

Finance and Empire: Sir Charles Addis, 1861–1945. London: Macmillan, 1988.

Dean, Austin. *China and the End of Global Silver, 1873–1937*. Ithaca, NY: Cornell University Press, 2020.

Denzel, Markus A. *Handbook of World Exchange Rates, 1590–1914*. Farnham: Ashgate, 2010.

Dernberger, Robert F. 'The Role of the Foreigner in China's Economic Development, 1840–1949'. In *China's Modern Economy in Historical Perspective*, edited by Dwight H. Perkins, 19–47. Stanford, CA: Stanford University Press, 1975.

Disconto-Gesellschaft. *Die Disconto-Gesellschaft 1851 bis 1901, Denkschrift zum 50 Jährigen Jubiläum*. Berlin: Reichsdruckerei, 1901.

Drayton, Richard, and David Motadel. 'Discussion: The Futures of Global History'. *Journal of Global History* 13 (2018): 1–21.

Du Xuncheng 杜恂诚. *Jindai Zhongguo qianye xiguanfa* 近代中國錢業習慣法:以上海錢業為視角 (Modern China's Customary Law in the Money Trade: From the Perspective of the Money Trade in Shanghai). Shanghai: Shanghai caijing daxue chubanshe, 2006.

Dzen, Tien Yue. *Das Bankwesen in China. Ein Beitrag zur Organisation und den Problemen der inländischen und ausländischen Banken in China*. Berlin: Wilhelm Christians Verlang, 1927.

Edvinsson, Rodney. 'Historical Currency Converter' (2016). www.historical statistics.org/Currencyconverter.html.

Edwards, E. W. *British Diplomacy and Finance in China*. Oxford: Oxford University Press, 1987.

Epkenhans, Michael. 'Einführung: Bismarck und die Wirtschaft: Pragmatiker oder Programmatiker?' In *Otto von Bismarck und die Wirtschaft*, edited by Michael Epkenhans and Ulrich von Hehl, 229–46. Paderborn: Schöningh, 2013.

Erickson, Erling A. *Banking in Frontier Iowa 1836–1865*. Ames: The Iowa State University Press, 1971.

Esherick, Joseph. 'Harvard on China: The Apologetics of Imperialism'. *Bulletin of Concerned Asian Scholars* 4, No. 4 (1972): 9–16.

'How the Qing Became China'. In *Empire to Nation: Historical Perspectives on the Making of the Modern World*, edited by Joseph Esherick, Hasan Kayali and Eric Van Young, 229–59. Lanham, MD: Rowman & Littlefield, 2006.

Reform and Revolution in China: The 1911 Revolution in Hunan and Hubei. Berkeley: University of California Press, 1976.

Fabozzi, Frank J. *Bond Markets, Analysis and Strategies*, 8th ed. Harlow: Pearson Education Limited, 2013.

Feng Tianyu 馮天瑜. *Zhang Zhidong pingzhuan* 張之洞評傳 (A Critical Biography of Zhang Zhidong). Zhengzhou: Henan jiaoyu chubanshe, 1985.

Ferguson, Niall. 'Political Risk and the International Bond Market between the 1848 Revolution and the Outbreak of the First World War'. *Economic History Review* 59, No. 1 (2006): 70–112.

Feuerwerker, Albert. *China's Early Industrialization: Sheng Hsuan-huai (1844–1916) and Mandarin Enterprise*. Cambridge, MA: Harvard University Press, 1958.

Field, Frederick V. *American Participation in the China Consortiums*. Chicago, IL: University of Chicago Press, 1931.

Flandreau, Marc, and Frédéric Zumer. *The Making of Global Finance, 1880–1913*. Paris: OECD Publishing, 2004.

Flandreau, Marc, and Juan H. Flores. 'Bonds and Brands: Foundations of Sovereign Debt Markets, 1820–1830'. *The Journal of Economic History* 69, No. 3 (2009): 646–84.

Fohlin, Caroline. *Finance Capitalism and Germany's Rise to Industrial Power.* Cambridge: Cambridge University Press, 2007.

Forman, Ross G. *China and the Victorian Imagination: Empires Entwined.* Cambridge: Cambridge University Press, 2013.

Frank, André Gunder. *ReOrient: Global Economy in the Asian Age.* Berkeley: University of California Press, 1998.

Frieden, Jeffrey A. *Global Capitalism: Its Failure and Rise in the Twentieth Century.* New York: W. W. Norton, 2006.

Gall, Lothar, Gerald Feldman, Harold James, Carl-Ludwig Holtfrerich and Hans E. Buschgen. *Die Deutsche Bank 1870–1995.* München: C. H. Beck, 1995.

Gallaher, Ruth A. 'The First Bank in Iowa', *The Palimpsest* 18, No. 3 (1937): 103–12.

Gao Xi 高晞. *De Zhen zhuan: Yige Yingguo chuanjiaoshi yu wan Qing yixue jindai hua* 德貞傳:一個英國傳教士與晚清醫學近代化 (A Biography of John Dudgeon: Medical Modernisation during the Late Qing and a British Missionary). Shanghai: Fudan Daxue chubanshe, 2009.

Gardella, Robert. *Harvesting Mountains: Fujian and the China Tea Trade, 1757–1937.* Berkeley: University of California Press, 1994.

Gasster, Michael. 'The Republican Revolutionary Movement'. In *The Cambridge History of China Vol. 11, Late Ch'ing, 1800–1911 Part 2*, edited by John K. Fairbank and Kwang-ching Liu, 463–534. Cambridge: Cambridge University Press, 1976.

Gerschenkron, Alexander. 'Economic Backwardness in Historical Perspective'. In *Economic Backwardness in Historical Perspective: A Book of Essays*, edited by Alexander Gerschenkron, 5–30. New York; Washington, DC; London: Frederick A. Praeger, 1962.

Glade, Dieter. *Bremen und der Ferne Osten.* Bremen: Carl Schünemann Verlag, 1966.

Goetzmann, William N., Andrey D. Ukhov and Ning Zhu. 'China and the World Financial Markets 1870–1939: Modern Lessons from Historical Globalization'. *The Economic History Review* 60, No. 2 (2007): 267–312.

Goldberg, Lawrence G., and Anthony Saunders. 'The Determinants of Foreign Banking Activity in the United States'. *Journal of Banking and Finance* 5 (1981): 17–32.

Gonjō, Yasuo 権上康男. *Furansu teikoku shugi to ajia: indoshina ginkōshi kenkyū* フランス帝国主義とアジア:インドシナ銀行史研究 (French Imperialism and Asia: A Study of the Banque de l'Indochine). Tokyo: Tōkyō daigaku shuppankai, 1985.

Greenwald, Bruce C., and Joseph E. Stiglitz. 'Asymmetric Information and the New Theory of the Firm: Financial Constraints and Risk Behavior'. *The American Economic Review* 80, No. 2 (1990): 160–5.

Griffith, James B. *Practical Bookkeeping.* Chicago, IL: American School of Correspondence, 1914.

Guo Yuqing 郭予慶. *Jindai Riben yinhang zai Hua jinrong huodong: Hengbin Zhengjin Yinhang* 近代日本銀行在华金融活动-橫濱正金銀行 (1894–1919) (The Financial Activities of Modern Japanese Banks in China: The Yokohama Specie Bank (1894–1919)). Beijing: Renmin chubanshe, 2007.

Hallgarten, George W. F. *Imperialismus vor 1914: Die soziologischen Grundlagen der Außenpolitik europäischer Großmächte vor dem Ersten Weltkrieg*, 2nd ed., 2 vols. Munich: C. H. Beck, 1963.

Hamashita Takeshi 濱下武志. *Chūgoku kindai keizaishi kenkyū: Shinmatsu kaikan zaisei to kaikōjō shijōken* 中国近代経済史研究 : 清末海関財政と開港場市場圏 (A Study of Modern Chinese Economic History: The Fiscal Administration of the Maritime Customs and the Market Sphere of the Opened Ports at the End of the Qing Dynasty). Tokyo: Tōkyō Daigaku Tōyō Bunka Kenkyūjo, 1989.

Hao Qingyuan 郝慶元. *Zhou Xuexi zhuan* 周學熙傳 (A Biography of Zhou Xuexi). Tianjin: Tianjin renmin chubanshe, 1991.

Hao Yanping 郝延平. *The Commercial Revolution in Nineteenth-Century China: The Rise of Sino-Western Merchant Capitalism.* Berkeley: University of California Press, 1986.

The Comprador in Nineteenth Century China: Bridge between East and West. Cambridge: Cambridge University Press, 1970.

Harris, Lane. 'Overseas Chinese Remittance Firms, the Limits of State Sovereignty, and Transnational Capitalism in East and Southeast Asia, 1850s–1930s'. *Journal of Asian Studies* 74, No. 1 (2015): 129–51.

He Wenkai. *Paths toward the Modern Fiscal State: England, Japan, and China.* Cambridge, MA: Harvard University Press, 2013.

Headrick, Daniel. R. *The Invisible Weapon: Telecommunications and International Politics, 1851–1945.* Oxford: Oxford University Press, 1991.

Heilongjiang jinrong lishi bianxie zu 黑龍江金融歷史編寫組. *Hua-E Daosheng Yinhang zai Hua sanshi nian* 华俄道胜银行在华三十年 (Thirty Years of the Russo-Chinese Bank in China). Heilongjiang: Heilongjiang Renmin Chubanshe, 1992.

Helferrich, Karl. *Georg von Siemens: Ein Lebensbild aus Deutschlands großer Zeit*, 3 vols. Berlin: Verlag von Julius Springer, 1923.

Henriot, Christian, and Robert Bickers. 'Introduction'. In *New Frontiers: Imperialism's New Communities in East Asia, 1842–1953*, edited by Christian Henriot and Robert Bickers, 1–11. Manchester: Manchester University Press, 2000.

Hibbard, Peter. *The Bund Shanghai: China Faces West.* Hong Kong: Odyssey, 2007.

Hillier, Andrew. *Mediating Empire: An English Family in China 1817–1927.* Folkestone: Renaissance Books, 2020.

Hirata Koji 平田 康治. 'Britain's Men on the Spot in China: John Jordan, Yuan Shikai, and the Reorganization Loan, 1912–1914'. *Modern Asian Studies* 47, No. 3 (2013): 895–934.

'The Sino-British Relations in Railway Construction: The Modernising State, Foreign Interests and Local Elites, 1905–1911'. In *Britain and China, 1840–1970: Empire, Finance and War*, edited by Robert Bickers and Jonathan Howlett, 130–47. London: Routledge, 2016.

Homer, Sidney, and Richard Sylla. *A History of Interest Rates*, 4th ed. Hoboken, NJ: John Wiley & Sons, 2005.

Hong Jiaguan 洪葭管. 'Cong Huifeng yinhang kan diguozhuyi dui jiu Zhongguo de jinrong tongzhi 從滙豐銀行看帝國主義對舊中國的金融統治 (Looking at Imperialism's Financial Domination of China from the Perspective of the Hongkong and Shanghai Banking Corporation)'. *Xueshu yuekan* 4 (1964): 35–47.

ed. *Shanghai jinrong zhi* 上海金融志 (A Financial Gazetteer of Shanghai). Shanghai: Shanghai shehui kexue chubanshe, 2003.

Zai jinrong shiyuan di li manbu 在金融史園地裡漫步 (Wandering in the Garden of Financial History). Beijing: Zhongguo jinrong chubanshe, 1990.

Hopkins, Antony Gerald. 'Gentlemanly Capitalism in New Zealand'. *Australian Economic History Review* 43, No. 3 (2003): 287–97.

'Informal Empire in Argentina: An Alternative View'. *Journal of Latin American Studies* 26, No. 2 (1994): 469–84.

Horesh, Niv. *Shanghai's Bund and Beyond: British Banks, Banknote Issuance, and Monetary Policy in China, 1842–1937*. New Haven, CT: Yale University Press, 2009.

Hou Chi-ming. *Foreign Investment and Economic Development in China, 1840–1937*. Cambridge: Cambridge University Press, 1965.

Hsiao Liang-lin. *China's Foreign Trade Statistics, 1864–1949*. Cambridge, MA: Harvard University Press, 1974.

Hsu, Mongton Chih. *Railway Problems in China*. New York: Columbia University Press, 1915.

Hua Changhui 華長慧. *Shanghai maiban zhong de Ningbo bang* 上海買辦中的寧波幫 (The *Ningbo bang* amongst Shanghai's Compradors). Beijing: Zhongguo wenshi chubanshe, 2009.

Huang Guangyu 黃光域. *Waiguo zai Hua gongshang qiye cidian* 外國在華工商企業詞典 (Dictionary of Foreign Commercial and Industrial Businesses in China). Chengdu: Sichuan Renmin chubanshe, 1995.

Huang Yasheng, *Selling China: Foreign Direct Investment during the Reform Era*. Cambridge: Cambridge University Press, 2003.

Huenemann, Ralph William. *The Dragon and the Iron Horse: The Economics of Railroads in China, 1876–1937*. Cambridge, MA: Harvard University Press, 1984.

Hummel, Arthur W. *Eminent Chinese of the Ch'ing Period (1644–1912)*, 2 vols. Washington, DC: Government Printing Office, 1944.

Jackson, Isabella. 'Who Ran the Treaty Ports? A Study of the Shanghai Municipal Council'. In *Treaty Ports in Modern China: Law, Land and Power*, edited by

Robert Bickers and Isabella Jackson, 43–60. London and New York: Routledge, 2016.

Ji Yu 季宇. *Duan Qirui zhuan* 段祺瑞傳 (Biography of Duan Qirui). Hefei: Anhui renmin chubanshe, 1992.

Ji Zhaojin. *A History of Modern Shanghai Banking: The Rise and Decline of China's Finance Capitalism.* Armon, NY: M. E. Sharpe, 2003.

Jiang Jianqing 姜建清, and Jiang Lichang 將立場. *Jindai Zhongguo Waishang Yinhang* 近代中國外商銀行 (A History of Foreign Banks in Modern China). Beijing: Zhongxin chubanshe, 2016.

Jiao Jianhua 焦建華. *Zhongguo caizheng tongshi, juan 8: Zhonghua Minguo caizheng shi* 中國財政通史,第八卷:中華民國財政史 (A Comprehensive History of Chinese Public Finance, Vol. 8: A History of Public Finance during the Republican Period). Changsha: Hunan renmin chubanshe, 2013.

Jing Chunxiao. *Mit Barbaren gegen Barbaren: Die chinesische Selbststärkungsbewegung und das deutsche Rüstungsgeschäft im späten 19. Jahrhundert.* Münster: LIT Verlag, 2002.

Jones, Geoffrey, ed. *Banks as Multinationals.* Oxford: Routledge, 1990.

'Banks as Multinationals.' In *Banks as Multinationals,* edited by Geoffrey Jones, 1–13. Oxford: Routledge, 1990.

British Multinational Banking 1830–1990. Oxford: Oxford University Press, 1993.

Entrepreneurship and Multinationals: Global Business and the Making of the Modern World. Cheltenham: Edward Elgar, 2013.

'Globalization'. In *The Oxford Handbook of Business History,* edited by Geoffrey Jones and Jonathan Zeitlin, 141–70. Oxford: Oxford University Press, 2008.

Multinationals and Global Capitalism from the Nineteenth to the Twenty-First Century. Oxford: Oxford University Press, 2005.

Kanada Shinji. 'Chūgoku kaikō-go no gaikoku ginkō 中国開港後の外国銀行 ('The Foreign Banks in China after the Opening of the Ports')'. *Shigaku zasshi* 107, No. 9 (1998): 1559–80.

Kent, Perry Horace. *Railway Enterprise in China: An Account of Its Origin and Development.* London: Edward Arnold, 1907.

Kerr, W. G. *Scottish Capital on the American Credit Frontier.* Austin: Texas State Historical Association, 1976.

Khanna, Tarun, and Krishna Palepu. 'Why Focused Strategies May Be Wrong for Emerging Markets'. *Harvard Business Review* (July/August 1997): 41–51.

King, Frank H. H. 'Extra-Regional Banks and Investment in China'. In *International Banking 1870–1914,* edited by Rondo Cameron and V. I. Bovykin, 371–405. Oxford: Oxford University Press, 1991.

Money and Monetary Policy in China 1845–1895. Cambridge, MA: Harvard University Press, 1965.

The History of the Hongkong and Shanghai Banking Corporation, 4 vols. Cambridge: Cambridge University Press, 1987–91.

Kirby, William C. *Germany and Republican China*. Stanford, CA: Stanford University Press, 1984.

'The Internationalization of China: Foreign Relations at Home and Abroad in the Republican Era'. *China Quarterly* 150 (1997): 433–58.

Kobrak, Christopher, Per H. Hansen and Christopher Kopper. 'Business, Political Risk, and Historians in the Twentieth Century'. In *European Business, Dictatorship, and Political Risk, 1920–45*, edited by Christopher Kobrak and Per H. Hansen, 3–21. New York: Berghahn Books, 2004.

Kobrin, Stephen J. 'Political Risk: A Review and Reconsideration'. *Journal of International Business Studies* 10, No. 1 (1979): 67–80.

Köll, Elisabeth. 'Chinese Railroads, Local Society, and Foreign Presence: The Tianjin-Pukou Line in Pre-1949 Shandong'. In *Manchurian Railways and the Opening of China: An International History*, edited by Bruce A. Eleman and Stephen Kotkin, 123–48. New York: M. E. Sharpe, 2010.

Kong Min 孔敏. *Nankai jingji zhishu ziliao huibian* 南開經濟指數資料彙編 (Nankai Collection of Economic Index Materials). Beijing: Zhongguo shehui kexue chubanshe, 1988.

Kong Xiangyi 孔祥毅. *Jinrong piaohao shilun* 金融票號史論 (Historical Discussion of Finance and Piaohao). Beijing: Zhongguo jinrong chubanshe, 2003.

Kuhlmann, Wilhelm. *China's Foreign Debt, 1865–1982*. Hannover: Wilhelm Kuhlmann, 1982.

Kwan Man Bun. 'Zhou Xuexi'. In *Berkshire Encylopedia of China*, edited by Cheng Linsun, 2646–7. Green Barrington, MA: Berkshire Publishing Group, 2009.

Leung Yuen-sang. *The Shanghai Taotai, Linkage Man in a Changing Society, 1843–90*. Honolulu: University of Hawaii Press, 1990.

Leutner, Mechthild. 'Deutsche Vorstellungen über China und Chinesen und über die Rolle der Deutschen in China, 1890–1945'. In *Von der Kolonialpolitik zur Kooperation: Studien zur Geschichte der deutsch-chinesischen Beziehungen*, edited by Kuo Heng-yü, 401–22. Munich: Minerva, 1986.

Li Enhan 李恩涵. *China's Quest for Railway Autonomy, 1904–1911: A Study of the Chinese Railway-Rights Recovery Movement*. Singapore: Singapore University Press, 1977.

Li Guoqi 李國祁. *Die Chinesische Politik zum Einspruch von Shimonoseki und gegen die Erwerbung der Kiautschou-Bucht: Studien zu den chinesisch-deutschen Beiziehungen von 1895–1898*. Münster: C. J. Fahle, 1966.

'Ming Qing liangdai difang xingzheng zhidu zhongdao de gongneng ji qi yanbian 明清兩代地方行政制度中道的功能及其演變 (The Function of the Daotai and the Change of This Function in the Local Administrative System of the Ming and Qing Dynasties). *Zhongyang yanjiuyuan jindaishi yanjiusuo jikan* 3 (1972): 139–88.

Zhongguo zaoqi de tielu jingying 中國早期的鐵路經營 (The Management of China's Early Railways). Taibei: Institute of Modern History, Academia Sinica, 1976.

Li Wenjie 李文杰. Guozhai zai jindai Zhongguo de mingyun 國債在近代中國的命運 (The Fate of National Debt in Modern China). MPhil Diss., Peking University, 2007.

Li Xizhu 利細珠. *Zhang Zhidong yu Qingmo xinzheng yanjiu*. 張之洞與清末新政研究 (A Study of Zhang Zhidong and the *Xinzheng* Reforms during the Late Qing Dynasty). Shanghai: Shanghai shudian chubanshe, 2003.

Li Xuefeng. 'Zaifeng and Late Qing Railway Policy'. In *China: How the Empire Fell*, edited by Joseph W. Esherick and C. X. George Wei, 89–106. London: Routledge, 2014.

Lin Man-houng 林滿紅. 'China's "Dual Economy" in International Trade Relations, 1842–1949'. In *Japan, China, and the Growth of the Asian International Economy, 1850–1949*, edited by Kaoru Sugihara, 179–97. Oxford: Oxford University Press, 2005.

Lin, Shuanglin. 'China to Curtail Local Government Debt'. *East Asian Policy* 8, No. 4 (2016): 69–81.

Liu Mingkang 劉明康. *Zhongguo yinhangye gaige kaifang 30 nian (1978–2008)* 中國銀行業改革開放 30 年(1978–2008) (The Chinese Banking Sector and 30 Years of Reform and Opening Up (1978–2008)). Beijing: Zhongguo jinrong chubanshe, 2009.

Ma Debin 馬德斌. 'The Rise of a Financial Revolution in Republican China in 1900–1937: An Institutional Narrative'. *London School of Economics and Political Science, Department of Economic History, Working Papers*, No. 235 (2016).

Ma Jinhua 馬金華. *Waizhai yu wan Qing zhengju* 外債與晚清政局 (Foreign Debt and the Political Situation during the Late Qing Dynasty). Beijing: Shehui kexue wenxian chubanshe, 2011.

Ma Linghe 馬陵合. *Qingmo minchu tielu waizhai guan yanjiu* 清末民初鐵路外債關研究 (A Study of Views on Using Foreign Debt for Railway Construction during the Late Qing and Early Republican Period). Shanghai: Fudan daxue chubanshe, 2004.

Wan Qing waizhaishi yanjiu 晚清外債史研究 (A Study of the History of Foreign Debt during the Late Qing Dynasty). Shanghai: Fudan daxue chubanshe, 2005.

MacKinnon, Stephen. *Power and Politics in Late Imperial China: Yuan Shi-kai in Beijing and Tianjin, 1901–1908*. Berkeley: University of California Press, 1980.

Mair, Johanna, Ignasi Marti and Marc J. Ventresca. 'Building Inclusive Markets in Rural Bangladesh: How Intermediaries Work Institutional Voids'. *Academy of Management Journal* 55, No. 4 (2012): 819–50.

Malik, Hassan. *Bankers and Bolsheviks, International Finance and the Russian Revolution*. Princeton, NJ: Princeton University Press, 2018.

Mann Jones, Susan. 'Finance in Ningpo: The "Ch'ien Chuang" 1750–1880'. In *Economic Organization in Chinese Society*, edited by W. E. Willmott, 47–78. Stanford, Stanford University Press, 1972.

Matzat, Wilhelm. 'Cordes, Heinrich (1866–1927), Dolmetscher und Bankdirektor'. www.tsingtau.org/cordes-heinrich-1866-1927-dolmetscher-und-bankdirektor.

McElderry, Andrea. *Shanghai Old-Style Banks (Ch'ien-Chuang), 1800–1935*. Ann Arbor: Center for Chinese Studies, University of Michigan, 1976.

McKellar, Robert. *A Short Guide to Political Risk*. Farnham: Gower, 2010.

McLean, David. British Banking and Government in China: The Foreign Office and the Hongkong and Shanghai Bank, 1895–1914. PhD Diss., University of Cambridge, 1976.

'The Foreign Office and the First Chinese Indemnity Loan, 1895'. *The Historical Journal* 16, No. 2 (1973): 303–21.

Mi Rucheng 宓汝成. *Diguo zhuyi yu Zhongguo tielu* 帝國主義與中國鐵路 (Imperialism and Chinese Railways). Shanghai: Shanghai renmin chubanshe, 1980.

Moazzin, Ghassan. 'From Globalization to Liquidation: The Deutsch-Asiatische Bank and the First World War in China'. *Cross-Currents: East Asian History and Culture Review E-Journal* 16 (2015): 52–76.

'Investing in the New Republic: Multinational Banks, Political Risk, and the Chinese Revolution of 1911'. *Business History Review* 94, No. 3 (2020): 507–34.

'Sino-Foreign Business Networks: Foreign and Chinese Banks in the Chinese banking Sector, 1890–1911'. *Modern Asian Studies* 54, No. 3 (2020): 970–1004.

Monroe, Arthur E. 'The French Indemnity of 1871 and Its Effects'. *The Review of Economics and Statistics* 1, No. 4 (1919): 269–81.

Müller-Jabusch, Maximilian. *Fünfzig Jahre Deutsch-Asiatische Bank 1890–1939*. Berlin: Otto von Holten Verlag, 1940.

Münch, Hermann. *Adolph von Hansemann*. Munich: Drei Masken Verlag, 1932.

Ni Yuping 倪玉平. *Qingchao jiadao caizheng yu shehui* 清朝嘉道財政與社會 (Public Finance and Society during the Reigns of the Jiaqing and Daoguang Emperors of the Qing Dynasty). Beijing: Shangwu yinshu guan, 2013.

Nie Haochun 聶好春. *Maiban yu jindai Zhongguo jingji fabiao yanjiu* 買辦與近代中國經濟發展研究, 1840–1927 (A Study of Compradors and Modern China's Economic Development, 1840–1927). Guizhou: Guizhou renmin chubanshe, 2014.

Nield, Robert. *China's Foreign Places: The Foreign Presence in China in the Treaty Port Era, 1840–1943*. Hong Kong: Hong Kong University Press, 2015.

Nishimura Shizuya 西村閑也. 'The Foreign and Native Banks in China: Chop Loans in Shanghai and Hankow before 1914'. *Modern Asian Studies* 39, No. 1 (2005): 109–32.

'Honkon Shanhai Ginkō 1865–1913' 香港上海銀行 1865–1913 年 ('The Hongkong and Shanghai Banking Corporation 1865–1913'). In *Kokusai ginkō to Ajia* 国際銀行とアジア: 1870–1913 (International Banks and Asia: 1870–1913), edited by Nishimura Shizuya 西村閑也, Suzuki Toshio 鈴木俊夫 and Akagawa Motoaki 赤川元章, 539–610. Tokyo: Keiō Gijuku Daigaku Shuppankai, 2014.

Nishimura Shizuya 西村閑也, Ranald Michie and Suzuki Toshio 鈴木俊夫. 'Introduction'. In *The Origins of International Banking in Asia: The Nineteenth and Twentieth Centuries*, edited by Shizuya Nishimura, Ranald Michie and Suzuki Toshio, 1–12. Oxford: Oxford University Press, 2012.

eds. *The Origins of International Banking in Asia: The Nineteenth and Twentieth Centuries*. Oxford: Oxford University Press, 2012.

Nishimura Shizuya 西村閑也, Suzuki Toshio 鈴木俊夫 and Akagawa Motoaki 赤川元章, eds. 国際銀行とアジア: *1870–1913* (International Banks and Asia: 1870–1913). Tokyo: Keiō Gijuku Daigaku Shuppankai, 2014.

'Jobun' 序文 ('Introduction'). In *Kokusai ginkō to Ajia: 1870–1913* 国際銀行とアジア: 1870–1913 (International Banks and Asia: 1870–1913), edited by Nishimura Shizuya 西村閑也, Suzuki Toshio 鈴木俊夫 and Akagawa Motoaki 赤川元章, i–xiii. Tokyo: Keiō Gijuku Daigaku Shuppankai, 2014.

Nolan, Peter. *China and the Global Economy: National Champions, Industrial Policy and the Big Business Revolution*. Houndmills: Palgrave Macmillan, 2001.

Obstfeld, Maurice, and Alan Taylor. 'Globalization and Capital Markets'. In *Globalization in Historical Perspective*, edited by Michael Bordo, Alan Taylor and Jeffrey Williamson, 121–88. Chicago, IL: The University of Chicago Press, 2007.

Okazaki Tetsuji 岡崎哲二, and Okuno Masahiro 奥野正寛. 'Evolution of Economic Systems: The Case of Japan'. In *Institutional Foundations of East Asian Economic Development*, edited by Hayami Yujiro 速水佑次郎 and Aoki Masahiko 青木昌彦, 482–525. London: Palgrave Macmillan, 1998.

O'Rourke, Kevin H., and Jeffrey G. Williamson. *History and Globalization*. Cambridge, MA: MIT Press, 2001.

Osterhammel, Jürgen. *Britischer Imperialismus im Fernen Osten: Strukturen der Durchdringung und einheimischer Widerstand auf dem chinesischen Markt 1932–1937*. Bochum: Studienverlag Dr. N. Brockmeyer, 1982.

'Imperialism in Transition: British Business and the Chinese Authorities, 1931–37'. *China Quarterly* 94 (1984): 260–86.

The Transformation of the World: A Global History of the Nineteenth Century. Princeton, NJ: Princeton University Press, 2014.

Otte, Thomas G. '"The Bagdad Railway of the Far East": The Tientsin-Yangtze Railway and Anglo-German Relations, 1898–1911'. In *Railways and International Politics: Paths of Empire, 1848–1945*, edited by Thomas G. Otte and Keith Neilson, 112–36. New York: Routledge, 2006.

The China Question: Great Power Rivalry and British Isolation, 1894–1905. Oxford: Oxford University Press, 2007.

Oxbury, Harold. F. 'Aglen, Sir Francis Arthur (1869–1932), Official in the Chinese Service'. *Oxford Dictionary of National Biography* (23 September 2004). www.oxforddnb.com/view/10.1093/ref:odnb/9780198614128.001.0001/odnb-9780198614128-e-37097.

Pan Zihao 潘子豪. *Zhongguo qianzhuang gaiyao* 中國錢莊概要 (A Summary of Chinese *Qianzhuang*). Shanghai: Huatong shuju, 1931.

Parthasarathi, Prasannan, and Kenneth Pomeranz. 'The Great Divergence Debate'. In *Global Economic History,* edited by Giorgio Riello and Tirthankar Roy, 19–37. London: Bloomsbury, 2019.

Peng Zeyi 彭泽益. *Shijiu shiji houbanqi de zhongguo caizheng yu jingji* 十九世紀後半期的中國財政與經濟 (Chinese Public Finance and Economy during the Second Half of the 19th Century). Beijing: Zhongguo renmin daxue chubanshe, 2010.

Pintjens, Stefan. 'The Internationalisation of the Belgian Banking Sector: A Comparison with the Netherlands'. In *The Competitiveness of Financial Institutions and Centres in Europe,* edited by Donald E. Fair and Robert J. Raymond, 301–12. Boston, MA: Kluwer Academic Publishers, 1994.

Plumpe, Werner, Alexander Nützenadel and Catherine Schenck. *Deutsche Bank: The Global Hausbank.* London: Bloomsbury, 2020.

Pohl, Manfred. 'Das Ostasiengeschäft der Deutschen Bank'. *Beiträge zu Wirtschafts- und Währungsfragen und zur Bankengeschichte* 15 (1977): 447–85.

— ed. *Handbook on the History of European Banks.* Cheltenham: Edward Elgar, 1994.

Pohle Fraser, Monika. Noisy Optimists: Risk Management in French and German Banks in the 19th and Early 20th Centuries. PhD Diss., European University Institute, 1998.

Pomeranz, Kenneth. *The Great Divergence: China, Europe, and the Making of the Modern World Economy.* Princeton, NJ: Princeton University Press, 2000.

Pratt, Mary Louise. *Imperial Eyes: Travel Writing and Transculturation.* London: Routledge, 1992.

Quested, Rosemary. *The Russo-Chinese Bank: A Multinational Financial Base of Tsarism in China.* Birmingham: University of Birmingham Slavonic Monographs, 1977.

Rajan, Ramkishen S. 'Booms and Busts in Private Capital Flows to Emerging Asia since the 1990s'. In *Emerging Asia: Essays on Crises, Capital Flows, FDI and Exchange Rates,* edited by Ramkishen S. Rajan, 3–8. Basingstoke: Palgrave Macmillan, 2011.

Ratenhof, Udo. *Die Chinapolitik des Deutschen Reiches 1871 bis 1945. Wirtschaft, Rüstung, Militär.* Boppard am Rhein: Harald Boldt, 1987.

Rawski, Thomas G. *Economic Growth in Prewar China.* Berkeley: University of California Press, 1989.

Reitmayer, Morten. *Bankiers im Kaiserreich. Sozialprofil und Habitus der deutschen Hochfinanz.* Göttingen: Vandenhoeck & Ruprecht, 1999, 120–47.

Remer, Charles Frederick. *Foreign Investments in China.* New York: Macmillan Company, 1933.

Rhoads, Edward J. M. *Stepping Forth into the World: The Chinese Educational Mission to the United States, 1872–81.* Hong Kong: Hong Kong University Press, 2011.

Robertson, Roland. 'Glocalization: Time-Space and Homogeneity-Heterogeneity'. In *Global Modernities,* edited by Scott Lash, Roland Robertson and Mike Featherstone, 25–44. London: Sage, 1995.

Rose, Andreas. 'Otto von Bismarck und das (außen-)politische Mittel der Handels- und Schutzpolitik'. In *Otto von Bismarck und die Wirtschaft,* edited by Michael Epkenhans and Ulrich von Hehl, 77–96. Paderborn: Schöningh, 2013.

Roth, Ralf, and Günther Dinhobl. 'Introduction: Across the Borders'. In *Across the Borders: Financing the World's Railways in the Nineteenth and Twentieth Centuries,* edited by Ralf Roth and Günther Dinhobl, xxiii–xxxviii. Aldershot: Ashgate, 2008.

Satō Junpei 佐藤淳平. 'He Sheng Yuan piaohao de riben fenhao yu dongya de guoji jinrong 合盛元票號的日本分號與東亞的國際金融 (The Japanese Branch of the He Sheng Yuan Piaohao and East Asia's International Finance)'. *Shehuishi yanjiu* 4 (2016): 114–27.

Sattler, Friederike. *Herrhausen: Banker, Querdenker, Global Player: Ein deutsches Leben.* Munich: Siedler Verlag, 2019.

Schaefer, Karl Christian. *Deutsche Portfolioinvestitionen im Ausland 1870–1914: Banken, Kapitalmärkte und Wertpapierhandel im Zeitalter des Imperialismus.* Münster: LIT Verlag, 1995.

Schiltz, Michael. *Accounting for the Fall of Silver: Hedging Currency Risk in Long-Distance Trade with Asia, 1870–1913.* Oxford: Oxford University Press, 2020.

The Money Doctors from Japan: Finance, Imperialism, and the Building of the Yen Bloc, 1895–1937. Cambridge, MA: Harvard Asia Center, 2012.

Schmidt, Vera. *Deutsche Eisenbahnpolitik in Shantung.* Wiesbaden: Otto Harrassowitz, 1976.

Schneider, Jürgen, Oskar Schwarzer, Friedrich Zellfeder and Markus A. Denzel. *Währungen der Welt IV: Asiatische und Australische Devisenkurse im 19. Jahrhundert.* Stuttgart: Franz Steiner, 1992.

Schneider, Jürgen, Oskar Schwarzer und and Markus A. Denzel. *Währungen der Welt V: Asiatische und Australische Devisenkurse im 20. Jahrhundert.* Stuttgart: Franz Steiner, 1994.

Schönhärl, Korinna. 'Introduction'. In *Decision Taking, Confidence and Risk Management in Banks from Early Modernity to the 20th Century,* edited by Korinna Schönhärl, 1–12. Basingstoke: Palgrave Macmillan, 2017.

Schrecker, John. *Imperialism and Chinese Nationalism: Germany in Shantung.* Cambridge, MA: Harvard University Press, 1971.

Schumpeter, Joseph. *Capitalism, Socialism and Democracy.* London: Harper & Brother, 1947; reprint, London: Routledge, 2003.

Schwarzer, Oskar, Markus A. Denzel and Friedrich Zellfelder. 'Ostasiatische, indische und australische Wechselkurse (1800–1914)'. In *Währungen der Welt. IV, Asiatische und australische Devisenkurze im 19. Jahrhundert,* edited by Jürgen Schneider, Oskar Schwarzer, Friedrich Zellfelder and Markus A. Denzel, 1–65. Stuttgart: Franz Steiner, 1992.

Scranton, Philip, and Patrick Fridenson. *Reimagining Business History.* Baltimore, MD: The Johns Hopkins University Press, 2005.

Shandong sheng difang shizhi bianzuan weiyuanhui 山東省地方史志編纂委員會. *Shandong sheng zhi: jinrong zhi* 山東省志.金融志 (Provincial Gazetteer of Shandong: Gazetteer on Finance). Jinan: Shandong ren min chu ban she, 1996.

Sheehan, Brett. *Industrial Eden: A Chinese Capitalist Vision.* Cambridge, MA: Harvard University Press, 2015.

'The History of Chinese Money and Banking: A Mini Explosion'. *Chinese Business History* 14, No. 1 (2004): 1–10.

Trust in Troubled Times: Money, Banks and State-Society Relations in Republican Tianjin. Cambridge, MA: Harvard University Press, 2003.

Simmel, Georg. *Die Philosophie des Geldes.* Munich; Leipzig: Duncker & Humblot, 1922.

Smith, Andrew. 'A LBV Perspective on Political Risk Management in a Multinational Bank during the First World War'. *Multinational Business Review* 24, No. 1 (2016): 25–46.

So, Billy K. L. 'Modern China's Treaty Port Economy in Institutional Perspective: An Introductory Essay'. In *The Treaty Port Economy in Modern China: Empirical Studies of Institutional Change and Economic Performance,* edited by Billy K. L. So and Ramon H. Myers, 1–27. Berkeley: University of California Press, 2011.

Song Peiyu 宋佩玉. *Jindai Shanghai waishang yinhang yanjiu (1847-1949)* 近代上海外商銀行研究 (1847-1949) (A Study of Foreign Banks in Modern Shanghai (1847-1949)). Shanghai: Shanghai yuandong chubanshe, 2016.

Stent, James. *China's Banking Transformation: The Untold Story.* Oxford: Oxford University Press, 2016.

Stoecker, Helmut. *Deutschland und China im 19. Jahrhundert: Das Eindringen des deutschen Kapitalismus.* Berlin: Rütten & Loening, 1958.

Stoskopf, Nicolas. 'From the Private Bank to the Joint-Stock Bank: The Case of France (Second Half of the 19th Century)'. 6th Annual Congress of the European Business History Association (EBHA), August 2002, Helsinki, Finland. https://hal.archives-ouvertes.fr/hal-00934946.

'La Fondation du Comptoir National D'escompte de Paris, Banque Révolutionnaire'. *Histoire, économie et société* 21, No. 3 (2002): 395–411.

Strange, Susan. *States and Markets*. London: Bloomsbury Academic, 1988; reprint, 2015.

Strasser, Karl. *Die Deutschen Banken im Ausland: Entwicklungsgeschichte und Wirtschaftliche Bedeutung*. Munich: E. Reinhardt, 1925.

Strauss, Julia. *Strong Institutions in Weak Polities: State Building in Republican China, 1927-1940*. Oxford: Oxford University Press, 1998.

Sun E-tu Zen. *Chinese Railways and British Interests, 1898-1911*. New York: King's Crown Press, 1954.

Sun Fang 孫芳. 'Xinhai Geming bainian yanjiu zongshu 辛亥革命百年研究綜述 ('A Summary of the Research on the 1911 Revolution Published after Its 100th Anniversary')'. *Jiangxi shifan daxue xuebao* 46, No. 2 (2013): 95–110.

Tamagna, Frank. *Banking and Finance in China*. New York: International Secretariat Institute of Pacific Relations, 1942.

Tang Chuansi 唐傳泗, and Huang Hanmin 黃漢民. 'Shilun 1927 nian yiqian de Zhongguo yinhang 試論 1927 年以前的中國銀行 (An Attempt to Discuss China's Banking Sector before 1927)'. *Zhongguo jindai jingjishi ziliao* 4 (1986): 57–89.

Tatewaki Kazuo 立脇和夫. 'Senzen shio no zainichi gaikoku ginkō (ue) 戦前期の在日外国銀行(上) (The Foreign Banks in Japan in the Period before the War, Part One)'. *Waseda shōgaku* 358 (1994): 43–74.

Zainichi gaikoku ginkōshi: bakumatsu kaikō kara jōyaku kaisei made 在日外国銀行史: 幕末開港から条約改正まで (The History of Foreign Banks in Japan: From the Opening of the Ports during the late Tokugawa Period to the Revision of the Treaties). Tokyo: Nihon Keizai Hyōronsha, 1987.

Taylor, Jeremy E. 'The Bund: Littoral Space of Empire in the Treaty Ports of East Asia'. *Social History* 27, No. 2 (2011): 125–42.

Teichmann, Gabriele. *Mehr als eine Bank. Oppenheim in Köln*. Cologne: Greven Verlag, 2004.

Tilly, Richard. 'Zur Entwicklung des Kapitalmarktes und Industrialisierung im 19. Jahrhundert unter besonderer Berücksichtigung Deutschlands'. *VSWG: Vierteljahrschrift für Sozial- und Wirtschaftsgeschichte* 60 (1973): 145–65.

Torp, Cornelius. *Die Herausforderung der Globalisierung. Wirtschaft und Politik in Deutschland 1860-1914*. Göttingen: Vandenhoeck & Ruprecht, 2005.

Trevor-Roper, Hugh. *Hermit of Peking: The Hidden Life of Sir Edmund Backhouse*. London: Macmillan, 1979.

Tuncer, Ali. *Sovereign Debt and International Financial Control: The Middle East and the Balkans, 1870-1914*. London: Palgrave Macmillan, 2015.

van de Ven, Hans. *Breaking with the Past: The Maritime Customs Service and the Global Origins of Modernity*. New York: Columbia University Press, 2014.

'Globalizing Chinese History'. *History Compass* 2, No. 1 (2004): 1–5.

'Public Finance and the Rise of Warlordism'. *Modern Asian Studies* 30, No. 4 (1996): 829–68.

'Robert Hart and Gustav Detring during the Boxer Rebellion'. *Modern Asian Studies* 40, No. 3 (2006): 631–62.

'The Onrush of Modern Globalization in China'. In *Globalization in World History*, edited by Antony Gerald Hopkins, 167–94. London: Pimlico, 2000.

van der Putten, Frans-Paul. Corporate Behaviour and Political Risk: Dutch Companies in China, 1903–1941. PhD Diss., Leiden University, 2001.

Varg, Paul A. 'The Myth of the China Market, 1890–1914'. *American Historical Review* 73, No. 3 (1968): 742–58.

Vinnai, Volker. *Die Entstehung der Überseebanken und die Technik des Zahlungsverkehrs im Asienhandel von 1850 bis 1875*. PhD Diss., Johann Wolfgang Goethe-Universität, Frankfurt am Main, 1971.

von Glahn, Richard. *The Economic History of China: From Antiquity to the Nineteenth Century*. Cambridge: Cambridge University Press, 2016.

Waibel, Michael. *Sovereign Defaults before International Courts and Tribunals*. Cambridge: Cambridge University Press, 2011.

Wang Jingyu 汪敬虞. '19 shiji mo ye waiguo zai Hua yinhang de touzi huodong 19 世紀末葉外國在華銀行的投資活動 (The Investment Activities of Foreign Banks in China at the End of the 19th Century)'. *Jindaishi Yanjiu* 7 (1997): 60–81.

Jindai Zhongguo ziben zhuyi de fazhan he bufazhan 近代中國資本主義的發展 何不發展 (The Development and Non-Development of Chinese Capitalism). Beijing: Zhongguo caijing chubanshe, 2002.

Waiguo ziben zai jindai Zhongguo de jinrong huodong 外國資本在近代中國的 金融活動 (The Financial Activities of Foreign Capital in Modern China). Beijing: Renmin chubanshe, 1999.

Wang Luman. *Money and Trade, Hinterland and Coast, Empire and Nation State: An Unusual History of Shanxi Piaohao, 1820–1930*. PhD Diss., University of Southern California, 2014.

Wang Yejian. 'Zhongguo jindai huobi yu yinhang de yanjin (1644–1937) 中國近 代貨幣與銀行的演進 (1644–1937) (The Development of Modern Chinese Currency and Banks (1644–1937))'. In *Qingdai jingji shilun wenji* 清代經濟 史論文集 (Collected Essays in the Economic History of Qing China), by Wang Yejian, 3 vols, 1: 161–274. Taibei: Daoxiang chubanshe, 2003.

Wang Zhimin, ed. *Shandong zhongyao lishi renwu di si juan* 山東重要歷史人物第 四卷 (*Important Historical Figures of Shandong, Vol. 4*). Jinan: Shandong renmin chubanshe, 2009.

Wasserstrom, Jeffrey N. 'Cosmopolitan Connections and Transnational Networks'. In *At the Crossroads of Empires: Middlemen, Social Networks, and State-Building in Republican Shanghai*, edited by Nara Dillion and Jean C. Oi, 206–24. Stanford, CA, Stanford University Press, 2008.

Wehler, Hans-Ulrich. *Bismarck und der Imperialismus*, 3rd ed. Cologne: Kiepenheuer & Witsch, 1972.

Deutsche Gesellschaftsgeschichte, Dritter Band: Von der 'Deutschen Doppelrevolution' bis zum Beginn des Ersten Weltkrieges, 1849–1914. Munich: Verlag C. H. Beck, 1995.

Wei Guangqi 魏光奇. 'Qingdai houqi zhongyang jiquan caizheng tizhi de wajie 清代後期中央集權財政體制的瓦解 (The Disintegration of the Centralised System of Public Finance in the Late Qing Dynasty)'. *Jindaishi yanjiu*, No. 1 (1986): 207–30.

Wen Bingzhong 温秉忠. *Zuixian liu Mei tongxue lu* 最先留美同學錄 (Record of the First Students to Study in America). Beijing, 1924.

Wen, Wei Pin. *The Currency Problem in China*. PhD Diss., Columbia University, New York, 1914.

White, Richard. *The Middle Ground: Indians, Empires, and Republics in the Great Lakes Region, 1650–1815*. Cambridge: Cambridge University Press, 2011.

Wilkins, Mira. *The History of Foreign Investment in the United States to 1914*. Cambridge, MA: Harvard University Press, 1989.

Wilson, Craig, and Fan Yang. 'Shanxi Piaohao and Shanghai Qianzhuang: A Comparison of the Two Main Banking Systems of Nineteenth-Century China'. *Business History* 58, No. 3 (2016): 433–52.

Wong, John D. *Global Trade in the Nineteenth Century: The House of Houqua and the Canton System*. Cambridge: Cambridge University Press, 2016.

Wong, R. Bin. *China Transformed: Historical Change and the Limits of European Experience*. Ithaca, NY: Cornell University Press, 1997.

Woo-Cumings, Meredith, ed. *The Developmental State*. Ithaca, NY: Cornell University Press, 1999.

Wright, Mary C., ed. *China in Revolution: The First Phase, 1900–1913*. New Haven, CT: Yale University Press, 1968.

Wright, Stanley Fowler. *China's Customs Revenue since the Revolution of 1911*. Shanghai: Statistical Department of the Inspectorate General of Customs, 1935.

Hart and the Chinese Customs. Belfast: Queen's University, 1950.

Wright, Tim. 'Imperialism and the Chinese Economy: A Methodological Critique of the Debate'. *Bulletin of Concerned Asian Scholars* 18, No. 1 (1986): 36–45.

Wu, Shellen Xiao. *Empires of Coal: Fueling China's Entry into the Modern World Order, 1860–1920*. Stanford, CA: Stanford University Press, 2015.

Wu Yunxian 巫雲仙. *Huifeng Yinhang yu Zhongguo jinrong yanjiu* 匯豐銀行與中國金融研究 (A Study of the Hong Kong and Shanghai Banking Corporation and Chinese Finance). Beijing: Zhongguo zhengfa daxue, 2007.

Xia Liangcai 夏良才. 'Guoji Yinhang Tuan he Xinhai Geming 國際銀行團和辛亥革命 ('The International Banking Group and the 1911 Revolution')'. *Jindaishi yanjiu*, No. 1 (1982): 188–215.

Xu Dixin 許滌新, and Wu Chengming 吳承明. *Zhongguo ziben zhuyi fazhan shi* 中國資本主義發展史 (The History of the Development of Chinese Capitalism), 3 vols. Beijing: Renmin chubanshe, 2005.

Xu Guoqi 徐國琦. *China and the Great War: China's Pursuit of a New National Identity and Internationalization*. Cambridge: Cambridge University Press, 2005.

Xu Jiqing 徐寄廎. *Shanghai jinrong shi* 上海金融史 (A Financial History of Shanghai). Shanghai: 1926; reprint, Taibei: Xuehai chubanshe, 1970.

Xu Yi 許毅, Wang Xiaoguang 王曉光, Pan Guoqi 潘國旗, Jin Pusen 金普森 and Kong Yongsong 孔永松. *Cong bainian quru dao minzu fuxing* 從百年屈辱到民族復興 (From One Hundred Years of Humiliation to National Rejuvenation), 4 vols. Beijing: Jingji kexue chubanshe, 2002-5.

Xu Yi 許毅, Jin Pusen 金普森, Long Wuhua 隆武華, Kong Yongsong 孔永松 and Wang Guohua 王國華. *Qingdai waizhai shilun* 清代外債史論 (A Historical Discussion of Foreign Debt during the Qing Dynasty). Beijing: Zhongguo caizheng jingji chubanshe, 1996.

Xu Yisheng 徐義生. 'Jiawu zhongri zhanzheng qian Qing zhengfu de waizhai 甲午中日戰爭前清政府的外債 (The Foreign Debt of the Qing Government Prior to the Sino-Japanese War)'. *Jingji yanjiu* 5 (1956): 105-27.

Zhongguo jindai waizhai tongji ziliao 中國近代外債史統計資料 (Statistical Materials on Foreign Debt in Modern China). Beijing: Zhonghua shuju, 1962.

Yabuki Susumu, and Stephen M. Harner. *China's New Political Economy, Revised Edition*. Boulder, CO: Westview Press, 1999.

Yan, Dong. 'The Boxer Indemnity and Late Qing Financial Governance, 1901-1911', unpublished manuscript (December 2019).

Yang Yinpu 楊蔭溥. *Minguo caizheng shi* 民國財政史 (A History of Public Finance during the Republican Period). Shanghai: Shanghai caizheng jingji chubanshe, 1984.

Shanghai jinrong zuzhi gaiyao 上海金融組織概要 (A Summary of the Financial Organisations of Shanghai). Beijing: Shangwu yinshuguan, 1930.

Yang Yonggang 楊勇剛. *Zhongguo jindai tielushi* 中國近代鐵路史 (A History of Modern Chinese Railways). Shanghai: Shanghai shudian chubanshe, 1997.

Young, Arthur N. *China's Nation-Building Effort, 1927-1937: The Financial and Economic Record*. Stanford, CA: Hoover Institution Press, 1971.

Young, Ernest P. *The Presidency of Yuan Shih-k'ai: Liberalism and Dictatorship in Early Republican China*. Ann Arbor: The University of Michigan Press, 1977.

Zarrow, Peter. *China in War and Revolution, 1895-1949*. London: Routledge, 2005.

Zhang Guohui 張國輝. *Wan Qing qianzhuang he piaohao yanjiu*. 晚清錢莊和票號研究 (A Study of Qianzhuang and Piaohao Banks during the Late Qing Dynasty.) Beijing: Shehui kexue wenxian chubanshe, 2007.

Zhongguo jinrong tongshi: Di er juan: Qing Yapian zhanzheng shiqi zhi Qingmo shiqi 中國金融同史: 第二卷: 清鴉片戰爭時期至清末時期 (A General History of Chinese Finance, Volume 2: From the Period of the Opium War during the Qing Dynasty to the Late Qing Period). Beijing: Zhongguo jinrong chubanshe, 2003.

Zhang Kaisen 張開森. '1918 nian zaihua Deqiao chuzhi an yinfa de Zhongwai jiaoshe 1918 年在華德僑處置案引發的中外交涉 (The Sino-Foreign Relations Caused by the Handling of the Germans in China in 1918)'. *Jindaishi yanjiu*, No. 3 (2011): 80–9.

Zhang Kaiyuan 章開沅. 'Xinhai Geming yanjiu de huigu yu qianzhan 辛亥革命研究的回顧與前瞻 (Research on the 1911 Revolution: Review and Outlook)'. *Wenshi zhishi*, No. 9 (2001): 4–10.

Zhang Kaiyuan 章開沅, and Tian Tong 田彤. 'Xin shiji zhi chu de Xinhai Geming shi yanjiu 新世紀之初的辛亥革命史研究 (Research on the 1911 Revolution at the Start of the New Century)'. *Zhejiang shehui kexue*, No. 9 (2010): 89–98.

Zhang Xiaosong 張曉松, and Li Wei 李煒. *Zhongguo jinrong ye 'zou chuqu' fabiao zhanlüe yanjiu* 中國金融業'走出去'發展戰略研究 (A Study of the Strategy of Developing the 'Going Out' of the Chinese Financial Industry). Beijing: Zhonggong zhongyang dangxiao chubanshe, 2002.

Zhang Yongjin. *China's Emerging Global Businesses: Political Economy and Institutional Investigation*. Basingstoke: Palgrave Macmillan, 2003.

Zhang Zhiyong 張志勇. 'He De yu Ying De xujie kuan 赫德與英德續借款 (Robert Hart and the Second Anglo-German Loan)'. *Jiangsu shehui kexue*, No. 4 (2014): 154–63.

Zheng, Xiaowei. *The Politics of Rights and the 1911 Revolution in China*. Stanford, CA: Stanford University Press, 2018.

Zhongyang yanjiuyuan jindaishi yanjiusuo 中央研究院近代史研究所. *Jindai zhongguo dui xifang ji lieqiang renshi ziliao huibian, disan ji di er fence* 近代中國對西方及列強認識資料彙編, 第三輯第二分冊 (Compendium of Materials on Modern China's Understanding of the West and the Powers, 3rd ed., Vol. 2). Taibei: Zhongyang yanjiuyuan jindaishi yanjiusuo, 1986.

Zhou Yumin 周育民. *Wan Qing caizheng yu shehui bianqian* 晚清財政與社會變遷 (Late Qing Public Finance and Social Change). Shanghai: Shanghai renmin chubanshe, 2000.

Zhou Zhichu 周志初. *Wan Qing caizheng jingji yanjiu* 晚清財政經濟研究 (A Study of Public Finance and the Economy during the Late Qing Dynasty). Jinan: Qilu shushe, 2002.

Zhu, Xiaohuang, Song Lin, Lin Wang, Wenqi Wu and Quanli Qin. *A Study of the Turning Point of China's Debt*. Singapore: Springer, 2018.

Zhu Ying 朱英. *Wan Qing jingji zhengce yu gaige cuoshi* 晚清經濟政策與改革措施 (Economic Policy and Reform Measures during the Late Qing Dynasty). Wuhan: Huazhong shifan daxue chubanshe, 1996.

Zhuang Zheng 莊正. *Zhongguo tielu jianshe* 中國鐵路建設 (China's Railway Infrastructure). Tangshan: Zhongguo tiedao chubanshe, 1990.

Ziegler, Dieter. *Eisenbahnen und Staat im Zeitalter der Industrialisierung: Die Eisenbahnpolitik der deutschen Staaten im Vergleich*. Stuttgart: Franz Steiner Verlag, 1996.

INDEX

Printed in the United States
by Baker & Taylor Publisher Services